ST ALBANS

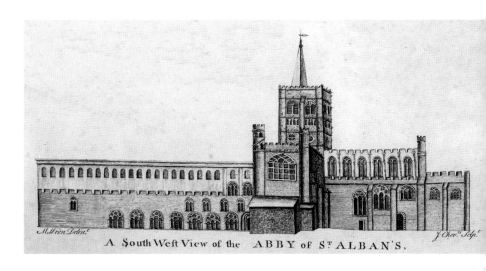

M. Wren Delin.

J. Chev.º Sclp.

A South West View of the ABBY of St ALBAN'S,

For Tamsin Beal

ST ALBANS

A history
by Mark Freeman

Town and city histories available from Carnegie:
Prof. David Hey, *A History of Sheffield*
Prof. John K. Walton, *Blackpool*
Prof. Graham Davis and Dr Penny Bonsall, *A History of Bath: Image and Reality*
Peter Aughton, *Bristol: A People's History*
Dr John A. Hargreaves, *Halifax*
Dr Andrew White (ed.), *A History of Lancaster*
Peter Aughton, *Liverpool: A People's History*
Prof. Alan Kidd, *Manchester*
Dr Jeffrey Hill, *Nelson*
Malcolm Neesam, *Harrogate Great Chronicle, 1332–1841*
Dr Derek Beattie, *A History of Blackburn*
Peter Shakeshaft, *St Anne's-on-the-Sea*

Forthcoming town and city histories:
Prof. Carl Chinn, *Birmingham*
W.A. Maguire, *Belfast* (2009)
Dr John Doran, *Chester*
Michael Baumber, *A History of Haworth* (2009)
Dr John A. Hargreaves, *Huddersfield*
Dr Andrew White, *Kendal* (2009)
Dr Trevor Rowley, *A History of Oxford*
Prof. Bill Sheils, *A History of York*
Dr Evelyn Lord, *Cambridge*
Anthea Jones, *Cheltenham*
Prof. Fred Gray, *Brighton*
Dr Andrew Walker, *Lincoln*
Dr David Hunt, *Preston* (2009)
Dr Joan Allen and Dr Richard Allen, *Newcastle*
Prof. Richard Rodger (ed.), *Leicester: A Modern History*

Full details on www.carnegiepublishing.com

Copyright © Mark Freeman, 2008

First edition

Published by Carnegie Publishing Ltd
by Carnegie Publishing Ltd
Carnegie House
Chatsworth Road, Lancaster LA1 4SL
tel: 01524 840111
www.carnegiepublishing.com

ISBN 978-1-85936-139-9 *hardback*
ISBN 978-1-85936-190-0 *softback*

British Library Cataloguing-in-Publication data
A catalogue record for this book is available from the British Library

Designed and typeset by Carnegie Book Production, Lancaster
Printed and bound in the UK by Cambridge University Press

FRONTISPIECE
'The Michaelmas Fair, St Albans, 1852'. This watercolour by J.H. Buckingham (1800–81) shows a disorderly scene from the fair on St Peter's Street. The town's first royal charter, in 1553, permitted the corporation of St Albans to hold a twice-weekly market, and fairs on Lady Day (25 March), St Alban's Day (22 June) and Michaelmas Day (29 September). Buckingham's picture also shows the rather primitive sanitary arrangements in the streets of early Victorian St Albans.
© ST ALBANS MUSEUMS

Contents

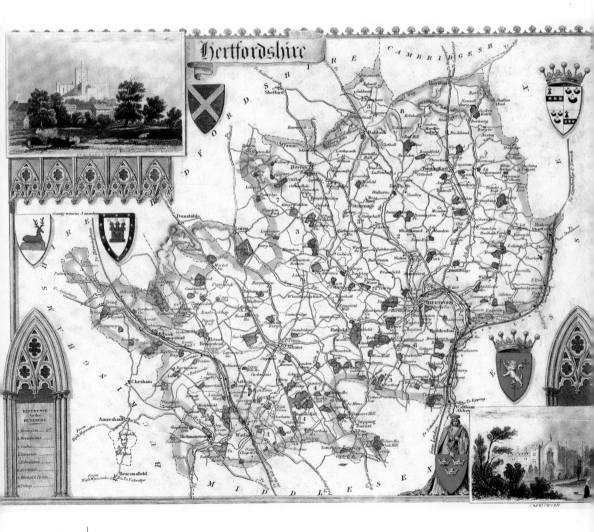

Introduction

I N HIS FOREWORD to the souvenir programme of the St Albans historical pageant in June 1948, the mayor, councillor W.R. Hiskett, eloquently explained the appeal of the history of the city:

> The fascination which history has for us is not a merely curious interest in a dead past, it arises from an intimate conviction that past and present are inseparably linked. A community is a living organism, with its roots in bygone days, and the attraction of age is not its remoteness, but its links with the present … We in St Albans are members of a community with an ancient and illustrious record, for, times out of number, on this spot history has been made.

This book traces that history, charting what Hiskett called 'the story of struggle and progress, of failure and success, which has brought us where we stand today'. In the case of St Albans, this is a story which stretches back more than two millennia. Some towns and cities impinge upon the wider national experience for only a relatively brief period or for just a single reason: Manchester, for instance, was not even an incorporated borough before industrialisation put it on the international map; Salisbury has never regained the importance it once had in the medieval period; and some formerly grand Roman towns such as Aldborough in Yorkshire are now little more than villages or abandoned altogether. Relatively few – Bath, York, Exeter and Lincoln might be cited as examples – have enjoyed (or endured) a significant place in the national experience at more than a single period. St Albans can be included in this select list. It is particularly notable for its remarkable and important British and Roman past, of course, and for the grandeur of its medieval abbey. Yet it has also experienced long periods of relatively consistent prosperity, witnessed by the survival of a good range of vernacular architecture, and it has rarely been unimportant in its regional sphere. Two aspects of the St Albans experience will emerge repeatedly in the chapters which follow: the city's relationship with London, and the role of history and tradition in its life and culture.

St Albans's much larger neighbour – the country's capital for most of its history – has played an important role in shaping the economy, social life and politics of St Albans. For most of the Roman period, the government of this outpost of empire was centred on London, and the Roman town of Verulamium, itself one of the more important urban centres, was linked to the capital by Watling Street, one of the country's principal Roman roads. In medieval and early modern times, St Albans's geographical situation, a day's journey from London, made it an important 'thoroughfare town', as well as a key strategic location in the civil wars of the fifteenth and seventeenth centuries. The proximity of the metropolis has also affected the agriculture of the surrounding countryside, the industrial character of St Albans, and even the politics of the borough: the parliamentary seat, close to the capital, was an attractive enough target for would-be MPs to allow a substantial culture of bribery to emerge in the eighteenth and nineteenth centuries. Since the arrival of the railway – three lines served St Albans by the end of the nineteenth century – commuting to London has made St Albans an important dormitory city, in common with other towns in Hertfordshire and the Home Counties.

The second long-standing theme in the history of St Albans is the ever-present nature of the city's own past, and, increasingly, tensions between the demands of the past and the present. Most obviously, the ruins of Roman Verulamium have had a significant, continuing presence: for the builders of the medieval abbey of St Albans, the ancient ruins were a source of building materials; and during the early modern and modern periods, these same ruins have been invaded by successive generations of archaeologists, who have given us new insights into the life of the ancient town.

In its historical geography St Albans is perhaps uniquely fortunate. Unlike London, York or Bath its site of occupation has migrated over time, so that both the ancient British site of Verlamion and the Roman site of Verulamium have not been built over by successive generations. The latter lies remarkably close to the medieval and modern city, yet safe from development under the turf of Verulamium Park. York's Viking past was uncovered only when the Coppergate redevelopment allowed archaeologists a brief opportunity to dig below layers of later occupation; and the Roman city north of London Bridge has never been available for systematic excavation. In St Albans uncovering the city's past is almost literally a stroll in the park.

History and the remains of the past were important for the medieval abbey, too. Home to some of the greatest historians and chroniclers of the time, its long and distinguished history was emphasised in the monks' repeated attempts to justify their religious and political liberties. The people of the town, too, had their own sense of history, which was well demonstrated in their bitter grievances against the authority of the abbey in the fourteenth and fifteenth centuries. In modern times, the growing public and official awareness of the rich history of the city has spawned a widespread interest in local studies, and several societies have been established to promote urban conservationism and the pursuit of local history. Managing the development of the modern city of St Albans has often brought planners into conflict with those who wish to preserve the historical urban environment, a theme that can be identified as early as the nineteenth century, and seems ubiquitous today.

Several key political events shape the narrative of St Albans's past. The first is the martyrdom of St Alban, without which the city would not exist in the form that it does, and of course would have a different name. The foundation of the town itself, reputedly by abbot Ulsinus in 948, and the re-formation of the abbey in the Anglo-Saxon period, were also of critical importance, although we are still, as historians, relatively poorly informed about these developments. The Norman conquest, and with it the arrival of abbot Paul de Caen and his great Norman successors, marked another stage in the history of abbey and town. The repeated uprisings by the townspeople of St Albans, against the authority of the abbey, culminating in the peasants' revolt of 1381, are described in detail in chapters 3 and 4; and the dissolution of the monasteries, which finally freed the town from its subjection to the abbot and monks, represented another highly significant moment in the development of St Albans. Subsequently, the concession of charters by Edward VI and his successors shaped the structure of the politics and government of St Albans for centuries to come. Similarly, the disenfranchisement of the borough in 1850, the establishment of the diocese of St Albans in 1877, and the creation of the City and District in 1974, have all contributed to the evolution of the city that we know today.

However, the main focus in what follows is on the economic, social and cultural life of St Albans. The first chapter, on Verulamium, examines the economic prosperity and decline of the Roman town, and pieces together some aspects of its cultural life, notably its importance as a religious centre. The book examines how St Albans grew from a small settlement of some 500 people at the time of the Norman conquest, to a larger, but still small, town of around 2,500 at the time of the peasants' revolt, and then to around 4,000 at the dissolution of the monasteries. The population reached 7,000 in 1851; it stood at 16,000 at the end of the nineteenth century, and around 45,000 in 1951. I have focused on the economic foundations of the city's growth, which have always been influenced by the proximity of London, but have moved in very different directions at different times. St Albans was a city of innkeepers, victuallers and market traders in the medieval and early modern period, but grew in importance as a manufacturing centre in the nineteenth and early twentieth centuries, before this sector in turn declined in the second half of the twentieth century. Throughout the whole of the history of St Albans, the market has been a central aspect of its economic life; and it is only in

comparatively recent times that the relationship between the urban centre and the surrounding countryside has not been of great economic importance. Alongside these changes, the social life of the city – as manifested in its churches, schools, hospitals, voluntary organisations, governmental and civic institutions, parks, pubs and cinemas – as well as the development of housing, will be examined in this book.

The book is divided into nine chapters, which move chronologically through the history of St Albans. There are also twelve 'boxes', dealing in more depth with specific themes and events, including the martyrdom of St Alban, the medieval monastic chroniclers, the Wars of the Roses and the Civil War, the parliamentary politics of the borough and the role of education and civic pageantry in the modern period. The chapter endnotes are all at the end of the book, but the boxes themselves contain their own references. The first time a source is referred to in the book, the full reference is given; this may therefore be either in a box or in the endnotes. A full bibliography would have proved too long, and there is therefore a short bibliographical note at the end of the book. There is also an appendix, which gives the sources for the tables and charts which appear in chapters 7, 8 and 9.

My own association with St Albans began when I was born in the maternity ward of the city hospital in 1974. I lived in the city until the age of 18, attending Skyswood JMI school and then St Albans School. At the latter, compulsory twice-weekly services in the cathedral, and lessons in the abbey gatehouse, exposed pupils to the history of the city from an early age. The enforced trips to the 'abbey' (as the cathedral is usually known in St Albans, perhaps correctly if one takes a long-term perspective) were resented at the time, but it would be appropriate to identify in them the origins of my interest in history. However, it was at the school itself that I began to take a deeper interest in the study of the past, supported by an enthusiastic group of history teachers, who shared a passion for the subject and a commitment to teaching it. In my later years at St Albans, I was particularly encouraged by Tim Martin, Nigel Williams and, above all, Mike Hudis, whose premature death in 1996 was a great loss to the school. The experience of studying history with them exercised a powerful influence on my subsequent career. Although I have lived in three other cities since the age of 18, I still spend a lot of time in St Albans, and writing its history has been the source of great interest and pleasure.

A selection of
pottery from
Verlamion, *c*.AD 10–
40. Although most
was native to the
region, some was
made from material
imported from
continental Europe.
This pottery was
unearthed during
Mortimer Wheeler's
excavations in the
1930s.
AUTHOR COLLECTION

Verlamion and Verulamium

The Iron Age and Roman town

THE FIRST KNOWN URBAN SETTLEMENT near the site of modern St Albans was an Iron Age town dating from the first century BC, some of the remains of which lie in Prae Wood, to the north-west of the modern Bluehouse Hill road, which runs from Hemel Hempstead past the village of St Michael's and towards the Batchwood estate in St Albans. The banks and ditches in the wood were excavated by Sir Mortimer and Tessa Wheeler in the early 1930s, and described by Mortimer Wheeler as 'relics of a city which was at one time no less than the metropolis of a considerable part of Britain'.[1] The Wheelers found a series of defensive ditches, which had apparently been dug quickly and were reinforced by palisades on the inner side, similar to defences also found in prehistoric settlements in Devon and Sussex. The ditches had been filled with ash and pottery dating from the late first century BC to around AD 40, and sealed with a layer of Roman brick and pottery from the first century AD. A causeway ran across one of the ditches, close to which prehistoric wheel tracks were found, along with some shallow 'rubbish tips', also containing prehistoric pottery. There was no trace of any houses, but some bricks were found, which were clearly Iron Age in origin and differed from the bricks used by the later builders of the nearby Roman town. The Prae Wood settlement also provided evidence of a small domestic textile industry and of some iron working. There were small amounts of imported Italian pottery, rather more pots from Gaul and Belgium, and some locally produced imitations of inferior quality. Subsequent excavations by Sheppard Frere in the 1950s and 1960s showed that the town was not confined to Prae Wood, but spread into the valley of the river Ver, on the south-west bank of which the later Roman town stood.

3034. St-ALBANS - Ancient British Causeway

Whereas the Wheelers had believed that the settlement was in dense woodland, newer techniques of pollen analysis have shown that they were mistaken, and that considerable arable agriculture was being pursued in the region of the town in the first century BC. The discovery of a large cemetery at King Harry Lane, many pre-Roman coins and evidence of a large local mint, together with a large system of agricultural enclosure and trackways, all point to a heavily populated district with considerable and varied economic activity. The town is referred to as Verlamion, distinct from the Roman town of Verulamium which grew up on the same site; coins from the Iron Age period use the name Verlamio. The name Verlamion – Romanised as Verulamium – may mean 'above the pool': there was a large fishpond on the other side of the river, which caused political controversy in the medieval period.[2]

The Wheelers' excavations had revealed a considerable Iron Age town, and if its characterisation as a 'metropolis' was perhaps rather exaggerated, by the time of the Roman conquest of Britain in AD 43 Verlamion was certainly one of the two main urban centres in the territory of the Catuvellauni and Trinovantes tribes, the other being Colchester.[3] The Catuvellauni territory was bordered on the south by the river Thames, and extended some 80 miles northwards, and probably from the Cherwell valley in the west to the Lea valley in the east, a total of some 4,000 square miles.[4] The Trinovantes occupied the territory to the east of the Catuvellauni, in modern-day Essex and east Hertfordshire;

their capital was at Colchester. Politically, the tribes were united under the leadership of king Tasciovanus, or his successor Cunobelin (the *Cymbeline* of Shakespeare), who ruled from *c.*AD 10–40, although economic and cultural unity seems to have occurred somewhat earlier.[5] If we were to accept the description of the people of southern Britain by Julius Caesar, who remembered the 'barbarians' that he encountered in 55 and 54 BC, we would believe that these Iron Age tribes were brutal and uncivilised:

> Inland, the people for the most part do not plant corn-crops, but live on milk and meat and clothe themselves in animal skins. All the Britons paint themselves with woad, which produces a dark blue colour: this means they appear more frightening in battle. They have long hair and shave their bodies, all except for the head and upper lip. Groups of ten or twelve men share their wives in common, particularly between brothers or father and son. Any offspring they have are held to be the children of him to whom the maiden was brought first.[6]

Caesar's derogatory description, one of the few that survives from the period, was adopted many centuries later by historians who saw the Roman conquest of Britain as a civilising imperial mission. For example, Charles H. Ashdown, in a lavishly presented and attractively illustrated book on St Albans published

Beech Bottom Dyke is an impressive Iron Age ditch, which probably marked the boundary of the *oppidum* known as Verlamion, which existed before the Roman town of Verulamium. It runs in a north-easterly direction from the Ancient Briton junction for over a kilometre before it is crossed by the Midland Railway line. The earthwork continues to St Albans Road, which runs north towards Sandridge and Wheathampstead.

PHOTOGRAPH: CARNEGIE

in 1893, described the 'primeval barbarism' and 'primeval darkness' of the ancient Britons before the coming of the Roman invaders.[7] In a period when the British empire was supposedly civilising much of the distant world, it was easy to draw parallels with the Roman empire doing the same thing in northern Europe. In fact, as noted above and in contrast to Ceasar's claim, there is clear archaeological evidence of arable agriculture being practised in this part of Hertfordshire in the first century BC, and no evidence of the polyandry described by Caesar among the Catuvellauni and other Celtic tribes.[8] There was intensive farming and, as Wheeler showed, some industrial production: this part of the country was 'far from being a backwater' in the mid-first century when Caesar arrived.[9] In the following century, before the successful Roman invasion under Claudius in AD 43, the economic and social life of the region became more sophisticated and cosmopolitan.

At the time of Caesar's invasions of Britain, Verlamion was not a substantial settlement. The largest in the area was at nearby Wheathampstead, which was heavily occupied in the mid-first century BC but abandoned around 15–10 BC. Wheeler suggested that Wheathampstead was the stronghold where the tribal chief Cassivellaunus held out against Caesar's army, but there is no definitive proof of this. There were also large settlements near Baldock and Braughing in north-eastern Hertfordshire. By contrast, there was little evidence of urban settlement around Verlamion in the mid-first century BC. Whereas in Baldock and Braughing imported pottery has been found dating to the early part of the century, along with elite burials suggesting continental cultural influence, at Verlamion 'knowledge of precisely what if anything was going on ... is still very much a matter for speculation'.[10] What is clear is that, in the late first century BC and the early first century AD, Verlamion expanded rapidly, apparently at the same time that occupation of the nearby Wheathampstead site declined. Burial practices familiar in north-east Hertfordshire some time earlier began to be adopted in Verlamion, and imported goods also appear in the archaeological record from this period.

Verlamion was an *oppidum* (plural: *oppida*), a new type of settlement that emerged in the late Iron Age, as populations shifted from hill-forts to valleys, often near river crossings. *Oppida* were characterised by the development of zones delimited by function and the use of dykes for defensive purposes or to mark boundaries, and were often the site of 'high status metalworking'.[11] Some were enclosed by earthworks, as at Winchester and Dorchester (Oxfordshire); others, including Verlamion and Braughing in Hertfordshire together with Canterbury, 'were apparently without significant boundaries'.[12] The development of *oppida* is imperfectly understood, but the Iron Age historian Barry Cunliffe sees it as representative of 'the change from a pre-urban to a fully urban system'.[13] The *oppidum* at Verlamion stood on a plateau above the Ver, and was enclosed by the ditches and palisades excavated

'... knowledge of precisely what if anything was going on ... is still very much a matter for speculation.'

Mortimer Wheeler and his wife Tessa excavated Verulamium in the early 1930s. Tessa Wheeler died in 1936, but Mortimer became a well-known writer and broadcaster, dying in 1976. He was made a Companion of Honour in 1967.

© ST ALBANS MUSEUMS

by Wheeler. The 'Devil's Dyke', running westwards from the Ver towards Gorhambury, and the nearby Beech Bottom Dyke, which runs parallel to the modern Beech Road north of St Albans, probably marked the boundaries of the *oppidum*. The area of the *oppidum* may have been some 1,250 acres.[14] There was a cemetery outside the enclosed area, and ovens have also been found. As noted above, textiles and metals were worked in Prae Wood, and within the wider area, two Iron Age mints have been discovered. The distribution of coins minted here by Tasciovanus and Cunobelin – they have been found across south-eastern England and as far north as the Humber – further emphasises the economic importance of the *oppidum* at Verlamion. One of these mints was at Gorhambury, later the site of a large Roman villa; another was near the river and within the walls of the later Roman town. The coins minted here reflect continental influences in design, providing evidence of cultural links with the Roman empire. Rosalind Niblett, an archaeologist and historian of the period, suggests that cultural exchange may have been fostered by the practice of hostage-taking by the Romans, which was commonplace following treaties, such as those signed under Julius Caesar, and under Augustus prior to the invasion of Britain in AD 43.[15] Another example of Roman influence is the increasing popularity of cremation of the dead rather than inhumation: of 472 burials at the cemetery excavated at King Harry Lane, dating from *c*.AD 1–60, 455 were cremations.[16] Expanding links with Rome may also help to

explain the relatively peaceful occupation of the area by the Romans following the successful invasion of AD 43.

A key to the economic success of the Catuvellauni *oppidum* at Verlamion lies in its geographical position. It lay on an important trade route from south-west to north-east Hertfordshire. In the south-west the area around Berkhamsted was well populated in this period: iron was worked at Northchurch and at the site known as Cow Roast, on the Roman Akeman Street. In the north-east, Braughing and Baldock continued to thrive, while Welwyn (to the east of Verlamion) had a pottery industry. Wheathampstead seems to have declined; but Verlamion was well placed to take advantage of communication with the other sites.[17] However, Verlamion also had wider economic links, reflecting its importance in the life of the tribes who dominated the region. The road which ran to the south of the nucleus of the *oppidum*, along what is now Bluehouse Hill, was part of a road leading to Braughing, and then on to Colchester, the other main urban centre in the Catuvellauni/Trinovantes territory. Mortimer

This reconstruction of part of the Catuvellauni *oppidum* at Verlamion shows the river Ver and the area known as the 'Central Enclosure', with surrounding agricultural lands and smaller settlements. The original Roman town was centred on this area.
© ST ALBANS MUSEUMS

ST ALBANS: A HISTORY

Wheeler emphasised the importance of this road when he first excavated the site.[18] The Colchester road, before the bridging of the Thames and the building of Watling Street from London to the north-west, was Verlamion's main trade artery: as Wheeler suggested, 'at this period, the relationship between [Verlamion] and Colchester must in some sense have anticipated the later relationship between Roman Verulamium and London; and it may be said that, whilst the Roman Verulamium looked southwards to the Thames, its predecessor faced rather towards the east and the Essex coast'.[19] Imports and exports travelled along this road: we know that silver, iron, cattle, crops, animal skins, dogs and slaves were all exported from prehistoric Britain to the Roman empire, and many of these (though not silver and iron) could be produced in Hertfordshire.[20] This relationship with the east was not only economic; it was also political. Under the leadership of either Tasciovanus or Cunobelin, it appears that the seat of tribal government for the Catuvellauni/Trinovantes region moved from Verlamion to Colchester. Yet even after this migration of tribal government, coins were still minted at Verlamion, which in the words of the historian of the Catuvellauni tribe, Keith Branigan, continued to play 'an important administrative role of some sort in the organisation of [Cunobelin's] kingdom'.[21]

At the *oppidum* itself, there were also significant changes in the early first century AD. Earthworks, probably forming boundaries between land holdings,

Verulamium is now a large park, with a lake next to the river Ver. The lake was built by unemployed workers from Wales and the north of England in the 1930s, following the excavations led by Mortimer Wheeler.

were being developed, and the centre of economic gravity of the town was beginning to shift. Close to the river Ver, on the site where the Roman forum was later constructed, a development, referred to by archaeologists as a 'Central Enclosure', has been identified, surrounded by a large ditch and comprising more than 5 acres in extent. Sheppard Frere suggested that the mint, and maybe a royal residential and administrative centre, were located here; others have suggested a temple.[22] Socially, a highly polarised society evolved at Verlamion. The discovery of the King Harry Lane cemetery has presented archaeologists with evidence of considerable social inequality.[23] The graves of wealthy and poor inhabitants were found, some in enclosed plots. The wealthy burials included pots, coins and jewellery; other bodies were buried unaccompanied. At other sites, inhumations provide evidence that the poorest members of society suffered from 'a variety of illnesses and deficiencies', and 'physical traumas'.[24] The recent discovery at Folly Lane of the tomb of a wealthy and powerful native leader, who had experience of service in the Roman army, is evidence of the region's growing links with Rome, and of the potential for the acquisition of wealth that these links facilitated.[25] It also illustrates the hierarchical nature of Iron Age society, a far more complex social structure than the reader of Caesar's accounts of Britain would infer. Socially the elite were receptive to Roman influence, while militarily the region seems to have been unprepared to resist: there is little evidence of military activity among the Catuvellauni in the vicinity of Verlamion.

There is no indication that the economic and social life of the town was seriously disrupted by the [Roman] conquest.

The Romans successfully invaded Britain during the reign of Claudius in AD 43. Although Julius Caesar claimed to have conquered the province almost a century earlier, there had been no formal establishment of Roman rule. Economic and cultural links had been fostered following Caesar's visits, and some treaties concluded, and the development of Verlamion in the late first century BC and early first century AD reflected the increasing continental influence on Iron Age communities in southern Britain in this period. The receptiveness to Roman influence probably helped to smooth the transition to Roman rule in the Catuvellauni region; most of the evidence points to a peaceful conquest and aftermath. Sheppard Frere suggested that there was a fort at the early Roman settlement of Verulamium, but it had been abandoned by AD 48–9.[26] The town certainly had no significant military presence by AD 61.[27] There is no indication that the economic and social life of the town was seriously disrupted by the conquest. Other parts of the country were not so easily pacified: in Colchester, for example, the behaviour of Roman soldiers and the aggressive promotion of the imperial cult aroused local resentment and anger.[28] At Verulamium, the early result of the conquest appears to have been a shift in the pattern of settlement. Population shifted towards the area of the Central Enclosure, near the river, and there was a move away from the sites higher up the valley slopes around Prae Wood in the second half of the first century AD. The early Roman town clustered around the Central Enclosure, and a causeway featuring a timber tower was built across the marshes south and west of the Ver (where an artificial lake is now situated).[29] Further causeways were built across some of the Iron Age ditches to facilitate access to the Central Enclosure area from the other parts of the *oppidum*. One large block of buildings dating from the early Roman period is thought to have been a speculative retail development, with space rented out to tradesmen, mostly metalworkers.[30] By AD 61 the town had expanded somewhat, but remained small: the early Roman town comprised some 116 acres.[31]

In AD 61 the great revolt against Roman rule by the Iceni and Trinovantes tribes, led by the Iceni queen Boudicca, took place. It arose because of the treatment of the natives by the Roman conquerors in East Anglia. According to Tacitus,[32] the Roman soldiers plundered the kingdom of the Iceni, raping the king's daughters and attacking the king's wife Boudicca. The Iceni, together with members of the Trinovantes tribe who were angered by the arrogance and lawlessness of the military veterans who occupied Colchester,

Thomas Thornycroft's statue of Boudicca, on the Victoria Embankment, London, near Westminster Bridge, dates from 1850. Boudicca, queen of the Iceni, led the revolt against Roman rule in AD 61, burning the towns of Colchester, London and Verulamium before suffering defeat in battle.

PHOTOGRAPH: CARNEGIE

took the opportunity afforded by the absence of the Roman governor Suetonius Paulinus to rebel against the imperial authority. While Suetonius was occupied with campaigns in the north-west of England, the rebels attacked Colchester, where the ninth legion was massacred. As Tacitus explained, London and then Verulamium were attacked, abandoned to their fate by Suetonius:

> Nor did the tears and weeping of the people [in London], as they implored [Suetonius's] aid, deter him from giving the signal of departure and receiving into his army all who would go with him. Those who were chained to the spot by the weakness of their sex, or the infirmity of age, or the attractions of the place, were cut off by the enemy. Like ruin fell on the town of Verulamium, for the barbarians, who delighted in plunder and were indifferent to all else, passed by the fortresses with military garrisons, and attacked whatever offered most wealth to the spoiler, and was unsafe for defence. About seventy thousand citizens and allies, it appeared, fell in the places which I have mentioned. For it was not on making prisoners and selling them, or on any of the barter of war, that the enemy was bent, but on slaughter, on the gibbet, the fire and the cross, like men soon about to pay the penalty, and meanwhile snatching at instant vengeance.[33]

RIGHT
This map shows Verulamium and its surroundings in the Roman period. The key position of the town on the roads leading north from London (Watling Street) and east towards Colchester is clearly indicated. There were a number of known villas, as well as several centres of industry.
PHOTOGRAPH: CARNEGIE

They did indeed soon 'pay the penalty', because Suetonius's army defeated Boudicca's in a pitched battle, in which as many as 80,000 Britons may have been killed, if Tacitus is to be believed. In the wake of this defeat, further reinforcements were sent from among the Roman legions in Germany, and the natives quelled. Famine ravaged the country, according to Tacitus, because the natives had been 'careless about sowing corn, people of every age having gone to war', and the problems were exacerbated by the Roman soldiers confiscating some of the crops. Eventually the country was pacified under a more conciliatory imperial authority.[34]

As far as Verulamium is concerned, Tacitus's account is supported by archaeological evidence of a fire at about the time of the revolt, although the small size of the town at this period means that this evidence is scanty: as Niblett has suggested, Verulamium 'was still very much an emerging town where there was, as yet, comparatively little to destroy in terms of "Roman" buildings'.[35] It is likely that Verulamium was chosen for attack because of the pro-Roman stance of many of its inhabitants. The villa at nearby Gorhambury may also have been damaged by fire during the rebellion.[36] The town (and the villa) took some years to recover following the destruction by the rebels: some buildings were not replaced until the mid-70s AD, an example being the early retail development near the Central Enclosure.[37] However, by the late first century AD the town was flourishing, with large-scale public and private development. Following the rebellion of the Iceni and Trinovantes, Roman policy in Britain was much more successful, and the development of structures of imperial governance proceeded without serious interruption. As Niblett notes, the Folly Lane burial – of a native leader who evidently had cultural associations with Rome – is evidence of the persistence of a native elite under the Roman imperial authority, and the use of this elite as an instrument of the policy of 'Romanisation', which was followed in Britain and other colonies.[38] It is not clear who the wealthy and powerful individual interred at Folly Lane was, but in Niblett's words,

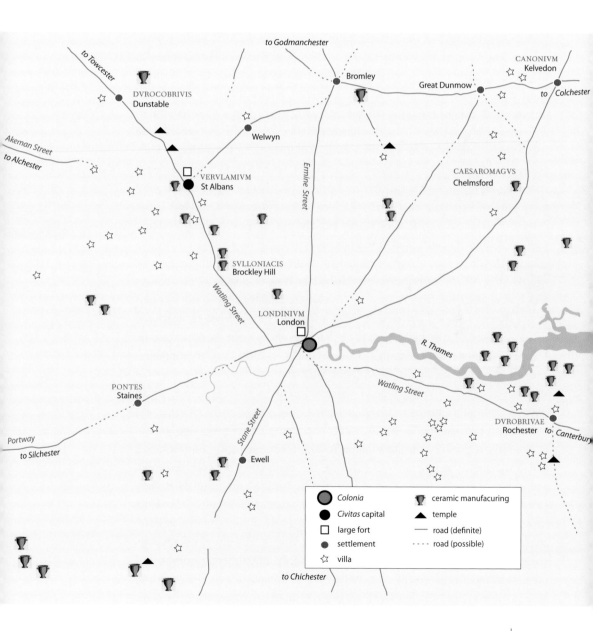

The ... burial suggests that there was an element among the native elite locally that could be relied upon to cooperate, controlled by a powerful individual who had seen service in the Roman army. Whether he was a client king ... or a *princeps civium* [chief citizen] is impossible to say, but we can safely assume that he was a man who had displayed sufficient pro-Roman sympathies at the time of the conquest to allow him to retain his wealth and position for over a decade after the conquest.[39]

Developments at Verulamium, then, reflected the success of the Romanising policy in the Catuvellauni territory, and increasingly elsewhere in Britain. It is important to emphasise the centrality of urbanisation to the process of Romanising Britain and the other colonies. Towns were central to the Roman way of life, from the imperial capital itself to the smaller urban centres in the outlying parts of the empire. The ancient world was based on city-states, and the political structure of the Roman empire reflected this form of social organisation. Britain and other colonies were organised into *civitates* (singular: *civitas*), the boundaries of which approximated to those of the pre-existing tribal areas. One example was the *civitas* comprising the Catuvellauni area, centred on Verulamium. The *civitates* were, in Peter Salway's words, 'city-states of varying status but all striving towards the character and condition of assemblies of Romans, with their own local constitutions and customs based more or less closely on that of Rome herself and subject to the overriding control of Roman magistrates'.[40] In practical terms, this meant that a town was responsible for its own government and for that of the surrounding region, or *civitas*. Some of the early towns established in Roman Britain were *coloniae*, which were chartered from Rome, and which were established to house veterans of the Roman legions. The first of these in Britain was Colchester, chartered in AD 49, where, as we have seen, the behaviour of the veterans provoked the Iceni and Trinovantes to rebellion. The second was Lincoln (date unknown) and the third Gloucester (AD 96–8); and York was also later promoted to the status of a *colonia*. Another type of chartered town was a *municipium*, which differed from other towns in being governed mainly by Roman citizens, and in having a surrounding *territorium* under the town's direct rule. Verulamium is 'the only reasonably certain example' of a *municipium* in Britain (Leicester and York might be others).[41] In practice, the distinction between *municipia* and other towns was minimal, and becoming even less significant as Roman citizenship spread in the second century AD. An edict of the emperor Caracalla in AD 212 gave Roman citizenship to all free-born subjects of the empire, confirming an existing trend in the western provinces. Therefore, whatever its status, the governance of Verulamium was probably little different from that of other Romano-British towns of a similar size and importance. Along with at least 15 other towns – Silchester, Cirencester, Canterbury, Exeter, Aldborough,

Chichester, Leicester, Winchester, Caistor-by-Norwich, Caerwent, Wroxeter, Brough-on-Humber, Dorchester, Carmarthen and Chelmsford – Verulamium was the seat of government of a *civitas*.[42] As capital of the Catuvellauni civitas the town underwent rapid growth in the early Roman period, after the setback of Boudicca's revolt.

Although Iron Age *oppida* had marked the beginnings of British urbanisation, the historian John Wacher remarks that 'few ... would have contained more than a haphazardly placed collection of huts, and none would have provided fully the functions which were expected of a town by the Roman provincial administration'.[43] Under Roman rule, the town stood at the centre of the *civitas*, which was divided into *pagi*, or counties; the town itself was divided into *vici*, or wards. A town was governed by an *ordo*: an elected council of 100 members, who were later known as *curiales*. To be elected to the *ordo* candidates had to meet a property qualification, and had to live in the town (although some towns, such as Silchester, were too small for the residential qualification to be enforced). The minimum age was 30. The *ordo* appointed magistrates: a town had two senior and two junior magistrates. The senior magistrates had control over criminal cases, although these powers were gradually ceded to assize courts; they also oversaw various military and religious matters, including the imperial cult. The junior magistrates had powers over public buildings and amenities. By the second century, elections were dying out and being replaced by co-option to the *ordo*; and the *ordo* and magistracy were 'virtually self-perpetuating'.[44] Nevertheless, it became increasingly common for those eligible for service – the curial class – to avoid taking office, as the duties were often onerous and the expenses great: a fee was payable on election or co-option to the *ordo*, and councillors were expected to make donations for public works in the town. However, in the early years of Roman rule, the governance of towns functioned quite effectively, and resulted in substantial development, at Verulamium and in the other *civitas* capitals. In a town so far from Rome, considerable autonomy could be exercised in practice by the *ordo*. Martin Henig has emphasised that 'as far as local people were concerned, the real power ... lay less in distant Rome than in the town council'.[45] Given the importance of local power structures, it is a measure of our limited knowledge of the history

The inscription on the Verulamium basilica has been reconstructed from fragments excavated in the 1950s. A full translation can be seen on p. 22. The basilica was the legal, religious and administrative centre of the Roman town.

© ST ALBANS MUSEUMS

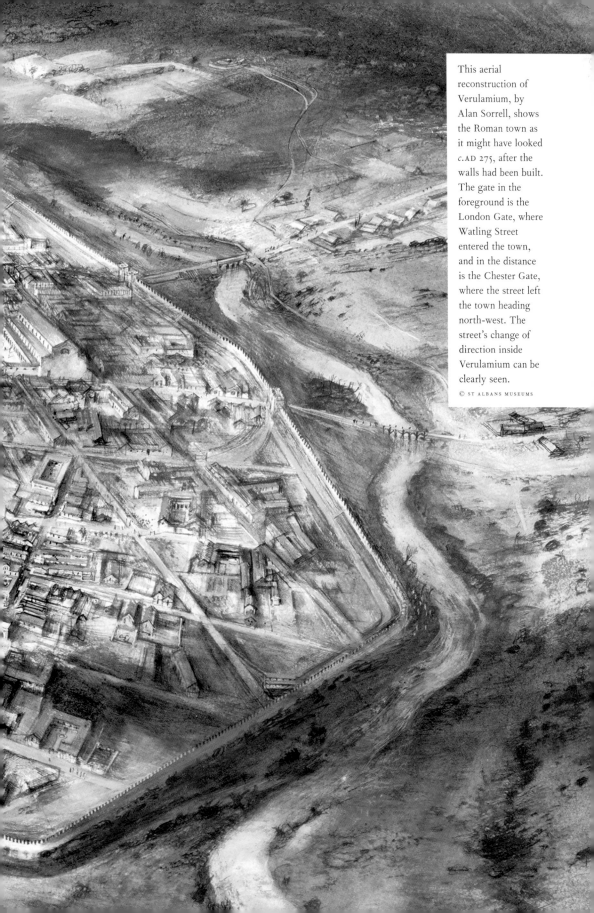

This aerial reconstruction of Verulamium, by Alan Sorrell, shows the Roman town as it might have looked *c*.AD 275, after the walls had been built. The gate in the foreground is the London Gate, where Watling Street entered the town, and in the distance is the Chester Gate, where the street left the town heading north-west. The street's change of direction inside Verulamium can be clearly seen.

of Verulamium that we know almost nothing about its governance: we can assume that it was ruled by an *ordo* and a magistracy, yet we do not even know the name of a single Verulamium magistrate.[46]

The economic, governmental, social and cultural functions of Roman towns, and their very similar political structures, resulted in physical developments that were common to many of them. It was usual for a forum and basilica to be constructed, to function as the main administrative centre of the town: the perceived importance of this physical manifestation of Roman governance was such that evidence has been found in some towns of the erection of temporary wooden structures prior to the construction of more permanent stone basilicas.[47] Large public bath-houses were usually built, and in many towns theatres or amphitheatres, market halls and temples. This pattern of urban development was reflected at Verulamium. In the late first century AD, when confidence had been steadily restored following the destruction of the town in AD 61, considerable development of public and private buildings took place. A forum and basilica were constructed on the site of the old Central Enclosure: the forum court measured 98 × 88 metres, and the basilica 45 × 120 metres.[48] An inscription on the basilica, dating from AD 79, marked the completion of the main public buildings of Verulamium; this has not survived in full, but has been reconstructed as follows:

'During the governorship of Gnaeus Julius Agricola ... the town of Verulamium pays homage by erecting this ornate civic centre.'

> To the Emperor Titus Caesar Vespasian, son of the deified Vespasian, Chief Priest, holding the power of a tribune for the eighth time, declared commander-in-chief for the fifteenth time, holding the office of consul for the seventh time, and already chosen to be consul for the eighth time, with the title of 'censor' and 'father of his country', and to Ceasar Domitian, son of the deified Vespasian, holding the office of consul for the sixth time and already chosen to be consul for the seventh time, leader of youth and priest of all the priestly orders. During the governorship of Gnaeus Julius Agricola, representative of the Emperor and with the rank of praetor, the town of Verulamium pays homage by erecting this ornate civic centre.[49]

The language of the inscription reflects the deification of Roman emperors; although in the case of this inscription, the name Domitian, whose posthumous reputation was poor, was later erased.[50]

In the same period, baths, an aqueduct, a market hall and various temples were all constructed, and the built-up area of the town extended. One of the temples was triangular, built in the late first century, and owed its shape to its position within Verulamium at the point where the road from London diverged.[51] Expansion continued into the second century, 'a period of almost uncontrolled development', in John Wacher's words.[52] The first theatre was

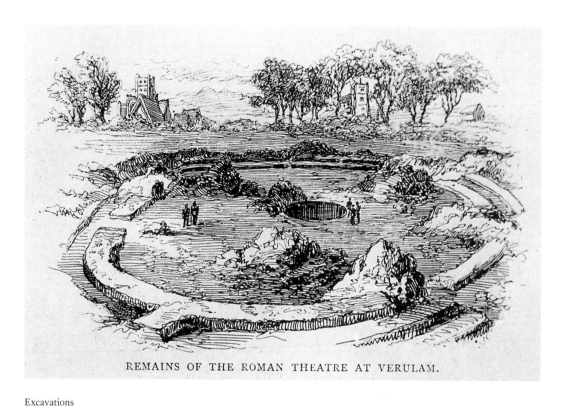

REMAINS OF THE ROMAN THEATRE AT VERULAM.

built in c.140: it was close to a temple, and as was common in the Roman world, its function was probably as much religious as dramatic.[53] An old ditch that had had been dug around the town in the first century was now filled in and covered to allow the town to expand, and a new earthwork, known as the Fosse and dated by Niblett to c.125–50, was constructed. The purpose of the Fosse is not entirely clear, but it surrounded a much larger area than the previous ditch.[54] Although memories of the old ditch lasted well into the third century – archways on Watling Street marked the places where the street crossed the ditch – it was 'systematically levelled' between 150 and 170.[55] The prosperity of Verulamium seems to have arisen from a combination of its administrative importance as the capital of the Catuvellauni *civitas*, its position at the heart of a well populated agricultural and industrial district, and its proximity to London, which became the headquarters of the Roman imperial authority. Watling Street linked Verulamium with the capital and facilitated trade; one reason for the rather late development of Iron Age Verlamion may have been its distance from the major ports of import and export. With the development of the port at London and the transport links to Verulamium, the location on the Ver became less isolated.[56] The Ver itself was small: its flow was used to power mills, but it was probably never a significant navigable river. However, it was canalised in the late second or early third century, and Niblett has

suggested that heavy items may have been moved 'by flat-bottomed boats or barges'.[57] Between *c*.AD 50 and *c*.150, locally produced pottery supplied many distant markets, before declining somewhat, but still serving a local market.[58] Insofar as the importance of a town can be measured by its size, at Verulamium's peak only the walls of London and Cirencester, among British towns, enclosed a larger area.[59] Niblett estimates the population of the town to have grown from around 1,000 at the time of the Boudiccan revolt to perhaps 5,000 in the mid-second century.[60]

If the public buildings of Roman Verulamium were impressive, some of the private homes of the curial class were no less so. Before suffering under the economic and political pressures of the later Roman Britain, this class enjoyed a high standard of living, in large and well-appointed houses. One building excavated by Sheppard Frere in the 1950s is a good example.[61] This house was built some time around AD 180, on the site of a previous house that was demolished. The house had two wings and a large courtyard. One wing was 57' 6" long, with rooms 19' 6" wide and ceilings 11' high. The walls were painted to simulate marble panels: the panels were red, each featuring a yellow candelabra, floral patterns and doves; and the room also had a red frieze. The ceiling was painted red or purple with a design containing wheat stalks and,

One of the highest
surviving stretches
of the Roman city
wall, just south from
the London gate.

Sheppard Frere
excavated a large
private house in
Verulamium in the
1950s, finding this
mosaic, featuring a
lion carrying in its
mouth a stag's head
with blood dripping
from it. The house
and mosaic date
from the late second
century AD.

again, doves. One room had a mosaic depicting a lion carrying a stag's head dripping with blood – as Frere pointed out, similar scenes appear in another Verulamium mosaic and in one found at Orbe in Switzerland.[62] This symbol of death was surrounded by four vessels containing wine: Martin Henig suggests that 'the floor can be read as a memento mori, "drink while your star gives you time for life"'.[63] The other wing of the house was even longer, at 67′ 6″, and continued to be developed in the early fourth century, after the first wing had been destroyed. On the courtyard wall there was a large painting, which is now in the British Museum. The decorative art on display in the domestic interiors of Verulamium's ruling elite reflected respect for the power of nature, a deep concern with death, and a belief in the power of salvation. Above all, however, it reflected the opulence and grandeur of the political elite. As Henig suggests, the private homes of the curial class were part of the physical apparatus of urban governance, and shared with the forum and basilica an important public role:

> The city councillors who ran the … city and commissioned wall paintings and mosaics would have been fully conscious of the need to overawe their clients who visited each day and to impress their equals who dined with them in the evenings: the *domus* was no more a private

place in Verulamium than it was in Rome. Here, it is possible that real decisions would have been taken by cabals of magistrates at dinner in advance of more formal sessions in the Curia. Under such circumstances private decoration had to have something of the character of a public monument.[64]

The status of elite residents of the town was bound up with their patterns of consumption, and these in turn stimulated the cultural and political life of Verulamium. Many homes were heated by hypocausts – an example of which can still be seen in the park at Verulamium – whereby heat was generated in an external furnace, and transmitted through pipes and flues through the floors and walls of the house.[65]

'Real decisions would have been taken by cabals of magistrates at dinner ...'

Members of the curial class are also likely to have occupied villas in the countryside surrounding Roman towns. Around Verulamium we know of a number of Roman villas: excavations have taken place at Lockleys, Dicket Mead, Park Street, Netherwilde, Munden, Gadebridge Park, King's Langley, Boxmoor, Northchurch, Childwickbury and Gorhambury. The last named was the closest villa to the town, lying north-west of Verulamium, close to Watling Street. As at other sites, pre-conquest buildings pre-dated the Roman villa; and, as noted above, there is evidence of the destruction of a building here at the time of Boudicca's revolt. After c.AD 100, masonry was used in a 'major reconstruction' of the buildings, transforming the site into 'a fully Romanised villa of some luxury'.[66] The main building had five rooms and two verandahs; fragments of stucco and a mosaic have been found; a hypocaust was added later; and the complex also featured a bath house and an avenue of trees.[67] Other villas at Boxmoor and Park Street also contained mosaics.[68] The economic life of the villa revolved around agriculture: there was a granary, and evidence of pastoral and arable farming. There may have been artificially created ponds for watering livestock, and rectangular enclosures suggest market gardening on the site. There are remains of cattle, suggesting dairy farming, and sheep and pigs, probably slaughtered for meat. The main market for the produce, presumably, was Verulamium. The workforce was probably housed at the villa, or elsewhere on the estate; it may have been augmented by residents of Verulamium. Villas, then, at Gorhambury and elsewhere, housed members of the urban elite, and were also centres of practical farming, and in some cases of industry – for example, bricks were produced, and flints quarried, at some Roman villas. Near Verulamium, there were kilns used for pottery at Verulam Hills Field, Prae Wood farm, and, southwards along Watling Street, at Bricket Wood, Radlett, Aldenham, Elstree and Brockley Hill.[69] At Gorhambury, and many other villas, a small semi-rural community, numbering perhaps between 30 and 50, had an intimate relationship with the nearby Roman town, and the economic fortunes of villa and town were inextricably linked. This meant

This floor mosaic was unearthed by Mortimer Wheeler's excavations of Verulamium in the 1930s. It was in a private house, with a hypocaust (an underfloor heating system), and is on display in a small purpose-built museum in Verulamium.

This male skeleton, in a lead-lined limestone coffin, was found at the Roman villa at Park Street. A nearby coffin contained a female skeleton, perhaps the wife of this man. Inhumation burials replaced cremations as the normal method in the early third century AD.

© ST ALBANS MUSEUMS

Watling Street entered Verulamium from the south-east through the London Gate, the foundations of which can be seen in Verulamium today. The reconstruction by P.M. Andrews, drawn at the time of Mortimer Wheeler's excavations, dates the gate and town walls to the second century AD, but it is now thought that they were not built until the early or mid-third century.

PHOTOGRAPH: CARNEGIE; DRAWING: © ST ALBANS MUSEUMS

PLAN OF EXISTING REMAINS

that a crisis, or a series of crises, could affect both. As the excavators of the Gorhambury villa point out,

> Until the late Antonine period [c.AD 150] it is possible to relate the growth of the town houses and villas. It was a period of stability and the countryside around Verulamium was sufficiently fertile to merit investment in land. Markets for produce were close at hand and either considerable surpluses and profits were being produced to pay for the construction of the villas, and perhaps ultimately the town houses, or the land was deemed sufficiently profitable to be accepted as collateral for loans to pay for building work. In such a situation any upset, whether national or local, could alter the economic balance and create insecurity.[70]

In or around AD 155 just such an 'upset' occurred: a fire destroyed much of Verulamium, perhaps a third of the town, including the forum, basilica and public baths. The cause of the fire is not known. As with the first-century destruction of the town, the recovery from the second-century fire was slow: for example, the town's baths lay in ruins for as long as 50 years.[71] However, the later second and early third centuries, when the town was again rebuilt, provide evidence of 'very considerable wealth' in Verulamium.[72] Many private houses from the period contained mosaics and hypocausts; and burials of members of the urban elite contain evidence of prosperity. One inhumation burial dating from around AD 200 – inhumation was coming back into fashion and was the normal method by c.250[73] – of a man aged about 50 featured a lead coffin decorated with scallop shells, symbolising the oceans across which the dead had to travel in the afterlife. This body was packed in chalk to aid preservation; and the man had very good teeth, a sign of a good diet probably featuring plenty of seafood – itself showing that Verulamium traded with many distant places.[74] Other burials took place with food – lentils, hazelnuts, wheat and cabbage – in jars beside the human remains.[75]

The continuing civic pride of Verulamium was shown in the reconstruction of the forum and basilica after the fire. The erection of arches over the site of the old ditch, a new gate, and the town walls, are all evidence of wealth, prosperity and confidence. The Verulamium walls enclosed an area of over 200 acres;[76] they were probably more than 4 metres high. Disagreements among archaeologists over the dating of the walls remind us how conjectural much of our knowledge of the urban history of Roman Britain remains. Wheeler dated them to the mid-second century, and Frere to the later third, but the early or mid-third century is now favoured. The walls featured five gates, three of which have been excavated: the London Gate, where Watling Street entered the town from the south-east; Chester Gate, where Watling Street left the town to the north-west; and Silchester Gate, on the south-western side of the town. Two more gates are known, referred to as the North Gate and North-East Gate, but they have not been excavated. The London and Chester Gates seem to have been impressive structures, probably quite ornate, although artists' impressions such as the one reproduced by the Wheelers (see page 30) are, in Niblett's words, 'of course conjectural'.[77] The walls enclosed a larger area than the built-up part of Verulamium, and although the increasingly uncertain political situation may have been one motive for their construction, display and civic pride was certainly another. In Niblett's words, Verulamium's walls were a manifestation of the 'self-confidence and prosperity' of the Roman town.[78] It has been estimated that 66,000 tons of flint were required to construct the walls.[79] Unsurprisingly, perhaps, their construction may have imposed a heavy cost on the urban elite: there is evidence of the temporary abandonment of Gorhambury and other villas near Verulamium in the late second or early third century, and it has been suggested that the cost of the town's defences may have severely affected the villa-owning class.[80]

Although the villas were re-occupied after the temporary decline, and although urban life at Verulamium continued to thrive, from the mid-third century onwards the economic and political difficulties of the Roman Empire as a whole were beginning to make themselves felt in Britain, and Verulamium

Jewellery, especially necklaces, was popular in the Roman empire, as these examples from Verulamium show. This picture also shows brooches, used to fasten clothes, and hairpins. The hairpin on the left-hand side of the photograph was found in a cremation burial.

The Roman theatre
from the west. The
theatre was built
in the mid-second
century, and
extended in the
third. It had fallen
into disuse by the
late fourth century.
It is thought that
the theatre was
associated with a
religion as much
as with dramatic
entertainment.

was no exception. There is increasing evidence of crisis in urban communities. Inflationary pressures meant that less money was available for construction of either private or public buildings, and it was not until the later third or early fourth century that, in John Wacher's words, 'people once more became interested in erecting new and comparatively useless public monuments', a tendency that was reflected in Verulamium by the construction of a triumphal arch over Watling Street and an extension to the theatre.[81] In general terms, the governance of towns was becoming more difficult. The freedom of action enjoyed by the *ordo* in the earlier Roman period was increasingly restricted, as the imperial bureaucracy expanded and centralising tendencies predominated. By the fourth century, laws were being passed to prevent the avoidance of office that was increasingly common among the curial class; and when, under the Christian emperor Constantine I (306–37), the endowments of pagan temples were confiscated, the resultant municipal funding deficit threw urban government into crisis. This was worsened by the transfer of urban lands to the emperor under Constantius II (337–61), after which the *curiales* themselves had to meet all the expenses of public works personally.[82] At Verulamium, there is evidence that the curial class was struggling to maintain its standard of living: several nearby villas seem to have experienced difficulties during the third century. The problems were exacerbated by the decline of some local industries, including iron workings in the Berkhamsted region; there is also evidence of the dilapidation of shops within Verulamium itself.[83] Although there are clear signs of economic recovery in the later third and early fourth centuries – for example, a row of shops along Watling Street dates from around 275 – it seems that Verulamium had passed its peak in terms of wealth and status.

Archaeologists have disagreed about the pattern of decay in Verulamium, and its similarities and differences to the decline of other Roman towns in Britain. The Wheelers identified a period of decline in the third century, followed by a 'Constantinian renaissance' in the early fourth, but their pessimistic view of mid-fourth-century Verulamium was of a town in ruins, and a 'return to a condition of barbarism'.[84] By contrast, Sheppard Frere argued that the economic vitality of the town was undiminished in the later third century, and identified much greater continuity of occupation well into the fifth century. It now seems clear that the wealth and size of the town was declining in the later fourth century: there is evidence of nearby villas at Gorhambury and Park Street, and of homes in the south of Verulamium itself, being abandoned. Houses continued to be built and refurbished into the fifth century, but the built-up area, which had spread beyond the original earthworks in the first and second centuries, was now beginning to contract.[85] Building and refurbishment were now concentrated in the area of the forum and basilica – the old Central Enclosure of the Iron Age *oppidum*. The forum and basilica themselves, and at least one of the temples, remained in use; roads and public squares continued to be maintained; and although the theatre was disused by the late fourth century, Niblett suggests that this may have been because of the decline of the religious cult for which it was used, rather than for any other reason.[86] Frere excavated a water-main, which suggested that the aqueduct was still working as late as 450, and from this he inferred occupation of Verulamium into the late fifth century, although another historian considered this to be 'rather a lot to read into a single pipe'.[87] Even if there was continued occupation this late, which is plausible given the slow penetration of the Anglo-Saxon invaders into Hertfordshire, it is not clear who the occupants were, or how they were governed. It is probable that 'slow decay' was the experience of Verulamium and most other British towns, although Wacher has also suggested that the process of decay may have been significantly accelerated by one or more outbreaks of epidemic disease, which are certainly referred to in some of the sources for the period.[88] Land was being vacated, which implies a falling population, and there is evidence of bodies going unburied in some towns, together with a marked reluctance of Anglo-Saxon incomers to settle in towns, which could be explained by disease as well as by their increasingly ramshackle buildings.[89] Although a Christian community survived somewhere near Verulamium, and although a small population probably continued to live in increasingly poor conditions, Verulamium, like other Roman towns, gradually declined along with the civilisation that had given rise to it.

'Religion may have been a more significant feature of the town than previously thought.'

The account of the rise and fall of Verulamium presented here has focused on the economic and political status of the town, but recent research has suggested alternative explanations of its importance. We know that religion played a key role in the life of the Roman Empire, ranging from the early promotion of the cult of the emperors as gods, to the mystical religions centred on the cults of Mithras and Cybele (who may both have inspired temples in Verulamium), and the Christian conversion under Constantine. In Verulamium, the site of the martyrdom of St Alban (see box 2), religion may have been a more significant feature of the town than previously thought. The excavation of the Catuvellauni burial site at Folly Lane, while providing valuable evidence of the early Romanisation of the *civitas*, has also suggested that Verulamium retained an ongoing importance as a religious centre through most of the period of Roman rule. This clearly has significant implications for the subsequent history of the abbey and town that were later built on the site of the martyrdom of St Alban. In the early 1990s, under the direction of Rosalind Niblett, a team from St Albans Museums excavated a burial dating from the mid-first century AD, near Folly Lane, overlooking Roman Verulamium from the other side of the river Ver. The rich cremation burial was that of an unknown Catuvellauni chieftain, with Romanesque decoration, on a scale 'so far unparalleled in late Iron Age Britain'.[90] It was suggested that this burial was of a 'client king', who died not long after the Claudian invasion. As noted above, this provides evidence of the close relationship that existed between the Catuvellauni and the Romans. However, the excavations went on to reveal a temple built on the Folly Lane site some time in the early second century AD, which seems to have retained its religious importance until the late third century. This has significant implications for our understanding of the cultural geography of Verulamium. The importance of temples in the Roman town has long been known, and it is also clear that the theatre, attached to a temple, served a religious function, as in other towns. However, the scale of the Folly Lane discoveries suggests that Verulamium was a major religious centre in the Roman period, probably a site of pilgrimage and host to a substantial temporary population – perhaps as large as the permanent population[91] – at times of ritual observances associated with

This mosaic depicting a scallop shell is also known as the 'sunrise pavement', and is one of the best known images of Roman Verulamium. It was unearthed by Mortimer Wheeler in the 1930s, and dates from the second century AD.

© ST ALBANS MUSEUMS

Many private households in Verulamium had their own shrines, at which daily offerings were made to the gods. This figure of Venus, the goddess of love and beauty, was part of a domestic shrine. She is holding a piece of fruit – a pomegranate or an apple – in her left hand: Venus was also associated with nature and the coming of spring.

© ST ALBANS MUSEUMS

Amphorae (singular: *amphora*) were ceramic jars with two handles and narrow necks, used for transporting liquids such as oil and wine. They are an important feature of the archaeological record of the ancient world. Their contents were traded across the Roman empire, and often beyond. Evidence from Iron Age hillforts, such as Danebury in Hampshire, shows that amphorae were imported well before the Roman invasion of Britain. Verlamion, with its wide economic links, is likely to have participated in this trade.

© ST ALBANS MUSEUMS

the Folly Lane site. This interpretation is strengthened by the presence of a bath-house on the road between the town and the temple complex, which was intermittently used, presumably when the religious site was also in use.[92] The Folly Lane temple was connected to the forum and basilica by the main road that ran to Braughing and Colchester, and by another road to the theatre.

Niblett argues that the Folly Lane site provides evidence of a long tradition of a religious cult at Verulamium, which began in the first century AD and was therefore 'deeply rooted in local custom' by the late third century, over 200 years later.[93] The reconciliation of Celtic and Roman religious cultures certainly seems to have been more successful than at Colchester, where the insensitive promotion of the imperial cult stirred the town to rebellion in the early years of Roman rule. It is by no means clear which cult, or cults, were worshipped at Folly Lane, or whether the focus of worship changed over time. Niblett hints at a water cult, associated with the marsh between Verulamium and the river Ver, which was crossed by the roads linking temple and town. As many as 40 pits close to the temple suggest various religious uses during the Roman period. It is fair to say that the full implications of the findings at Folly Lane have not yet been digested by archaeologists, but they have undoubtedly stimulated, and will continue to stimulate, new interpretations of Verulamium and its role in the life of Roman Britain. Isobel Thompson emphasises the potential for new archaeological findings to transform our view

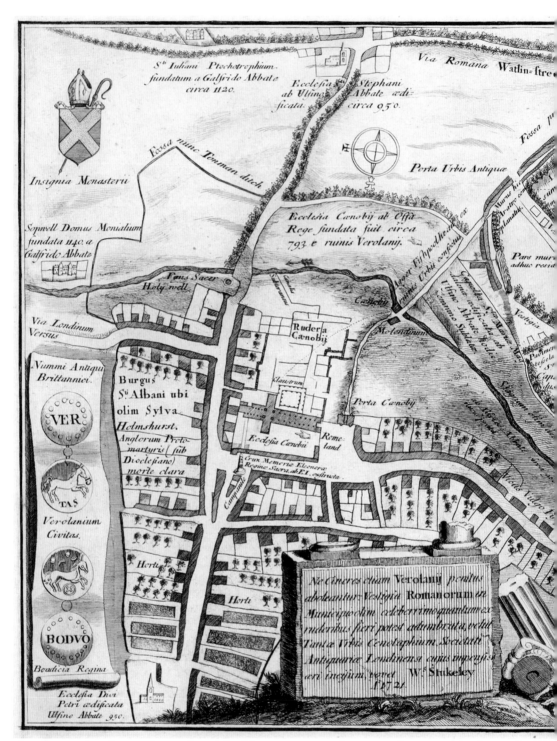

This early map of Verulamium, showing the position of the Roman town in relation to St Albans, was produced in 1721 by William Stukeley (1687–1765), an antiquarian and medical man best known for his work on Stonehenge. The map shows south at the top. The Roman street layout is speculative.

of the distant urban past: in her words, the Folly Lane discovery 'has altered entirely our view of Verulamium, and yet it was completely unsuspected until the excavation of 1991–93. It is an object lesson in reminding us that current models and theories are not necessarily the truth.' [94] In its wake, scholars have emphasised the religious and spiritual aspects of the history of Verulamium: for example, Martin Henig proposes that 'the most important public buildings [in the town] seem to have been temples'.[95] He also draws attention to the spiritual character of many decorations in private houses, which were similar to those found in London, Colchester, Cirencester and Silchester.[96] Daily offerings were made in private houses at domestic shrines made of bronze or pipeclay; private devotion is in evidence alongside public religious ritual.[97]

'A proud city with deeply conservative traditions'

It is not clear why the Folly Lane temple was abandoned around the turn of the third and fourth centuries, although this seems to have been the fate of similar sites elsewhere in the northern Roman empire during this period.[98] At Verulamium, it may have been part of the general tendency for the outlying parts of the town to be abandoned while the central areas remained buoyant. It would be tempting to suggest that the influence of Christianity played its part, but there is little evidence of any Christian community, or places of worship, in Roman Verulamium, and this explanation remains conjectural. In the next chapter we will examine the development of the site of the martyrdom of St Alban into a place of religious worship, but it is appropriate here to emphasise the older religious history of the town as a centre of native and Roman cults. Much of the twentieth-century archaeology of Verulamium played down this aspect of the town's history. The cultural influence of the Roman town did not necessarily diminish at the same rate as its population or its economic importance. The 'vigour' of the religious life of the town persisted well into the fourth century and beyond: as Henig explains, the depredations of late antiquity may have taken their toll on Verulamium, but the religious and cultural fires of the town were not easily extinguished:

What had changed? Undoubtedly there had been economic decline, the urban population was smaller and in purely material terms Verulamium was failing. But it was still a proud city with deeply conservative traditions … the voices of the ancient gods were not to be quickly silenced.[99]

Kingsbury and St Albans

The Anglo-Saxon abbey and town

W HEREAS our knowledge of Verulamium, and other Roman towns, is
scanty in the written record, and derives mostly from archaeological
excavations, for the Anglo-Saxon period we have more written evidence, but
written evidence which presents considerable difficulties of interpretation. The
very early post-Roman period – between the early fifth century and the arrival
of St Augustine in 596 – is, in the words of J. N. L. Myres, 'the most difficult
and obscure in the history of this country';[1] while the period from the early
seventh century to the Norman conquest in 1066 has left a relative abundance

The triforium in
the south transept
of the abbey church
contains unusual
baluster shafts,
which probably
date from the Saxon
period, and which
were incorporated
into the Norman
church. Above the
shafts, the plaster
has been removed,
and the Roman
bricks used in the
construction of
the church, under
the direction of
abbot Paul de Caen
(1077–93), can
clearly be seen.

PHOTOGRAPH: CARNEGIE

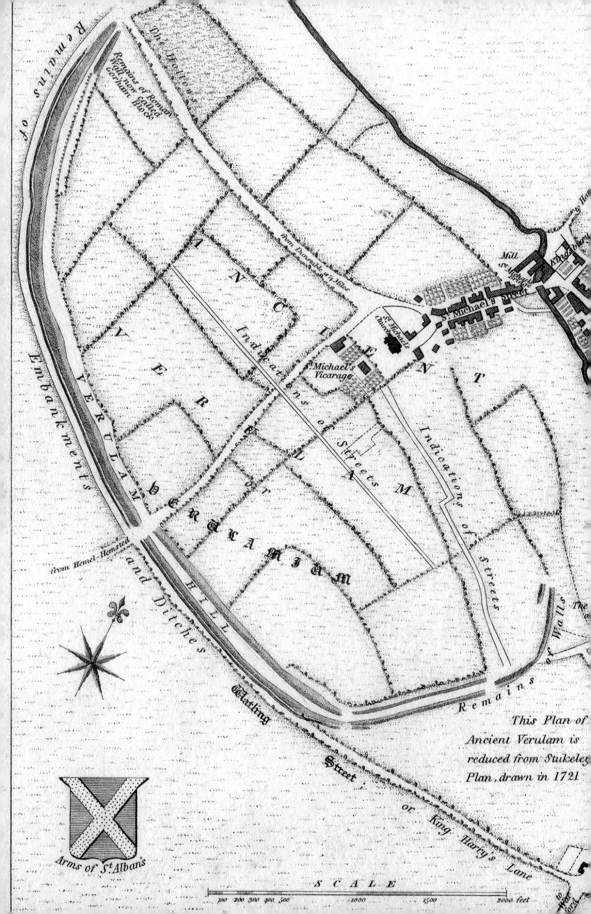

This Plan of
Ancient Verulam is
reduced from Stukeley
Plan, drawn in 1721

Arms of St Albans

SCALE

100 200 300 400 500   1000   1500   2000 feet

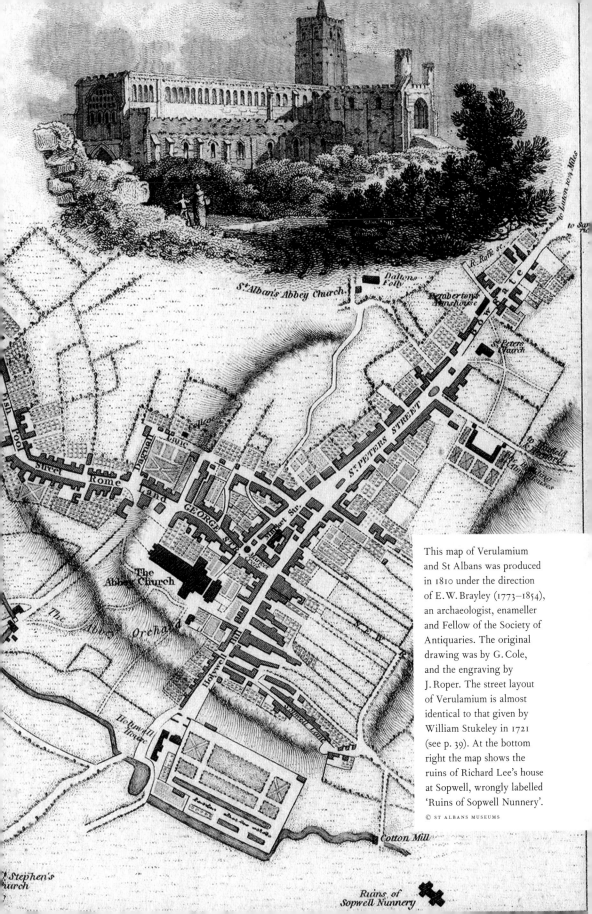

This map of Verulamium and St Albans was produced in 1810 under the direction of E. W. Brayley (1773–1854), an archaeologist, enameller and Fellow of the Society of Antiquaries. The original drawing was by G. Cole, and the engraving by J. Roper. The street layout of Verulamium is almost identical to that given by William Stukeley in 1721 (see p. 39). At the bottom right the map shows the ruins of Richard Lee's house at Sopwell, wrongly labelled 'Ruins of Sopwell Nunnery'.

of written material, but which must be used with particular care. On the other hand, in contrast to the rich archaeological record of the Roman era, material remains of Anglo-Saxon England are relatively sparse. The historian David Wilson remarks that many see the Anglo-Saxon period 'as a no-man's-land, across which flit insubstantial, semi-legendary figures – Hengist and Horsa, Arthur, Alfred and Offa'.[2] If the phrase 'Roman Britain' describes four or five centuries, when we refer to 'Anglo-Saxon England' we are speaking of a period of 600 years or more, beginning with an England divided into several kingdoms, and ending with the development of a recognisable political entity and the beginning of a modern line of monarchs. The 'dark ages', as it was once fashionable to call this period, saw the emergence of the English language and literacy, the slow conversion of England to Christianity, the establishment of the Benedictine monastic order, and the decline and re-emergence of a vigorous urban life. St Albans played a part in these developments.

'a radical and remarkable influence on the part of the incoming English'

Historians disagree about the extent to which the decline of Roman rule and the establishment of the Anglo-Saxon ascendancy represented a fundamental discontinuity in the economic, political and cultural history of England. In political terms, barbarian attacks destabilised Roman rule in Britain in the early fifth century: the 'traditional date for the end of Roman involvement with Britain' is 410.[3] The withdrawal of Roman troops had been happening for some time, and there is evidence of a small Saxon presence even before the Romans had left. Historians admit to being 'poorly informed' about what replaced the Roman system of government in Britain;[4] but there is no evidence of immediate discontinuity of political structures. The semi-independent *civitates* of the Roman occupation, such as Verulamium, may have continued to operate more independently under the rule of 'shadowy local potentates' or warlords,[5] while the native Romano-British population offered a mixed response to repeated Saxon incursions into their territory. However, by the end of the fifth century much of the south of England had fallen under Saxon control. In the sixth century, they expanded further into a island that seems to have been 'torn with political and military conflict'.[6] The Anglo-Saxon settlement of England was certainly slow. However, it was successful: for example, it has been emphasised that the survival of Roman place-names was very limited, as the influence of the English language spread between the fifth and the seventh centuries. As Stephen Johnson has argued, 'the success of English both as a spoken language and as a medium for naming places suggests a ... radical and remarkable influence on the part of the incoming English, over a period of time'.[7] In the case of Verulamium, the old name did not disappear from memory, but the Saxon name Waeclingceaster or Verlamchester was used in the eighth century, and Watlingchester in the tenth.[8]

Anglo-Saxon communities were predominantly agricultural. The unreliable sixth-century observer Gildas (see box 2) suggested that, following the decline

A small detail on the western end of the shrine of St Alban, showing the martyrdom of the saint.

of Roman authority, even agriculture broke down, and that 'the whole province [of Britain] was deprived of its food supply except for the resources of hunting'.[9] However, this was an exaggeration: for example, at Gorhambury near Verulamium, although the Roman villa itself was abandoned, agricultural operations appear to have continued.[10] In Gaul, the life of the Roman villas continued into the post-Roman period, but in England they were probably already in ruins by the time of the Anglo-Saxon settlement. However, the close proximity of many Roman villas to the manors recorded centuries later in Domesday Book (1086) suggests that we should be wary of assuming any wholesale transition in the practice of agriculture between the Romans and the Anglo-Saxons. As Martin Welch has asserted, '[i]f by continuity we mean that there was no time in the fifth and sixth centuries when the landscape of lowland Britain ceased to be inhabited, ploughed, pastured or otherwise exploited by human society, then surely there was continuity.'[11] Although there is impressionistic evidence of a 'drastic fall' in the rural population in the late fourth and early fifth centuries, there is no evidence of major

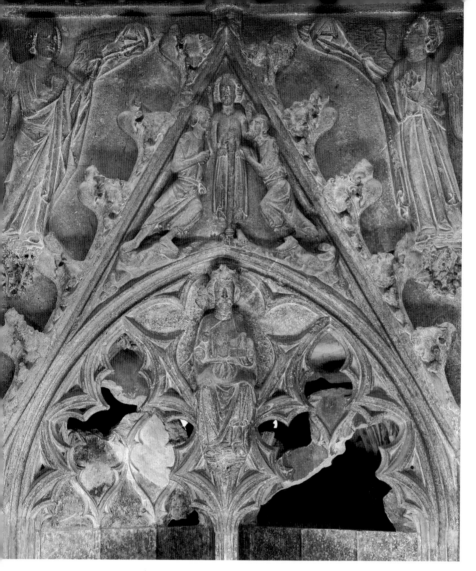

This detail from the
shrine of St Alban
depicts king Offa
of Mercia, who
reputedly discovered
the bones of Alban
and established the
abbey in 793. He
is shown holding a
model of the church.

PHOTOGRAPH: CARNEGIE

ecological change, or of the malnutrition that we would expect to result from
an abandonment of agriculture.[12] Certainly it was not long before the patterns
of Anglo-Saxon agriculture were established. The Anglo-Saxons grew barley,
wheat and oats, and raised sheep, cattle, pigs and goats. Flax was grown, and
wool was exported. The agricultural population used heavy ploughs, pulled by
oxen; there was also small-scale industry in the countryside, such as weaving.
Milling of corn took place in the countryside: Hatfield, near St Albans, had
four mills by the time of Domesday Book, while St Albans itself had three.[13]
The rural population was organised into villages comprising small huts with
sunken floors; as Wilson points out, the majority of the population lived like
this, whereas 'only a few specialists dwelt in the towns'.[14] Only about 10 per
cent of the English population at the end of the first millennium was urban:

one historian spoke of the 'town-hating Angles and Saxons'.[15] This idea is something of an exaggeration: in some parts of England at least, there were a number of 'proto-urban centres' from the seventh century, which could be described as 'truly urban' by the tenth century.[16] Among these were royal and monastic centres, such as the one that emerged at St Albans.

Despite this gradual emergence of towns, it is clear that the urban life of the Anglo-Saxons differed greatly from that of their Roman predecessors. Continuity is more difficult to find in the urban context, although many Roman towns were occupied, in one way or another, during the Anglo-Saxon period. Some were completely abandoned – Silchester is the best example – while Canterbury survived, 'albeit miserably', and some of the Roman buildings were used by the occupants the new Kentish capital.[17] Colchester, similarly, provides evidence of continuity. In London, Mortimer Wheeler suggested that life after the Roman withdrawal is likely to have continued largely unchanged, and that sub-Roman political authority persisted into the fifth and sixth centuries. However, the dramatic changes in the layout of London's streets, together with the disappearance of the episcopal authority and the difficulties experienced by St Augustine in reviving it, due to opposition from the pagan Saxons, suggest discontinuity in the urban economic and political life of the Roman capital.[18] In general terms, it is certain that the urban population of England fell after the Roman period, although it should be noted that the rural population also declined, perhaps in part because of a major environmental crisis or epidemic disease. In the case of Verulamium, for which a population of some 5,000 has been estimated at its Roman peak,[19] town life as the Romans knew it completely disappeared. When St Germanus (see box 2) visited Verulamium (for the second time) in the 440s, he stayed in a thatched hut, in Myres's words, 'hardly the accommodation for a distinguished bishop from Gaul had anything better been available'.[20]

The final decline of Verulamium probably occurred somewhat later than that of other Roman cities in Britain. One reason for this was probably the relatively late penetration of the area by the Anglo-Saxons, and the survival of a Romano-British population. The Chiltern region provides comparatively little evidence of early Anglo-Saxon settlement in terms of place-names or archaeological remains; and the fact that the Saxons captured a number of British strongholds in the region as late as 571 is clear evidence that some kind of sub-Roman culture survived here late into the sixth century.[21] Even if the main urban centres were largely deserted, unbroken occupation probably continued in rural areas. In the late sixth century, Hertfordshire burials contained Kentish objects, suggesting that Kent was the 'paramount power' in the region among the Anglo-Saxon kingdoms: it has been suggested that Kent was eager to control the Roman roads north of London, on which Verulamium stood.[22] However, although the Hertfordshire area was originally placed in

'town life as the Romans knew it completely disappeared ...

The building of
St Albans abbey,
following king
Offa's discovery of
the saint's relics, is
shown in this picture
from Matthew
Paris's chronicle.
It is now widely
believed that the
traditional account
of the building of
the abbey under
Offa's patronage
obscures the even
longer history
of a Christian
community in or
near St Albans.

the bishopric of London, established as early as 604, the midland kingdom of Mercia was politically dominant in the region by the late seventh century.[23] As a result, in the words of Martin Biddle, Hertfordshire was probably 'at least nominally Christian' by the third quarter of the seventh century, and had therefore been under pagan Saxon rule for only a century or less.[24]

In this context, the survival of a Christian community near Verulamium is not surprising, especially given the long-standing religious importance of the Roman town, which new archaeological evidence has pointed to, as discussed in the last chapter. A small community living on or near the site of the martyrdom of St Alban probably evolved into the abbey, which became the dominant local political and economic power by the time of the Norman conquest. The early history of the abbey is uncertain. The traditional account of its establishment is derived from the medieval monastic chroniclers Roger of Wendover and Matthew Paris (see box 1), whose accounts remain among the most important, and most troublesome, sources for the study of Anglo-Saxon history. In Paris's account, which followed Roger's, king Offa of Mercia, at

Bath in 793, was visited by an angel, who told him to create a worthy shrine for the relics of St Alban, in atonement for the murder of Ethelbert of East Anglia by Offa's wife Quendreda. Offa, accompanied by a large crowd including three bishops, then went to Verulamium, where he re-discovered the lost relics. At a synod held in the same year, 793, Offa gave a large endowment for the establishment of a monastery at the site. The monastery was given further endowments by Offa and his son Egfrith, and was organised according to the Rule of St Benedict.[25]

Although one historian writing in the early twentieth century, William Page, thought Paris's account of Offa's establishment of the abbey was 'doubtless correct' (with the exception, presumably, of the visit by the angel),[26] few historians would now accept the medieval monk's story at face value. Offa of Mercia certainly had an interest in St Alban – his 'palace chapel' at Wood Street in London, and the church which succeeded it on the same site, were dedicated to Alban[27] – and may well have had a direct involvement in the monastery, but the fanciful story of the rediscovery of the buried relics and the angelically inspired foundation of a Benedictine house actually obscures the even longer history of the Christian community at St Albans. Martin Biddle describes Offa's

continued on page 54

A seventeenth-century wall painting of Offa high above an arch in the north presbytery aisle, not far from the shrine of St Amphibalus.

PHOTOGRAPH: CARNEGIE

Box 1: 'A marvellous record of the past': historians and chroniclers at St Albans

As Chapter 2 makes clear, much of our imperfect knowledge of Anglo-Saxon St Albans is derived from the historical accounts of Roger of Wendover, Matthew Paris and other monks from the later medieval period. Chapter 4 will draw heavily on the roughly contemporaneous account by Thomas Walsingham of the struggle between the abbey and town of St Albans. It is important to understand these historians' and chroniclers' place in their own time, and in the abbey of St Albans, which became one of the leading centres of English intellectual life in this period.

There is little evidence of education or scholarly activity in the abbey before the time of abbot Paul de Caen in the late eleventh century: although the traditional date of establishment of the school is 948, there is no supporting evidence for this. The Rule of St Benedict required monks to spend a part of every day of the year reading, except during Lent. It is not clear what books the monks of St Albans actually read: the very imperfect surviving evidence suggests that, even at the height of the abbey's fame as a centre of intellectual pursuits, there were rather fewer books available at St Albans than at comparable institutions elsewhere.[1] The scriptorium at St Albans, where monks wrote, was not built until the abbacy of Paul de Caen, in the late eleventh century. The first great document known to have been produced at the abbey was during the abbacy of Geoffrey de Gorham (1119–45): the St Albans Psalter was an illuminated manuscript of over 400 pages, containing scenes from the lives of Christ and St Alexis, as well as the psalms. This was produced (for reasons that are not entirely certain) for Christina of Markyate, a well-known hermit who became an adviser to abbot Geoffrey and, in 1145, prior of a newly founded house in Markyate. Christina had made a secret vow of celibacy at St Albans, but had been forced to marry, and, having refused to consummate the marriage, underwent a long struggle to obtain its annulment.[2] Nevertheless, her relationship with abbot Geoffrey gave rise to 'gossip and jealousy', and there were veiled references among the monks to sinful behaviour between the two.[3] The psalter has been called 'one of the fullest and most vivid accounts of a woman's life to survive from the twelfth century'.[4] It appears to have been kept at Markyate for several centuries, perhaps until the dissolution of the monasteries, and then in the mid-seventeenth century was found again near Hildesheim in Germany; it is now in the cathedral library at Hildesheim.[5]

It was not until the early thirteenth century, and the appearance of the chronicle written by Roger of Wendover, that the abbey began to become known for the historical scholarship that would soon spread its fame across the Christian world. Roger probably wrote his historical chronicle in the 1220s and 1230s; he is known to have died in 1236.[6] He had been prior of Belvior, a dependent cell of the abbey that had been acquired during the abbacy of Paul de Caen.[7] His chronicle, known as the *Flores Historiarum*, covered many centuries of history, going back to the creation, although only the sections dealing with the thirteenth century itself appear to have involved him in original composition. His history of earlier times was 'essentially based on a compilation of well-known authorities ... which Roger ... may have inherited from a single St Albans text to which one or more St Albans

---

[1] Still, *Abbot and the Rule*, pp. 169–71.

[2] C. H. Talbot, 'Markyate, Christina of (*b.c.*1096, *d.* after 1145)', *Oxford Dictionary of National Biography*.

[3] Jane Geddes, *The St Albans Psalter: A Book for Christina of Markyate* (London: British Library, 2005), pp. 8, 13–14.

[4] Talbot, 'Markyate, Christina of'.

[5] Geddes, *St Albans Psalter*, p. 7.

[6] See David Corner, 'Wendover, Roger of (*d.*1236)' rev. Henry Summerson, *Oxford Dictionary of National Biography*.

[7] See below, p. 70.

This portrait is of Matthew Paris, from the *Catalogue of the Benefactors of St Albans Abbey*, which calls him an 'incomparable chronicler' (in the last line on this page). Paris lived from *c*.1200 to 1259, and his chronicles are important, if problematic, sources for the history of the abbey and town of St Albans, and for other aspects of the ecclesiastical and political history of the medieval period.

historians had already contributed'.[1] His work, however, has been criticised as being riddled with inaccuracies, relatively poorly written and 'shallow' in its learning. Nevertheless, Roger is a crucially important source for the history of St Albans, because his account of the martyrdom of St Alban and subsequent events on the site, although not original, was improved upon by his successor Matthew Paris and became 'the version of the history of the monastery of St Albans which the monks wished to propagate'.[2] This version is described in chapter 2.

Matthew Paris was probably the greatest of all the medieval monastic scholars at St Albans, and, as chapter 3 shows, played a considerable role in developing the public image of the abbey. Paris was born around 1200; he joined the abbey in 1217 and lived there for the remainder of his life, dying in 1259. He also travelled in the north of England and in Norway, where he was sent in 1248 by Pope Innocent IV to reform one of the country's leading monasteries.[3] However, his greatest fame rests on the *Chronica Majora* – a wide-ranging history, going back, like the *Flores Historiarum*, to the creation – and a number of other chronicles, which developed the work of Roger of Wendover and also broke considerable new ground. His *Gesta Abbatum Monasterii Sancti Albani* told the history of the abbots of St Albans from the supposed foundation of the house by Offa in 793. Some of Paris's historical reconstructions were 'highly imaginative', and consisted of dialogue which he cannot possibly have heard.[4] Other parts of the histories were based on the work of his unreliable predecessor Roger of Wendover, and on some older sources, which were also of doubtful accuracy. As a monk of St Albans, Paris was always concerned to present the abbey's point of view, and was particularly keen to document the papal recognition of the privileges of the abbey by Adrian IV.

[1]   Corner, 'Wendover, Roger of'.
[2]   Still, *Abbot and the Rule*, p. 11.
[3]   Simon Lloyd and Rebecca Reader, 'Paris, Matthew (*c*.1200–1259)', *Oxford Dictionary of National Biography*.
[4]   Still, *Abbot and the Rule*, p. 21.

His chronicles were carried right up to his own time; and, in in common with other monastic chroniclers, he can be characterised as 'more of a reporter, a journalist, than a historian'.[1] However, it was during the time of Matthew Paris that St Albans became 'the greatest centre of historical writing in England', which it remained for a century and a half after his death.[2] Paris was also an artist and illustrator of some note.

Paris was followed by several lesser known chroniclers, including William Rishanger, who continued the chronicle from 1259 to 1296, but whose achievements did not match his predecessor's. The continuance of the St Albans historical tradition was encouraged by abbots John de Maryns and Hugh de Eversdene in the early fourteenth century, during which time 'an extraordinary revival in learning and historical writing took place' at the abbey.[3] Under these abbots, and Michael de Mentmore, St Albans followed in a contemporaneous 'movement for improved monastic education', which resulted in improvements to the library and a greater encouragement to prospective monks to attend university.[4] In later years, one of these monks was Thomas Walsingham, who studied at Oxford, 'some time before 1376'.[5] Walsingham became the next, and last, great St Albans chronicler, who also followed scholarly activities in other areas, notably music and classical poetry. Although he spent most of his adult life at St Albans, in the years 1394–96 Walsingham was prior of Wymondham, a dependent cell of the abbey. He continued Paris's *Gesta Abbatum Monasterii*

Sancti Albani, but is best known for his *Chronica Majora*, which was also an explicit continuation of Paris's work, and, as chapter 4 shows, contained the same pro-abbey and anti-town bias that Paris had exhibited. This chronicle is an important historical source for the events of 1381, especially those which took place in St Albans itself, but Walsingham also casts some light on other events of the period.[6] Walsingham himself recognised that he was no equal of Paris, on whose memory he poured praise:

> Matthew Paris, monk of St Albans and an eloquent and famous man full of immeasurable virtues, a magnificent historian and chronicler, an excellent author … Diligently compiling his chronicle from the earliest times up to the end of his life, he fully recorded the deeds of magnates, both lay and ecclesiastical, as well as various and wonderful events; and left for the notice of posterity a marvellous record of the past … it is thought that there has been no equal to him since in the Latin world.[7]

[1] Richard Vaughan, 'Intorduction', in *Chronicles of Matthew Paris: Monastic Life in the Thirteenth Century* (Gloucester: Alan Sutton, 1984), p. 5.
[2] Still, *Abbot and the Rule*, p. 172.
[3] Ibid., pp. 173–5.
[4] Ibid., pp. 175ff.
[5] John Taylor, Wendy R. Childs and Leslie Watkiss, 'Introduction', in *The St Albans Chronicle: The Chronica Maiora of Thomas Walsingham, I: 1376–1394* (Oxford: Clarendon Press, 2003), p. xx; John Taylor, 'Walsingham, Thomas (c.1340–c.1422)', *Oxford Dictionary of National Biography*.

[6] Taylor, 'Walsingham, Thomas'.
[7] Quoted in Lloyd and Reader, 'Paris, Matthew'.

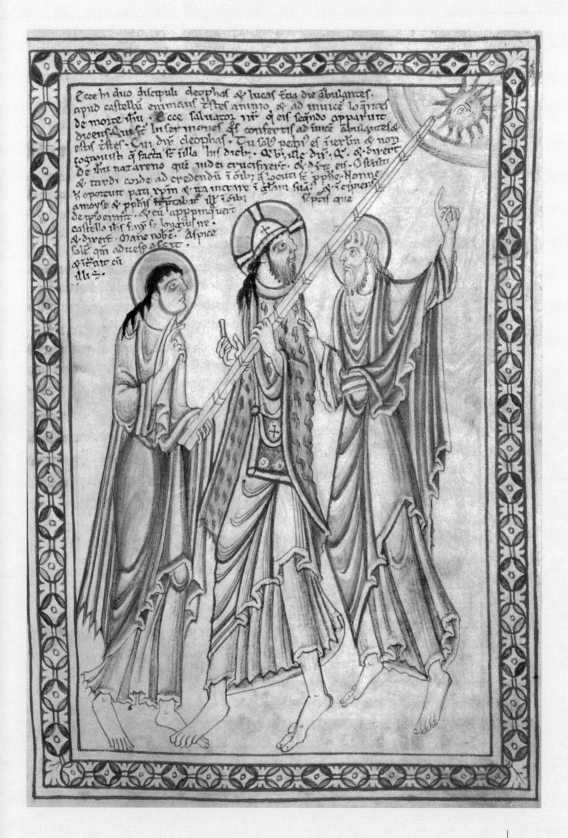

foundation of the abbey as 'St Albans tradition – it is barely more'; indeed, he emphasises the probability of a virtually unbroken Christian community on the site of the martyrdom of St Alban for several centuries before the supposed foundation of the abbey in the late eighth century.[28] In fact, Alban is unique among British saints in that there is 'evidence as clear and as consistent as could possibly be expected for the continued existence of a cult of St Alban centred on a church of Roman origin built on or near the site or sites of his martyrdom and burial'.[29] Bede, writing in the early eighth century, certainly believed that the cult had been continually present on the site. As discussed in the last chapter, the recent scholarly emphasis on the religious functions of Verulamium in the early Roman period suggests that the town's history as a place of pilgrimage is even older than St Alban himself. We can be reasonably sure that there was a continuous, or almost continuous, Christian community on the hill overlooking Verulamium, and that this evolved into a monastic settlement, based on the Benedictine Rule, some time before the late eighth century.

'there was a continuous ... Christian community on the hill overlooking Verulamium'

The Benedictines, or the 'black monks', were the dominant monastic order between the mid-sixth and the mid-twelfth centuries in non-Celtic Europe, from Italy northwards. Knowledge of the Rule of St Benedict, who died in 543, spread gradually through Europe in the subsequent decades, and was brought to England by St Augustine at the end of the sixth century. Although in the north of England, especially Northumbria, there was a powerful tradition of Celtic monasticism, by the time of Bede the Rule of St Benedict had spread to Wearmouth and Jarrow, the heartland of the Christian religion in the north. In the south, there was no alternative monastic tradition, and the Benedictine order spread more rapidly. The Rule emphasised a regular daily regimen, based on silence and contemplation. Although silence was not a requirement, monks often communicated by signs rather than the spoken word. Monks were to spend an average of four hours a day praying according to the liturgy – there were seven daily services, beginning with matins at 2 a.m. and ending with compline at 7 p.m. or 8 p.m. – four hours reading or in personal prayer, and six hours at manual work. The liturgy was chanted. Reading was from scripture and a limited range of prescribed literature of the early church. Although the manual work was not necessarily very heavy – local labour would be employed for tasks such as harvesting – the agricultural and craft work of the Benedictine houses made them comparatively self-sufficient institutions. The Rule banned the consumption of meat, although this was usually interpreted as red meat, allowing the monks to eat poultry; they also grew vegetables and consumed nuts and dairy products. There was an element of democratic government in monasteries: the abbot was elected by the monks, although his term of office was for life. As a leading historian of monasticism has observed, the Benedictine monastery was intended to be 'a unit, completely self-contained and self-sufficient, both economically and constitutionally'.[30]

The Rule of St Benedict was suited to the idea of the monastery as a 'little world',[31] where boys were often taken in infancy – the only formal education of any kind in Anglo-Saxon England was in religious houses – and spent their lives in contemplation. However, the Anglo-Saxon abbeys also served wider social functions. They provided a limited medical service through abbey infirmaries, offering spiritual and physical remedies. Through the education of boys, and in the scriptorium, where monks dutifully copied texts and, in some cases, composed their own chronicles, the monasteries exercised an 'effective monopoly over the written word' in Anglo-Saxon England.[32] Moreover, they were local employers and, increasingly, local landowners. Monasteries took control of increasing amounts of agricultural land in the Anglo-Saxon period, and St Albans provides just one example. The early accounts of the abbey suggest that Offa and Egfrith between them endowed the abbey with some 60,000 acres of south-west Hertfordshire, followed shortly afterwards by considerable lands in Buckinghamshire.[33] The leading religious houses became 'the economic centres of their communities'; they 'grew to be vast institutions, the centres of widespread economic and territorial organizations'.[34] The increasing involvement of monks in worldly activities had two results: first, the spread of the custom that monks would normally enter holy orders, and participate more fully in local community life; and second, a move away from active participation in agricultural work among monks, and a consequently enhanced social divide between monks and the local labourers whom they employed. The more land that the monasteries acquired, the greater the economic and social power of the monks. In the case of St Albans abbey, there is some doubt about the extent to which the Rule of St Benedict was followed at all in the eighth and ninth centuries: the abbey's territorial strength suggests that it was far from the 'little world' envisaged by Benedict, while Matthew Paris implied that the early abbots lived with their families, which would not have been possible were the Rule being strictly observed.[35] Both men and women lived at the early monastery – according to Paris, the women of the convent poisoned the unpopular third abbot, Wulsig – and it was, in the words of William Page, 'always distinctly an aristocratic house'.[36]

Across Britain, Benedictine monasticism was in decline in the ninth century, soon after Offa had, supposedly, established the abbey at St Albans. This decline mirrored developments on the continent, but in Britain the monasteries suffered with particular severity from the depredations of the Vikings. The Danish raiders caused particular damage to the great Northumbrian monastic houses at Jarrow and Wearmouth, whose geographical position left them especially vulnerable; but even in Wessex and south Mercia, more distant from the direct attacks of the Danes, the political and economic impact was felt. By the mid-ninth century many abbeys in the south of England were extinct or almost so: they did not necessarily cease to function – St Albans, Winchester,

'vast institutions, the centres of widespread economic and territorial organizations'

uerris possessiones siue libertates beati
albi monastio conferas· Et uid pui
legio isto ro borabimus co sequente·
Et monasterium illud inspecialem
romane ecce filiam adoptabimus·z
isto illud apostolatui subiacemus· nul
lo epo siue archiepo mediante. Vnde
h audiens illustris rex offa ut plibatu
est quid digne tante largitati respon
dento recompenset pr actat secam. Di
uinaq isprante gra· scolam anglo
rum ingredit que tunc rome flora
t i gressus, dedit ibi ad sustinacione
gentis regni sui illuc uenientis sing

ulos argenteos de familijs sin
gulis omnib; in posterum diebus
singulis annis· quib; uidelicet
sore tu contulit at domibus in
palatis· ut rriginta argente
orum paun excedet· Vt in tanta
busicas largicone optineret ut
de regno anglice nullus publice
penitens pexecuctione s iuuicte
penitencie subiret exillium· Ce
lebrata g conacone pdcam z suscep
ta ut plibatum confessione
z patru remissione cum benedicti
ne ··· ad ipa rex magnitatis pl

Christ Church Canterbury and others continued in existence, but appear to have been in the hands of clerics other than monks – but monastic life as promoted by St Benedict declined.[37] St Albans lay just outside the Danelaw, the area of Danish settlement and rule that covered much of the north and east of England, and was agreed upon in a treaty between the English king Alfred (871–99) and his Danish counterpart Guthrum in 886. The boundary of the Danelaw followed the line of Watling Street southwards towards Dunstable, and then the river Lea through Hertfordshire.[38] Culturally, Hertfordshire was not subject to heavy Danish influence – there are few Scandinavian place-names[39] – but there were some military incursions into the county, notably in 896 when the Danish fleet travelled up the river Lea to reach Hertford, and in 930 when St Albans itself was attacked, and the shrine of St Alban ravaged.[40] Nevertheless, the organisation of the estates of the abbey seems to have continued, and in later years the abbey benefited from the gifts of wealthy Danish settlers who prospered during the reigns of king Canute (1016–35) and his successors.[41]

The political uncertainty and conflict of the ninth century resulted in the construction by king Alfred of fortified settlements known as *burhs* across England, designed to withstand Danish attacks. Some of these *burhs* were in new places, previously non-urbanised, which subsequently evolved into larger towns – Oxford is a good example – whereas others made use of old ramparts and defensive works.[42] One example of the latter is the royal *burh* near St Albans abbey, known as Kingsbury. It has usually been thought that Kingsbury stood on the site of the area of St Albans known by the same name today, across the river Ver from the Roman town and to the south of

the recently discovered religious site at Folly Lane. It has been described as 'a Saxon town of considerable size, protected by earthen ramparts on all sides'.[43] The remains of earthworks can be seen in the area. However, it has recently been pointed out that very little Anglo-Saxon archaeological evidence survives from the area of modern Kingsbury, where most of the remains are Roman or medieval, and that the supposed 'ramparts' of Kingsbury were not defensive structures at all.[44] As a result it has been suggested that Alfred's *burh* was actually situated in the remains of Roman Verulamium itself.[45] Three pieces of evidence lend credence to this view: the fact that, in the medieval period, the name Kingsbury was used for the area of St Michael's church, which is on the site of the Roman forum and basilica; the long history of Fishpool Street, which was the main route between the abbey and Kingsbury in the tenth century; and the pattern of re-using old defences that can be observed elsewhere in Anglo-Saxon England.[46]

The modest amount of urban development that took place in the *burh* of Kingsbury caused considerable political disquiet in the area. Because it was established when monastic life at St Albans – and elsewhere – was at its nadir, and because of its strategic location and royal foundation, Kingsbury was at first able to exercise relatively unchallenged authority in the area. The royal 'servants' who lived there made themselves unpopular. For example, at some point, on the northern side of the Ver between Kingsbury and the abbey, a royal fishpond was dug, and according to Matthew Paris,

> The fishpond, which was called 'Fishpool', was too close to the Abbey and was causing a nuisance. For it was a royal fishpond, and the King's servants and fishermen were a trouble and a burden to the monastery and the monks. They continually used their status as King's men to behave in a rude and oppressive manner towards the servants of the monastery.[47]

Even at the distance of several centuries, Paris was hardly a neutral commentator on the relationship between the abbey and its neighbours. However, it is easy to see how the establishment of a royal *burh* on the abbey's doorstep could lead to resentment, and it is unsurprising that rivalries between the royal and religious foundations sprang up in the tenth and eleventh centuries.

These rivalries were intensified by the revival in the fortunes of English monasteries in the mid-tenth century. It is in the wake of this revival that we can identify the beginnings of the history of the modern town of St Albans. Following the assimilation of the Danish settlers in England, the pacification of the countryside and the coasts, and the unification of the country under a single political authority, a monastic revival became possible. Although monasticism had largely died out, its traditions and some of its institutions had not, and under the leadership of a trinity of monastic bishops – Dunstan of

RIGHT
This engraving of St Michael's church was made by Joseph Clayton Bentley (1809–51) from an original study by the landscape painter Charles Marshall (1806–90). It dates from the late 1830s or 1840s, and depicts a burial taking place in the foreground. Victorian refurbishment considerably altered the appearance of St Michael's, which was one of three churches reputedly established by abbot Ulsinus or Wulsin in AD 948.

FROM THE COLLECTION OF TONY BAXTER

Canterbury, Oswald of Worcester and Ethelwold of Winchester – this revival was effected. Dunstan was associated with Glastonbury, which can be seen as the centre of the revival, but across England monasteries and monastic culture were re-established, and the economic and political strength of the Benedictine order re-asserted. St Albans abbey was re-formed in c.969, which has been attributed to Oswald, but the first abbot of the re-formed house was Aelfric of Abingdon, who is known to have been influenced by bishop Ethelwold.[48] The new monasteries fostered artistic achievement, especially the creation of illuminated manuscripts: according to the monastic historian Dom David Knowles, St Albans was one of the abbeys where 'creative genius' was to be found in the later tenth century.[49] Economically and politically, royal support, especially in the person of king Edgar (959–75), was essential to the success of the monastic revival. Edgar was anointed in 973, giving his kingship the authority of the church; and prayers were said for the royal family in monasteries, under the authority of the *Regularis Concordia*, a document prepared at a synod in Winchester c.970 under the influence of the three

monastic bishops.[50] In return, a succession of kings and members of the noble elite gave land to religious houses, which became very rich in the tenth and eleventh centuries, owning nearly a sixth of the total income of England, as recorded in Domesday Book.[51]

St Albans abbey benefited economically from its re-formation and the monastic revival, although it was not as wealthy as some of the largest monasteries in late Anglo-Saxon England. Our chronology of the abbey's history derives from Matthew Paris, and is not wholly reliable, but we can identify a period of considerable growth, in terms of land holding and local political power. Under successive abbots, St Albans abbey expanded its power and prestige. According to Paris, after complaining about the behaviour of the king's servants in the royal *burh*, abbot Aelfric bought the controversial fishpond from King Edgar, promptly draining as much of it as possible, leaving a small part for his own use: a fishpond is mentioned in Domesday Book.[52] There is evidence, dating from the 960s or 970s, of new building in the grounds of the abbey itself, as well as a cemetery featuring distinctively late Saxon burial practices.[53] At some point in the mid- to late tenth century, or perhaps the early eleventh, abbot Ulsinus or Wulsin built three churches: St Stephen's, St Michael's and St Peter's, all on sites where churches of the same names stand today. Paris dated these foundations to 948, which is also the traditional (but unsupportable) date of foundation of St Albans School.[54] Although the exact dating is speculative, the establishment of three churches on the main approaches to St Albans is evidence of the abbey's self-confidence in a period of expansion.[55] St Michael's church was built under the walls of the Roman forum and basilica, which may still have been partly standing; if this was the site of Alfred's Kingsbury, then the construction of a church by the abbey seems to represent another significant victory over the royal *burh*. In the early eleventh century, during the reign of Canute, Kingsbury itself was sold to the abbey, and mostly demolished, although a small remnant was left, which was not destroyed until the mid-twelfth century.[56]

This last acquisition was part of a number of developments, all of which have left a somewhat blurred historical record. The sale of Kingsbury was at least closely related to the acquisition of the ruins of Verulamium, which occurred in 1005; the two things may in fact have been the same event.[57] Aelfric died in the same year, and, although no longer abbot, left property in the area to the abbey, which further confuses the picture. While extensive demolition took place at Kingsbury, the abbot – who may have been Ealdred or Leofric, depending on which chronicler's account is believed[58] – also began work on the ruins of the Roman town. Paris's account of this work reflects the durability of the disused Roman buildings, and emphasises the moral decay of Verulamium, which was used mostly by unsavoury characters for nefarious purposes:

The interior of St Stephen's church today bears little resemblance to the medieval church that was reputedly built in 948. This picture shows the nave. To the right can be seen a replica of a distinctive brass eagle lectern, which was hidden during the Civil War and rediscovered in the mid-eighteenth century. The font in St Stephen's was built in the mid-fourteenth century (see page 157).

[The abbot] knocked down, filled in and blocked up the rough passages and streets, together with the underground passages, which had been solidly and skilfully built with arches, some of which formed the underground water system which had once flowed round much of the city. For they had become hiding places for robbers, cut-throats and strumpets. So far as he could, he levelled the ditches and caverns in which criminals and outlaws had come out of the thick neighbouring woods to take refuge.[59]

While the abbey secured its position as the greatest power in the area, it also began its own programme of urban development, and established a market; Matthew Paris also attributed this to abbot Ulsinus and dated it to 948, although this is no more reliable than Paris's dating of Ulsinus's three churches. Ulsinus is supposed to have encouraged the settlement of a township in the vicinity of the abbey and started the market somewhere to the north, between the abbey and St Peter's church, not far from where the market is held today. Roman Watling Street was diverted, taking it around the north of the abbey: the diversion comprises modern-day Holywell Hill, High Street and George Street, and travellers could continue down Fishpool Street to re-join the Roman trunk road at St Michael's. The new churches of St Stephen's and St Michael's stood at either end of this diversion. Archaeological evidence from these two churches suggests that the late tenth or early eleventh century is a more likely date than the traditional 948 for their construction, and therefore also for the development of the Anglo-Saxon town.[60] To attract residents, the monastery provided timber for settlers to use; it is also likely that, in common with procedures adopted elsewhere to encourage urban settlement, land was provided rent-free for a period of somewhere between three and seven years.[61] If the town was laid out prior to the acquisition of Kingsbury, then it may have been a deliberate attempt to strengthen the economic power of the abbey in relation to the royal *burh*; however, it probably makes more sense to see the acquisition and destruction of Kingsbury as a roughly contemporaneous development. It is certainly the case that deliberate urbanisation, on a small scale, represents the beginnings of the history of the modern town of St Albans. This may also have been when the town became known as St Albans, which was the name it was given in Domesday Book.

The establishment of the abbey's township needs to be seen in the wider context of urban development in tenth- and eleventh-century England. It has been suggested that the laying out of streets as part of the development of *burhs* in the late eighth and early ninth centuries was an attempt to foster commercial activity in towns alongside their defensive functions, although other historians argue that urbanisation was modest until the tenth century.[62] During the reign of Athelstan (924–39) there was a concerted attempt 'to concentrate the marketing, minting and defensive functions in one place', and there was a further urbanisation of the *burhs*.[63] By the tenth century the word 'borough' was understood, legally, to mean a 'port or trading place'.[64] Tenth-century kings tried to give towns monopolies on commerce above a certain value, and to develop a network of mints in urban centres.[65] The economic expansion, under careful royal and aristocratic guidance, encouraged the settlement of planned towns, such as St Albans. It is clear that urban life was deliberately fostered by the landed elites of Anglo-Saxon England. As Richard Britnell has explained,

> at every stage in this period [600–1300] the fortunes of towns were shaped to a large degree by the decisions of landlords rather than entrepreneurial choices of townsmen. Investment in urban development, and infrastructure, the location of large households, garrisons and armies, and the choice of schemes for provisioning them, were all predominantly matters for decision by the king, the magnates and the greater churches.[66]

St Albans was one of a small number of planned towns established before the time of the Norman conquest by Benedictine monasteries: other examples include Bury St Edmunds ('certainly a considerable, perhaps a major, town' by

the time of Domesday Book),[67] Glastonbury, Peterborough and the Longport borough at Canterbury; in addition, Evesham, Sandwich, Coventry and Rye may also pre-date the conquest. Others such as Sherborne, Battle and Ely were laid out after 1066.[68] Characteristic of these monastic towns was a triangular market place, along the base of which the abbey gatehouse usually stood, although not at St Albans, where the gatehouse stood at Romeland, which was the site of a medieval fair, but not the town's market.[69] The reason for the different location of the market place at St Albans may lie in the relationship between the royal *burh* and the abbey: if the king still had the land to the north of the abbey gatehouse, the abbot could not develop his market on the site. T. R. Slater, in an examination of the layout of the housing plots in St Albans, has argued that there were two phases of town planning, carried out by separate authorities: an earlier phase, around Dagnall Street, which was carried out under the auspices of the *burh*; and a second phase, along the east side of Holywell Hill and St Peter's Street as far as St Peter's church, which was fostered by the abbey.[70] The latter was characterised by long thin plots of land, a feature of other settlements of the period, and suggesting the presence of gardens and orchards.[71] As Slater explains, the early development of this planned town at St Albans prefigured the urban experience at many other places in the medieval period:

RIGHT
The Reverend Henry Fowler (1827–1900) was a master at St Albans School from 1863. A keen archaeologist, he prepared this detailed plan of the abbey and its precincts. It now hangs at the western end of the cathedral's north aisle.
PHOTOGRAPH: CARNEGIE

> It is reasonably clear that St Albans is of considerable significance in the history of urban development in England. Its topography is very different from that of the more or less contemporary *burhs* of Wessex and midland England and, whereas in the *burhs* it was royal decision-making that was to the fore and Benedictine institutions were generally fringe features of the towns, in St Albans it was the abbot who took the initiative and the king's palace that was to become a fringe and, ultimately a derelict, feature. St Albans has none of the rectangular grid of streets that have come to be regarded as typical of the most developed of the *burh* towns and characteristic of their planned nature ... but the plan of St Albans points the way to the hundreds of new single-street market towns that were to [be] laid out by secular and ecclesiastical lords in the twelfth and thirteenth centuries to enhance the economic development of their estates in all parts of the kingdom.[72]

This account of the development of St Albans has been questioned by Isobel Thompson, who suggests that the original market and urban development actually took place within the precinct of the abbey, rather than at the modern market place and along Chequer Street and Holywell Hill, and that an earlier diversion of Watling Street ran across the abbey orchard; if this is the case, then the development of housing plots on Chequer Street and Holywell Hill was

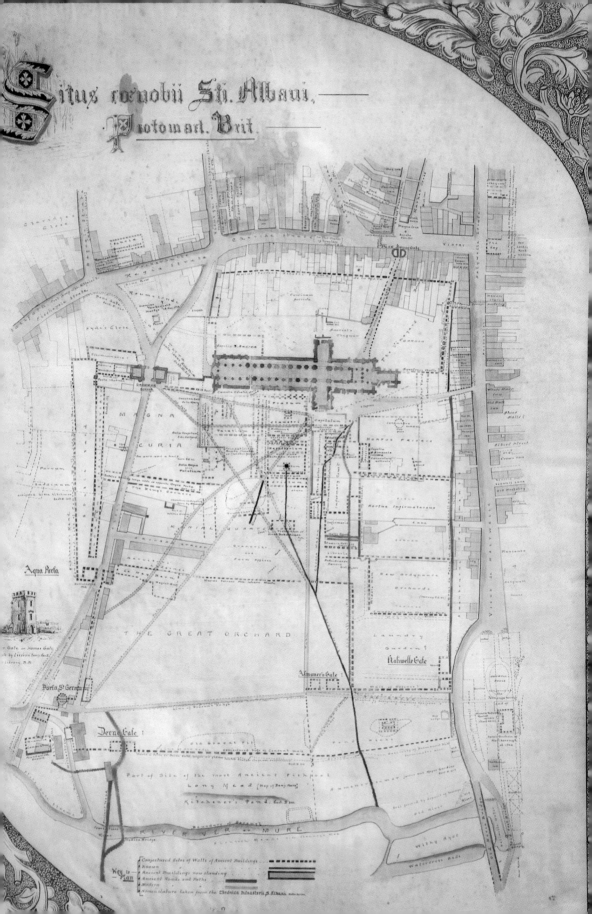

Situs cœnobii Sti. Albani,
Protomart. Brit.

somewhat later than previously thought, probably in the early to mid-twelfth century.[73] This was, in Thompson's account, also when the roads were diverted to their present course. Dagnall Street, known as Dagnall or Dagnal Lane in the medieval period, was occupied at the same time or a little later;[74] again, this calls into question the location of the incipient town, but not its existence. It is clear that St Albans was planned and managed by the abbey, in common with many other medieval towns – a feature of its origins and governance that would cause repeated conflict in the following centuries – and in this respect, in Thompson's words, 'St Albans takes its place alongside other towns with comparable histories'.[75]

By this time the influence of the abbey reached well beyond the local area. Aelfric, for example, became bishop of Ramsbury in 990 and archbishop of Canterbury in 995.[76] One of his successors, Leofstan, abbot at St Albans from the late 1040s according to Matthew Paris, was a member of the royal household, and, probably using his royal influence, acquired yet more land for the abbey from the nobility, and from the wealthy Danish settlers who are known to have supported the abbey in the eleventh century.[77] By the time of the Norman conquest, St Albans was a well-endowed Benedictine house, which owned a substantial amount of land locally, and by the time of Domesday Book had 'a comfortable income' of £270 annually.[78] Although many monasteries were richer than St Albans – the wealthiest was Dunstan's Glastonbury, with £828 – many were much poorer, four having an annual income of less than £40.[79] St Albans was the twelfth richest in England at the time of Domesday Book.[80] Along with many abbeys, St Albans had a feudal obligation to provide a small number of knights to serve the king in the early Norman period;[81] but it was also owed many feudal obligations by its tenants. Politically, it was probably stronger than most monastic houses, with its succession of powerful abbots, itself perhaps the legacy of the 'aristocratic' character of St Albans. The abbey's victory over the royal *burh* of Kingsbury, and its oversight of controlled local urbanisation, illustrate the benefits of the re-formation under Aelfric, and the successful stewardship of the monastery by his successors during the following century. Abbot Leofstan died in January 1066, shortly before the Norman conquest; as the monastic chronicler of St Albans remembered, he died leaving his abbey 'overflowing with all good things'.[82]

CHAPTER THREE

Norman Conquest to Black Death

A LTHOUGH we are better informed about the urban history of St Albans
after the Norman conquest than before it, there remain significant gaps
in our knowledge of the town. The archaeological record is patchy, and the
documentary relics of the period tell us more about the history of the abbey
than about the town and its people, except for the moments when the two came
into conflict, which were often violent. Even the abbey's surviving records are
deficient compared with those of comparable monastic houses. We cannot even
be certain, before the twelfth century, exactly where the urban settlement of
St Albans was. One historian remarked that 'although a borough of St Albans
apparently existed at the time of the Domesday survey, it long remained very
obscure'.[1] We know that it was small: Domesday Book records that St Albans
in 1086 had 81 householders, from which it has been estimated that there was
an urban population of around 500.[2] Estimates for the largest towns in England
in 1086 give the population of London as about 12,000, York about 8,000,
Norwich and Lincoln around 5,000 each, Thetford 4,000, Oxford 3,500 and
Colchester 2,000.[3] Hertfordshire had no towns approaching this size. Hertford
itself had been laid out in 912, according to the *Anglo-Saxon Chronicle*, and
was probably the only town in Hertfordshire that could rival St Albans in
size during the early post-conquest period.[4] The wealth of Hertfordshire was
'almost wholly derived from its rural manors' in 1086.[5] (The manor was the
standard unit of territorial organisation in medieval England: the word refers
to an estate of land owned by a lord, such as the abbot of St Albans, together
with the services that were owed to the lord from the tenants of the land.)
Even as the largest centre of population in the county, St Albans at this time
was low down the English urban hierarchy: of the 112 towns named in the
Domesday survey, St Albans was one of the smaller, ranked at 72nd in one
historian's very tentative list.[6] Its size and importance increased significantly
during the next two centuries; and much of this expansion was fostered by the
abbey that had created the town.

The manuscript illumination contains the following Latin text:

ginti solidos. predictam uero tram dicta spe
lipa dari procuraut huic ecclie p aima pnoris
maniti siu vlfi

Oolf quidam danus pre
potens minister sancti Colbar
di Regis filu Ethelredi Regis
Anglie. dedit nobis tram que
uocatur Estuua cum ommi
bz ad eam ptinentibz. 7 Orlbi
eam. atqz umu calicem 7 umu
missale 7 umu torsale:

Sadlbpinus te Cadingdone
dedit huic monasterio tram
que uocat Ibaterforde 7 Beoron
team. 7 leg. uut msup biginti
boues 7 biginti baccas huic loco.

Egellbpinus pe Slbarte 7
Ibpnfleda bror eius dederunt
teo 7 sancto albano tempore Re
gis Colbardi ultum ante co
questum Redburnam. Gie
neburlbe. Langeleiam. Thiban
tinam. Et Ibpnfleda uxor e
iustem dedit huic ecclie unam

This page of
the *Catalogue of
Benefactors of St
Albans Abbey* depicts
three laymen who
had given land
and other gifts to
the abbey. Those
shown here are
Tolf (a Danish
benefactor), Eadwyn
of Caddington
and Egelwyn the
Swarthy, with his
wife Wynfleda.
The *Catalogue
of Benefactors*
was begun in
1380 by Thomas
Walsingham.

REPRODUCED BY KIND
PERMISSION OF THE
BRITISH LIBRARY

Monasticism and the power of religious houses expanded significantly after the Norman conquest. In 1066 there were around 60 'houses of monks and nuns' in England, with 1,000 or slightly more inhabitants; by 1216 there were about 700, with a population of some 13,000.[7] Even at the time of Domesday Book, in 1086, Benedictine houses held around a sixth of the land of England south of the Humber, and this was before the onset of what was 'arguably a golden age for monasticism in England' in the century after the conquest.[8] A feature of the period was the establishment of dependent cells or daughter houses: separate priories under the rule of an abbey. There was also an influx of new monastic orders: whereas the Benedictines were the dominant order before the conquest, in the late eleventh and early twelfth centuries several Cluniac monasteries were founded; and ascetic orders such as the Cistercians established many abbeys, often, like those of Yorkshire, in the countryside. Foundations of Augustinian houses, organised on a smaller scale than the large Benedictine establishments, peaked in the second half of the reign of Henry I (1100–35): an example in Hertfordshire was the community of Augustinians at Royston, with just seven canons.[9] By contrast, the largest monasteries, such as St Albans, probably had about 100 monks in residence at their peak.

Although they benefited in the long term, most English monasteries struggled in the immediate post-conquest period. They were suspected by the Norman incomers of being sources of opposition, not unreasonably in many cases, as some Anglo-Saxon abbots had fought against king William in 1066. One of these was abbot Fritheric of St Albans, who had succeeded Leofstan in 1066.[10] The early post-conquest years were 'difficult' ones for the abbey of St Albans. In the first decade after 1066, it lost some of its land, at Aldenham and Flamstead, and also the manor of Great Gaddesden, which were seized by the Crown. In the short term, the value of the abbey's lands

Part of the ruins of Tynemouth priory, in Tyne and Wear. This Benedictine house was one of a number acquired by the abbey of St Albans in the second half of the eleventh century. The priory had an eventful history. Abbot Richard de Wallingford exiled some of his monks to Tynemouth as a result of their sympathy with the townspeople in the rebellions of the early fourteenth century, and some monks fled there during the peasants' revolt of 1381.

CROWN COPYRIGHT, NMR

fell by about a quarter, although this needs to be seen in the context of a 30 per cent decrease in the value of land in Hertfordshire as a whole.[11] Most of the abbey's land at this time was in Hertfordshire, with a little in neighbouring Bedfordshire, Buckinghamshire and Berkshire. Yet by the time Henry I died in 1135, St Albans was flourishing: in Emma Cownie's words, it 'possessed an unparalleled number of dependent cells and priories and its landed interests, together with those of its dependants, stretched from Northumberland, through Yorkshire, Lincolnshire, Leicestershire, Northamptonshire, Norfolk, Buckinghamshire, Bedfordshire, Berkshire, Oxfordshire and Hertfordshire to Middlesex and Essex'.[12] This remarkable increase in endowments was achieved without significant royal patronage: Bury St Edmunds and a number of other abbeys got far more from the Norman kings. St Albans was endowed by the Anglo-Norman landed aristocracy and their tenants, and enjoyed the active support of Lanfranc, archbishop of Canterbury from 1070 to 1089. Lanfranc's nephew Paul de Caen was abbot of St Albans from 1077 to 1093, and under his rule the abbey recovered various estates lost under Edward the Confessor (1042–66) and in the early post-conquest period, including the local manors of Childwick, Redbourn, Napsbury and Kingsbury.[13]

St Albans 'had a lot going for it' in this period …

Paul de Caen also attracted new benefactors to St Albans, many of whom gave land in far-flung parts of England to the abbey; and several dependent cells of monks were established during his abbacy and those of his successors. For example, Belvoir in Leicestershire was given to the abbey by Robert de Tosny, explicitly intended to be a dependent cell; and Wallingford priory in Berkshire was established following a gift of churches and land. In the 1080s distant Tynemouth priory, in the north-east of England, was given to St Albans by Robert de Mowbray, later earl of Northumbria, who was 'acting with the good wishes of the king and archbishop Lanfranc', according to the abbey's chronicler.[14] Other dependent cells were established at Hertford – founded by another benefactor, Ralf de Limesi[15] – and Binham (Norfolk) during the abbacy of Paul de Caen. Following abbot Paul's death, the abbacy was vacant for four years, but under his successor Richard d'Aubigny (1097–1119) the endowments continued, with lands being acquired in Norfolk, Essex, Bedfordshire, Warwickshire and elsewhere. The abbey also acquired the priories of Wymondham and Hatfield Peverel, and the dependent cell at Tynemouth itself acquired more land in the north. Richard d'Aubigny came from a family of benefactors of St Albans: for example, his brother Nigel d'Aubigny had given land in Berkshire worth £10 in 1086.[16] Nigel, and many of the other benefactors, were key figures in the new Norman aristocracy, and their patronage ensured that, unlike some other religious houses, St Albans 'had a lot going for it' in this period.[17] Richard was succeeded as abbot by Geoffrey de Gorham (1119–45), who was less well-connected than his two predecessors and therefore less successful at attracting benefactors on a national scale, but continued to augment the abbey's local land holdings, and established Sopwell nunnery in or around 1140 and St Julian's leprosy hospital on Watling Street at around the same time. Later in the twelfth century under abbot Warin (1183–95), St Mary de Pré was established on the Redbourn road as hospital to treat female leprosy sufferers. St Albans was fortunate to have a succession of competent and well-connected abbots: in post-conquest England, many successful abbots came from Normandy, especially Caen (Paul may have originated from Pavia in northern Italy, but he came to England from Caen),[18] although not all the incomers had the positive impact of abbot Paul. For example, the first Norman abbot of Peterborough, Turold (1070–98), through his poor management, 'brought disaster down upon his house' from which it had not recovered by the mid-twelfth century.[19]

The abbey was given wide powers of jurisdiction ... over its large Liberty

The abbey of St Albans had rapidly become one of the largest and most important in the country: Michelle Still has called it 'the premier Benedictine monastery of all England' from the mid-twelfth century.[20] It benefited from the patronage of Pope Adrian IV (1154–59), who, as Nicholas Breakspear, had been refused entry to the abbey (to which his father had retired) and become an Augustinian monk instead. Adrian was not the first pope to grant privileges to St Albans: Calixtus II (1119–24) had granted an indulgence (a remission of punishment for sin) of 12 days to visitors to the abbey at the feast of St Alban, and this was confirmed by Adrian.[21] Adrian was visited in Rome by abbot Robert de Gorham (1151–67): perhaps understandably given his earlier rejection by the abbey, the pope was, apparently, unwelcoming at first, but was – according to the St Albans chronicler – mollified by flattering words from the mouth of the abbot. Adrian granted 17 bulls to the abbey during his short papacy. One of these confirmed the independence of the abbey from the bishop of Lincoln – in whose diocese St Albans was, by this time, situated – and of the dependent cells from their respective diocesan bishops. Another bull, in 1157, established the Liberty of St Albans, a large group of parishes which were to be, in the bull's words, 'entirely free from subjection to any bishop'.[22] The abbey was given wide powers of jurisdiction over St Peter's, St Michael's and St Stephen's parishes – the three churches traditionally attributed to abbot Ulsinus in the tenth century – and also Watford, Rickmansworth, Abbots Langley, Redbourn, Codicote, St Paul's Walden, Hexton, Norton, Newnham and Barnet in Hertfordshire, as well as Winslow and Aston Abbots in Buckinghamshire; these parishes were not all contiguous.[23] Despite the fierce opposition of the bishops of Lincoln in the twelfth century, and their attempts to overturn the exemption of St Albans from their control, subsequent papal interventions confirmed the abbey's privileges, and extended some of them, so that, in Still's words, 'by 1290 the position of St Albans was assured as an exempt monastery, free from the interference of the diocesan and subject only to the papal see'.[24] It had almost complete control over its large Liberty.

The growing independence and power of the abbey was reflected in its buildings. Whereas the very early post-conquest monastic churches were 'comparatively modest' – for example, William I's abbey at Battle – the churches at St Albans and Durham, in Colin Platt's words, 'display their security in their scale'.[25] The most spectacular development at St Albans was the construction of the new abbey church, commenced under Paul de Caen and completed under Richard d'Aubigny. The architect was Robert the Mason, who was probably a Norman, and was an 'inspired' choice according to one architectural historian.[26] The new church was larger even than the new church built by Lanfranc at Canterbury, and featured a vaulted chancel, a nave more than 50 metres long and a crossing tower, which is the only eleventh-century example still standing at a major church in England.[27] Roman bricks from the ruins at Verulamium were used in the construction of the church; and Eileen Roberts remarks that 'the Saxon masons must have been amazed at the thick, sturdy walls' erected by Robert the Mason, 'so different from the thin, plain walls they had used' in their churches before the Norman conquest.[28]

The new church, consecrated by the bishop of Lincoln in 1115, was a prominent symbol of the 'overweening pride and opulence' of which some critics accused St Albans abbey in this period.[29] Paul de Caen may also have built the chapel of St Andrew, which stood against the nave of the abbey church

The abbey church, now St Albans cathedral, was begun in the eleventh century by abbot Paul de Caen. The tower, built under Paul's direction by the architect Robert the Mason, dates from this period and is still standing. Roman materials from nearby Verulamium were used in this phase of construction.

PHOTOGRAPH: CARNEGIE

RIGHT
The tower from the south-west.

PHOTOGRAPH: CARNEGIE

along the northern wall, and which was used by the people of the town as their place of worship.[30] Further developments at the abbey precinct improved the monks' accommodation and enhanced the standing of the house: Paul de Caen established a scriptorium (a writing room);[31] a new shrine of St Alban was built by the 'monk-goldsmith' Anketil under abbot Geoffrey de Gorham in 1129;[32] Robert de Gorham built the chapter house, a parlour and the east walk of the cloister;[33] the scriptorium was improved under abbot Simon (1167–83); and under John de Cella (1195–1214) the monks abstained from wine for 15 years to pay for the construction of a new dormitory, which was completed by William de Trumpington (1214–35), who also made further improvements to the interior of the abbey church and glazed the windows.[34] These improvements included the wall murals in the church, designed by Walter de Colchester, who was sacrist in the abbey in 1213.[35] John de Cella had also built a new refectory, and rebuilt the chapel of St Andrew.[36]

Not all abbot John's schemes were successful. As Platt has remarked, St Albans abbey 'suffered from the excessive wealth which might tempt its abbots into schemes that proved eventually beyond them'.[37] John's attempted rebuilding of the church's west front proved catastrophic, as the ambitious construction by the mason Hugh de Goldclif, featuring expensive and time-consuming carvings, took so long that the soft stones broke up and, in the words of the abbey's chronicler, 'the wall ... with its columns, bases and capitals, slipped and fell by its own weight; so that the wreck of images and flowers was a cause of smiles and laughter to all those that saw it'.[38] The abbey was rich enough to survive this – a simpler west front was constructed under John's successor William de Trumpington – but it was an embarrassing

The monks' walled vintry garden, inside the precinct of St Albans abbey, is at the north-east corner of the cathedral. Re-landscaping took place in 2005, including the resurfacing of paths, planting of new flowers and herbs, and repairs to the walls. A memorial was also unveiled to the five schoolchildren, from Verulam and Beaumont schools, and one teacher, who were killed in a coach crash at Ledignan in France in 1985.

PHOTOGRAPH: AUTHOR

episode. Later in the thirteenth century, further constructions proved more successful: for example, following earthquake damage in 1250, the presbytery was rebuilt, and the east end of the church repaired. The presbytery featured a timber vault, probably using wood given by Henry III.[39] Both Henry III (1216–72) and Edward I (1272–1307) were regular visitors to the abbey at St Albans, and to other saints' shrines across England.[40]

The shrine of St Amphibalus stands in the north aisle of the presbytery of the abbey church. Built *c.*1350, it replaced an earlier structure dating from the late twelfth century, that was damaged when a large section of the church collapsed in 1323. Like the shrine of St Alban, this shrine was broken during the dissolution of the abbey, and reconstructed in the nineteenth century. St Amphibalus was reputedly the Christian priest whom Alban had sheltered, and his relics were 'discovered' at Redbourn during the abbacy of Simon (1167–83).

PHOTOGRAPH: CARNEGIE

The cult of St Alban was actively fostered by the monks, especially in the thirteenth and early fourteenth centuries, as part of a more general assertion of the rights and traditions of the abbey. As early as 1195 a shrine was built, in the eastern apse of the church, dedicated to St Amphibalus, reputedly the Christian priest whom Alban had sheltered, and who had also been martyred (see box 2). Amphibalus's relics were 'discovered' during Simon's abbacy (1167–83) at Redbourn, by monks led by a vision of the townsman Robert Mercer, and St Mary de Pré was established by Simon's successor Warin at the place on the Redbourn road where the relics had met those of St Alban, which were carried there for this ceremonial purpose.[41] The discovery of the relics of Amphibalus was an early example of the promotion of relics and the revival of dormant saints' cults that became a feature of English monasticism in the thirteenth century. In 1257 what was believed to be the original mausoleum of St Alban himself was discovered, and this was used to promote the abbey as a place of pilgrimage.[42] In the time of Matthew Paris (c.1200–59; see box 1), the monks employed relics and other objects to ward off ill-fortune and the power of nature, which was demonstrated by the earthquake of 1250. These superstitious precautions did not always have the desired effect. In or around 1235, the chronicle recorded:

Twice within three years the church of St Albans was set on fire by lightning, which no one remembered to have seen before, or to have heard of. And as it is no use to rely upon the privileges or indulgences of the Saints, so the papal seal, on which is figured the Agnus Dei, which is placed on top of our tower, did not avert the lightning, although it is said to have virtue and power to drive away such storms.[43]

By contrast, Paris recorded how, in early autumn 1257, the monks fasted, as was usual in such circumstances, because too much rain was threatening to spoil the crops. There was also a procession of the bier of St Alban to the church of 'St Mary-in-the-Fields' (Paris presumably meant St Mary de Pré – pré means 'meadow'), with the result that, 'on the same day, through the merits of the martyr, the destructive rain ceased'.[44]

Not only were SS Alban and Amphibalus themselves repeatedly invoked by the monks, but during the thirteenth century St Albans abbey was more aggressive in promoting the historical origins of its liberties. This was partly because of the growing bitterness of the conflict between abbey and town, which is discussed at length below, but also in part because of the encroachments of other ecclesiastical and secular authorities onto the privileges of the abbot and his monks. The importance of king Offa – whose legendary foundation of the abbey had been recorded by the chroniclers Roger of Wendover and Matthew Paris (see box 1)[45] – was emphasised in the abbey's propaganda, which also noted the papal authority under which the independence of the abbey and its dependent cells had been established. This authority was symbolically represented in the placement of the papal seal at the top of the church tower. In 1248, Paris recorded that the bishop of Durham 'began to harass' the priory at Tynemouth, disregarding the liberty that the house enjoyed from diocesan authority under the terms of Adrian IV's bull. When the abbey of St Albans complained about this treatment of one of its dependants, the king, Henry III, rebuked the bishop in a letter. Paris then commented: 'By the aforesaid letter then is clearly manifest the injury done to the said prior and his convent, who enjoyed the same privileges and liberties as the church of St Alban's, on which church was conferred as much privilege as can lawfully be conferred on any abbot by the supreme pontiff in spiritual matters; and in temporal ones, whatever the royal authority could grant to it, was bestowed by its pious founder Offa, and other kings of England.'[46] It is in the light of this thirteenth-century emphasis on Offa that we should interpret Paris's retrospective criticism of the late abbot Paul de Caen, whom he rebuked for not having managed to obtain Offa's body for reburial within the abbey.[47] In 1256, Paris again recorded that 'Offa established the freedom in temporal matters, as far as any king could do, of the convent of St Alban's, of which he was the noble founder'; and in the same year it was decreed that the words 'May the soul of King Offa repose in peace' should be added to the abbey's prayers, 'and that this should be observed inviolably and for ever'.[48]

This carved head depicts Henry Wy, the mason who oversaw the repairs following the collapse of a section of the abbey church in 1323. It stands on a spandrel, above one of the piers on the south side of the nave.

PHOTOGRAPH: CARNEGIE

The thirteenth century marked the economic high point of the fortunes of St Albans abbey, but by the early fourteenth century, the monks were beginning to feel the pressures of change, which generated a defensive attitude on their part towards the management of their estates. Inflation created a 'harsh economic climate' in the early fourteenth century, especially for those landlords, like the abbots of St Albans, who had taken manors into direct management during the thirteenth century, when the profits available from agriculture had been especially high.[49] Famine, livestock epidemics and crop failures in the years 1315–22 were worsened by the high taxes levied to fund wars with Scotland and France: the Scots were a particular problem for St Albans abbey, because of cross-border attacks on the dependent priory at Tynemouth.[50] In 1305, 1309 and 1327 the finances of the abbey were so stretched – and so obviously mismanaged by incompetent abbots – that the king appointed a custodian to manage the abbey's affairs. In 1305 the custodian was William de Bolum, who remained in charge for most of the following year, but failed to put the house in order.[51] Heavy borrowing – some of the abbey's manors and mills were mortgaged in the early fourteenth century – could not be repaid. Matters were worsened in 1323 when a large section of the church and cloister collapsed, taking many years to rebuild.[52] The rebuilding was done in the Gothic style, and has attracted considerable criticism from subsequent architectural scholars: it 'was not completed according to plan and is thus considered a botched job'. Although recently the architectural merits of the work have been more positively re-assessed,[53] it was still very expensive.

The high costs that the monks had to bear included the occasional heavy expenses of electing a new abbot: the monks had the right to elect their leader, but he was then required to travel to Rome to have his election confirmed by the pope. This journey could be very expensive, and usually required a loan.[54] Abbot Hugh de Eversdene (1308–27) tried to avoid this expense by sending representatives instead, but they returned with a papal order for Hugh to attend in person.[55] There were also cultural pressures, which affected the whole Benedictine order: the growth of the universities was providing competition in terms of resources, recruitment, and intellectual and cultural pre-eminence; and the expansion of the ascetic orders of monks, and the arrival of Franciscan friars who were critical of the opulence of the Benedictine houses, painted the Black Monks in a bad light.[56] At St Albans itself, ill-discipline was rife among the monks during the abbacy of John de Maryns (1302–08) and Hugh de Eversdene. In 'serious lapses' from the Benedictine Rule, monks were 'wandering about alone', and disobeying the rules of silence and chastity.[57] John and Hugh were weak abbots who failed to sort the problems out; and Hugh's successor Richard de Wallingford (1327–36) was hampered in his efforts by his ill-health – he reputedly suffered from leprosy[58] – and the difficult relationship he had with some of his senior monks. Richard was rather obsessed with an

astronomical clock which he was building in the abbey church, which many monks disliked because of the money and time that Richard spent on it.[59] Eventually, in 1333, the pope himself ordered a thorough investigation into the affairs at the abbey, and Richard and his successor Michael de Mentmore (1336–49) were able to restore some control. During the difficult abbacies of the early fourteenth century, the monks also found themselves in bitter conflict with their neighbours in both countryside and town.

While the abbey was gaining in size, and in economic and cultural strength, the history of the post-conquest town is rather harder to trace. The fortunes of the small urban settlement were clearly bound up with those of the abbey: the increasing numbers of pilgrims to the shrines of SS Alban and Amphibalus must have brought money to St Albans.[60] The reasons for the planned layout of the town by the Saxon abbots included the provision of local services to visitors, the supply of goods to the monks, and the economic improvement of the immediate vicinity of the abbey. It has recently been suggested that the original Saxon town, or at least its market, was actually located within the precinct of the abbey itself: Rosalind Niblett and Isobel Thompson, in their survey of St Albans archaeology, have shown that there is no evidence of any settlement around the current market place before the twelfth century.[61] Niblett and Thompson suggest that the urban settlement recorded in Domesday Book was centred on the abbey orchard, south of the church, and may have been moved northwards during or after the extensive rebuilding work of Paul de Caen. The markets of two other monastic towns, Peterborough and Bury St Edmunds, are known to have been relocated by their landlords in the twelfth century,[62] and this may also have been the case at St Albans. Other historians, such as T. R. Slater, have suggested an earlier, pre-conquest layout of the main

continued on page 85

This image of St Alban dates from the early fifteenth century, and appeared in an edition of the very popular *Golden Legend* by Jacobus de Voraigne, a thirteenth-century collection of saints' lives. Alban is pictured in a cloak: this is likely to represent the cloak that, in many accounts of his martyrdom, he exchanged with St Amphibalus. The invention of St Amphibalus was the result of a mistranslation of the Latin word for 'cloak' by Geoffrey of Monmouth.

Box 2: The martyrdom of St Alban

ST ALBAN is believed to have been the first Christian martyr, or the 'protomartyr', in Britain. The traditional account of the martyrdom gives the location as the hill outside the Roman city of Verulamium, which could coincide with the site of the present abbey church. The first known written reference to Alban refers to AD 429, when St Germanus, bishop of Auxerre, accompanied by bishop Lupus of Troyes, visited Britain in an attempt to suppress the heresy of Pelagianism – named after a British monk, Pelagius, who spread the doctrine of free will and denied the transmission of original sin. Having defeated the heresy, according to Germanus's biographer Constantius of Lyons, writing in the third quarter

of the fifth century, 'the priests went to the tomb of the blessed martyr Alban to give thanks through him to God'; St Germanus also took some of the relics of St Alban.[1] Constantius gave no details of the circumstances of the martyrdom: the first account comes from the sixth-century historian Gildas, who dated it to the persecution of Christians under 'the tyrant Diocletian' (AD 284–305). During this time, 'the churches throughout the whole world were overthrown, all the copies of the Holy Scripture which could be found burned in the streets, and the chosen

---

[1] Quoted in Martin Biddle, 'Alban, d. *c*.303', *Oxford Dictionary of National Biography*.

pastors of God's flock butchered, together with their innocent sheep'.[1] In Britain, the first of these was 'Alban of Verulam', who

> for charity's sake saved another confessor who was pursued by his persecutors, and was on the point of being seized, by hiding him in his house, and then by changing clothes with him, imitating in this the example of Christ, who laid down his life for his sheep, and exposing himself in the other's clothes to be pursued in his stead.[2]

According to Gildas, between his confession and death, Alban

> was honoured with the performance of wonderful miracles ... the martyr, with a thousand others, opened a path across the noble river Thames, whose waters stood abrupt like precipices on either side; and seeing this, the first of his executors [sic] was stricken with awe, and from a wolf became a lamb; so that he thirsted for martyrdom, and boldly underwent that for which he thirsted.[3]

By the time the Venerable Bede wrote his history of the English church in AD 731, more details had been added to the story; it appears that Bede (and maybe also Gildas) was drawing on an account, or 'passion' of St Alban that may have been written by Germanus himself.[4] Bede certainly knew an account written by the early seventh-century bishop of Poitiers, Venantius Fortunatus. In Bede's story of the martyrdom, also dated to the time of Diocletian, Alban was a 'pagan', in the city of Verulamium, who 'gave

entertainment' to a Christian priest who was fleeing persecution.[5] Alban 'began to imitate the example of faith and piety which was set before him, and ... cast off the darkness of idolatry, and became a Christian in all sincerity of heart'. When the priest's place of concealment was discovered, soldiers were sent to Alban's house, whereupon Alban 'immediately presented himself to the soldiers, instead of his guest and master, in the habit or long coat which he wore, and was led bound before the judge'. Alban told the judge that he was now a Christian, and refused to offer sacrifices to the pagan gods when ordered to do so. He was then tortured in an attempt to make him recant, which he would not; and his execution was therefore ordered. 'Being led to execution, he came to a river, which, with a most rapid course, ran between the wall of the town and the arena where he was to be executed' – Gildas had identified this as the Thames, but if the location of the martyrdom was Verulamium, it must have been the Ver, which runs between the Roman city and the hill on which the abbey church stands. The bridge over the river was blocked by a 'multitude' of men and women, 'who were doubtless assembled by Divine instinct':

> St Alban, therefore, urged by an ardent and devout wish to arrive quickly at martyrdom, drew near to the stream, and on lifting up his eyes to heaven, the channel was immediately dried up, and he perceived that the water had departed and made way for him to pass. Among the rest, the executioner, who was to have put him to death, observed this, and moved by Divine inspiration hastened to meet him at the place of execution, and casting down the sword which he had carried ready drawn, fell at his feet, praying that he might rather suffer with the martyr, whom

[1] Gildas, *History*, parag. 9; in *The Works of Gildas, Surnamed 'Sapiens', or the Wise*, in J. A. Giles (ed.), *Six Old English Chronicles* (London: Henry G. Bohn, 1848).

[2] Gildas, *History*, parag. 11.

[3] Ibid.

[4] Biddle, 'Alban, d. *c*.303'.

[5] The account below is drawn from Bede, *The Ecclesiastical History of the English Nation* (London: J.M. Dent. 1910), book I, chapter 7.

he was ordered to execute or, if possible, instead of him.[1]

Alban and the 'multitude' then ascended the hill on the other side of the river, a distance, according to Bede, of some 500 paces; at the top, Alban prayed for God to send him water, and a spring duly appeared. When Alban – together with the executioner who had refused to perform his duties – was beheaded, 'he who gave the wicked stroke, was not permitted to rejoice over the deceased; for his eyes dropped upon the ground together with the blessed martyr's head'. Having witnessed the miracles of St Alban, the judge who had condemned him ordered the persecution of Christians to be ended. More than four centuries later, according to Bede, at the site of the martyrdom 'there ceases not to this day the cure of sick persons, and the frequent working of wonders'.

The dating of Alban's martyrdom has been disputed by scholars, some arguing that the early third century was the most likely date, during the time of the emperor Severus (AD 193–211), and others in the mid-third century.[2] As Niblett explains, 'at present there is no consensus as to the date of Alban's martyrdom, other than that it must have occurred sometime in the third or fourth centuries'.[3] Martin Biddle, in the *Oxford Dictionary of National Biography*, gives the date as *c*.303.[4] It appears that a cemetery church existed in the late Roman period, and that this may have marked either the site of Alban's martyrdom, or the place of his burial, or both; this stood on the later site of the Saxon abbey. It is known, as mentioned above, that St Germanus visited the tomb of St Alban in 429: according to Constantius, Germanus

tore up a lump of earth from the actual spot where the martyr's blood had flowed.

This desecration was justified, since the stain of the blood could still be seen. This was a great sign shown clearly to all men, of how the martyr's blood had reddened the earth as his persecutor grew pale.[5]

There is, as Biddle and others have shown, a strong argument that a continuous or almost continuous Christian presence existed on or near the site of Alban's burial, and that the origins of the Saxon monastery of St Albans lay in this community.[6]

During the medieval period, encouraged by the monks of St Albans abbey, the story of St Alban was embellished, the site promoted as a place of pilgrimage, and the relics of the saint 'invented' and dispersed. Owing to a mistranslation by Geoffrey of Monmouth, the historian and bishop of St Asaph, writing in the twelfth century, the priest whom Alban sheltered was given the name Amphibalus, and a cult was soon established around him by the monks of St Albans, who 'discovered' his relics at Redbourn in the twelfth century.[7] Matthew Paris, the most influential of the chroniclers of the medieval abbey of St Albans (see box 1), wrote an account of Alban and Amphibalus, and depicted both saints carrying a distinctive coptic cross; he also discovered, or acquired, a cross of the same shape to add to the relics at St Albans.[8] According to Paris, the relics of St Alban, or at least some of them, were stolen during a Danish raid in the ninth or tenth century, and removed to Odense. Two monks from St Albans then claimed to have stolen the relics back from Odense; the relics were then sent by abbot Aelfric to Ely for protection. Later, the monks of Ely sent some

[1] Ibid.
[2] Biddle, 'Alban, d. *c*.303'.
[3] Niblett, *Verulamium*, p. 138.
[4] Biddle, 'Alban, d. *c*.303'.

[5] Quoted in Niblett, *Verulamium*, p. 138.
[6] Biddle, 'Alban and the Anglo-Saxon Church'; see above, pp. 48–9.
[7] See above, pp. 75, 77; Geoffrey of Monmouth, *British History*, book V, chapter 5, in Giles, *Six Old English Chronicles*.
[8] Birthe Kjølbye-Biddle, 'The Alban Cross', in Henig, *Alban and St Albans*, 85–110.

other bones back to St Albans, and kept the relics; however, the abbot of St Albans then declared that the relics originally sent to Ely had not been genuine. Eventually, Pope Adrian IV – Nicholas Breakspear, who as a local man was likely to be supportive of the claims of the abbey of St Albans – ruled that the relics at St Albans were the genuine ones. As one commentator has remarked, 'as the bones in question were unlikely to have been those of [St Alban] in the first place, probably neither St Albans nor Ely nor Odense ever had the gruesome relics that each laid passionate claim to'.[1] Some more relics of the protomartyr, perhaps taken by St Germanus in 429, apparently found their way to the church of St Pantaleon in Cologne.[2] In June 2002 a group from St Pantaleon presented a shoulder bone from

among the relics held there to the cathedral at St Albans; this bone was then placed in the shrine of St Alban, which had recently been restored. On this occasion the dean of St Albans explained: 'Whether this relic is one of the bones of St Alban can never be known, but there is a distinct possibility that it is.'[3]

---

[1] Brian J. Bailey, *Portrait of Hertfordshire* (London: Robert Hale, 1978), pp. 83–4.

[2] Biddle, 'Alban, d. *c*.303'.

---

[3] *St Albans and Harpenden Review*, 3 July 2002, p. 5.

streets,[63] but there is little archaeological evidence of settlement beyond the abbey precinct before the twelfth century.

By the mid-twelfth century, the centre of gravity of the urban settlement had moved to the triangular market place and Chequer Street. The first houses and shops, including those on Chequer Street, were timber-framed, and used Roman tiles from the ruins of Verulamium.[64] Several buildings had

RIGHT

A modern reconstruction, in St Albans cathedral, of the astronomical clock constructed by abbot Richard de Wallingford in the fourteenth century. The clock struck the hours and showed the positions of the stars that could be seen from St Albans. The time spent by abbot Richard on the clock was a source of concern to many of the monks in the abbey.

PHOTOGRAPH: CARNEGIE

large tile ovens, probably for grain; as noted in the last chapter, the plots on this street were very long, and wheat may have been grown at the back of the houses.[65] High Street, along the northern wall of the abbey precinct, George Street, Fishpool Street and Sopwell Lane were also probably built up in the twelfth century;[66] and a bridge was built over the Ver at the bottom of Holywell Hill in 1143 or earlier.[67] The east side of Holywell Hill was certainly occupied by houses from the later twelfth century; and it is probable that in this period Sopwell Lane marked the southernmost extent of the built-up part of the town.[68] There is evidence of thirteenth-century occupation of St Peter's Street.[69] The earliest buildings on French Row and Dagnall Street may have been built in the fourteenth century: there is no archaeological evidence of any before this date. By the late twelfth century, St Albans had experienced a considerable improvement in its economic fortunes, and was able to make a substantial contribution to the ransom that was raised in England to release king Richard I from his imprisonment in Austria. The local historian James Corbett explains that

George Street, formerly known as Church Street or Cook Row, formed part of the main road through St Albans until the construction of Verulam Road in the 1820s. This timber-framed building dates from the early fifteenth century. Formerly an inn called the George and Dragon, it was more recently known as the Tudor Tavern. Along with other pubs in St Albans, including the Cricketers and the King's Arms, this is now a restaurant.

PHOTOGRAPH: CARNEGIE

The size of the ransom reflected both the increasing wealth of the country and the rising prosperity of the towns, including St Albans, where changes for the better were evident. Clay-tiled roofs had been replacing inflammable thatch for half-a-century and the occupants of the houses had become accustomed to using locally made pottery, distinctively glazed in a rich shade of orange. Livings were earned from agriculture, brewing, the making of leather goods and, of course, cloth.[70]

'the town was ... deeply affected by the number of people who travelled through it ... [and] widely known for the number of inns it contained.'

The cloth industry was 'well established' in St Albans by the late twelfth century. Cloth fulling (or milling – the process of cleansing and thickening the cloth) was carried out south of the river Ver, in the vicinity of St Stephen's. In the medieval period a road known as Fullers Street ran from Holywell Hill to the causeway that runs along the south-eastern wall of Verulamium.[71] In 1202, the people of St Albans paid two marks (£1 6s. 8d.) to King John to renew the cloth trading rights that they had enjoyed under Henry II (1154–89), although this agreement required them to use the abbey's fulling mill, which caused resentment.[72] In Hertfordshire as a whole, and St Albans in particular, cloth did not attain the predominance that it held in some other parts of medieval England: in general, the towns of Hertfordshire, including St Albans, did not specialise in a single industry or sector, and nor did they develop a 'diverse manufacturing base' in the medieval period.[73] However, a wide range of trades and services were performed in St Albans: a register of those liable for taxation in 1307 revealed 88 taxpayers, with names such as Thomas le Coupere, Benedict Tanner, John le Taillur, Simon le Viniter, William le Maltleder and Robert le Barbur giving a flavour of the occupational diversity of the town.[74] Estimates of the population of St Albans vary considerably: one historian has suggested around 940 in 1290, while another proposes 2,025.[75]

The market and the service sector were probably the most important features of the economy of the town in this period: St Albans was becoming a 'thoroughfare town',[76] benefiting from its geographical position a day's journey from London, as well as developing as a centre for local agricultural marketing and services. The road to London, running along Sopwell Lane, was certainly 'established' before 1200.[77] St Albans 'was a town of traders and innkeepers, primarily serving the Abbey, visitors both staying and passing through, and the surrounding countryside'.[78] As Michelle Still remarks, 'the town was ... deeply affected by the number of people who travelled through it ... As a result St Albans was widely known for the number of inns it contained'.[79] Serving the needs of the pilgrims who visited the abbey was one aspect of this development: by the early fourteenth century there was a pilgrims' hostel, on the site of the White Hart hotel; while in the mid-thirteenth century abbot John de Hertford (1235–63) had bought a large house on the corner of George Street and Spicer Street to use as additional accommodation for the abbey's guests.[80]

Chequers-st
St Albans, 1902

E. A. Phips

The 'highway town' was a feature of twelfth- and thirteenth-century England, the result of the growth of trade in the country as a whole.[81] Not only did the Norman conquest initiate an increased international trade in luxury goods, but there was what Colin Platt has called 'a flowering of trade on a local level': the number of markets expanded, and many new towns were established, in this period.[82] St Albans was becoming an important local centre for the trading of agricultural produce; the by-products of this trade, most notably wool and leather, were used in local industry. As Platt suggests, agriculture was very important in most medieval towns, 'and for the smaller market settlement it perhaps always retained its original dominant role'.[83]

In the case of St Albans, proximity to London was crucial in this respect, as it was in others. The town was 'land-locked', in that it did not stand on an easily navigable river such as the Lea, which was the main route by which grain grown in east and south-central Hertfordshire was carried to London; as a result, St Albans 'lay just beyond the outer edge of London's regular provisioning zone'. However, some grain was carried to London by road through St Albans, and here and at other towns was 'combined the basic

Chequer Street is one of the oldest streets in St Albans, and was laid out in the tenth, eleventh or twelfth century. This watercolour by E. A. Phipson dates from the early twentieth century, and was part of a large group of Phipson paintings acquired by the museum in St Albans during this period.

© ST ALBANS MUSEUMS

function of servicing a small agricultural hinterland with provisioning the traffic which passed along one of the main routeways to London'.[84] By the early thirteenth century the changes in the town included the development of permanent structures at the market, and an increasing specialisation of market trading: stalls selling the same goods were all situated in the same street or area. The market became separated into 'zones': the meat market was in the 'lower part' of Market Place; the fish market was higher up, at the corner of Market Place and Dagnall Street; the 'women's' market (selling butter, eggs and poultry) was on French Row; and wheat and leather were sold between French Row and Dagnall Street.[85] Such spatial zoning was also a feature of other market towns in this period.[86] In the reign of Henry III, St Albans, in political importance if not in size, 'ranked with what were then some of the larger boroughs, and was frequently called upon with them to supply the royal household and army with provisions'.[87] The growing size and prosperity of St Albans was reflected in its increasing liability for taxation: by 1334 the taxable wealth of the town was £266, placing St Albans 48th in a list headed by London (£11,000), with Bristol second (£1,900). Other monastic towns were of a similar size and wealth to St Albans: Bury St Edmunds is 26th on the list with £360, and Abingdon 46th with £269.[88] St Albans was 'comfortably the largest and most important town' in Hertfordshire, although this fact emphasises the lack

of urban development in the rest of the county as much as the growth of St Albans itself.[89]

Mainly because of the economic and political strength of the abbey, the town of St Albans was gaining in political importance in the twelfth and thirteenth centuries, and found itself caught up in various disputes, often to its inhabitants' cost. In 1142 the town was the site of a 'skirmish' in the civil war between the forces of king Stephen and queen Matilda; and in 1143 Stephen's court met at St Albans.[90] On Stephen's instructions, the last remnants of the Saxon royal *burh* of Kingsbury were destroyed, although as this happened in the time of Robert de Gorham (who became abbot in 1151), this cannot have been at the same time as the meeting of the court.[91] It is probable that the town's defences were strengthened at this time, but this did not stop the abbey from having to surrender the gold and jewels from the shrine of St Alban as a ransom to prevent the town from being burned.[92] In 1173, some of the barons who had been defeated in a rebellion against Henry II took sanctuary at the abbey. King John's turbulent reign (1199–1216) proved difficult for St Albans: the king ordered that the abbot, John de Cella, should ignore the papal interdict which banned public worship in England, and when the abbot refused, the abbey was placed under the rule of the king's representative Robert of London, who extracted money from the abbey as a penalty for disobedience.[93] In the years leading up to Magna Carta in 1215, meetings were held at St Albans, London and Bury St Edmunds, attended by barons and leading churchmen; and after king John had conceded, and then retracted, the charter of liberties, he entered St Albans with an army in December 1215, and pillaged several local villages. A year later, French troops threatened to burn the abbey and town, and a ransom of 80 marks (£53 6s. 8d.) was paid; then, early in 1217, a gang of 'cut-throats' led by the French mercenary Falkes de Breauté extorted a ransom of 100 marks (£66 13s. 4d). It was probably little consolation to the inhabitants of St Albans that Breauté later repented and asked for absolution from the abbot.[94] According to a possibly exaggerated account by Matthew Paris, the abbot (William de Trumpington) had to spend more than £2,500 to protect the abbey during the turmoil of these years.[95] In the mid-thirteenth century, the rudimentary Norman defences were replaced by the Tonman Ditch, which also served a function as the boundary between the lands of the abbey and the town.[96] The defences were needed in 1265, when the armies of Henry III and Simon de Montfort, leader of the barons' rebellion, were both in the vicinity of St Albans. The town 'sympathised' with de Montfort in this rebellion, and a group of townsmen publicly beheaded the governor of Hertford Castle, Gregory Stokes, who entered the town as a supporter of the king. As a result Henry fined the town 100 marks.[97] However, the status of St Albans was undiminished, and this was reflected in the fact that the 'Model Parliament' met in the abbey in 1295, the first occasion on

... a group of townsmen publicly beheaded the governor of Hertford Castle.

which two representatives were summoned to Parliament from 'every city, borough, and leading town'.[98]

The government of St Albans was dominated by the abbey, which also exercised a powerful control over its rural land holdings. In both town and country, the jurisdiction and policy of the abbey were increasingly challenged during the thirteenth and early fourteenth centuries, culminating in an explosive urban rebellion at St Albans. The Norman conquerors had brought with them a strict feudal form of social organisation which was deeply engrained into their culture.[99] At St Albans, feudal rights were enforced with particular severity as part of an 'extremely authoritarian' regime.[100] The English rural peasantry, on the St Albans abbey estates as elsewhere, comprised two main groups. Villeins paid labour rent to their feudal superiors – in other words, they were required to work for a set number of days in a year on the lord's land – and they were required to pay fees on the marriages of their children, on their deaths and at other times, and faced severe restrictions on the sale of their land. According to one historian, villeins lived in 'a state of economic slavery'.[101] The second group, tenants-in-scotage, had rather more freedom to sell land, and usually paid rent in money, although they were sometimes required to pay labour rent at especially busy periods in the agricultural calendar such as harvest and hay-making. Villeins lived at the mercy of their feudal lords, and although in many places, including on the St Albans estates, some were able to build up substantial holdings through land transfers, landlords did not like the villein land market, and tried hard to suppress it. Abbot Roger de Norton (1262–90) barred villeins from selling their land, 'for this is most damaging'.[102] Villeins could also be compulsorily settled onto vacant land, and abbot Roger 'ordered diligent enquiry to be made about the whereabouts of sons of [villeins], so that they could be sought out and planted on vacant holdings'.[103]

Other feudal obligations owed by peasants to their landlords caused particular friction on the St Albans estates: the payment of labour rent was one example. At the manor of Park, which was close to the abbey and amounted to a 'suburb' of St Albans,[104] peasants were required to provide four weeks' labour at haymaking. This was no more than was generally required from other lords, but it provided a focus for the discontents that arose from the other impositions that the abbey made on its tenants. There were examples of labour rent 'strikes' at Park in 1246, 1265 and in the 1270s, and again in 1309 and every year from 1318 to 1327 inclusive.[105] As Rosamund Faith has shown, there seems to have been a group of peasant families who, for several generations, protested against the authority of the abbey by withholding their labour rent, and a tradition of disobedience and rebellion grew up, both in rural manors and in the town of St Albans itself. However, even more than labour rent, the most significant theatre of conflict was milling. As Faith explains,

The Abbot's villein tenants 'owed suit' to the Abbot's own mills: that is to say that they had to take their own grain there to be ground, and their cloth to his fulling-mills for fulling. A proportion of the grain had to be paid to the Abbot. The system was expensive and a nuisance; the tenants naturally preferring to grind their own grain at home in hand-mills ... The Abbey's eagerness to enforce suit to its own mills is understandable in the light of the considerable profits that could be made from milling and of the fact that it had made a heavy capital investment in its mills and their machinery ... The Abbey mills were large, modern and expensive; the peasants' hand-mills were small, basic and cheap: in part it is a conflict over technology.[106]

A hunting dog captures a rabbit, and a shepherdess plays a pipe while minding her flock. Details from the early fifteenth-century St Albans watching loft.

There is evidence of refusal to use the abbey's mills on the manor of Park as early as 1237, and conflicts over milling became a feature of both rural and urban struggle for a century and a half, culminating in the peasants' revolt of 1381.[107]

Other, more primitive, rebels against 'the supreme local power base'[108] of the abbey poached game and timber from the abbey's land. Matthew Paris recorded a dispute about the abbey's warren in 1240, which, like the long-running labour rent strikes, suggests a powerful sense of history and tradition among those who protested against the authority of the abbey – no less powerful and significant than the traditions being fostered by the monks of the abbey itself in this period. According to Paris's heavily biased account, 'certain knights and others' – Geoffrey de Childwick and his four sons, William de Gorham, Thomas de Wauz and his two sons, and Adam de Sumery and David de Garpenville – had been 'given permission [by the abbot] to hunt for a time in the free warren of St Alban's', but now, 'abusing the favour granted to them, and infected by the vice of ingratitude, claimed this favour as a standing custom and perpetual right, and endeavoured to deprive, or rather disinherit, the church of its rights'. Abbot John de Hertford complained to the king, Henry III, who ordered a jury to meet at Cambridge to decide the matter. The defendants pleaded that their ancestors had been hunting hares on the same land during the reign of the king's grandfather, Henry II. The jury – perhaps unsurprisingly given Henry III's evident support for the abbey of St Albans in many ways – found in favour of the abbot and required the offenders to pay damages.[109] An appeal eight years later failed; but one of the offenders, Geoffrey de Childwick, who had influence at court, obtained a charter from Henry III in 1250 that protected his personal right to hunt on the abbey's lands.[110] Under John de Hertford the abbey continued to exert its rights and authority over those under its jurisdiction: in 1258 John granted a charter to his monks – confirmed by Henry III – that was intended to ensure them a sufficient supply of bread and beer to feed themselves and their guests, which would be supplied from the proceeds of certain specified tithes and manors owned by the abbey.[111] It was already the responsibility, on the St Albans and other abbey estates, of manors to provide the monks with provisions: 52 of the St Albans manors did this, each for one week per year, and another manor was required to provide utensils for the abbey's kitchen.[112]

The feudal relationship between the abbey and the town of St Albans was also the cause of conflict during this period. St Albans is perhaps the most spectacular example of what happened in several monastic towns where increasing economic prosperity was not matched by corresponding advances in urban political independence. As at Park and other rural manors, the root causes of the disputes between the monks and the people of the town lay in the aggressive insistence by the monks on their feudal rights. The disputes mirrored those experienced in similar urban theatres in the thirteenth and fourteenth centuries, where a 'violent revolutionary element' ensured that, from the end of the twelfth century until the dissolution, the monastic towns were in 'a constant state of political unrest'.[113] The urban historian N. M. Trenholme attributed this state of affairs to two general causes: first, 'the failure of the monastic corporations to recognize the growing corporate spirit of the townsmen and to concede to them rights of self-government and of commercial control such as were obtained by royal boroughs'; and second, the strictness with which monasteries exacted feudal obligations. 'The result was that sooner or later conflicts arose over town government, trading rights ... and numerous other questions.'[114] At St Albans and elsewhere, the monks needed the income from tolls, taxes and feudal obligations, and the townsmen tried to abolish the 'old services' that they owed to the abbey. Whereas the townspeople fought hard to gain the privileges of a borough, the abbot, in Michelle Still's words, had 'to fight hard to ensure that the town remained only a manor governed autocratically by the monks'.[115] A borough was distinguished from a manor by certain freedoms enjoyed by the burgesses who lived there: unlike villeins on a manor, burgesses in a borough held their land by burgage tenure, 'a peculiar form of scotage tenure', for which they usually paid money rent, labour rent being very rare in boroughs.[116] The restrictions on land transfers that characterised villeinage in English manors were absent in boroughs. A borough had its own courts, and most borough charters protected burgesses from being called to other courts in the county or the hundred (the hundred was a unit of administration below the level of the county). Borough charters prevented arbitrary fines from being levied, and often set upper limits on the amount that burgesses could be fined.[117] Some charters allowed for the establishment of a merchant guild, which could regulate trading within a borough and pass by-laws; and most burgesses were exempt from tolls levied at markets and fairs within the borough.[118]

... the right of the townspeople to use a common seal was ... widely asserted ...

The king, a baronial landlord or an abbey could issue a charter to a town and elevate it to the status of a borough, but many places that never received charters were known as boroughs. There is evidence of guilds, or 'fellowships', existing in some English towns before the conquest, and exercising some local governmental functions;[119] but the growth of industry and commerce after the Norman invasion, bringing with it urban prosperity and the emergence of 'real municipal life', led to an acceleration in the concession of charters by the Crown to royal boroughs, under Henry I and his successors.[120] Charters usually established a corporate body that was responsible for the government of the borough. However, many such charters merely confirmed existing practices and privileges, and towns could be thought of as boroughs without having been officially so designated. M. W. Beresford and H. P. R. Finberg's 'hand-list' of English medieval boroughs lists 'places which in their day were reckoned to be boroughs': St Albans, which was not chartered except for a brief period in the early fourteenth century, was one such place. Domesday Book referred to St Albans as a borough, declaring that 46 of its 81 householders were burgesses.[121] Later, St Albans had its own jury at Henry III's eyre court (an itinerant court of royal justices) in 1248, which suggests some elements of burghal status.[122] The distinction between chartered boroughs and unchartered villages was not as clear in the twelfth century as it later became: in many towns the burgesses acted like a corporate body well before they were legally incorporated by charter.[123] Oxford, for example, used a common seal – which legally established corporations had the right to do – in the early thirteenth century, whereas the borough was not formally incorporated until 1605.[124] In

St Albans, the right of the townspeople to use a common seal was a widely asserted claim during the struggles for independence from monastic rule that erupted in the early fourteenth century.

The confusion as to the exact status of towns such as St Albans was reflected in the inconsistency with which they were represented in Parliament. In the case of St Albans and Hertford, the latter only was represented, by two members, at the Parliament of 1298, the sheriff of Hertfordshire having stated that there were no other boroughs in the county. In 1301 and 1302, Hertford was again represented; in 1305, the sheriff reported that Hertford and St Albans had been asked to send representatives, but had not replied. He had made the same report for St Albans in 1301. Hertford sent representatives in 1306, and St Albans sent two in 1307; it is probable that both sent representatives in 1309; while in 1311 and 1312 Bishop's Stortford sent two burgesses to Parliament. St Albans may have been represented in 1311, but there is no record again of members being sent before the end of the reign of Edward II in 1327.[125] The townspeople blamed the abbot for their lack of representation: a petition from the town in 1314 asked that St Albans be allowed to send two representatives to Parliament, as it had previously done, claiming that the abbot had unduly influenced the sheriff of Hertfordshire to refuse to allow the names of their burgesses to be put forward. The king replied that St Albans should be allowed to send members if the record showed that it had formerly done so, but this reply does not seem to have been acted upon, and the town remained without representation.[126] For taxation purposes, St Albans was *not* regarded as a borough: in Hertfordshire, for payment of the lay subsidies of 1307 and 1334, only Hertford and Bishop's Stortford were considered as boroughs. This oversight was probably less annoying than others for the inhabitants of St Albans, as boroughs paid the subsidy at a higher rate (a fifteenth of the assessed value of moveable property in 1307, while the rest of the county paid a twentieth).[127]

The struggle for parliamentary representation was just one aspect of the ongoing dispute between town and monastery at St Albans, which also affected the internal governance of the town. The ways in which St Albans was governed in the twelfth and thirteenth centuries are not entirely clear.[128] The legal cases of the townspeople were almost all held in the court of the Liberty of St Albans, which sat in the abbey courtyard and corresponded to a hundred court. The borough court – held on St Margaret's Day (20 July) – dealt with only a limited range of matters: market prices, weights and measures, and the view of frankpledge (a feature of medieval law and order whereby members of the community, in groups, bound themselves and each other to keep the peace). A charter of 1253 allowed a measure of independence from the abbot's courts, but the abbey attempted to negate this independence by altering the structures of government in place in the town. An appeal before the justices in eyre (the

'... *compelling them to answer ... against the customs and liberties of the town*' itinerant royal court) in 1262 heard a complaint that the abbot's steward had called the men of St Albans 'to a foreign hundred court, compelling them to answer there against the customs and liberties of the town'.[129] It appears that a separate borough court, with powers corresponding to those of a hundred court, was established in St Albans, but it was abolished by abbot John de Maryns (1302–09) in the early fourteenth century, and the legal position of the townspeople remained insecure. As early as the thirteenth century, the abbey divided the town into four wards to ensure its better government; and in the fourteenth century abbot Richard de Wallingford appointed constables for each of the wards, which existed until the reform of the municipal corporations in 1835. The four wards were St Peter's (the part of the parish of St Peter's that was within the town); Middle Ward (the parish of St Andrew, or the Abbey parish); Holywell Ward (the urban part of St Stephen's parish 'and somewhat more'); and Fishpool Ward (the urban part of St Michael's).[130] The abbots also appointed a bailiff from 1284 onwards (a reeve, fulfilling the same functions, was appointed between 1270 and 1284). The bailiff, 'although usually a townsman, was the officer of the abbot, and did not represent the interests of the town, but was constantly at variance with it'.[131] He collected fines, administered the orders of the abbot, and enforced the rulings of the courts. The abbots ran the town from the moot hall, where the borough court met; this was replaced by a new town hall in the sixteenth century.[132]

The townspeople of St Albans were aggrieved by the attempts of the abbot to restrict their independence of government, but, like the villeins of Park, their most significant grievance was the extent of their feudal obligations to the abbey, and especially the requirement to use the abbey's mills. The earliest known date for urban resistance to this requirement at St Albans is 1274. In this year some townsmen had constructed their own domestic hand-mills, in defiance of their obligation to use the abbot's mills. The abbot, Roger de Norton, sent 16 men to seize the goods of the ring-leaders in the dispute, Michael Bryd and Henry de Porta. The two men were imprisoned, amid widespread local discontent. The townsmen established a common chest to fund their campaign, often used in such urban disputes and an indication of a degree of corporate identity on the part of the burgesses in their opposition to the 'particularly obnoxious obligation' of owing suit to the abbey's mills.[133] During the dispute Edward I's queen Eleanor visited the town, and the burgesses tried to impress upon her their sense of grievance, at a time when the king was carrying out an investigation into feudal privileges. Despite these representations, the result of the investigation was that the rights of the abbey were upheld, and Bryd and de Porta imprisoned. However, on this occasion the dispute ended amicably, as the abbot was lenient to the perpetrators, and made various concessions to the town, including the abolition of an unpopular beer tax. In return, the townspeople presented him with ten tuns of wine, but,

in the spirit of compromise, he accepted only five of them.[134] Sixteen years later, when queen Eleanor died in 1290, her body was carried from Lincoln to London, and a memorial cross built at each place at which the procession rested for the night. St Albans was one of these places, and the Eleanor Cross – built by John de la Battaille and completed by 1294 – stood in the market place until the early eighteenth century.[135]

The revolt of 1274 reflects what Trenholme called 'the growth of a spirit of municipal liberty and independence on the part of the burgesses of many of the monastic towns', which also resulted in the establishment of merchant guilds that came into conflict with abbeys in several places, including Reading, Coventry and Bury St Edmunds.[136] At Bury, as early as the eleventh century there had been a discernible 'desire for municipal privilege and burghal solidarity' among the inhabitants; and in the late twelfth and early thirteenth centuries there were ongoing conflicts over various dues that were owed by the town to the abbey. The mid-thirteenth century was quiet, but discontent erupted again in 1264, at the time of the barons' revolt against Henry III.[137] Other monastic towns – such as Dunstable, where a settlement between town and priory was reached following refusals to pay tithes and perform feudal services in the early thirteenth century, and a period of peace was followed by 'serious disturbances' in the fourteenth[138] – followed a similar trajectory of discontent, and although there is no evidence of any trouble in St Albans before 1274, it is by no means certain that none occurred.

A siege of the abbey followed, during which the townsmen attacked the monks with missiles ...

The most spectacular outbreak of urban discontent at St Albans in this period was in 1327, when the townsmen gained a temporary victory over the abbey. Following the death of Edward II, when London was beset by political instability during the minority of his son Edward III, the townspeople of Bury St Edmunds staged an uprising against the authority of their abbey, and the inhabitants of St Albans, more than 50 years after the first recorded dispute over hand-mills, followed suit, seizing the opportunity to demand more freedom from the tyranny of the abbot.[139] Their protests became violent, and one of the abbot's servants was attacked. He in turn killed one of the townsmen; and they responded by building a scaffold in the market place and threatening to kill anyone who did not support them. They demanded that the town be made a borough, that they be given the right to use the abbey's fishponds and to hunt in its woods (the offence for which Geoffrey de Childwick and others had been arraigned nearly a century before), and that they be allowed to use their own hand-mills. They cited the authority of Domesday Book, which named St Albans as a borough. A siege of the abbey followed, during which the townsmen attacked the monks with missiles; the monks in turn were defended by a force of some 200 men, who had been hired by abbot Hugh de Eversdene. A royal writ authorised force to be used against the besiegers, as a result of which they withdrew; however, they managed to convince the teenage king Edward, following consultation with his chamberlain and treasurer, that St Albans should indeed be a borough, and the abbey was ordered to confirm its burghal privileges. Under protest, abbot Hugh gave in, and St Albans gained a charter; however, the abbey retained its milling rights. The townspeople, celebrating their victory and eager for more, pulled down hedges and 'invaded' the abbey's ponds and warren; they also began to use a common seal, mimicking the practice of chartered boroughs, and set up around 80 hand-mills in defiance of the abbey's feudal privileges. The claims of the town gained wider recognition: between 1327 and 1334 St Albans sent two representatives to Parliament on five occasions, the only borough in Hertfordshire to do so; and both Hertford and St Albans were represented in 1336.[140] The borough court, abolished by abbot John de Maryns, was reinstated, and probably remained in existence until after the revolt of 1381.[141]

In most respects, however, the victory over the abbey was short-lived. In September 1327 abbot Hugh died, and was succeeded by Richard de Wallingford, one of 'the three greatest abbots', according to St Albans historian Elsie Toms.[142] Although, as noted above,[143] Richard had some difficulties with the management of the abbey, and certain eccentricities which displeased some of the monks, he proved adept at winning back the rights of the abbey in its battles with the town. In 1331, in an act of deliberate provocation, he summoned a townsman to his court on a charge of adultery, and made it clear that he intended to exert his authority over the town in moral matters.[144] This precipitated a riot, during which two of the abbot's clerks and a townsman were killed, and after which some 60 people were imprisoned in the abbot's jail. The townsmen then made a tactical error, believing that they could convict the abbot of murder by indicting him, and packing the jury. However, the jury acquitted the abbot, who then tried some of the burgesses as accessories to murder, and for perjury, before two royal justices. The abbot 'feasted' the justices, who promptly convicted the accused.[145] The new abbot had succeeded in reasserting his authority over the town of St Albans: the townsmen surrendered their charter in 1332, and Richard de Wallingford ceremoniously broke their common seal.[146] The townsmen agreed to pay the abbey £48 a year to use its fulling mill, and the 80 hand-mills were also surrendered. Richard set some of the millstones in the floor of the abbey to commemorate his victory; these stones were smashed half a century later, by the next generation of St Albans rebels, during the peasants' revolt of 1381.[147] Michelle Still attributes the victory of the abbey to the personality and effectiveness of abbot Richard, who took decisive action during the crisis: for example, on discovering that some of his monks were sympathetic to the townspeople's cause, he promptly exiled them to the abbey's dependent cell at Tynemouth.[148]

The townsmen were quelled, and order returned to St Albans; and there seems to have been peace for a time on the abbey's rural manors as well.

However, the memory of the revolt of 1327–32 remained with the rebels, and with their descendants, who would participate in the greatest revolt of all in 1381. The corporate identity of the town of St Albans had been forged through several decades of rebellion, culminating in the temporary success of 1327. Rosamund Faith, emphasising the abbey chronicler's comments about the apparent solidarity among the rebels, suggests that 'this struggle was by no means simply one of an urban proletariat alone, but involved, and was probably led by, a self-confident and politically sophisticated urban ruling class'.[149] Moreover, the town and its surrounding manors were united in their detestation of the abbey's insistence on its milling rights, and concerted opposition to the rule of the abbot and his men could be mobilised. In a period when the abbey itself had been weakened by debt, by the economic challenges facing early fourteenth-century agriculture, and by the incompetent leadership of several abbots, there was an opportunity for the townspeople to demonstrate their strength and self-confidence. By the 1330s, the wealth of St Albans had increased significantly; and the town's relative importance in the urban wealth of England was to increase during the next two centuries. On the eve of the Black Death, St Albans had a dynamic and increasingly complex urban economy, and a political culture that expressed the frustrations of an urban elite who wished to exercise more power over their affairs than their feudal overlords were willing to concede. In future decades the conflict between abbey and town would deepen in its intensity.

From the Black Death to the dissolution of the monasteries

T HE PLAGUE known as the Black Death swept across Europe from 1348–49, killing 'between a third and a half' of the population of England, including abbot Michael de Mentmore and 47 monks of St Albans.[1] The effects on the population of the town itself are less clear: one historian suggested that it was 'decimated', but if this word is used in its original sense, meaning reduced by a tenth, this is probably an underestimate.[2] James Corbett speculates that St Albans may have lost half its inhabitants to the plague, but there is no archaeological evidence to support an estimate.[3] In rural England, including the St Albans estates, the labour shortages that resulted from the sharp decline in the population gave villeins the opportunity to press for improvements to their conditions of work. The immediate increases in wages following the plague were addressed in 1351 by the Statute of Labourers, which set upper wage limits, but this proved 'impossible to enforce'.[4] An increasingly confident peasant class in the 1350s and 1360s proved resistant to lords' attempts to enforce labour rents and other feudal services, many of which had already, as we have seen, provoked intense conflict on the St Albans estates.

The situation was becoming more complicated in the decades following the Black Death, as a changing tenantry, many from London, moved onto the St Albans estates, and the monks tried hard to insist on the 'old customs' that had characterised life on their manors.[5] They were similarly insistent, following their victory over the townspeople in 1332, on their rights over their urban manor; and the dominance of the abbey was physically emphasised by the construction of the great gatehouse in the 1360s, during the long abbacy of Thomas de la Mare (1349–96). This imposing construction – the only building, except the church, left standing today from the abbey of St Albans – formed a physical, and psychological, barrier between abbey and town, and

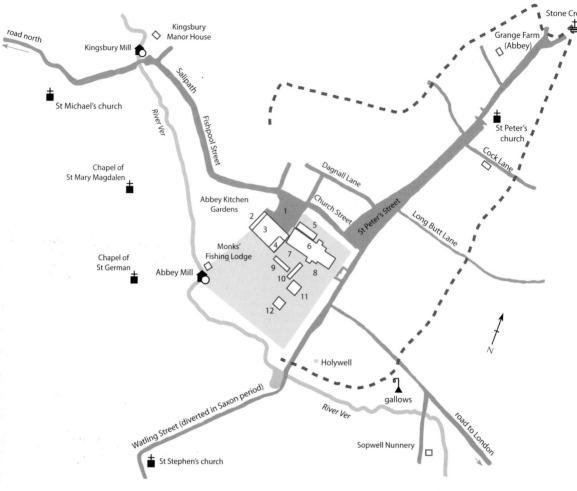

Map labels:
- road north
- Kingsbury Mill
- St Michael's church
- Kingsbury Manor House
- Sallpath
- River Ver
- Fishpool Street
- Chapel of St Mary Magdalen
- Abbey Kitchen Gardens
- Dagnall Lane
- Church Street
- St Peter's Street
- Long Butt Lane
- Cock Lane
- St Peter's church
- Grange Farm (Abbey)
- Stone Cross
- Monks' Fishing Lodge
- Chapel of St German
- Abbey Mill
- Holywell
- Watling Street (diverted in Saxon period)
- River Ver
- gallows
- St Stephen's church
- Sopwell Nunnery
- road to London
- N

(Numbered features on map: 1, 2, 3, 4, 5, 6, 7, 8, 9, 10, 11, 12)

ABOVE

This map shows the main streets and features of medieval St Albans, prior to the dissolution of the monasteries. The dotted line represents the Tonman Ditch, which featured in the battles of St Albans, and which formed the borough boundary when St Albans was chartered in 1553. The chapel of St German was established in the ninth or early tenth century, to commemorate the visit of St German or Germanus to the place of Alban's martyrdom in 429 (see box 2). The chapel of St Mary Magdalen was established, according to Matthew Paris, by abbot Ulsinus or Wulsin in the tenth century. The 'holy well' to the south was used for dipping bread by the nuns of Sopwell.

replaced an earlier structure which was destroyed by a storm in 1362.[6] The use of the gatehouse as a prison further emphasised the political and social control exercised by the abbey. On the other hand, the monks continued to provide for the poor of the town, notably by the provision of hot cross buns at Easter, a tradition that is supposed to have been initiated in St Albans by the cook, known as Father Rocliff, in 1361.[7]

Meanwhile, the town of St Albans was growing, despite setbacks such as the Black Death, which was followed by smaller but still serious outbreaks of plague in 1361 and 1368–69. In 1334, as we have seen,[8] St Albans ranked

French Row,
photographed here
looking north from
beside the clock
tower, was along
the western side of
the original large
market place of St
Albans. The Fleur-
de-Lys inn on the
left was reputedly
where king John
of France was
briefly imprisoned
following the battle
of Poitiers in 1356.

among the top 50 towns in England by taxable wealth. Records from the
poll tax of 1377 – which helped to spark the peasants' revolt of 1381 – do
not survive for St Albans, but the total population of the town at this date
has been estimated at around 2,500.[9] This represents a considerable increase
on the estimated population of some 500 at the time of Domesday Book,[10]
reflecting the growing prosperity of medieval St Albans. According to James
Corbett, in 1353 St Albans was 'a bustling town', home to 'four bakers, three
taverners, seven hostellers, 11 butchers, 10 fishmongers, three cooked-meat
sellers, six drapers, nine tailors, 14 tanners, eight skinners, one saddlemaker, 13
cobblers, two spicers, four smiths, four metalworkers, one plumber, 11 weavers,
six fullers, five dyers, one cornmonger, two saltmongers and … 81 brewers'.

Many of the latter had other employment in addition to brewing.[11] Agriculture remained important in the economy of the town, not least because of its market. During the fourteenth century more permanent structures between Chequer Street and Market Place were erected.[12] Three fairs were held each year, at Romeland, in front of the abbey gatehouse. Manufacturing was also growing in importance, probably more so at St Albans than at other towns in the region: the long-standing, escalating and bitter disputes over fulling-mills are evidence of this.[13]

LEFT
Thomas de la Mare was abbot of St Albans from 1349 to 1396. He led the response of the abbey to the peasants' revolt of 1381. This brass of abbot Thomas, one of the finest and largest surviving ecclesiastical brasses in the country, probably dates from the 1360s, and shows him wearing his Mass vestments, as well as his mitre. He is flanked by saints.

PHOTOGRAPH: CARNEGIE

These disputes, the origins of which were explored in the last chapter, culminated in the events of 1381, when a rebellion against the monks of St Albans took place against the backdrop of the peasants' revolt across the south and east of England, which tested to the limits the power of royal and feudal authority. The revolt was the first of several convulsions that shook St Albans between the mid-fourteenth and mid-sixteenth centuries, which are explored in this chapter, and despite which the town continued to grow and prosper. However, it remained politically under-represented: for example, in the Parliaments of 1373 and 1375–76, Hertford was the only borough in the county that sent representatives.[14] The revolt

of 1381, in its local context, was a trial of strength between the townsmen and peasants on one side, and the abbey and the forces of law and order on the other; although the abbey eventually prevailed, the events demonstrate the growing spirit of independence among the people of St Albans, and the tensions to which the feudal order was subjected during the demographic and political upheavals of the fourteenth century.

The main primary source for the events of 1381 is the chronicle written by Thomas Walsingham, a monk of St Albans abbey who recorded in great detail the events of his day, both at St Albans and across the south of England. He was the successor to Matthew Paris (see box 1), although he does not seem to have achieved the national and international prominence of his predecessor, and nor did he have the same range of intellectual interests, although he was a classical scholar who had probably studied at Oxford.[15] Walsingham's account is unashamedly biased towards the abbot and the monks, and he was disdainful of the townsmen and peasants who took part in the rebellion. He usually referred to them as 'villeins', emphasising their lack of burghal privileges, and sneered at the other words they used to describe themselves, such as 'burghers', 'citizens' or 'commons'.[16] In one historian's words, the use of the term 'villeins' (*villani* in Walsingham's Latin) conveyed an 'implied assimilation of St Albans to the status of a mere village'.[17]

The revolt of 1381 seems to have begun in Essex and Kent: on 10 June the rebellious peasants marched on Canterbury, led by Wat Tyler, the best known of the rebel leaders. Three days later they entered London – an 'army' of some 100,000 men, according to Walsingham[18] – where the urban poor were

already attacking the Savoy Palace, home of the duke of Lancaster, John of Gaunt. Following further attacks on the Temple Bar and St John's Hospital, the young king Richard II conceded to the demands of the rebels, who then occupied the Tower of London and executed three men, including the king's treasurer Sir Robert Hales, on 14 June. On the same day – 'a day of wrath, a day of affliction and anguish, a day of calamity and grief'[19] – a delegation of sympathisers from St Albans and Barnet met the London rebels at the church of St Mary-of-the-Arches (St Mary-le-Bow). At the same time, the abbot had sent his knights to help to defend London against the rebels. Once in London, the 'villeins' of St Albans and Barnet demanded various freedoms: according to Walsingham, they

> began to discuss their subservience to the monastery, and the means by
> which they could achieve what they had secretly wanted for a long time
> … that they should enjoy new boundaries around the town, within which

LEFT

The gatehouse is
the only part of
St Albans abbey,
except the church
itself, that still
stands. It was built
in the 1360s, and its
size and imposing
exterior represented
the power and
authority of the
abbey over the
people of the town.
This view is from
inside the abbey
precinct, from the
south-east. The
gatehouse was used
as a prison, and was
a focus of discontent
in the peasants'
revolt of 1381. It
now forms part of St
Albans School.

PHOTOGRAPH: CARNEGIE

they might freely pasture their animals, obtain fishing rights in certain places with impunity, have rights of hunting and fowling again in certain places, and erect hand-mills that they could freely use whenever they wished. They also demanded that the bailiff of the liberty [of St Albans] should not interfere at all within the limits of the town, and that the bonds which their parents had once made to Abbot Richard of Wallingford of blessed memory [on the occasion of their surrender in 1332], should be given back to them as well as other charters if these were prejudicial to them, or indeed any of the muniments at all ... which were in the abbey, that were a support to them or harmful to the monastery.[20]

It is clear that the events of 1381 in St Albans cannot be understood outside the context of the long tradition of opposition to monastic authority that existed in the town and in the surrounding countryside. Certainly many of the demands of the rising of 1327 were repeated in 1381, and a strong folk memory of their parents' and grandparents' struggles against the feudal authority of the abbey informed the actions of the St Albans rebels. Walsingham's account of the rebels' demands for the righting of the wrongs done to them by abbot Richard de Wallingford emphasises this aspect of their revolt.

After this meeting and the articulation of their demands, the rebels returned to St Albans, where they threatened to burn the abbey and murder the monks if these demands were not met. Some rebels were more cautious, suggesting that they should apply to Richard II and request a letter instructing the abbot to grant the desired liberties to the townsmen. In this more moderate group was William Grindcobbe, an inhabitant of St Albans who, according to Walsingham, 'was under great obligation to the monastery, not only because he had been educated, brought up and fed there, but also because of his close relationship with some of the monks who had been his relatives and still were'.[21] Grindcobbe's relationship with the abbey had been soured following his excommunication for assaulting two monks during a property dispute; and although he was among the more cautious of the rebels, he rapidly became the leading figure in St Albans. Grindcobbe conducted the negotiations with the king, and obtained the desired letter; however, he and his companions also managed to persuade Wat Tyler to agree to come to St Albans 'if it was deemed necessary' to enforce concessions from the abbey.[22] Rumour of Tyler's coming reached the abbey very quickly, and some of the monks, including the prior John Moot, fled to the dependent cell at Tynemouth: this journey itself was one involving 'considerable dangers'.[23] Meanwhile, Grindcobbe and and his lieutenants returned, followed by the St Albans 'villeins' from London; and a series of deliberate acts of rebellion followed. The mob broke down the abbot's enclosures, and destroyed the sub-cellarer's house, which 'was thought to impede the view of the burghers and to insult the nobility of the citizens

The Peasants Revolt 1381.

This depiction of the peasants' revolt of 1381 was created for the St Albans pageant in 1907 (see below, pp. 249–51), in which the revolt was one of the historical scenes that were re-enacted.

– for that was what they now called themselves'.[24] All this happened on one day – Friday 14 June 1381 – and precipitated a month of crisis, and a temporary victory for the townspeople that was not reversed until the middle of July.

On the following day, Saturday 15 June, the rebels declared that all able-bodied men in the town should take up arms and join them, on pain of execution. The local peasantry also joined them, having been 'stirred up' by the townsmen and summoned from the villages within the Liberty of St Albans. There were 'two thousand or more of these scoundrels', who 'hastened with great arrogance to the gates of the monastery to show what great power they had obtained from Wat Tyler', whom they believed to be coming to assist them.[25] At the gatehouse, which had recently been rebuilt, the mob released the abbot's prisoners, except for one, whom they summarily beheaded in the middle of Romeland. The others they allowed to go free on condition that they supported the rebellion. Shortly afterwards, Richard of Wallingford – 'the most important of the villeins of St Albans' and incidentally a namesake of the late abbot who had recovered the abbey's privileges after the rising of 1327 [26] – returned to the town carrying the letter from Richard II that Grindcobbe had, as Walsingham's claimed, 'extorted' from the king. Abbot Thomas was sent for, and although he 'had long ago decided to die protecting the liberty of the monastery sooner than do anything prejudicial to his church', he was persuaded by his monks to give in to the rebels. The letter from Richard II read:

Beloved in God. At the petition of our beloved loyal subjects of the town of St Albans, we wish and command that you hand over certain charters which are in your possession, made by our forefather, King Henry, to the burgesses and good people of the said town concerning the common land, pasture, fishery, and certain other possessions mentioned in those charters, as stated in them, as the law and right require, so that they may have no grounds for complaining to us in future in this matter. Given under our signet at London, the fifteenth day of June, in the fourth year of our reign.[27]

The distinctive St Albans clock tower was built between 1403 and 1412, a symbol of civic pride in a town which was repeatedly striving for independence from the authority of the abbey. The construction of the clock tower, directly opposite the Waxhouse Gate entrance to the abbey, can be seen as a gesture of confident defiance towards the abbot and monks.

PHOTOGRAPH: CARNEGIE

The abbot was still reluctant to concede to the rebels, but, under threat of the destruction of the abbey, he agreed to draw up new charters releasing the townsmen from the pledges they had made at their surrender to abbot Richard in 1332.

It was at this point that the 'mob', still unsatisfied with the concessions made by the abbot, began to demand that he produce a charter that had, apparently, been given to the townsmen by king Offa in the eighth century. Offa had become 'a figure of popular local legend', something of a hero to the townspeople.[28] There is a certain irony in this, as in the thirteenth century the monks themselves, especially Matthew Paris, had cited the authority of the abbey's royal benefactor and traditional founder to enhance their own claims to local hegemony.[29] Bernard Spichfort, a member of an established family of opponents of the abbey, was apparently in the forefront of a group that was 'leading the young people of the town astray by telling them tales of Offa and his charter',[30] and the clamouring for this charter emphasises the importance of the 'sense of tradition and history' that animated the St Albans rebels of 1381.[31] In 1327 the rebels had referred to Domesday Book, in which the inhabitants of St Albans (or some of them) were described as burgesses;[32] in 1381 the appeal was to a still older authority. Offa's charter, of course, did not exist, and had almost certainly never existed, and it was clear that the townsmen would have to be content with a new charter, which the abbot was willing to concede. However, the anger of the 'villeins' having been aroused, the crowd was unwilling to wait for the charter of liberties to be drawn up, and 'the rascals entered the cloister with implements and lifted up the mill-stones on the outside of the parlour which were on the floor by the parlour entrance, laid there as a memento and memorial of the ancient agreement between the villeins and the monastery in the time of abbot Richard' – in other words, the mill-stones that abbot Richard de Wallingford had set in his floor following his victory over the townsmen in 1332, and which still stood as a symbol of the abbey's suppression of the town.[33] The mill-stones were smashed to pieces and the remnants distributed among the rebels. To buy time, and to prevent the destruction of the abbey, a brief truce was agreed, and the abbot agreed to produce the 'irrecoverable charter' by noon the next day, Sunday 16 June.[34] The monks made plans to follow the example of their prior and some of their colleagues, and to flee.

The next morning, the mood of the rebels was quietened when they heard reports of the death of Wat Tyler, who had been killed in London, and when a messenger arrived carrying a letter from Richard II extending his protection to the abbey of St Albans. The rebels, who were still anxious to obtain their charter, 'acted with less commotion, and less insolence, than previously', although Walsingham believed that their politeness and peaceability was 'feigned'.[35] It was accepted that Offa's charter could not be found, and a

'the rascals entered the cloister with implements and lifted up the mill-stones.'

new charter was given, the terms dictated by the rebels, and the abbot's seal attached.[36] Walsingham described a 'miracle', whereby, through the power of St Alban, whose image was on the abbot's seal, the wax 'could by no means whatsoever, even after three attempts, be stripped or removed from the seal'.[37] Eventually, however, the seal was attached and the charter secured, and the townsmen promptly displayed it at the market cross. This success prompted the villeins of Barnet, Rickmansworth and Watford to demand similar charters, permitting them to hunt and fish on abbey lands, and to use their own hand-mills; and ultimately a charter was given by the abbot to all the 'bondmen' of the St Albans abbey estates, after the concession of which 'these countrymen thought that they were noblemen superior to royal lineage, and should be freed from all subservience and from supplying in the customary service'.[38] Walsingham was clear that the rural rebellion on the St Albans estates was stirred up by the townsmen of St Albans, who certainly, if his account is to be believed at all, both encouraged the peasantry to rebel, and threatened them with ill-treatment if they did not.

'a self-confident and politically sophisticated urban ruling class'

The situation in St Albans differed from that of some towns in the rebellion of 1381, but was paralleled in others, especially the monastic borough of Bury St Edmund's. As Rodney Hilton explains, in some towns the disturbances 'were simply the continuation, or revival, of struggles having a purely urban context, and which took place because of the generally disturbed condition of the country at large': examples were York, Winchester and Bridgwater. By contrast, elsewhere, including St Albans and Bury, 'while the same factors of inner-urban conflict might have existed, a new situation emerged, constituting a conscious effort by rebels of town and country to take advantage (at least) of a temporary coincidence of revolutionary interests'.[39] These monastic boroughs were 'political anachronisms', whose economic strength was not matched by the relative political independence that was common in other boroughs by the later fourteenth century. As a result, townsmen and peasants made common cause, finding themselves in the same situation, as the chronicler's demeaning use of the term 'villeins' demonstrates.[40] Thus the urban leaders of the rebellions at St Albans and Bury were not the 'rank and file', but members of urban elites such as William Grindcobbe, with his relatives at the monastery, and William Cadindon, a St Albans baker.[41] The suppression of the urban elites' claims to self-government made rebels of them; as in 1327, what Rosamund Faith has called 'a self-confident and politically sophisticated urban ruling class' led the rising of 1381 in St Albans.[42]

The rebels' victory, as in 1327, was temporary; in this case it lasted only a month. As Richard II and his government regained control of London and the rest of south-eastern England, royal authority was reasserted in the rebellious towns. On 2 July, a letter from Richard revoked the liberties that he had conceded under the pressure of the rebellion in London;[43] and at around the same time he instigated an inquiry into events at St Albans. His first instinct was to inflict serious punishment on the town, but he was restrained by his knight Sir Walter atte Lee, who was from St Albans himself, and hoped that the town might not be destroyed. Lee, an MP, JP and sheriff of Hertfordshire, was sent to St Albans, where many of the rebels had already lost heart, but were kept from fleeing by the 'shameful boldness' with which, in Walsingham's phrase, William Grindcobbe continued to harangue them.[44] Lee met the rebels, and tried to reassure them that he was seeking a just solution to the crisis; but when he summoned a jury of twelve townsmen, they refused to indict any of their fellows, or to return the charters that the abbot had conceded, and which Lee now demanded.[45] Lee then caused Grindcobbe, Cadindon and their fellow rebel John Barbitonsor (or Barbour) to be arrested and conveyed to Hertford jail, where they were escorted by the abbot's knights. These arrests aroused more disturbance in St Albans and the surrounding manors, which in turn

provoked the fear that the undefended abbey would be destroyed. The abbot
summoned his knights back from Hertford, and Grindcobbe was bailed; and an
ultimatum was presented to the townsmen: return the charters, or Grindcobbe
would be executed. Grindcobbe urged the townsmen to stand firm; and in a
sign that the alliance of town and country had now run its course, the town's
spokesmen refused to return the charters, claiming the fear that, should they
do so, the men of Barnet, Watford and the other parts of the Liberty would
attack and burn St Albans.[46] This stalemate, and the failure of Lee to achieve
his purpose, prompted the king to go to St Albans himself.

Neither the abbot – who feared the destructive revenge of the king's forces – nor the townsmen themselves wanted the king to visit St Albans, and the townsmen appointed Sir William Crosier, a JP for Hertfordshire and Surrey, as their legal representative, in the hope that he would be able to broker an agreement between abbey and town.[47] A settlement was reached, whereby the townspeople were to compensate the abbot with two hundred pounds of silver, and to replace the mill-stones in the abbey floor with as many of their own stones as possible. In return, the abbot promised to ask the king to be lenient with the rebels, although he emphasised that he could not promise to secure any pardon. As Walsingham explained,

> About the time of vespers [on the evening of Friday 12 July] six millstones were brought, which was the number they had taken, and by the ministration of the villeins they were put down near the place from which the others had been removed. Furthermore, in their fear they humbly pleaded to be pardoned for having extorted the charters and bonds, and they returned the charters; also very many of them bound themselves over to give satisfaction which would compensate for the seriousness of their misdeeds. These things were done on the very day the king was due to arrive.[48]

'compelled to hang their fellow citizens again with their own hands ...'

When Richard did arrive, he was accompanied by Sir Robert Tresilian, who was to try the offenders. Grindcobbe, Cadindon and Barbitonsor, together with John Ball, one of the leaders of the revolt, were convicted and executed. Some fifteen men were 'drawn and hanged' in total, and 80 others from Hertfordshire were imprisoned, including Richard of Wallingford, who had carried the king's letter to St Albans a month earlier.[49] This defeat for the rebels was followed by a written requirement from Richard II for all the tenants of the St Albans abbey estates to 'render their accustomed services' to their feudal overlords, 'under pain of forfeiting all the things which they will in future be able to forfeit to us'.[50] The king then took a pledge of allegiance from all the Hertfordshire men who had been summoned to the court at St Albans. However, even this was not the end of the revolt. Soon after the king had left, some of the townsmen removed the bodies of the hanged rebels from their gibbets. Richard immediately ordered them to be re-hanged, and Walsingham sneeringly described how the rebellious townsmen

> were compelled to hang their fellow citizens again with their own hands ... Their bodies were now stinking with decay, swarming with worms, were putrid and stinking, and exuding their foul odour upon them. The men who had unjustly assumed the name of citizens deserved this loathsome duty, causing them aptly to be called, as they were in fact,

hangmen, thus incurring an everlasting reproach for their action, a reproach which will not be blotted out ... it was fitting that perjurors, and backbiters hateful to God, should be ... obliged to carry out so servile and disgusting a service.[51]

'a deliberate expression of defiance'

The end of the revolt of 1381 did not entirely crush the spirit of rebellion on the St Albans estates: for example, at Barnet in 1417 the villeins revived the old demand that they be allowed to trade in land without the approval of the abbot's court.[52] During the late fourteenth and early fifteenth centuries, the abbots were concerned about the spread of Lollardy in the town: Lollards, who criticised the established church and denied certain key doctrines such as transubstantiation, distributed tracts in St Albans and elsewhere; and Sir John Oldcastle, a Lollard preacher accused of heresy in 1413, went into hiding in various places, including a location near St Albans, evading capture until 1417, when he was executed.[53] In the town itself, a culture of defiance of abbatial authority was manifested in the building of the clock tower, between 1403 and 1412. Isobel Thompson explains that the tower's 'position facing the ... entrance to the Abbey precinct [on the High Street] can be seen as a deliberate expression of defiance'.[54] The clock played an important part in the management of the economic and social life of the town, and, together with other examples of town clocks such as the contemporaneous clock at Dunstable, another monastic town, can be seen as representing 'the attainment on the part of these secular societies of a degree of autonomy vis-à-vis their monastic lords, who had hitherto claimed a local monopoly on timekeeping as on other affairs'.[55] Although the St Albans clock tower is almost unique in England,[56] public clocks were being constructed in other towns in the early fifteenth century, for example Stratford-on-Avon, Bridgwater and Abergavenny.[57] At St Albans, the bell was older than the tower itself, and the local historian Elsie Toms speculated that it may have been donated by the abbey – its inscription reads *Missi de coelis habeo nomen Gabrielis* ('I bear heaven-sent Gabriel's name') – which would represent a degree of rapprochement between abbey and town.[58]

The abbot retained almost complete authority over St Albans in the mid-fifteenth century: in 1440 Henry VI confirmed the charters of his predecessor Henry II, allowing the abbot to hold all the courts in the area of the Liberty of St Albans, to appoint his own JPs with whom others could not 'interfere', and to hold all the assizes, including those of bread (which fixed prices) and of weights and measures.[59] This was confirmed by the new Yorkist king Edward IV following his accession in 1461.[60] Some other privileges of the abbey are less certain, but it is known that in the thirteenth century those who claimed sanctuary in the abbey could also live, and even trade, in the town of St Albans, a privilege that was also available in Westminster; and it has been suggested that this may have lasted into the fifteenth century.[61] Abbot John de Wheathampstead, who served two separate terms (1420–40 and 1452–65), extended the local holdings of the abbey, acquiring several manors including Garston; and vigorously defended the rights of the abbey, following Matthew Paris and the rebels of 1381 in citing the authority of king Offa for the privileges of St Albans.[62] In his second term, the chapel of St Andrew, which served the community of the parish of St Andrew – later the Abbey parish – was rebuilt, paid for by the parishioners.[63] There were also some notable works of re-decoration and construction within the abbey, including a roodscreen in the later fourteenth century; a watching loft (one of only two from the period that survives in England) built c.1400; the great west window; a new spire; traceried windows in the transepts; and, dating from 1484, the high altar screen.[64] Under John de Wheathampstead, the chantry chapel of Humphrey, duke of Gloucester,

RIGHT
The chantry chapel of Humphrey, duke of Gloucester, was built next to the shrine of St Alban (just off this photograph, to the left) in the abbey church in the 1440s. Humphrey was the 'principal councillor' to the king during the minority of Henry VI, but had been marginalised politically by the time of his death. He was an important patron of St Albans abbey.
PHOTOGRAPH: CARNEGIE

LEFT
The oak watching loft, on the northern side of the shrine of St Alban, was constructed c.1400. A watchman was stationed in it to guard the relics of the martyr. This would usually have been one of the abbey's tenants rather than one of the monks. The watching loft is one of only two surviving in England, and contains detailed carvings of religious and secular scenes.
PHOTOGRAPH: CARNEGIE

LEFT

One of a pair of doors built for the west front of the abbey church during the first of John de Wheathampstead's periods as abbot (1420-40). The doors are now displayed in the chapter house. They are made of four layers of wood, held together using wrought iron nails.

PHOTOGRAPH: CARNEGIE

was also constructed, to a design by John Thirsk, the master mason of Westminster abbey. Duke Humphrey was the son of Henry IV and brother of Henry V, and his chantry is similar in several respects to Henry V's own chantry at Westminster.[65]

The duke of Gloucester was a prominent participant in the political struggles that followed the death of his brother in 1422, the crowning of the infant king Henry VI, and the new king's long minority.[66] Gloucester became 'Protector, defender and principal councillor' to the new king, but was dissatisfied with the limited extent of the powers he had been given.[67] He disagreed with the conduct of the ongoing war against the French, and was the subject of repeated attempts by the other magnates of the realm to sideline him. Even after Henry VI had reached the age of majority, his ability to rule was in doubt – in the words of one historian, 'gradually ... the realisation dawned on those around the king that he was never going to grow up'[68] – and the struggle for control of the government continued. Gloucester was hampered by his repeated 'lack of judgement at home and abroad', by a personality that aroused the dislike of other leading political figures, and by a wife whose alleged involvement in necromancy caused him considerable embarrassment.[69] During the crises that beset his political career, Gloucester visited St Albans, and prominently 'cast himself as the patron of the monastery'.[70] In 1441 he decided to be buried at St Albans, and by 1443 his chantry had been commissioned. In 1447, at a Parliament meeting in Bury St Edmunds, Gloucester was arrested for treason, but died shortly afterwards, before he could be tried; there were many, predictable, allegations that he had been murdered.[71] It has been suggested that his patronage of St Albans abbey was 'a predatory assertion of status and pretension', and his chantry is decorated in a regal style.[72] However, although he was a political failure, Gloucester managed to present 'a favourable public image', partly through his

continued on page 122

Box 3: 'Stuft full with the Bodies of the Slain': the two battles of St Albans

A LTHOUGH the abbey at St Albans remained neutral during the Wars of the Roses, the town stood in a strategic location, and two battles, in 1455 and 1461, were fought there. The first of these was once thought of as the opening battle in the war between the Lancastrians and Yorkists, but is now seen as 'a stage on the high road to to the Wars of the Roses' rather than the beginning of the conflict itself.[1] (The term 'Wars of the Roses' was a later coinage, by Sir Walter Scott.)[2] An eighteenth-century antiquarian remarked that St Peter's churchyard was 'stuft full with the Bodies of the Slain in the Battles fought there';[3] most of these must have fallen in the second battle, because the first, in the words of the historian Christine Carpenter, was 'no more than an affray', at which 'few were killed'.[4] Another historian dismissed it as 'a short scuffle in a street',[5] albeit one with significant consequences, marking a significant escalation in the ongoing political

and dynastic conflict that characterised fifteenth-century England. Henry VI, the Lancastrian king who had reigned since 1422, the year after his birth, had emerged from a long coma late in 1454. During his incapacity, Richard, duke of York, had acted as protector, and used this power as an excuse to imprison one of his main political rivals and a favourite of the king, Edmund Beaufort, duke of Somerset. Richard of York was closely associated with the Neville family, including Richard Neville, the earl of Salisbury, and his son, also Richard Neville, the earl of Warwick.[6] When Henry regained capacity and control of his government, Somerset was released, and restored to his position at the royal court. Even after his recovery, Henry was unable to exercise real authority over his government, and Richard of York and his supporters withdrew from the court in May 1455. During this period, in Carpenter's words, 'the whole tone of politics was becoming more violent'.[7] This culminated, following the withdrawal of the Yorkists from the government, in the raising of an army by Richard, who led his men southwards from Yorkshire towards London. Henry VI, assisted by Somerset, mobilised his

---

[1] Anthony Pollard, 'Battle of St Albans 1455', *History Today*, vol. 55, no. 5 (2005), p. 29. See also Andrew Boardman, *The First Battle of St Albans, 1455* (Stroud: Tempus, 2006).

[2] Briggs, *Social History of England*, p. 130.

[3] Quoted in Niblett and Thompson, *Alban's Buried Towns*, p. 288.

[4] Carpenter, *Wars of the Roses*, p. 135.

[5] Quoted in Briggs, *Social History of England*, p. 132.

[6] This account is based mainly on Pollard, 'Battle of St Albans'.

[7] Carpenter, *Wars of the Roses*, p. 137.

forces, which were smaller in number, and took them to meet Richard's army; the two met at St Albans.

The details of the battle, on 22 May 1455, are not entirely clear. It has been suggested that Henry stayed at Hall Place, a large house near St Peter's church that was demolished in the early twentieth century, and that the Nevilles were at Salisbury Hall, to the south-east of St Albans.[1] The Yorkist army gathered at Key Field, to the west of the town, while negotiations took place, during which the king rejected Richard's demand for the removal of Somerset from the court. The battle commenced in the plots of land behind the houses on Holywell Street – the Yorkist army managed to enter the town, not through the gates that stood at the end of Sopwell Lane, but across the Tonman Ditch.[2] Advancing up Chequer Street, the Yorkists soundly defeated the king's army, in the process killing the duke of Somerset – at the corner of St Peter's Street and Victoria Street, where a blue plaque today marks the spot – and two other supporters of the king, the earl of Northumberland and Lord Clifford. Henry VI was captured, although the Yorkists presented the victory as an act of loyalty rather than of treason: they used the traditional justification that

they had freed the king from unsuitable advisers. Richard of York was restored to his position, and found himself at the head of another protectorate, as Henry's physical and mental condition again deteriorated. However, Richard was not fully trusted by the other leading magnates, and the Yorkists trod carefully, perhaps too carefully, 'clearly aware that [in killing three leading men of the realm] they had taken a step beyond what had hitherto been accepted as justifiable action'.[3] The Lancastrian loyalists rallied around Henry VI's wife, Margaret of Anjou, in the following years, and the rival political factions solidified, the first battle of St Albans having marked an important stage in this process. In the Parliament which followed the battle, the Commons presented a petition which called for Humphrey, the late duke of Gloucester, to be 'formally rehabilitated'; the popular duke was buried in the abbey of St Albans, and the Yorkists were adopting his memory in support of their cause.[4] Richard of York had tried to present himself as duke Humphrey's successor in the early 1450s.[5]

The second battle of St Albans took place six years after the first, on 17 February 1461. In 1460 the earl of Warwick captured Henry VI at the battle of Northampton, and Richard

---

[1] Niblett and Thompson, *Alban's Buried Towns*, p. 288; Toms, *Story of St Albans*, pp. 60–1.
[2] Niblett and Thompson, *Alban's Buried Towns*, p. 268. On the Tonman Ditch, see above, pp. 90, 102.

[3] Pollard, 'Battle of St Albans', p. 27.
[4] See below, p. 122; Carpenter, *Wars of the Roses*, p. 138; Harriss, 'Humphrey, Duke of Gloucester'.
[5] Carpenter, *Wars of the Roses*, pp. 117–18.

of York attempted to claim the throne, but was killed in December of the same year at the Battle of Wakefield. His son Edward, aged 18, succeeded him as duke and as claimant to the throne. Meanwhile, Margaret of Anjou marched the victorious Lancastrian army southwards from Wakefield, while Warwick brought his army northwards from London. Again, the two forces met at St Albans. The Yorkists under Warwick were in the town first, and Margaret's army attacked from George Street, where they met a 'strong barricade'.[1] The Lancastrians retreated, and re-entered St Albans from the north, this time more successfully: Warwick's army were forced to retreat to Bernard's Heath, where they were routed by Margaret's forces. Some fled as far north as Nomansland, south of Wheathampstead.

Henry VI was re-captured by the Lancastrians. Nevertheless, by June Edward of York had been crowned king Edward IV, and Henry was in exile. The impact of the battle of 1461 on St Albans was significant: the victorious Lancastrian army, as they had done elsewhere, pillaged both the town and the abbey. 'They robbed, assaulted and killed indiscriminately during their orgy of celebration.'[2] The bones of some of the dead of 1461 were, reputedly, found in the cellar of the Cock Inn during the twentieth century.[3] The impact of the battles, especially the second, probably contributed to the brief period of urban decline that can be identified in mid-fifteenth-century St Albans.

---

[1] Toms, *Story of St Albans*, pp. 61–2.

[2] Corbett, *History of St Albans*, p. 45.
[3] Niblett and Thompson, *Alban's Buried Towns*, p. 288.

RIGHT
The ceiling of the tower of the abbey church, dating from the sixteenth century, contains, in the four central panels, the arms of St Alban, England, St George and Edward the Confessor. Surrounding them are the roses of York and Lancaster, reflecting the importance of St Albans in the Wars of the Roses.

PHOTOGRAPH: CARNEGIE

support for St Albans abbey, as well as the University of Oxford, where he founded Duke Humphrey's Library.[73]

The memory of the duke of Gloucester was aggressively promoted by opponents of Lancastrian rule, in Jack Cade's rebellion of 1450 – when rumours of Gloucester's murder again circulated – and in the early years of the Wars of the Roses.[74] Two battles were fought in St Albans during this conflict, in 1455 and 1461 (see box 3), and as a result the town suffered considerable, but temporary, setbacks, with demolitions and vacant plots in evidence during the mid-fifteenth century.[75] It should be emphasised, however, that vacant plots and falling populations were by no means uncommon in English towns in the fifteenth century, and the period was known as one of urban poverty and decay across much of the country. As one historian has commented, 'falling populations often meant the amalgamation of plots, wasted holdings and empty tenements'.[76] There has been considerable disagreement among urban historians as to the extent and reality of 'urban decay', but it is undoubtedly an important theme of the later medieval period. Fifteenth-century towns repeatedly complained of their poverty in Parliament: the fee-farm of many boroughs (the fixed sum they paid to the king or another landlord in return for their burghal privileges) was reduced in mid-century, often considerably.[77] Borough revenues, along with populations, were falling, and the fee-farm was proving difficult to meet. Ironically, unchartered towns without self-government such as St Albans, or the ecclesiastical town of Salisbury that was governed as a manor of the Bishop of Salisbury, were in a better position in this respect: rather than paying fixed sums, feudal duties were paid as a proportion of their revenues, and therefore did not become more onerous when these revenues fell.[78] It is clear that, across England as a whole, the urban population of England suffered a decline in this period, something upon which both native and foreign observers remarked. An Italian commentator, writing in the 1490s, claimed that 'there are scarcely any towns of importance in the kingdom' of England, except for London, York and Bristol;[79] and both the latter were shrinking during this period.[80] Some blamed the falling population on economic decline – the cloth manufacturing industry was struggling, especially in the large towns – and others on the failings of urban government. As late as 1532, a character in a philosophical text could complain that '[e]very gentleman flieth into the country; few ... inhabit cities or towns; few have any regard for them; by the reason whereof in them you shall find no policy, no civil order, almost, nor rule'.[81]

'few ... inhabit cities or towns ... in them you shall find no policy, no civil order, almost, nor rule'

In fact, we should not overstate the decline of English towns during the fifteenth century, for three reasons. First, if the population of many towns was declining, this was no less true of the surrounding countryside. The total population of England fell from somewhere between 4.5 and 6 million on the eve of the Black Death in 1348, to around 2.75 million in 1541, and it may be that the urban population was falling more slowly than the rural.[82] The heavy rural population losses in the Black Death and subsequent epidemics would put less pressure on the supply of rural land, and reduce one of the 'push factors' that could cause rural-to-urban migration.[83] The number of markets declined sharply after the Black Death, from a figure of 2,000–3,000 that was almost certainly inflated by speculative ventures, to around 600 by the sixteenth century.[84] As the growth of urban markets in the twelfth and thirteenth centuries had been driven by surplus agricultural production, the decline suggests a general contraction of economic activity under the impact of severe population loss. Second, although there may have been considerable corporate poverty in urban England in this period, this does not mean that individuals within towns were necessarily impoverished to the same extent. The difficulties that boroughs found in meeting the financial demands that were made upon them – difficulties that, in any case, were probably exaggerated – were not necessarily shared by individuals living in boroughs, who continued to build houses, and to contribute money to impressive civic projects such as town halls. The third reason to doubt the 'urban decay' thesis is that many towns – including St Albans – actually grew during the fifteenth century, certainly in population and perhaps in wealth. Although all population figures for this period can only be approximations, the population of St Albans grew from about 2,500 in 1377 to about 3,770 at the time of the lay subsidy of 1524–25, from which population sizes can be estimated.[85] Another estimate for St Albans at the latter date is 5,000, but this seems improbably high.[86] Nevertheless, St Albans may have been the 15th largest town in England at this time, and had 580 taxpayers.[87] The other towns that experienced growth were mostly in East Anglia, the south-east and south-west, including Crediton, Exeter, Huntingdon, Maidstone, Norwich, Reading, Rochester and Taunton. Many of the shrinking towns were in the north and east of the country, including York, Nottingham, Leicester, Hull, Beverley, Boston and Lincoln.[88]

These changes reflected a shift in the economic balance of power within England, away from the north, east and midlands and towards East Anglia, the west country and the counties around London.[89] Although each town had its individual story of growth or decline, general factors in the changing economic climate included the falling-off of foreign trade, especially the collapse of cloth exports in the mid-fifteenth century; the instablility caused by the Wars of the Roses – a particular problem for St Albans; and repeated outbreaks of bubonic plague, which in the fifteenth century tended to affect towns rather than the countryside.[90] However, despite these economic challenges, many towns prospered, for various reasons. In St Albans, the plots left vacant after the battles of 1455 and 1461 probably did not remain vacant for very long. The main reason for the continued prosperity of St Albans was the same as the reason why two battles were fought there in the mid-fifteenth century: its strategic location on the main road north of London. In the two centuries after

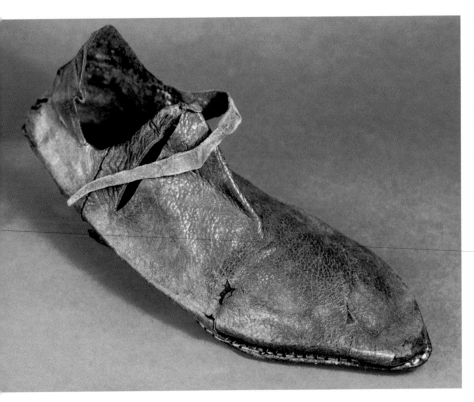

This leather shoe dates from the fifteenth century, and was found in Chequer Street in 1981. The Company of Shoemakers was one of the four guilds of freemen of St Albans that emerged in the sixteenth century.

© ST ALBANS MUSEUMS

the Black Death, London grew in economic importance: its port trade grew at the expense of Bristol, Southampton and other ports, and its population expanded from around 40,000 in 1377 to over 100,000 by the mid-sixteenth century.[91] One estimate suggests that London's wealth increased fifteen-fold between 1334 and 1515, and its share in the total taxable lay wealth of England from 2.0 per cent to 8.9 per cent.[92] The growth of London was good news for the surrounding towns: some produced goods for the metropolitan market, for example bread at High Wycombe and saffrons at Walden in Essex. Other towns' service sectors benefited, as Christopher Dyer explains: 'The inns at Newbury in Berkshire and St Albans in Hertfordshire did a busy trade because they provided convenient stopping places for travellers on two of the busiest main roads into London.'[93] In terms of taxable wealth, St Albans climbed steadily up the urban hierarchy: from 48th in 1334,[94] it reached 31st by 1524–25.[95] Some years later, in 1577, this 'little town' had no fewer than 27 inns, which probably had room to stable almost 2,000 horses.[96]

The general political uncertainty in the second half of the fifteenth century did not help the town and its tradesmen, but by the end of the century the inhabitants were beginning to gain some political independence from the abbey. The abbey was increasingly willing to compromise with the town. As early as the late fourteenth century, there is evidence that the abbey precinct wall was moved further inwards to allow the constricted tenement plots on High Street and Holywell Hill to expand; in some cases, they had already expanded over the wall.[97] Later, abbot John de Wheathampstead developed some of the High Street tenements, and may have constructed the Waxhouse Gate at the same time.[98] There are suggestions that, by the early sixteenth century, there was even some 'affection' among townsmen for the abbey, or at least for the church building itself.[99] Even in the fifteenth century, it was not uncommon for townspeople to leave property in their wills to relatives in local nunneries and monasteries: these bequests 'remind us of the many personal ties which bound our families of St Albans to the religious houses of the district'.[100] By the late fifteenth or early sixteenth century the offices of bailiff and clerk of the market, and the incomes of the town's court leet (a court that dealt with minor disputes), had been leased by the abbot to inhabitants of St Albans: in 1519, for example, the two offices and the income from the court were leased to John Gelly for a term of 31 years; and subsequently Raynold Carte took the lease, paying an annual rent of £13 6s.[101] Some years earlier, in 1485, the clock tower was leased to Robert Grane, a smith, who was required to maintain the clock, and to ring the bell at 4 a.m. and 8 p.m. daily.[102]

At the same time, in a development that was paralleled in other towns during the fifteenth century, a form of independent or quasi–independent local government, the guild or fraternity of All Saints, had emerged in St Albans.[103] The ostensible purpose of the guild – also known as the Charnel Brotherhood – was to maintain chaplains to serve in the chapel of St Andrew and at St Peter's, where there was a chapel or 'charnel house' in the churchyard. However, the functions of the guild extended beyond this. As the name 'Charnel Brotherhood' suggests, it conducted funerals for its members, many of whom left money to the guild in their wills; and it probably exercised 'some executive powers in the management of the affairs of the town'.[104] Both men and women were members of the guild.[105] Its meetings were at the moot hall, which was the abbey's 'seat of government' in St Albans.[106] Although it has usually been assumed that the moot hall was on the corner of Dagnall Street and Market Place, on the site of the new town hall that was built c.1570,[107] it has also been suggested that it may have stood on the site of the 'charnel house' in St Peter's churchyard.[108] The importance and 'ubiquity' of guilds like this has been commented upon by Heather Swanson, who discusses the practical role of the guilds in the provision of urban amenities, and their cultural role in promoting civic harmony and pride. In some cases, guilds

effectively took the place of governmental institutions, providing not only a chaplain, but a school, a market and the town's water supply ... even in towns where [unlike St Albans] civic officers and council had long since adopted these functions, a close link remained between the members of prestigious guilds and civic government, the social gatherings of the guild reinforcing the solidarity of the civic elite ... The status of the guild would be made explicit in the kind of feasting that it could provide for its members – the importance of eating together to articulate a sense of community cannot be overemphasised.[109]

Guilds were involved in the management of charity and education, the settlement of local disputes and the supply of services, including funerals, to the urban population.[110] In St Albans, the guild of All Saints seems to have had at least some independence from the abbot, as it lasted until 1548, some years after the abbey was dissolved; and at the latter date it had a 'considerable' annual income from land and houses of £23 2s. 2d., and was 'the wealthiest of all such foundations in Hertfordshire'.[111] A short-lived guild of St Alban had been established by abbot Thomas de la Mare in 1377, but had been dissolved, along with two other incipient guilds, following the events of 1381.[112] The guild of All Saints can be seen as a forerunner of the corporation established to govern St Albans in the terms of the charter received by the town in 1553.[113]

'... scenes of pageantry ... added colour and picturesqueness to the town'

The importance, probably growing, of the guild of All Saints is reflected in the fact that 'most, if not all, of the wealthier townsmen made bequests [to the guild] and evidently belonged'.[114] A study of 371 wills made in St Albans in the period 1471–1508 has shown that 77, or 21 per cent, made bequests to a guild or fraternity, mostly to the guild of All Saints.[115] The evidence of wills in the later fifteenth century shows that, at very least, the townsmen of St Albans 'maintained a position of moderate wealth and comfort'.[116] Long lists of items bequeathed by some testators suggest 'considerable wealth', especially among tailors and tanners, while the presence in the town of a pewterer and a goldsmith demonstrates the availability of expensive luxury goods.[117] Bequests to charities for the poor, and to the guilds and churches of St Albans, suggest a public-spiritedness among the leading citizens, and the resources to express it. The chapel of St Andrew, as noted above, was rebuilt in the mid-fifteenth century, as was the nave of St Peter's some time later; these projects, together with the building of the 'charnel house' and the Cornwall chapel, which also stood in the churchyard at St Peter's, provide evidence of the public wealth of St Albans.[118] Public display, in the form of elaborate funerals and other rituals, was evidence of civic self-confidence. As the historian William Page explained,

The quiet of the town was frequently relieved by scenes of pageantry – kings with their retinues, nobles and ecclesiastics with their attendants, merchants with their wares, pilgrims and beggars were constantly coming and going, while processions of religious persons and guildsmen in their liveries passing through the streets must have added colour and picturesqueness to the town.[119]

By the early sixteenth century, the power of the Church in England, and of the monasteries, was under attack on several fronts. Under the impact of Lutheran doctrines, which made headway in England from the 1520s, the clergy's neglect of pastoral duties was heavily criticised; the 'exactions' of the Church – in the form of tithes and fees for services and legal processes – were arousing resentment, as was clerical immunity from the penalties of the common law. Increasing lay involvement in the Church, through its parochial institutions and offices, drew further attention to the need for reform.[120] The wealth of monastic houses, especially the great Benedictine foundations such as St Albans, was an obvious target for a Crown that was seeking to increase its revenues. Monasteries had about half the total income of the Church.[121] Outside the monasteries, the plural church livings enjoyed by many clerics, giving them large incomes and preventing them from undertaking pastoral duties, came under attack: one particularly obnoxious example of this was Cardinal Thomas Wolsey, who held plural livings as well as several key clerical and lay offices. Wolsey was archbishop of York and Lord Chancellor, and attracted widespread unpopularity.[122] The monasteries, and their inhabitants, were presented as corrupt and avaricious: writing more than a century later, in 1679, bishop Gilbert Burnet described how the monks of the later middle ages had promoted the cults of saints, as a result of which the 'credulous multitude ... brought the richest things they had to the places where the bodies or relics of those saints were laid', and, encouraged by the available gains, monks rapidly discovered new relics, and wrote new accounts of saints, miracles and martyrdoms, and profited from 'the simplicity of the people'.[123] It was widely argued that the great, and perhaps ill-gotten, wealth of monasteries should be 'used more positively for the common good', especially for educational purposes.[124]

According to Burnet, the abbey of St Albans was among those particularly culpable: 'the monks, especially of Glastonbury, St Alban's, and St Edmundsbury, vied with one another who could tell the most extravagant stories for the honour of their house, and of the relics in it'.[125] It is certainly true that the monks continued to promote their abbey as a destination for pilgrims throughout the fifteenth century and after. Abbot Thomas de la Mare built a new guest house to accommodate them in the second half of the fourteenth century.[126] Pilgrims to St Albans in the fourteenth and fifteenth centuries could take souvenir badges away with them, depicting the martyrdom; however, these were of limited quality and developed little over time. Thus Geoff Egan has concluded:

... the 'credulous multitude ... brought the richest things they had ...'

St Albans seems to have been content with its standard — on close inspection, fascinatingly gruesome — souvenirs, while badge makers elsewhere [for example, Canterbury and Walsingham] rang the changes and devised new lines in profusion to bring in more money. The impression ... is of a second-league attraction, which, to judge from the numbers of souvenirs recovered, was fairly popular among Londoners (who lived less than a day's journey distant), but it was not one of the most significant, 'must-visit' destinations for all those who ventured on pilgrimage.[127]

In this context, we might question how far the monks of St Albans were particularly remarkable for the extent of their profiteering from tourism in this period, although Christopher Brooke has suggested that the layout of the abbey church was changed to ensure that pilgrims approaching the shrine of St Alban would pass by the collection boxes.[128] Such attempts to increase abbey revenues reflected the increasingly challenging climate in which the monks operated.

At St Albans, the abbacy of Thomas Ramryge (1492–1519) was characterised by incompetence and financial difficulties, worsened by the general economic climate, which was one of heavy inflation. Many of the abbey's lands had been leased out at fixed rents, which meant that income could not keep pace with steadily increasing expenditure. It appears that the abbey's control over the town of St Albans was diminished, and the abbey itself suffered 'long-term dilapidation'.[129] Its debts were increasingly heavy. In 1521 Cardinal Wolsey was appointed as the non-resident abbot of St Albans. In the words of James G.Clark, this 'would suggest that [the abbey's] independence from the Crown had been thoroughly compromised'.[130] The appointment of Wolsey – it seems unlikely that he was freely elected by the monks – was an ominous one. In his belief that 'education constituted the best way to reform the clergy, and that the diversion of resources from declining monasteries to vigorous educational foundations was essential to this end',[131] Wolsey suppressed thirty monasteries between 1525 and 1528, using the proceeds to endow Cardinal College in Oxford (later refounded as Christ Church).[132] As abbot of St Albans, Wolsey

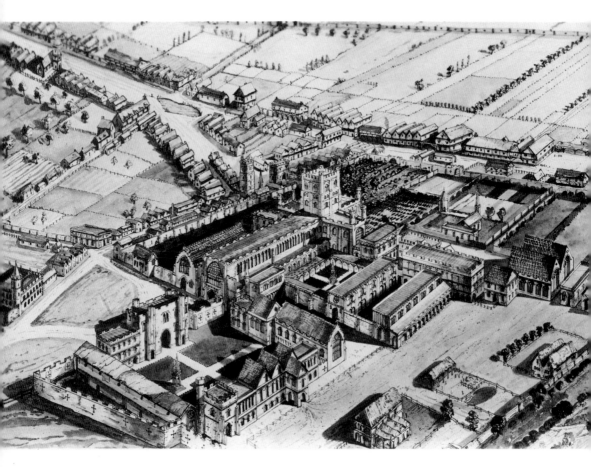

suppressed the dependent cell at Wallingford in 1528 for the same educational
purpose; and following his death in 1530, the abbacy stood vacant for some
months, and the abbey in the hands of the Crown, while Henry VIII took
some of its estates into his own possession.[133]

In the 'increasingly critical environment' that surrounded the Church in
the early sixteenth century,[134] matters were brought to a head by Henry VIII's
proposed divorce from Catherine of Aragon. Wolsey's refusal to support the
divorce lay behind his fall from royal favour in the years before his death.
The question of the divorce, together with wider issues surrounding the
relationship between the Crown, papacy and Church, and the administration
and endowments of the Church, were addressed by the Parliament which met
in 1529 and sat until 1536. By a series of legislative enactments, this Parliament
– later dubbed the 'Reformation Parliament' – replaced papal authority over
the clergy with royal headship of the Church, increased the taxation due from
Church to king, and appointed commissioners to ascertain the value of Church
incomes. Thomas Cromwell, who was appointed as the king's vice-regent in

1535, carried out a visitation of monasteries, and instituted their dissolution. This proceeded in two stages: first, 374 'lesser houses', and then 186 'great and solemn monasteries', of which St Albans was one.[135] Cromwell's management of the dissolution was careful: monasteries' tenants did not lose their leases, and many were engaged as surveyors to oversee the process of dissolution.[136] In 1539, when the process was close to completion, Parliament confirmed the vesting of monastic property in the Crown. In the main, the dissolution was carried out, in W. J. Sheils's words, 'remarkably peacefully' – partly because of the moderate policy regarding leases, and partly because pensions were provided for the monks – although some abbots, notably those at Colchester, Reading and Glastonbury, refused to co-operate, and were executed.[137]

At St Albans, although there was no such refusal to co-operate with Cromwell, there had been widespread opposition to the Reformation from the early 1530s. Unlike many Benedictine groups, the monks of St Albans 'formed a vigorous and vocal body of opposition to the King, to Cromwell, and to the work of the early Protestants'.[138] The leader of the opposition within the monastery seems to have been Richard Boreman, prior of the abbey from c.1535 and abbot from 1538, who has sometimes, wrongly, been seen as a 'placeman' of Cromwell's and a willing participant in the suppression of the abbey.[139] Boreman's predecessor, Robert Catton (1531–38), willingly transferred several manors of the abbey to the Crown, and was unpopular with his monks for doing so: like Wolsey, his appointment was probably not the result of a free election among the monks.[140] In fact, in both monastery and town there was widespread opposition to Cromwell. Thomas King, a local preacher, protested against the Reformation in his sermons, and was reported to Cromwell in 1535; and Thomas Ashwell, a long-standing member of the St Albans monastic community, was similarly reported in 1536 'for speaking against the King, his ministers and the recent religious changes'.[141] King had close links with the abbey, as did most of the local priesthood. In both these two cases, the informant was a townsman, Ralph Rowlatt. Within the abbey, two parties were emerging. On the one side, there were the opponents of the Reformation, led by Boreman and a 'secular priest' John Gwynneth, who lived 'alongside' the monks and collaborated with Boreman on a defence of traditional doctrine printed by the abbey's printer in 1536 (on printing in St Albans, see box 4). On the other side, there was a pro-Reformation group of monks, led by abbot Catton, who enjoyed a 'growing intimacy' with Cromwell.[142] Catton complained to Cromwell about the 'uncourteous flock of brethren' in his abbey,[143] and seems to have been willing to surrender the abbey to the Crown; but somehow his strategy failed, and in late 1537 or early 1538 he was deprived of the abbacy. Following Boreman's election as abbot, there was a 'sharp deterioration in relations with the government': Boreman failed to pay some of the new taxes that were due to the Crown, and was placed under house arrest in the abbey;

continued on page 134

Box 4: Hawking, hunting and heresies: printing in late medieval St Albans

FOR TWO SHORT PERIODS, between 1479 and 1486, and again between 1534 and 1539, St Albans was an important centre of early printing. In both cases, the printing press was probably within the precincts of the abbey. The first press may have been the third in England, but has for centuries been the subject of some controversy.[1] Eight books were produced by the press, but the printer himself is, in the words of one historian, 'obstinately anonymous', described vaguely as 'one sometyme scolemayster of Saynt Albons' in a source dating from the 1490s.[2] There is no contemporaneous confirmation of a printing press in the abbey's own records, or those of its school; and it was once suggested that St Albans was not the location of this press at all, but that it was on a manor of Westminster abbey which was known as 'St Albons', and that the printer was a former schoolmaster of Westminster.[3] However, there is other compelling evidence that St Albans was in fact the site of the press, especially from the last two books, which were both in English and announced themselves to have been compiled ('compylyt' or 'copylyt', in the spelling of the period) at St Albans. These two books, The Chronicles of England and the so-called Book of St Albans, date from 1483 and 1486 respectively, and the latter contains the St Albans coat of arms.[4] William Caxton himself, the father of English printing, is known to have had links with St Albans.[5]

The Book of St Albans is one of the most interesting and important early printed English books. It is attributed to Dame Juliana Berners or Barnes, whose name appeared on the early printed editions of the text, of which the 1486 edition was the first, although not in earlier manuscript versions; a fuller title by which the book was known is The Book of Hawking, Hunting and Blasing of Arms. Little is known of Berners, who may or may not have been the author, and was apparently alive in 1460. She was referred to as the prioress of Sopwell, and as a member of the Berners family of Essex, although Julia Boffey, in a recent account of Berners and the Book of St Albans, is sceptical of both claims. Boffey does remark, however, that 'the attribution of the text to a female author is not implausible'.[6] The book contains advice on hunting and hawking, reflecting the popularity of these sports in the period; and the chapter on fishing 'is said to be the best before [Izaak Walton's] The Compleat Angler, which appeared in 1653.[7] The fishing chapter did not in fact appear in the printed versions of the Book of St Albans until 1496.[8] It is not clear why the first St Albans press produced no more books after the Book of St Albans.

The printing press of the 1530s was used to disseminate doctrine and propaganda in the religious conflicts of the period, and a total of seven books were printed. The printer was John Hertford – not to be confused with the thirteenth-century abbot of the same name – and Richard Boreman, the last abbot, was heavily involved with the operation of the press.[9] Hertford also printed a 4,700-line verse account of the Life of SS Alban and Amphibalus at the request of Robert Catton, the penultimate abbot, in 1534: the author was John Lydgate, who had written it at the request of abbot John de Wheathampstead in 1439. Lydgate had been a prolific poet, and died

---

[1] See Page, Story of the English Towns, pp. 59–61.

[2] Kilvington, Short History of St Albans School, p. 6; H. R. Plomer, 'Printing', VCH Herts, vol. 4, p. 258.

[3] Plomer, 'Printing', pp. 258–9.

[4] Ibid., p. 260.

[5] Rachel Hands, 'Introduction', in English Hawking and Hunting in the Boke of St Albans (Oxford: Oxford University Press, 1975), pp. xv–xvi.

[6] Julia Boffey, 'Berners, Juliana (fl.1460)', Oxford Dictionary of National Biography.

[7] Toms, Story of St Albans, p. 63.

[8] W. L. Braekman, 'Introductory', in The Treatise on Angling in the Boke of St Albans (1496) (Brussels: Scripta, 1980), p. 7.

[9] See above, p. 131.

in 1449 or 1450.[1] In 1536, a defence of traditional religious doctrine was printed at the press by John Gwynneth and Richard Boreman, and two further books were printed, explicitly for Boreman, in 1538, the year when he took over the abbacy.[2] In the following year, less than two months before the surrender of the abbey, Hertford printed a controversial book, which Boreman disclaimed any knowledge of, denouncing it as a 'little book of detestable heresies'. Boreman sent Hertford to Thomas Cromwell for punishment, although it is not clear what this punishment was. This event, and the dissolution of the abbey, spelt the end for the second St Albans printing press, although Hertford himself operated a press in London from 1544 until his death in 1548. From the later sixteenth century, legislative restrictions were in place against printing presses, and only in London, Oxford, Cambridge, and later York, was printing allowed.[3]

[1] Douglas Gray, 'Lydgate, John (c.1370–1449/50)', *Oxford Dictionary of National Biography*.
[2] See above, p. 131; Plomer, 'Printing', p. 261.

[3] Plomer, 'Printing', p. 261.

RIGHT
The *Book of St Albans* dates from 1486; it was printed by the first printing press at St Albans, which was probably in the abbey. The famous chapter on fishing, the first page of which is shown here, was not added to the book until ten years after the first printing. The *Book of St Albans* contained a list of collective nouns for groups of animals, believed to be the first such collection in the English language.

it is also possible that he collaborated on another anti-Reformation treatise printed at the abbey.[144]

Eventually, it proved impossible for Boreman to do anything other than surrender the abbey, which he did in December 1539. The surrender was signed by 39 monks (including the abbot), all of whom received pensions from the Crown. In total, the dissolution removed some 9,000 monks and nuns from religious houses, and pensions were expensive.[145] They were somewhat cheaper at St Albans than elsewhere, because the abbot was penalised for the plunder that took place prior to the arrival of the king's servants. According to bishop Burnet, the monks 'saw the dissolution of their houses approaching, and so every one was induced to take all the care he could to provide for himself and his kindred'. When evidence of these activities was discovered, the abbot's pension was reduced to 400 marks (£266 13s. 4d.) per year, compared with the 500 marks (£333 6s. 8d.) paid to the abbot of Bury St Edmunds, where there was no such evidence of plunder.[146] Soon after the surrender of the abbey, the shrine of St Alban was stripped of its treasures, including over 100 ounces of pure gold, and the buildings quickly demolished, with the exceptions of the church, the gatehouse and the stables.[147] In 1542 St Albans was made an archdeaconry of the diocese of Lincoln, from which the abbey's territory had formerly enjoyed independence in the form of the Liberty of St Albans. The king had proposed a scheme of fifteen new dioceses, of which St Albans would have been one, along with several other former monastic centres. However, only six of these were actually created, and St Albans did not become a diocese until the nineteenth century (see box 10).[148] In 1550 St Albans was moved to the diocese of London.[149] There was a short-lived proposal during the reign of queen Mary (1553–58), supported by the queen herself, to re-establish St Albans abbey, but this came to nothing.[150] The subsequent history of St Albans is the history of a town completely free, for the first time, from the control of its monastic founders.

... completely free ... from the comfort of its monastic founders.

Chartered borough and 'thoroughfare town', 1539–1700

FOLLOWING the dissolution of the monasteries, the large estates of St Albans abbey passed to the Crown, and were then distributed among various members of the local landed class. The abbey precinct itself, together with Sopwell nunnery, was granted to Sir Richard Lee, a military engineer, surveyor of Calais and closely connected with Thomas Cromwell and other political leaders. Lee demolished the nunnery at Sopwell and built a house for himself there, using the material from the ruins.[1] He later sold the site of the abbey to the last abbot, Richard Boreman, who hoped (in vain) to re-establish a community of monks on the site.[2] Ralph Rowlatt, who had informed on the anti-Cromwell preachers in St Albans in the mid-1530s,[3] received Gorhambury (see box 6), Sandridge, Napsbury and a number of other manors.[4] St Michael's was acquired by Henry Gape, who had been a monastic official and who already held property in the town.[5] The abbey gatehouse was kept by the Crown, and used as a prison. It housed a number of prisoners of conscience during the sixteenth and early seventeenth centuries, when St Albans experienced the political and religious turbulence of the Reformation. One martyrdom took place in the town: George Tankerfield, a cook from London who refused to accept the doctrine of transubstantiation during the reign of the Catholic queen Mary, was imprisoned in Newgate and then burnt at the stake in St Albans – at Romeland – in 1555. Another martyrdom, this time of a Catholic, took place at Tyburn in 1642: Alban Roe, who had visited St Albans and changed his first name from Bartholomew to Alban following his conversion to Catholicism by a prisoner in the abbey gatehouse jail, was executed after a long imprisonment for illegal preaching.[6]

Politically, the dissolution freed the town of St Albans from the control of the abbot and monks. For a few years there was some 'confusion', as the

The ruins of Sir Richard Lee's house at Sopwell stand on the site of Sopwell nunnery, a dependent cell of the abbey of St Albans, dissolved in 1539. The ruins are often wrongly believed to be those of the nunnery itself (see, for example, Brayley's map of Verulamium and St Albans on pages 42–3 above).

PHOTOGRAPH: AUTHOR

guild of All Saints was wound up in 1548 and something of a vacuum in local government may have arisen,[7] but in 1553, the town was formally elevated to the status of a borough, with a mayor and corporation, by a charter of king Edward VI. Between 1539 and 1553, the town had experienced difficulty in paying its dues to the Crown, which had replaced the abbey as the authority to which its monetary obligations were owed, and the status of an incorporated borough was actively sought by petitioning the Crown.[8] According to the urban historian Robert Tittler, in towns such as St Albans, 'which had been governed by such restrictive ecclesiastical landlords that almost no effective institutions of

These floor tiles come from the house of Sir Richard Lee (see above). Lee Hall, as the house was known, was built following its owner's acquisition of the land at the dissolution of the abbey in 1539.

© ST ALBANS MUSEUMS

self-government had been allowed to emerge ... the impact of the Reformation era on local political powers was little short of revolutionary'.[9] St Albans was one of many monastic towns – including Banbury, Boston, Reading and, somewhat later, in 1606, Bury St Edmunds – that were chartered for the first time in the years following the dissolution. The Tudor period (1485–1603) was notable for a large number of borough incorporations: 388 boroughs obtained charters of incorporation or 'privileges' in this period.[10] St Albans's charter was confirmed by Edward VI's successors Mary, Elizabeth I and James I, and again by Charles I in 1632; this last charter made some adjustments to the government of the town, but these probably reflected the evolving practices in St Albans, and did not initiate anything new.[11]

As the last chapter has shown,[12] Tittler's suggestion that 'almost no effective institutions of self-government had been allowed to emerge' under monastic rule may be somewhat exaggerated as far as St Albans was concerned. The guild of All Saints, founded under the authority of the abbey, perhaps as early as the late fourteenth century, continued in existence after the dissolution, lasting until 1548.[13] However, the status of the town was undoubtedly enhanced by the charter of 1553, which established a corporation named 'The Mayor and Burgesses of the Borough of St Albans'. Among its provisions were the holding of a market every Wednesday and Saturday, and three fairs, on Lady Day (25

March), St Alban's Day (22 June) and Michaelmas Day (29 September).[14] The moot hall – previously the abbey's 'seat of government' within the town[15] – was given to the corporation, which was to be run by the mayor and 10 'principal burgesses'. These principal burgesses held office for life – provided they were resident in the borough – and the mayor was annually elected from among them. The election was by acclamation, and took place on St Matthew's Day, 21 September; all householders in the borough could vote, although in practice the election was a formality.[16] The mayor took his oath of office on Michaelmas Day. There were penalties for refusing office. The mayor was a Justice of the Peace for the borough and the Liberty of St Albans – the Liberty was the area previously under the direct rule of the abbot, as provided for by pope Adrian IV [17] – and also acted as clerk of the market. In this capacity, the mayor oversaw the setting of prices, and the accuracy and enforcement of weights and measures; there was also a Court of Pie Powder, which predated the charter, and which enforced the rules of the market.[18] Other officials included the steward, who was the main legal officer of the borough; and the chamberlain, who carried out the chief clerical tasks of the corporation.[19] The clock tower, which had been managed by a body of trustees since 1427, was given to the corporation by the charter,[20] which also described the boundaries of the borough, and enshrined the right of the burgesses to elect two MPs.[21] It also ruled that part of the abbey church or 'another convenient place within the said borough of St Albans' should be used to house the school, which went into abeyance after the dissolution, but which had been re-established in the town in 1549.[22] The responsibility for running the school was placed with the corporation; this was a common provision of urban charters (for example, at Stafford and Stratford-upon-Avon) during Edward VI's reign.[23] For the charter, and the independent government which it provided, the borough paid an annual 'fee farm' of £10 to the Crown.[24]

Subsequent charters made some changes to the provisions of 1553.[25] Elizabeth I's charter in 1570, secured through the influence of Sir Nicholas Bacon (see box 6), licensed the town's wine trade; the revenues from these licences were to be used to support the school.[26] The corporation was permitted to sell two licences, but in return was required to pay a salary of £20 a year to the master of the school.[27] Other charters modified the institutions, procedures and offices of borough government. In 1632 Charles I's charter replaced the chamberlain with the town clerk or common clerk, who took minutes of the proceedings of the corporation, collected the rents and other monies owing to it, and undertook other clerical duties. This charter also mentioned the high steward, an office which in practice had existed well before 1632. The high steward of St Albans, as in many other towns from the sixteenth century onwards, received a small fee for a role which has been summarised thus: 'to be a friend of the borough at court and in the country: to advance its interests

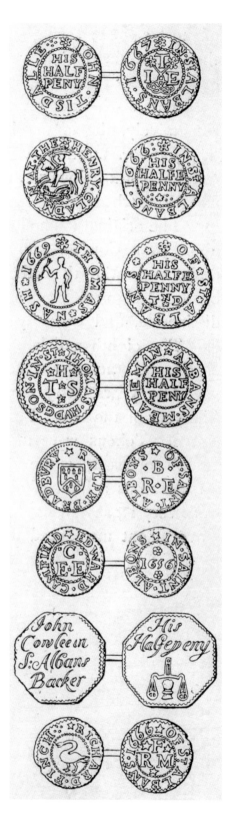

at Westminster and in the shire, and to exercise his "good lordship" wherever he could'.[28] Between c.1579 and 1588, Robert Dudley, earl of Leicester, was high steward of St Albans, an office he also held in many other towns, as far apart as Bristol, Andover and Great Yarmouth.[29] In the seventeenth century, the office was held by local eminences, including the second earl of Salisbury, Sir Harbottle Grimston (see box 6) and John Churchill of Holywell House, which stood at the south end of St Albans, at the bottom of Holywell Hill. The high steward was distinct from the steward, whose functions were taken over by the recorder in 1632: elected by the mayor and corporation, the recorder undertook the chief legal work of the borough.

Following the Restoration in 1660, St Albans received another new charter in 1664. This charter renamed the principal burgesses the aldermen and increased their number from 10 to 12. The corporation was also renamed: 'The Mayor, Aldermen and Burgesses of the Borough of St Albans'.[30] It was now provided that elections to borough offices required the approval of the king, a normal provision of borough charters in this period. From 1632 onwards, the corporation charters provided for the appointment of 24 assistants, one rank below the principal burgesses or aldermen: although 1632 marked these officers' first appearance in a charter, they had certainly existed long before this, probably since 1553 or shortly afterwards. Their offices, like those of the aldermen, were held for life, but were often vacant, until from 1677 more effort was made to fill them.[31] From among the assistants, two bailiffs were annually chosen: the corporation farmed out the profits of the fairs, markets and courts to the bailiffs, who paid a fixed sum in return for them, which in the second half of the seventeenth century ranged from £40 to £80, and was the largest single source of revenue for the corporation.[32]

The assistants were originally drawn from among the members of the guilds or companies of freemen, although by the seventeenth century the appointments were made by the mayor and aldermen. Freemen of the borough were the only people in the town allowed to

LEFT

This aerial view shows High Street at the top of the picture, Market Place to the left and French Row to the right. When the town of St Albans was first laid out, there were no buildings between Market Place and French Row, or between Market Place and Chequer Street. The whole area was a large market square, which was only gradually filled in with buildings. In this photograph, the corn exchange (1857) can be seen to the left; 'the Gables' (1637) is opposite the corn exchange across Market Place; and the clock tower (1403–12) and Waxhouse Gate (mid-fifteenth century) are at the top of the picture.

WWW.WEBBAVIATION.CO.UK

RIGHT

The moot hall, or town hall, was built around 1570, on the corner of Dagnall Lane (now Upper Dagnall Street) and Market Place. It was improved in the 1690s, and eventually replaced by the new town hall, on St Peter's Street, in 1831.

PHOTOGRAPH: AUTHOR

trade, and had the exclusive right to practise crafts and employ apprentices. They were also exempt from market tolls, and could vote and hold offices in local government. The freedom could be conferred by birthright – the son of a freeman could join the freemanry by right – by serving an apprenticeship in the borough, or by paying a substantial fee.[33] The companies of freemen were in existence before the charter of 1553, during the time of the guild of All Saints,[34] 'but as to the relation they bore to the [guild of All Saints], or the powers they had, we have no information'.[35] At one time there were at least seven guilds,[36] but by the mid-sixteenth century there were four: the Company of Innholders, the Company of Mercers, the Company of Shoemakers and the Company of Victuallers. Their names provide some clues to the economic foundations of the town's prosperity, but by this time each was responsible for a wide range of crafts and trades. For example, the Victuallers included bakers, brewers, butchers and fishmongers; the Mercers embraced most of those working in the textile industry and related trades; and the members of the Company of Shoemakers were from such diverse crafts as saddle-making, cooperage, carpentry, bricklaying and surgery.[37] Each company had two wardens, who were supposed to be elected annually from among the 24 borough assistants, although, as the assistants' offices were often vacant, the wardens were in practice drawn from a wider circle.[38] The wardens' main tasks were to collect the quarterly payments that freemen were required to make to their company,

continued on page 145

Box 5: 'A menacing interlude': St Albans in the Civil War

WHEREAS two centuries earlier St Albans had been the site of two battles during the Wars of the Roses, there was no battle in the town during the Civil War, although a minor 'skirmish' took place in 1643, when Sir Thomas Coningsbury entered St Albans, in his capacity as high sheriff of Hertfordshire, offering, to widespread derision, a royal amnesty to supporters of Parliament.[1] Most of the major encounters of the conflict took place in Yorkshire and the north of England, where Scottish invaders were met with English resistance, and in south-central England: there was none in Hertfordshire or nearby.[2] However, St Albans became an important strategic location during the war, serving on three occasions as an army headquarters: the years of war were, in one historian's words, 'a menacing interlude' for the town.[3] In common with most of the rest of south-east England, including London, and East Anglia, Hertfordshire was in Parliamentary territory – a member of the Eastern Association of Parliamentarian counties – and St Albans, in the main, supported Parliament. A leading example was William Hickman, an ironmonger from the town, who, both during and after the war, was a treasurer of the county committee, an instrument of Parliamentary rule that governed Hertfordshire (and other counties) in the Eastern Association.[4] There were some supporters of the king, including the mayor and steward of St Albans, William New and John Howland, who were imprisoned as a result of their allegiance.[5] During the build-up to the outbreak of war in 1642, the Parliamentary army recruited vigorously in St Albans, through the agency of prominent supporters such as Colonel Alban Cox; and some 2,000 men, under the command of the earl of Essex, were stationed in the town en route to Edge Hill, the first major battle of the war.[6] The behaviour of these troops, and their successors in St Albans during the next few years of war, was irksome to the inhabitants, as was the expense of billeting them, and of paying for the conduct of the war. The wages of soldiers – when they were actually paid – and the capital costs of equipment and fortification increased significantly the financial demands of the state.

There were three main sources of income to pay for the war: the seizure of estates held by supporters of the enemy, a weekly levy, and the excise tax, which was introduced in the Parliamentary areas in July 1643 and by the king soon afterwards. The weekly levy was paid by each county in proportion to an approximation of its taxable wealth, and, within counties, it was divided between boroughs and rural areas. At the local level, constables would determine the distribution of the burden of the levy, but most people would be affected. In Martyn Bennett's words, 'the net was cast much more widely than in normal peacetime taxes, and initially would include most families or individuals in the community'.[7] There was considerable local discontent surrounding issues of taxation. Following the introduction of the excise tax, a riot was threatened by 300 soldiers at St Albans, and petitions and other forms of protest were common.[8] Excise was levied at markets, such as the one at St Albans, and because the tax, although initially on luxuries, was soon extended to basic foodstuffs, women were often at the forefront of violent protest. The cost of billeting soldiers was borne in addition to the tax burden. There were complaints of the 'great Burthen of free Quarter', and often compensation for billeting troops was promised

---

[1] Toms, *Story of St Albans*, p. 102; Corbett, *History of St Albans*, p. 61.
[2] Martyn Bennett, *English Civil War 1640–1649* (London: Longman, 1995), map at p. x.
[3] Roberts, *Hill of the Martyr*, p. 164.
[4] SAHAAS, *St Albans*, p. 98.
[5] Corbett, *History of St Albans*, p. 60.

[6] Toms, *Story of St Albans*, p. 101.
[7] Bennett, *English Civil War*, p. 56.
[8] Corbett, *History of St Albans*, p. 61.

but never paid.[1] Further costs arose from the violent behaviour of soldiers stationed locally, from the need to protect buildings – such as Gorhambury House, which required protection in October 1642 – and from the price inflation that resulted from the uncertainty of supply during the war.

St Albans's location, around 20 miles from London, resulted in the stationing of troops and prisoners in the town on several occasions during and after the Civil War. In late 1643, the Parliamentary army in St Albans was close to mutiny, and was restrained by the strategic positioning of the town stocks in the vicinity of the soldiers' billets.[2] In 1645, royalist prisoners captured at the battle of Naseby, and in 1648 prisoners from the siege of Colchester, were held in St Albans, at further cost to the inhabitants. In June 1647 the New Model Army, in open rebellion against the Parliamentary authorities in London, moved its headquarters from Cambridgeshire, via Royston, to St Albans, 'in order to be closer to London and thus put greater pressure on Parliament'.[3] Parliament had been victorious in the war, but was unable to raise money to pay the considerable arrears of wages owed to the New Model Army and the other armed forces, which had mounted up to a total of some £3 million.[4] Attempts to disband the army, without pay, had resulted in the emergence of 'agitators' among the soldiery, who voiced their grievances in a series of demands made to Parliament from various locations in southern England.[5] The New Model Army, under the leadership of Sir Thomas Fairfax, abducted king Charles, and marched towards London in early June 1647, demanding payment of arrears of wages. By this time a General Council of the Army had been established, although this was not formally constituted in the drawing up of the various demands. By early June 1647, with the army advancing from Cambridgeshire, and London in the grip of riots, the situation was dangerous. Parliament was attempting to raise a 'counter-force' from among army veterans, and hoping that some members of the New Model Army would desert to join it.[6]

The New Model Army reached Royston by 10 June 1647, and St Albans by 12 June. On 14 June, a 'Declaration' was issued from St Albans, containing a 'far-reaching' set of demands.[7] The army declared itself to be 'not a mere mercenary army, hired to serve any arbitrary power of a state, but called forth ... to the defence of our own and the people's just rights and liberties'.[8] The demands included the purging of MPs who had been corruptly elected to Parliament, and of those who had intrigued against the army; the establishment of fixed-term Parliaments, on a triennial basis, these Parliaments not to be dissolved by the king or the MPs themselves; a general amnesty for most of those involved in the war; and the redressing of local grievances that had emerged from the exercise of authority and the exaction of taxes by the Parliamentary government during the war. In the wordy language of the 'Declaration', it was demanded

That the large Powers given to
Committees, or Deputy Lieutenants [of
counties under Parliamentary rule], during
the late time of War and Distraction,
may be speedily taken into Consideration;
that such of those Powers as appear not
necessary to be continued, may be taken
away, and such of them as are necessary
may be put into a regulated way, and left

[1] SAHAAS, *St Albans*, p. 12.

[2] Toms, *Story of St Albans*, pp. 102–4.

[3] Bennett, *English Civil War*, p. 80.

[4] Austin Woolrych, *Soldiers and Statesmen: The General Council of the Army and Its Debates 1647–1648* (Oxford: Clarendon Press, 1987), p. 4.

[5] Ibid., chapter 4.

[6] Ibid., pp. 125–6.

[7] Ibid., p. 126.

[8] Quoted in Bennett, *English Civil War*, p. 80; for the full text of the 'Declaration', see Eric Cochrane, Charles M. Gray and Mark A. Kishlansky (eds), *Early Modern Europe: Crisis of Authority* (Chicago: University of Chicago Press, 1987), pp. 332–42.

to as little Arbitrariness as the nature and necessity of the things wherein they are conversant will bear.[1]

There was a certain irony in this protest against the role of local administration, because the soldiers also wanted money to be raised to pay their wages; and the concessions to the New Model Army that were made by Parliament aroused violent opposition in London, where a 'hard line' against the military was popular.[2] A month's pay was voted in response to the St Albans demands, but this did not pacify the army, which then moved closer to London, leaving St Albans on 24 June and moving its headquarters to Uxbridge, directly threatening the capital, before further concessions persuaded Fairfax to withdraw to Reading.[3] The New Model Army met in St Albans again, briefly in October 1648, when more demands were issued, and the possibility of invading London was again under discussion.[4]

Even after the end of the war, St Albans was often used for billeting soldiers: in 1650–51 some 400 men, plus officers and their horses, were stationed in the town, and in 1654–55 the provision of coals and candles for a regiment in St Albans cost the 'considerable sum' of £4 16s. 6d.[5] In 1659 and 1660, in advance of the Restoration of Charles II, regiments passed through St Albans on the way to London, probably causing 'huge disruption' and expense, not to mention apprehension about the coming events.[6] The financial exactions and restriction of urban independence during Cromwell's Protectorate – St Albans's charter had been revoked in 1652 – seems to have weakened local enthusiasm for Parliamentary rule,[7] and the Restoration in 1660 was welcomed, at least in public, by most of the townspeople. The bell in the clock tower was rung in celebration, and 'bonfires and boisterous merrymaking' characterised the town's response.[8]

---

[1] Cochrane *et al.*, *Early Modern Europe*, p. 341.

[2] Martyn Bennett, *The Civil Wars in Britain and Ireland 1638–1651* (Oxford: Blackwell Publishers, 1997), p. 277.

[3] Woolrych, *Soldiers and Statesmen*, chapters 5–6.

[4] Bennett, *Civil Wars in Britain and Ireland*, pp.

310–11.

[5] SAHAAS, *St Albans*, pp. 12–13.

[6] Ibid., pp. 13–14.

[7] Ibid., p. 14; Corbett, *History of St Albans*, p. 62.

[8] SAHAAS, *St Albans*, p. 59; Toms, *Story of St Albans*, p. 105.

to ensure that craft standards were maintained (probably almost impossible given the large number of crafts embraced by each company), and to enforce the exclusive rights of freemen within the town.[39] In or around 1667 the number of guilds was reduced to two – the Innholders and the Mercers.

A monthly court of principal burgesses or aldermen was held, at which the mayor presided, and at which reports were received from the constables of the four wards of the town,[40] from the wardens of the companies and from other borough officers. At this court orders were made for the better government of the borough and the leasing of corporation property. The court also admitted freemen to the borough, and investigated allegations of trading in the borough by non-freemen or 'foreigners'.[41] The amounts of money overseen by the mayor and aldermen were very small at St Albans, and at most other boroughs in this period. As noted above, the proceeds from the farm of tolls and profits to the bailiffs – known as the bailiwick – formed the largest item of revenue. In the 1570s, in a range of small towns including St Albans, the gross annual income and expenditure of each corporation lay in the 'very modest' range of £50 to £90.[42] Inflation in the later sixteenth century pushed these sums upwards, and the financial exactions of the Civil War (see box 5) put a particularly heavy strain on borough expenditure, requiring the exploitation of additional sources of revenue, but the overall expenditure of most urban corporations remained low. In the year 1699–1700 the total expenditure of the St Albans corporation was £120 8s. 6d. Even this sum – a considerable decrease from the exceptional previous year, when work on the town hall pushed spending up to over £150 – proved difficult to raise, because the bailiffs were unable to collect the full sum expected from the bailiwick, and paid only £70 instead of £80.[43] It was not unusual for the mayor and aldermen to be required to support the work of the corporation out of their own pockets; and there were fines for refusal to serve, which were levied repeatedly, in the later sixteenth century in particular.[44] Continual financial difficulties, throughout the later seventeenth century, required the corporation to borrow heavily on occasions to meet the demands made upon it.[45] The inhabitants of St Albans were often required to pay for large one-off expenses, most notably during the war years, but also, for example, in 1594, when the law courts were evacuated to the abbey church during an outbreak of plague in London, and a levy was raised on the inhabitants to pay for the necessary internal alterations to the building.[46]

Other expenditure on buildings included a new market house or corn exchange, on which work began in 1588; this was replaced with a new building in 1728, and again in 1857. A shelter was built at the Eleanor Cross at some point in the seventeenth century.[47] The government of the borough, in the period following the first charter, was based at the moot hall, but this was replaced c.1570 'by a building suited to new requirements and free from any taint of past subjection' by the abbey. The new town hall stood at the corner of Dagnall Lane and Market Place, and the borough court was held there, as well as meetings of the mayor and principal burgesses.[48] The town hall was refurbished in the 1690s, hence the heavy corporation expenditure in 1698–99. For the mayor and aldermen, the town hall was a 'symbol of their prestige and dignity';[49] town halls in this period have been described as 'architectural expressions of urban authority and identity'.[50]

The largest and most important public building in the town was the abbey church itself: this was kept by the Crown, and not given to Richard Lee following the dissolution. It was sold to the corporation in 1553 for £400. Under the terms of the charter, the school was moved into the Lady Chapel, and the old chapel of St Andrew, which had been used by the townspeople for services since the time of abbot Paul de Caen and had been rebuilt at the cost of the parishioners in the 1450s, was 'taken down'.[51] The parish became known as the Abbey parish, rather than St Andrew's. The upkeep of the abbey church became a substantial expense, which the corporation was often unable to bear, with the result that

> For the next three centuries the treatment of the abbey church was deplorable. To maintain so large a building in a state of good repair was indeed a heavy burden for the townspeople and royal grants were frequently being made and money collected to pay for essential repairs of the fabric.[52]

These dole cupboards date from the seventeenth century. They were used to store bread under lock and key before it was distributed to the poor on Sundays. They can be found in a recess in the south transept of the abbey church.

PHOTOGRAPH: CARNEGIE

From 1556, a charge of 4s. 6d. towards the upkeep of the church was levied on the sons of freemen wishing to enter the freemanry of the town, but this raised a negligible proportion of the funds required.[53] However, despite the neglect of the fabric, and despite the town's long history of struggle against the authority that the abbey church had embodied, the building became an important part of urban life in the sixteenth and seventeenth centuries. Eileen Roberts remarks that, on reading the records of the corporation, 'one is struck by the important role church attendance and ceremonial played in the civic consciousness': the mayor was required to attend services, wearing his mayoral robes, and he was accompanied by the aldermen and assistants.[54] The building remained costly to maintain: in the 1680s and 1690s, grants from the Crown to assist with repairs to the church totalled almost £3,000.[55]

'Dung, rotting vegetables, offal and other rubbish were dumped in various places ...'

The corporation and other public authorities were faced with significant problems of public health, sanitation, poverty and crime in the sixteenth and seventeenth centuries. Outbreaks of plague were quite regular: for example, in 1563, when there were 104 burials in Abbey parish, compared with just 22 in the previous year; and 1578, when 301 bodies were buried in the parish between May and November.[56] Further plagues occurred in 1604 and 1625.[57] The Abbey parish was particularly overcrowded, its population crammed into courtyards and alleyways. Some of the houses of the poorest members of the St Albans population were probably built of mud, although it is a source of frustration to the historian that 'hardly any clues remain to show the kind of houses occupied by the poor'.[58] Problems were compounded by industrial, agricultural and commercial waste, with the result that, in the words of the local historian Gerald Sanctuary,

> In the sixteenth century, St Albans stank. There were dung heaps in St Peter's Street, the Market Place, Dagnall Street, and no doubt many other places. Dung, rotting vegetables, offal and other rubbish were dumped in various places, and from time to time the corporation took action in the courts against stall-holders and property owners to force them to clear these heaps away. There were local regulations banning pigs from running loose in the market, and in 1588 a baker was fined for leaving a dead horse in Dagnall Street.[59]

The problems were no less serious a century later. In the second half of the seventeenth century, roads in St Albans remained unpaved; rubbish was still left in the streets; and there was a problem of the unlicensed use of the streets for the storage of trade materials. Twenty-five dung heaps were the subject of complaint in the court leet – the administrative court of record which heard minor cases – in 1663 alone: nine of these were in St Peter's Street. Dung heaps were permitted to stand for five days, but this limit was often exceeded.[60]

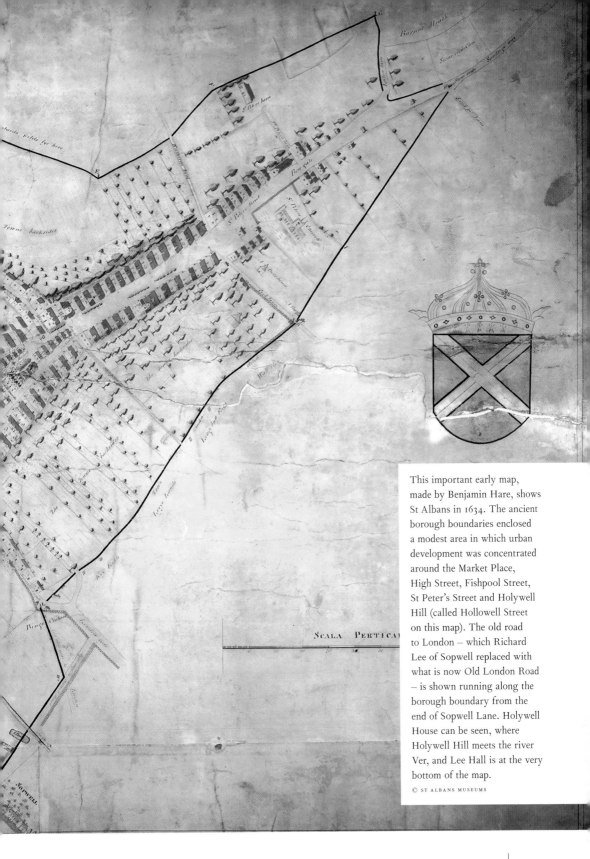

This important early map, made by Benjamin Hare, shows St Albans in 1634. The ancient borough boundaries enclosed a modest area in which urban development was concentrated around the Market Place, High Street, Fishpool Street, St Peter's Street and Holywell Hill (called Hollowell Street on this map). The old road to London – which Richard Lee of Sopwell replaced with what is now Old London Road – is shown running along the borough boundary from the end of Sopwell Lane. Holywell House can be seen, where Holywell Hill meets the river Ver, and Lee Hall is at the very bottom of the map.

Butchers' trade waste was also unpleasant, and could be found near the meat
market, which was at the bottom of St Peter's Street, near Dagnall Lane.
Tanning was another trade which had an unpleasant environmental impact:
it was carried on at the edge of the urban area, at the Gape family's premises
on Fishpool Street.[61] Epidemic disease was also common in the seventeenth
century: in the infamous plague year of 1665, St Albans was affected, especially
the area around Sopwell Lane; and there were outbreaks of smallpox in the
1650s, 1660s and 1670s.[62] Even where St Albans itself was not seriously affected
by disease, an outbreak elsewhere could cause significant economic dislocation
in the town: for example, in 1637, the corporation petitioned for relief of its tax
burden, pleading: 'The town consists chiefly of inns and victual houses, who
drive a trade upon the travelling of passengers, but have had no trade this year,
by reason of London having been so grievously visited with the plague.'[63]

As Londoners were well aware, fire was no less a hazard than plague in
seventeenth-century urban England, and St Albans experienced a number of
fires. The corporation records of the mid-1650s century remarked that 'many
sudden fires had happened to the undoing of some and great impairment of
the estates of divers others';[64] as a result a rate was levied to raise £40 in order
to purchase two fire engines in 1655.[65] Another two engines were acquired in
1675–76 at a cost of £25 (one of the old engines was given in part exchange),
and from 1677–78 Robert Gregory was paid 10 shillings annually to 'look after'
the fire engines.[66] In St Albans, the replacement of thatched roofs with tiles
in this period helped the town to avoid the catastrophic fires that occurred in
London and other places in the seventeenth and eighteenth centuries.[67]

England was a violent country in this period. Murder was not uncommon: in a famous St Albans case in 1662, a militia officer, Major Edward Crosby, shot a mourner dead in a dispute over the right of a Dissenter to officiate at a funeral at St Peter's church.[68] In this case, although a guilty verdict was brought in at the Old Bailey, the judge, Sir Harbottle Grimston (see box 6), coerced the jury into changing its mind. Travellers on the roads often met highwaymen; as a result, travel was usually undertaken in daylight only, which gave an added economic importance to St Albans, situated a day's journey from London.[69] The death penalty was widely used: in 1589 two men in St Albans were sentenced to death by hanging for theft, and another for clipping coins;

other offenders were whipped.[70] A century later whippings for petty larceny took place in the pig market.[71] In addition to public order offences such as leaving dungheaps, minor offences included gambling on the Sabbath, selling drink without a licence and public drunkenness.[72] There were various places for housing those convicted of crime: the old abbey gatehouse was used as the jail for the Liberty of St Albans, and as a house of correction for both borough and Liberty;[73] and the new town hall was also in use as a house of correction until 1679–80.[74] Houses of correction were established under the terms of an Elizabethan Act of Parliament (1575–76), and were 'intended to house those convicted of misdemeanours or other minor offences for which short sentences might be awarded, to keep "sturdy beggars" and tramps awaiting removal, or putative fathers of illegitimate children in bastardy cases'.[75] The jails in St Albans were also used to house ten mutinous soldiers during the Civil War.[76] A pillory stood outside the town hall, and a new one was built in 1686, with the maintenance contracted out as part of the terms of a lease of nearby market stalls.[77] The pillory, similar to the stocks where an offender was trapped and had abuse and objects thrown at him, was not abolished as a punishment in Britain until 1837.[78]

Urban poverty was a growing problem in the sixteenth and seventeenth centuries, in St Albans as elsewhere. In Asa Briggs's words, heavy inflation in the 1540s and 1550s, and again in the 1590s, 'significantly disrupted social relationships';[79] and poor harvests, together with the depredations of war and disease, worsened the lot of the poorest in society. At the same time, traditional patterns of relief were being undermined. The dissolution had removed an important source of relief for the poor, especially in monastic towns such as St Albans. The corporation made some attempt to provide for the poor in the sixteenth century: for example, firewood was provided, and a scheme to teach the poor spinning was established in 1588–89, followed by a similar one in 1618.[80] However, the main responsibility for the welfare of the poor was borne by the parishes.[81] Legislation of 1552 and 1572 required parishes to register their poor and make provision for them, and Acts in 1597 and 1601 allowed poor rates to be levied. Vestries – the governing bodies of the parishes – were given

ABOVE

The Abbey parish
poor box dates from
c.1650. It was (and
is) used to collect
charitable offerings.
The figure of a
beggar, which hangs
above the poor box
in the abbey church,
is a modern copy
of a seventeenth-
century original.
The dissolution of
the monasteries,
and the growing
problem of poverty
in the sixteenth
and seventeenth
centuries, led to
a growth of local
charities, and
legislation requiring
parishes to support
the poor.

PHOTOGRAPH: CARNEGIE

greater responsibilities, and churchwardens acquired more secular functions, including the administration of poor relief. The vestries elected overseers of the poor, whose duties were to set and collect the poor rate (which was often difficult), and to make the necessary payments to the poor. Sickness was a particularly expensive cause of pauperism, and the parish was often required to pay burial expenses. In Sandridge parish, the records repeatedly note payments made to individuals who had fallen into need 'by reason of sickness'.[82] Similarly, the records of St Peter's and the Abbey parish, recently examined in detail by a group of historians from the St Albans and Hertfordshire Architectural and Archaeological Society (SAHAAS), show a range of emergency payments to the sick poor. These parishes also paid pensions, ranging from two to 12 shillings per month, as well as school fees, and sometimes rent; and they also supported apprenticeships for the young, both locally in St Albans and in London.[83] In the 1660s, payments made to the poor by the Abbey parish usually totalled between £140 and £160 per year, higher than the total expenditure of the St Albans corporation.[84]

Parishes were responsible for the support of their own poor, and after 1662 for all those who had a 'settlement' in the parish. It was in a parish's interests to prove that paupers, especially those who might require long-term support, were chargeable elsewhere. In the case of three children abandoned in the Abbey parish in 1664–65 – whose upkeep for several years would be very expensive

– the parish authorities spent a total of £7 7s. in a successful attempt to prove that two distant parishes should bear the cost.[85] Pressure from ratepayers was regularly applied to restrict the amount of money spent on relief. Usually only a minority of householders were required to pay the poor rate: in the second half of the seventeenth century, an annual average of around 175 parishioners in the Abbey parish were liable for rating.[86] In the surrounding rural parishes, the costs of pauperism, and consequently the rates, were even more onerous. In Sandridge in 1687, around a third of the population of was in receipt of some kind of relief, and the pensions paid were in the same range as those in St Albans. Just 44 householders in Sandridge, probably slightly over a tenth of the population, paid the poor rate, at 9d. in the pound. As the parish was assessed at £1,643, this would have raised a little over £61.[87] Another problem that the parishes were required to deal with was vagrancy, a problem which Hertfordshire, and St Albans in particular, encountered a lot of, due to the proximity of London; there is plenty of evidence of the cost of vagrancy in the parish accounts.[88]

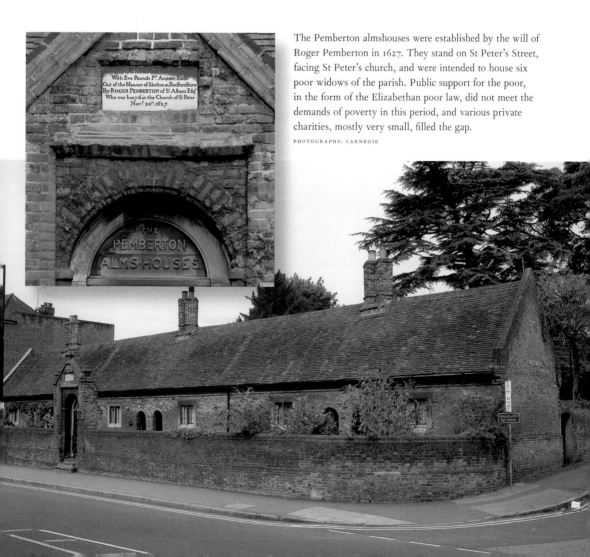

The Pemberton almshouses were established by the will of Roger Pemberton in 1627. They stand on St Peter's Street, facing St Peter's church, and were intended to house six poor widows of the parish. Public support for the poor, in the form of the Elizabethan poor law, did not meet the demands of poverty in this period, and various private charities, mostly very small, filled the gap.

PHOTOGRAPHS: CARNEGIE

The inadequacy of public support for the poor in St Albans left the field open for private charity. The seventeenth century in particular saw the establishment of a range of charities to support the poor, and other parochial objectives; but some date from the sixteenth century. Evidence is scanty for the activities and even existence of many charities: there was never a 'comprehensive listing', and the confusion caused problems in the eighteenth century.[89] There was only a handful of almshouses. In 1569 the will of Richard Raynshaw left three properties in Spicer Street in trust to the corporation, to be given rent-free for life to 'such honest poor persons as should seem most in need of charity';[90] and in 1605 John Clarke built six almshouses on St Peter's Street, three for the inhabitants of the Abbey parish and three for the inhabitants of the urban part of St Peter's. In 1627, Roger Pemberton's will established almshouses on St Peter's Street, opposite the church: these were intended to house six widows, two from St Peter's, two from St Stephen's, one from St Michael's and one from Shenley.[91] This rather limited provision meant that just 15 people could be housed in almshouses in St Albans by the second half of the seventeenth century, a deficiency in provision that was only partially addressed by the construction of the Marlborough almshouses in 1736.[92] Other charitable provision was concentrated in the Abbey parish and St Peter's, although there were some charities in the other parishes, and some which provided for more than one parish. Most charities were small, such as the bequest of £3 9s. 4d. by Thomas Knowlton in 1645, which was intended to support the distribution of 16 penny loaves to the poor of St Peter's parish on every Sunday.[93] From the Abbey parish, an early example is Thomas Lathbury's charity, which consisted of two tenements left by Lathbury to the corporation, which was to use the revenues to provide gifts to the poor of the town.[94] The provisions of some charities were complex: as the authors of the *Victoria County History* for Hertfordshire explained, a deed made by Robert Skelton in 1628 gave two properties or 'messuages' to the mayor and principal burgesses,

> to hold the same upon trust [and] with the rents and profits thereof to distribute twenty-six penny loaves unto twenty-six poor people of the parish on every Sunday in the year in the south aisle of the parish church [i.e. the abbey church], and upon the Friday next before Whitsunday to give at the place aforesaid thirty groats unto thirty poor widows. The overplus after reparations of the said two messuages to be accumulated and applied in the purchase of additional lands for the further relief of the poor of the parish.[95]

Other charities supported both church and poor: for example, the Cross Keys Charity, established in 1618, was endowed both to repair the abbey church and to provide for the poor of the Abbey parish and St Peter's.[96]

... the problems of poverty and public health in St Albans contributed to the high death rates ...

Despite the intervention of public authorities and local philanthropists, the problems of poverty and public health in St Albans contributed to the high death rates and, especially, high rates of infant mortality, which in turn kept the population relatively low. A little more than 50 per cent of all children born in St Albans died during infancy, while birth rates were relatively low compared with other places in the same period. Although the evidence of surnames in the town suggests that there was in-migration to St Albans from a range of English towns, out-migration, mostly to London, probably removed some young members of the adult population.[97] The returns from the hearth tax, introduced in 1662 and levied on ratepayers at the rate of a shilling per hearth, can be used to calculate the population of towns in the 1660s and 1670s. One historian, using these sources for St Albans, has estimated that the population of the three parishes of Abbey, St Michael's and St Peter's in 1668 was 3,066;[98] this would represent a decline from the 3,770 estimated for the 1520s,[99] and would reflect the sixteenth-century 'decay' of Hertfordshire towns. The number of taxpayers in St Albans, and the total number of inhabitants, declined in the second half of the sixteenth century, at the expense of the surrounding rural areas, such as Sandridge, St Michael's and Park.[100] In the seventeenth century the population of the town appears to have been fairly stable: 'It seems reasonable to suppose that the total population of the urban Abbey parish and the semi-urban St Michael's and St Peter's parishes in the latter half of the seventeenth century varied around 3,200.'[101] Many other towns in England had grown significantly by this time, and this accentuates the relative decline of St Albans: whereas in 1524–25 St Albans may have ranked as high as 14th in the English urban hierarchy, it was nowhere near the top 20 by the second half of the seventeenth century. At this time, according to one estimate, the population of the twentieth largest city in Britain, Colchester, was 6,647.[102] Indeed, St Albans was probably well outside the top 40.

The government of St Albans had been temporarily shaken by the Civil War in the 1640s (see box 5), which also caused economic disruption and hardship, especially because of the cost of quartering troops and the demands of wartime taxation. However, the structure of political authority, in terms of both institutions and personnel, emerged relatively unchanged. There was 'remarkable continuity' of office-holding in the middle of the seventeenth century.[103] For example, Thomas Oxton was mayor of St Albans in 1636, 1644, 1656 and 1667, and Thomas Cowley held the office in 1639, 1650 and 1661.[104] The elites of the town did not change very much in terms of personnel, reflecting a county-wide desire for peace and an end to the 'anarchy' of the interregnum.[105] By the late seventeenth century, although 'Whig feeling was ... very strong' in Hertfordshire,[106] Toryism was steadily coming to dominate the politics of the corporation of St Albans. Following the Restoration in 1660, there was a growing Tory presence in municipal politics, although as the group

'the majority ... probably bowed to the prevailing wind'

of historians from the SAHAAS has recently suggested, 'the majority [of civic leaders] probably bowed to the prevailing wind, something which must have happened on a number of occasions'.[107] One such example occurred in 1684, when St Albans, along with many other boroughs, was forced to surrender its charter to king Charles II; this was part of an attempt by the Tories to take control of urban politics, and to restrict the activities of Dissenters.[108] In fact, at St Albans the mayoralty had already been in the hands of probable Tory sympathisers for some years.[109] On this occasion, John Selioke, the 'ardent Tory' mayor, willingly surrendered the charter, which was replaced in 1685 by a new charter obtained at some civic expense from the new king, James II.[110] This charter replaced the old governing body with a mayor and 18 aldermen, who could all be removed by the king; a number of these were non-residents, two of whom served as mayor in the next two years. The Whig Harbottle Grimston was replaced as high steward by John Churchill. In the bitterly contested parliamentary election that followed, the Tories George Churchill and Thomas Docwra were elected, defeating Sir Samuel Grimston and Sir Thomas Pope Blount for the Whigs. The Tory victory at this election, in which fewer than 100 freemen voted, occurred after mayor Selioke imprisoned the Whig supporters, created 46 new freemen to vote for the Tory candidates (a strategy that would be repeatedly employed in subsequent polls), and threatened to withdraw the liquor licences of innkeepers who voted for Grimston and Blount.[111] The short-lived charter of 1685 was annulled following the 'Glorious Revolution' in 1688 (causing further expense to the corporation), and most of the old aldermen were restored. However, the aldermen who took office in the 1690s were increasingly likely to have Tory sympathies.[112] In terms

This row of cottages on St Peter's Green, at the south entrance to St Peter's churchyard, dates from the seventeenth century. At the end of the road is the former St Peter's parish workhouse, now offices. A water pump was built at St Peter's Green in 1733, although it was often in disrepair by the early nineteenth century.

PHOTOGRAPH: AUTHOR

Early font in St Stephen's church. The figures of the Apostles around the shaft of the font have all been defaced, apart from that of St John the Baptist nearest the camera.

PHOTOGRAPH: AUTHOR

of parliamentary politics, beginning with the election of 1689 at which George Churchill and Sir Samuel Grimston were elected, St Albans usually elected as its two MPs one Tory and one Whig, a situation which prevailed for most of the eighteenth century (see box 8).

Continuity and broad tolerance in politics was mirrored in religious matters, at least as far as Dissenters were concerned. After the bitter conflicts of the Civil War and interregnum years (see box 5), when objects and paintings in the abbey church that offended the Puritan conscience were destroyed, including murals depicting SS Alban and Amphibalus,[113] things settled down in St Albans. The ecclesiastical offices in the town, for the most part, did not change hands during the upheavals of the mid-seventeenth century, although there were some changes, notably the departure of Nathaniel Partridge, minister at the abbey church from 1657, who refused to accept the terms of the Act of Uniformity in 1662, and left office (the Act made the use of the Book of Common Prayer compulsory).[114] Dissent flourished in the town: its strength can be attributed in part to the 'close relationship between St Albans and the City of London', and also to the proximity of the Chilterns, from where members of the large Dissenting community probably migrated into St Albans.[115] Although there were occasional outbreaks of conflict between the established Church and Dissenters, such as the case of Major Edward Crosby,[116] the large community of Nonconformists were quite well integrated into the life and politics of St Albans. This was atypical of English boroughs in this period, many of which were much more exclusively Anglican than St Albans. Fluidity characterised religious affiliations in the town. One man, Laurence Clarkson or Claxton (1615–67), who spent some time as a Baptist minister in Sandridge in 1646, adhered to six different religious denominations during his lifetime.[117] In St Albans, some Dissenters served as churchwardens in their parishes, while other leading inhabitants practised 'occasional conformity', a practice widely tolerated in the town, whereby Dissenters took communion in the Church of England occasionally in order to qualify for holding office.[118] Robert Pemberton – grandson of the founder of the almshouses in St Peter's – was licensed to hold Congregationalist meetings in his home in the more lenient legal environment of the 1670s, by which time there was also a community of around 60 Quakers meeting regularly twice a week in St Albans, and some 100 Presbyterians.[119] Baptists from the town gravitated towards Kensworth, south-west of Luton, where a register of 217 Baptists dating from 1675 included 27 from St Albans.[120] Baptists travelled this far 'partly to avoid persecution but also to seek strength in the company of like-minded believers drawn there by the preaching of certain individuals'.[121] By 1694, the total number of Baptists in membership of the Kensworth church was 365, comprising 136 men and 229 women, and the congregation moved to St Albans in or around 1700 (see box 7).[122] A reconstruction of the population of St Albans in 1675 gives an adult male population of 1,192, of which 263 can be identified as Dissenters, some 22.1 per cent, much higher than the national average of 4–5 per cent. If women are included, there were probably as many as 500 Dissenters in St Albans at this time.[123] In the eighteenth century, the Dissenters wielded significant political strength in the borough (see box 8).

The economy of St Albans during this period was increasingly dependent on the service sector. In the sixteenth century, the emergence of the four guilds

The economy of St Albans … was increasingly dependent on the service sector.

of freemen – the Innholders, Mercers, Shoemakers and Victuallers – reflected the dominant trades of the town: as A. F. H. Niemeyer commented, the list of guilds 'shows incidentally that St Albans was much more a thoroughfare town than an industrial centre'.[124] This was in fact true of most English towns in the sixteenth century: relatively little manufacturing took place within towns, except in places where the late medieval textile industry retained its importance.[125] This was not the case in St Albans, where there had been a cloth industry in the medieval period, but where, as elsewhere in Hertfordshire, cloth merchants were 'never ... a very strong body'.[126] When in 1588–89 the unemployed poor in St Albans were given spinning to do in return for relief, the work was organised by a 'Dutchman' (perhaps a German), Anthony Moner, and the machinery was obtained from as far away as Hertford, suggesting that 'even the small amount of cloth-making which had formerly existed in the county was dying out'.[127] However, the similar scheme of 1618 was propsed by Stephen Langley, a clothier whose name suggests more local roots.[128] Other industries, such as tanning, continued in St Albans, carried out by the Gape family of St Michael's, who provided the town with a range of aldermen, mayors and MPs in the seventeenth century.[129] Brewing also remained an important industry, serving the large number of inns in the town; and the construction of buildings in the seventeenth century supported a local brick making industry. Although some buildings, such as Sir Nicholas Bacon's house at Gorhambury (see box 6), were built of brick in the Elizabethan period, bricks became increasingly common in the construction of new buildings in the second half of the seventeenth century: examples include the Gapes' house at St Michael's in 1668.[130] Bricks were supplied from kilns at Bernard's Heath, St Stephen's, Hatfield, Hemel Hempstead and Aldenham. All these kilns were owned by 'St Albans men',[131] and there is also evidence of clay being dug for brickmaking at Napsbury in the early sixteenth century.[132] However,

continued on page 162

The manor of St Michael's was acquired by Henry Gape following the dissolution of St Albans abbey. This manor house was built in the late seventeenth century, on the site of an earlier house; one of the ceilings in the present house dates from 1586. The Gape family, one of the most important in St Albans, occupied St Michael's manor into the twentieth century. It was converted for use as a hotel and restaurant in the 1960s. This view shows the back of the house, from near the river Ver. The Gapes' tanning business operated on this site.

PHOTOGRAPH: AUTHOR

Box 6: The Bacons and Grimstons of Gorhambury

GORHAMBURY was 'the biggest estate by far' in the region of early modern St Albans.[1] It has a long history, as a villa during the Roman period (see chapter 1) and a medieval manor, sometimes known by its alternative name of Westwick. The name Gorhambury comes from abbots Geoffrey and Robert de Gorham, whose family held the manor in the twelfth century.[2] The abbey retained Gorhambury until the dissolution, when it was passed by the king to Ralph Rowlatt, one of the largest beneficiaries of the loss of estates by the abbey; Rowlatt was also given the manor of Pré, site of the nunnery, which adjoined, and was merged into, the Gorhambury estate.[3] Gorhambury remained in Rowlatt's family until 1560, when it was purchased by Sir Nicholas Bacon (1510–79), who in 1568 built the house whose ruins can still be seen in the grounds of the Gorhambury estate today. Bacon was the lord keeper of the great seal, a lawyer of note and a privy councillor, whose 'renowned eloquence and wit as the queen's spokesman' helped him to steer a moderate course through the religious controversies of the early years of Elizabeth I's reign.[4] Although he avoided the extreme anti-Catholic stance of some of his contemporaries, he 'sheltered and supported known puritans at Gorhambury', and was briefly out of favour at court because of an ill-judged intervention in a debate about who should succeed Elizabeth to the throne. However, he regained royal favour, and Elizabeth visited Gorhambury three times, each at considerable expense to Sir Nicholas.[5] Bacon's local involvement in St Albans extended to the school, which he patronised actively, and he also served as high steward of the Liberty of St Albans.[6]

Bacon's second son Sir Francis (1561–1626) succeeded to the Gorhambury estate on the death of his brother Anthony in 1601. Francis had also trained for the law, following his father to Cambridge; and by the 1590s he was sitting in Parliament for the county of Middlesex.[7] Politically, Bacon 'gained spectacular promotion' during the reign of James I, becoming solicitor-general, attorney-general and, in 1618, lord chancellor, gaining the title of Baron Verulam at the same time. He became Viscount St Alban in 1621. In the early 1620s he was accused of taking bribes – an offence to which he confessed – impeached by Parliament, and briefly imprisoned in the Tower of London. He was fined £40,000, and left in straitened financial circumstances: although he never paid the fine, king James had organised his release from prison, and Bacon owed the sum to the king. Forced out of politics, Bacon spent the rest of his life at Gorhambury, writing many of the philosophical essays and histories for which he is best known. He also constructed the fish ponds, or 'pondyards', at Shafford on the Gorhambury estate, near Watling Street, where coarse fish were bred, especially carp.[8] When he died in 1626, he left debts of over £20,000.[9] Before his death, he gave Gorhambury to trustees on behalf of Sir Thomas Meautys, the husband of Bacon's niece Anne, daughter of his half-brother Nathaniel Bacon. On Sir Thomas's death, the estate passed to his brother Henry, who then sold Gorhambury to Sir Harbottle Grimston (second baronet, 1603–85), who had become Anne Bacon's second husband in 1651.[10] Grimston's descendants still hold Gorhambury

[1] SAHAAS, St Albans, p. 10.
[2] Page et al., 'St Michael's, p. 393.
[3] Ibid., pp. 394, 400–1; see above, p. 135.
[4] Robert Tittler, 'Bacon, Sir Nicholas (1510–1579)', Oxford Dictionary of National Biography.
[5] Toms, Story of St Albans, p. 86.
[6] Ibid., p. 84.
[7] Markku Peltonen, 'Bacon, Francis, Viscount St Alban (1561–1626)', Oxford Dictionary of National Biography.
[8] Charles T. Part, 'Sport, Ancient and Modern', VCH Herts, vol. 1, p. 362.
[9] Peltonen, 'Bacon, Francis'.
[10] Page et al., 'St Michael's, p. 396.

Gorhambury House, the ruins of which are shown in this watercolour by J.H. Buckingham, was built by Sir Nicholas Bacon in 1568. When the new house was built in 1784, the old one was deliberately ruined. The ruins are in the care of English Heritage, and can still be visited.

© ST ALBANS MUSEUMS

today; and in the seventeenth, eighteenth and nineteenth centuries, successive generations of the family made a significant contribution to local and national politics.

Harbottle Grimston had played a prominent part in the disputes between king and Parliament leading up to the Civil War: he sat as an MP for Colchester, and vigorously attacked the taxes that Charles I was attempting to raise.[1] During the war he raised money for the Eastern Association of Parliamentarian counties; but he was imprisoned by the army in 1648 and 1649, before retiring – temporarily – from politics. After marrying Anne Bacon, Grimston moved to Gorhambury. He returned to politics as an MP for Essex in 1656, and, back again as a member for Colchester, was elected Speaker of the House of Commons in 1660. In this capacity he delivered the invitation to Charles II to return from exile, and was appointed to the commission that tried those who had killed Charles I in 1649. Following this, he became master of the rolls.[2] Charles II's charter of 1664 made Grimston high steward of St Albans, 'the watchdog of civic authority'.[3] He continued to sit as MP for Colchester. Grimston has been described as 'vehemently anti-popish', and established a long dynasty of Whig politicians

---

[1] Christopher W. Brooks, 'Grimston, Sir Harbottle, Second Baronet (1603–1685)', *Oxford Dictionary of National Biography*.

[2] Ibid.

[3] Corbett, *History of St Albans*, p. 67.

at Gorhambury.[1] He exhibited some sympathy with Dissenters, but used his power and influence to arrange the acquittal in 1662 of Major Edward Crosby for the murder of John Townsend, a Nonconformist mourner at a memorial service in the abbey church. The Reverend William Haworth, a minister who had been ejected from St Peter's following the Restoration, was prevented by the Act of Uniformity (which required that the Book of Common Prayer be used) from conducting divine service in a Nonconformist manner, but was asked to do so by the mourners on this occasion. When he conducted the illicit memorial service, a militia officer, Crosby, attacked the 'rebels' and Haworth in particular, at which point Townsend stepped in between Crosby and Haworth, and was shot.[2] Although the members of the jury at the Old Bailey wanted to convict Crosby, Grimston – who was the judge in the case – coerced them into changing their verdict.

Harbottle Grimston died in 1685, and his son Sir Samuel Grimston (1644–1700), the third baronet, succeeded to his title and to the Gorhambury estate. He was elected as one of the MPs for St Albans in 1668, and held the seat, with a couple of interruptions, from then until his death.[3]

He was generally rather inactive in the House, and, as far as his politics can be ascertained, has been described as 'more of a country whig than anything else'.[4] Dying without any living children, Samuel Grimston left his considerable estate, and an annual income of some £8,000, to William Luckyn, his great-nephew, on condition that he changed his name to Grimston. Luckyn did so, and as William Luckyn Grimston was elected as MP for St Albans in 1710, and later ennobled as the first Viscount Grimston (see box 8). In the seventeenth century the Grimstons increased the size of the Gorhambury estate and made notable improvements. For example, considerable repairs were made to the house in the 1670s, and a large fence was built to enclose the 'park', at a cost of £800.[5] The estate was enlarged by the acquisition of the manor of Windridge in 1679.[6] The great wealth that Samuel Grimston left to his heir was to be the foundation of the political strength of the family in the next century, when they engaged in a long struggle for power with their Tory rivals in St Albans (see box 8). The new Gorhambury house, which remains the residence, was built in 1784, and the old house deliberately ruined.

---

[1] Brooks, 'Grimston, Sir Harbottle'.
[2] See Corbett, *Secret City*, chapter 3.
[3] Stuart Handley, 'Grimston, Sir Samuel, Third Baronet

(1644–1700)', *Oxford Dictionary of National Biography*.
[4] Ibid.
[5] Page *et al.*, 'St Michael's', p. 397.
[6] Ibid., p. 399.

frustratingly for the historian, it is still the case that 'little of interest can be said about this industry, important though it undoubtedly was … as a source of employment'.[133]

The most distinctive feature of the economy of St Albans was the large number of inns. In the sixteenth century, inns flourished with the increasing amount of through traffic. Many inns predated the dissolution, and had been owned by, or owed much of their prosperity to, the abbey, but others were established independently, and catered for long-distance travellers, as well as those who travelled shorter distances to trade at the market. They were particularly concentrated on the road that entered St Albans from London

RIGHT
Ye Olde Fighting
Cocks, on the river
Ver at the end of
Abbey Mill Lane,
was originally the
abbey's fishing
lodge. The old
cockpit now forms
part of the pub,
which claims to be
one of the oldest in
England.

PHOTOGRAPH: CARNEGIE

BELOW
The White Hart inn
on Holywell Hill is
medieval in origin.
It was refurbished in
the 1930s, when the
old wooden frame
was uncovered from
below a brick front.

PHOTOGRAPH: CARNEGIE

along Sopwell Lane, twisted through the town, and left via Fishpool Street to ford the Ver at St Michael's and continue along Watling Street to Redbourn and the north. On Sopwell Lane the traveller could find the Goat, the Ram, the Cross-with-the-Hand and the Crown at the junction with Holywell Hill. On Holywell Hill itself were the Trumpet, Post Boy, Bull, White Hart, Saracen's Head, Horsehead, Dolphin, Mermaid, Peahen, Woolpack and Cross Keys, which stood to the north of the Peahen, where the new London road was built in the late eighteenth century.[134] Where the main road turned left along High Street the Vintry, Lyon (later the Great Red Lion) and the Corner Tavern could be found; and just off the main road, in French Row, were the St Christopher and the Fleur-de-Lys. The road continued down George Street (then known as Church Street), where the traveller could visit the George and Dragon and the Tabard, later the Antelope, on the corner of Spicer Street. The Tabard/Antelope had a courtyard surrounded by galleries, where theatrical entertainments could be staged.[135] Fishpool Street had the Red Lion (known as the Lower Red Lion), Angel, Queen, Mawdlyn and Dolphin. Back in the town centre, along the road running northwards from Holywell Hill, which became Chequer Street but was known in this period as Malt Market, were the Chequers, Half Moon and Blue Bell; the Castle Inn, outside which the duke of Somerset was killed during the first battle of St Albans (see box 3), was on St Peter's Street. By around 1600 the Fighting Cocks on Abbey Mill Lane had been built, and by the second half of the seventeenth century several new

These clay pipes, which date from the seventeenth or eighteenth century, were found in an archaeological excavation on Holywell Hill. Many of these pipes carry the insignia of the inn for which they were made, and of the manufacturer.

© ST ALBANS MUSEUMS

inns had appeared, including the Dog on French Row and the White Horse on George Street. In 1637 St Albans was described by the mayor and principal burgesses as consisting 'chiefly of inns and victual houses, who drive a trade upon the travelling of passengers'.[136]

The road links between St Albans and London were improved during the sixteenth century; this in turn enhanced the service economy of the town. Sir Richard Lee, who had acquired Sopwell following the dissolution, diverted the existing road from Shenley to Sopwell Lane and constructed what is now the Old London Road; following further improvements further down the road at Barnet, this road became a major route from London to St Albans, a rival to Watling Street.[137] As noted in the last chapter, by 1577 there was space in St Albans to stable some 2,000 horses.[138] By the seventeenth century, there was even more traffic passing through the town, mostly in form of pack-horses, travelling in strings, which in 1637 provided regular services to towns as distant as Coventry, Preston, Sheffield and Nottingham. On Thursdays alone, 12 carriers travelled through the town in each direction. There was also a 'waggon or coach' service operating twice-weekly to London (the Bell inn on Aldersgate Street): only Cambridge, Hatfield and Hertford had a similar service in this period.[139] Sixteenth-century legislation had required parishes to maintain the roads that passed through them; and from the 1630s onwards small coaches were operating between London and the surrounding towns, extending to Chester, York and even Newcastle by the 1650s.[140] However, in the early seventeenth century, according to one historian, road transport in England was 'still agonizingly slow'.[141] Following the Civil War, the standard of trunk roads was raised by statutory provision for rate-financed improvements, and journey times were shortened. Although this was not an unmixed benefit – speeds of up to 6 miles an hour meant that St Albans was now less than a day's journey from London and travellers could travel further north, as far as Dunstable or Leighton Buzzard – the increased volume of traffic was enough to bring more people into St Albans. By 1681 wheeled services passed through St Albans from places as far afield as Shrewsbury, Chester, Derby and Nottingham, and services using horses came from Holyhead and Carlisle, together with many destinations in Lancashire and the midlands, as well as the local area. In 1690, 14 coaches, 21 waggons and 23 pack-horse carriers passed through the town every week, in addition to the many services that started and terminated in St Albans itself. Moreover, many individuals travelled independently on their own horses. St Albans, at the heart of a dense network of local traffic, as well as standing at the junction of two roads from London, and two roads to the north – Watling Street and the road to Luton, Kettering and Nottingham – was well placed to take advantage of the growth of road transport.[142] There is even some evidence of Londoners visiting St Albans on 'pleasure trips', probably to visit the abbey church, and perhaps the retail premises in the town.[143] There

... at the heart of a dense network of local traffic ... standing at the junction of two roads from London ...

was certainly a developing retail trade in millinery and haberdashery, and in books.[144]

As well as being a transport hub, St Albans was an important market for local agricultural produce, and in this period it retained an intimate connection with the surrounding rural economy. The sixteenth and seventeenth centuries were a period of considerable change in the rural economy of Hertfordshire and the other counties around London. Many of the leading tradesmen in St Albans dealt in and worked with the produce of local – and sometimes more distant – agriculture. Mealmen, who traded in corn crops produced by local farmers and sold them on, and millers and maltsters, who traded in wheat and barley, and supplied flour to bakers and malt to brewers, were often wealthy members of the urban community.[145] Brewers themselves, working in an industry that had a long history in St Albans,[146] 'seem to represent an extreme example of a wealthy and influential group in the borough'.[147] Brewing families such as the Crosfeilds [sic], the Pollards and the Lofts provided a succession of mayors and aldermen in the second half of the seventeenth century. Tanners, such as the Gapes of St Michael's, bought from butchers and sold on to the shoemakers and

This undated line drawing shows a farm at the bottom of St Michael's street, where the Verulamium museum was built in the 1930s. Agriculture retained an important role in the economy of St Albans and the surrounding region well into the nineteenth century. Nearly 2,000 men in the census registration district worked in agriculture in 1841.

other traders in the town, and in the case of the Gapes, and the Oxton family, were prosperous and politically influential. Tallow chandlers, who were closely connected by their trade (and often by their family relationships) to butchers, were also sometimes very wealthy.[148]

The expansion of the population of London increased the size of the large market that already existed for the produce of Hertfordshire agriculture. As well as food and beer, Londoners required fodder for the large metropolitan horse population. The corn and malt trade around the capital expanded during the sixteenth century, and in the surrounding counties, including Hertfordshire, mills were being constructed.[149] There is considerable evidence of the leasing of mills in the vicinity of St Albans to new tenants in the sixteenth and early seventeenth centuries, and possibly the construction of new mills.[150] Farmers' wealth in Hertfordshire was increasing, certainly for those 'yeoman' farmers with sizeable holdings that they owned: the real value of the stock and crops recorded in a large sample of Hertfordshire farmers' probate inventories increased threefold between the 1550s and the 1690s.[151] Patterns of production were changing: stimulated by the growing demand for malt, the acreage under barley increased from around 15 per cent of Hertfordshire arable acreage in the period 1580–1619 to over 20 per cent in the period 1670–99, while the acreage under rye fell to an almost insignificant level. The trend towards increased barley production was particularly noticeable on larger farms, and in the northern and eastern parts of Hertfordshire, close to the malting centres at Hitchin and Ware.[152] In southern Hertfordshire, the cultivation of rye on poor soils gave way to the production of livestock for the metropolitan market; and this period also saw an increasing size of the average sheep flock, a shift towards dairying on many farms, and, after about 1640, more widespread ownership of horses.[153] Around St Albans, wheat remained the most important arable crop. Increasing specialisation by the late seventeenth century in the different regions of Hertfordshire mirrored developments elsewhere, and in turn influenced the trading at St Albans market. Here, corn trading was 'preeminently in wheat', in contrast to the neighbouring markets at Watford and Hemel Hempstead, where other grain crops were traded.[154] It appears that St Albans market was used by traders from various places, but especially to the north and east of the town, from Wheathampstead, Welwyn, Codicote and Hatfield. South of the town, even in the adjacent parish of St Stephen's, many traders appear to have travelled to Watford, rather than St Albans, to market their produce.[155] Yet the role of the market in the national network, and the importance of St Albans as the centre of a large rural hinterland, combined to ensure that, in the 1680s, one observer could proclaim that the market was 'perhaps the greatest for Corne of any Towne that is not a port in England'.[156] St Albans may have been small, but it remained a flourishing economic centre, at least for trade and services.

'perhaps the greatest [market] for Corne of any Towne that is not a port in England.'

continued on page 173

Box 7: 'A Divided Town': religion and education

As earlier chapters have shown, before the eighteenth century there was what one historian has called a long 'pre-history of dissent in St Albans';[1] and most of the Dissenting congregations expanded in St Albans in the eighteenth century. Indeed, the whole western half of Hertfordshire was described by Daniel Defoe as being 'Whiggish and full of Dissenters', in contrast to the east of the county, which was 'entirely Church, and all of the High Sort'.[2] A large Baptist congregation met at Kensworth in the seventeenth century, and could claim 136 men and 229 women in 1694, drawn from a large surrounding area.[3] Baptists established a presence in St Albans in or around 1700, and a meeting

[1] Turner, 'Origins of the St Albans Baptists', *Baptist Quarterly*, vol. 37 (1998), p. 402.
[2] Quoted in Simkins, 'Political History', p. 40.
[3] Turner, 'Origins of the St Albans Baptists', pp. 402, 405; see above, p. 158.

house was built on Dagnall Lane c.1720, and extended c.1760; in 1815 there were around 40 members of the church.[4] There was also a Quaker meeting house on Dagnall Lane, with a burial ground (the Quakers had another on Sweetbriar Lane, later Victoria Street), but the Society of Friends had very few adherents in St Albans, 'about four families' according to local resident Solomon Shaw in 1815.[5] Also at Dagnall Lane for most of the eighteenth century was a meeting house used by Presbyterians and Congregationalists (also known as Independents). The latter were served by Dr Samuel Clark, a noted local educationalist. As Independent numbers increased they moved out in 1794, and built the Independent Chapel in Spicer Street in 1811, 'a very modern brick building' costing more than £1,200, which could accommodate around 500 'hearers'.[6] By the end of the eighteenth century, Methodism was also growing in St Albans, as elsewhere: the Methodists' first meeting house was at the corner of George Street and Romeland in 1793, and they then moved to St Peter's Street, to a church which could accommodate about 150 members of this 'increasing sect'.[7] The Kentishes, who supported Samuel Ferrand Waddington in the election of 1796 (see box 8), were prominent members of the town's Methodist congregation. Politically, Dissenters were an important part of the St

[4] Shaw, *History of Verulam*, pp. 187–8.
[5] Ibid., pp. 189–90.
[6] Ibid., pp. 191–2; Corbett, *History of St Albans*, p. 76.
[7] Corbett, *History of St Albans*, pp. 75–6; Shaw, *History of Verulam*, pp. 190–1.

LEFT

The Independent (Congregationalist) chapel on Spicer Street was built in 1811. It replaced an earlier meeting house in Dagnall Lane, which was one of a number of centres of Nonconformist worship in eighteenth-century St Albans.

© ST ALBANS MUSEUMS

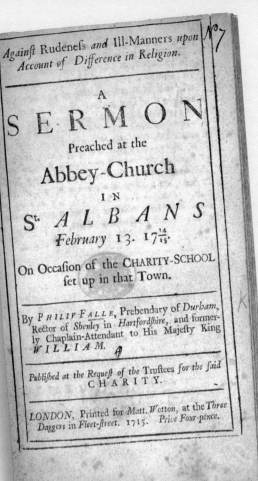

Against Rudeness and Ill-Manners upon
Account of Difference in Religion.

Nº 7

A
SERMON
Preached at the
Abbey-Church
IN
St ALBANS
February 13. 17¹⁴⁄₁₅.

On Occasion of the CHARITY-SCHOOL
set up in that Town.

By PHILIP FALLE, Prebendary of Durham,
Rector of Shenley in Hartfordshire, and former-
ly Chaplain-Attendant to His Majesty King
WILLIAM.

Published at the Request of the Trustees for the said
CHARITY.

LONDON, Printed for Matt. Wotton, at the Three
Daggers in Fleet-street. 1715. Price Four-pence.

donations that were invested in annuities. When
Philip Falle, rector of Shenley, was asked to
preach a sermon on the occasion of the foundation
of the school in February 1715, he explained
forcefully what he and others felt was the social
necessity for charitably provided education:

> You think that Money well laid out, which
> you give to have your streets cleaned, and
> the Dirt and Filth removed out of them.
> And can there be a greater annoyance than
> loose and disorderly Children, filling the
> Streets of a Town with unseemly Noise
> and Clamour, swearing, cursing, brawling
> and quarrelling, perhaps ... abusing and
> affronting Strangers and Travellers as they
> pass by? These generally are the Children
> of the Poor, whom Indigence keeps at
> home, deprived of the Benefit of Schools.
> Mark one of those Children, and observe
> from what such a beginning he grows up
> to! By the time he comes to be a Man,
> 'tis odds if you have him not a Wretch,
> without Principles, without Morals, ready
> for any Wickedness of Tongue or Hand,
> and against whom the Community and
> Neighbourhood must guard as against a
> dangerous Person. A small Charity given
> for his Education, might have made another
> Man of him.[3]

Albans electorate: the duchess of Marlborough
in 1743 regretted that, 'with the assistance of the
Dissenters, who are a great many, any person
would be easily chose' as MP for the borough.[1]
The long-serving MP James West (see box 8)
had the support of the Dissenting voters in the
borough, including influential families such as the
Pembrokes, the Iremongers and the Tombeses.[2]

Two charity schools, one Church, one
Dissenting, were established in the early
eighteenth century. The latter was organised by
Samuel Clark, supported by an annual sermon.
The Church's Bluecoat school was supported by

---

[1] Lansberry, 'Whig Inheritance', p. 49.
[2] Ibid., pp. 51–2.

[3] Philip Falle, *Against Rudeness and Ill-Manners upon
Account of Difference in Religion: A Sermon Preached at*

Falle cautioned against unhealthy rivalry between the Church and Dissenting establishments, referring to 'that School which stands in opposition to this'.[1] His language suggests tension between the congregations in St Albans. Falle hoped that 'the only Competition betwixt the Two Schools [would] be, which shall have the Glory of breeding up, and sending out into the World, the Civilest and the Best mannered Youths. Unless both Schools concurr in this Design, and pursue it jointly as their End, we labour in vain, and you must remain a Divided Town, and an Uneasy People for ever.'[2] By the early nineteenth century the Bluecoat school was educating 35 boys each year – the boys were 'fully clothed, instructed in the principles of the Christian religion according to the rites of the Church of England and taught to read, write and cast accounts' – and the Dissenting school clothed and educated 30 boys and 10 girls.[3] There were also a number of Sunday schools, established under various denominational auspices.

Meanwhile, the abbey school – known variously as the Grammar School, the Free School and St Albans School – was going through a period which its institutional historian has characterised as a 'dark age'.[4] In the 1720s there were revelations of heavy debts owed by the corporation to the school, and although in the wake of these the corporation made some efforts to improve the school, the number of pupils declined during the first half of the eighteenth century, until in 1762 there was none at all.[5] It appeared in the 1770s and 1780s that the school was not receiving the full sum to which it was entitled from the sale of wine licences in the town, which formed part of the school's endowment. It was not until a ruling in Chancery in 1787 that the matter at issue between the school and the corporation was cleared up.[6] Even in the early nineteenth century, the number of pupils at the school 'rarely exceeded seven or eight', mostly private pupils, although the financial position of school had improved somewhat, with income from leasing the wine licences and from lands let (somewhat controversially) to Alderman Thomas Kinder for £90 a year.[7] In 1815 the school was 'generally considered to be of little public service', although the school room itself, in the Lady Chapel, was 'a most excellent one'. As far as the library was concerned, 'there are but few books belonging to it, and most of these are but of little worth'.[8]

The abbey church itself, in which the school was housed, was in disrepair for most of the eighteenth and early nineteenth centuries. In 1703 a hurricane – which killed thousands of people in England and across north-western Europe – damaged the south transept, which was under scaffolding at the time. In the early 1720s it was found that the north wall was cracked and eighteen inches out of vertical; the south wall was also cracked, and 'the roof timbers were decayed and the whole building in a dangerous condition.'[9] An appeal for £5,775 was launched, and a body of 16 trustees appointed to oversee the building. Fire destroyed the old rectory in 1743; and in 1764 it was found that a further £2,500 worth of repairs to the church were required.[10] In 1818, following an Act of Parliament which made substantial funds available for the repair of churches, a survey was made by the architect Lewis Wyatt;[11] but in 1832 the collapse of a wall drew attention to the continuing deficiencies in the fabric of the abbey church (see box 10). Other churches in St Albans were also in disrepair for

---

the Abbey-Church in St Albans February 13, 1714/15, On Occasion of the Charity-School Set Up in that Town (London: Matthew Wotton, 1715), pp. 22–3.

[1] Ibid., p. 23. Original emphases.

[2] Ibid.

[3] Shaw, History of Verulam, pp. 211–12.

[4] Kilvington, Short History of St Albans School, chapter 6.

[5] Ibid., pp. 32, 37.

[6] Ibid., pp. 42–3.

[7] Ibid., pp. 41–4.

[8] Shaw, History of Verulam, pp. 210–11.

[9] Roberts, Hill of the Martyr, pp. 179–83.

[10] Ibid., pp. 183–5.

[11] Ibid., p. 191.

This engraving, produced by
Rock and Company of London
in 1862, shows St Peter's church
before the extensive restorations
carried out by Lord Grimthorpe
in the 1890s. St Peter's was one
of three churches supposedly
built by abbot Ulsinus in 948.
The cottages to the right-hand
side date from the seventeenth
century. St Peter's Green was
the site of one of the town's
water pumps.

much of the eighteenth century: in 1803 the tower
of St Peter's had 'become extremely ruinous,
and in danger of falling', and in that year an Act
of Parliament allowed trustees to levy a rate in
the parish to raise £4,000, as a result of which
considerable repairs were effected.[1]

Denominational rivalries continued to surface
at times in St Albans in the early nineteenth
century. Although relations were not generally bad,
Solomon Shaw believed that religious divisions
could be held partly responsible for the somewhat
stultified social life of the town.[2] When the St
Albans Branch Bible Society was established in
1812, under the presidency of Viscount Grimston
and with eleven vice-presidents including
the mayor and the town's two MPs, various
objections were raised which mirrored those that
had been aired against the Society at a national
level since its establishment in 1804. According
to Shaw, himself a member who donated a
pound and subscribed a guinea annually to the
Bible Society,[3] 'its merits were much agitated'

in St Albans, 'and it had to encounter with some
degree of opposition'.[4] Opposition centred on
the fact that the Society included members of
the established and Dissenting churches; some
felt that this weakened the Church of England.[5]
(Other criticisms reflected suspicions that the
Society distributed tracts, and a contrary concern
that it circulated bibles only, with no commentary
or other aid to understanding.) The St Albans
branch, which followed branches at Hertford and
Hitchin, did not flourish, and despite the 'very
distinguished patronage' of Grimston and others,
seemed to be 'rather upon the decline' by the time
Shaw was writing in 1815.[6] Although there were
religious divisions within the town, one practical
necessity restricted them: there was, simply, not
enough space in the abbey church, and as a result,
many parishioners, who would otherwise have
worshipped there, were forced to 'resort to the
dissenting chapels'.[7]

[1] Shaw, *History of Verulam*, p. 145.
[2] See below, pp. 206–7.
[3] *Report of the Proceedings at the Institution of the St
Albans Branch Bible Society, April 16th, 1812* (St Albans:

Shaw, 1812), list of subscribers, pp. 43–7.
[4] Shaw, *History of Verulam*, pp. 213–14.
[5] *Report of the Proceedings*, pp. 18–23.
[6] Shaw, *History of Verulam*, pp. 213–14.
[7] Quoted in Roberts, *Hill of the Martyr*, p. 191.

Economy, society and government, 1700–1835

LEFT

This soft ground
etching by Benjamin
Green (c.1739–98)
shows a rather
shabby-looking
clock tower, with
the market cross in
front. The picture
does not show the
shops on Market
Place that adjoined
the clock tower
to the north. The
market cross was
demolished in 1811.

© ST ALBANS MUSEUMS

T HE POPULATION OF ENGLAND grew steadily in the eighteenth
century, from around 5 million in 1700 to 7.8 million in 1801, when the
first national census was held. It grew more rapidly in the first three decades
of the nineteenth century, to 12 million in 1831.[1] The population of towns
followed the same pattern of growth: urbanisation in eighteenth-century
England was a 'gradual but distinctive process', a growth of population that
was more rapid, but not startlingly so, than for the population of the country as
a whole. Urban growth was 'modest' before c.1760, and there was 'more rapid
expansion thereafter'.[2] Less than 20 per cent of the population of England and
Wales lived in towns of 2,500 or more inhabitants in 1700, and this figure had
increased to around 30 per cent by the end of the eighteenth century.[3] By 1831,
it was 39.2 per cent; and in 1851 the decennial census revealed that, for the
first time, a majority of the population lived in urban areas. St Albans followed
the pattern of steady growth. Even by 1700, St Albans had already slipped
down the urban hierarchy, but remained a 'flourishing' town.[4] In 1724 Herman
Moll, in *A New Description of England and Wales*, called it 'a fair, large, and
well-inhabited Thoroughfare Town'.[5] Recent estimates suggest a 'fairly stable'
population until the later eighteenth century, followed by a 'rapid increase'.[6] As
noted in the last chapter, the population of the three urban parishes of Abbey,
St Peter's and St Michael's has been estimated at 3,066 in 1668.[7] By 1801 the
three parishes contained 4,679 people; and by 1831 the population had reached
7,592, an increase of 147.6 per cent on 1668.[8] There are many examples of
more rapid urban expansion in eighteenth-century England, especially in the
industrialising areas of the north and midlands, but St Albans was perhaps
more typical of the slower urban growth that characterised the counties around
London. The larger part of the increase in population took place in the parishes
of St Peter's and St Michael's, where there was more room for expansion: the
Abbey parish was already crowded by the late seventeenth century, and grew
between 1668 and 1831 from 1,585 to 3,092, or 95.1 per cent. By contrast, St

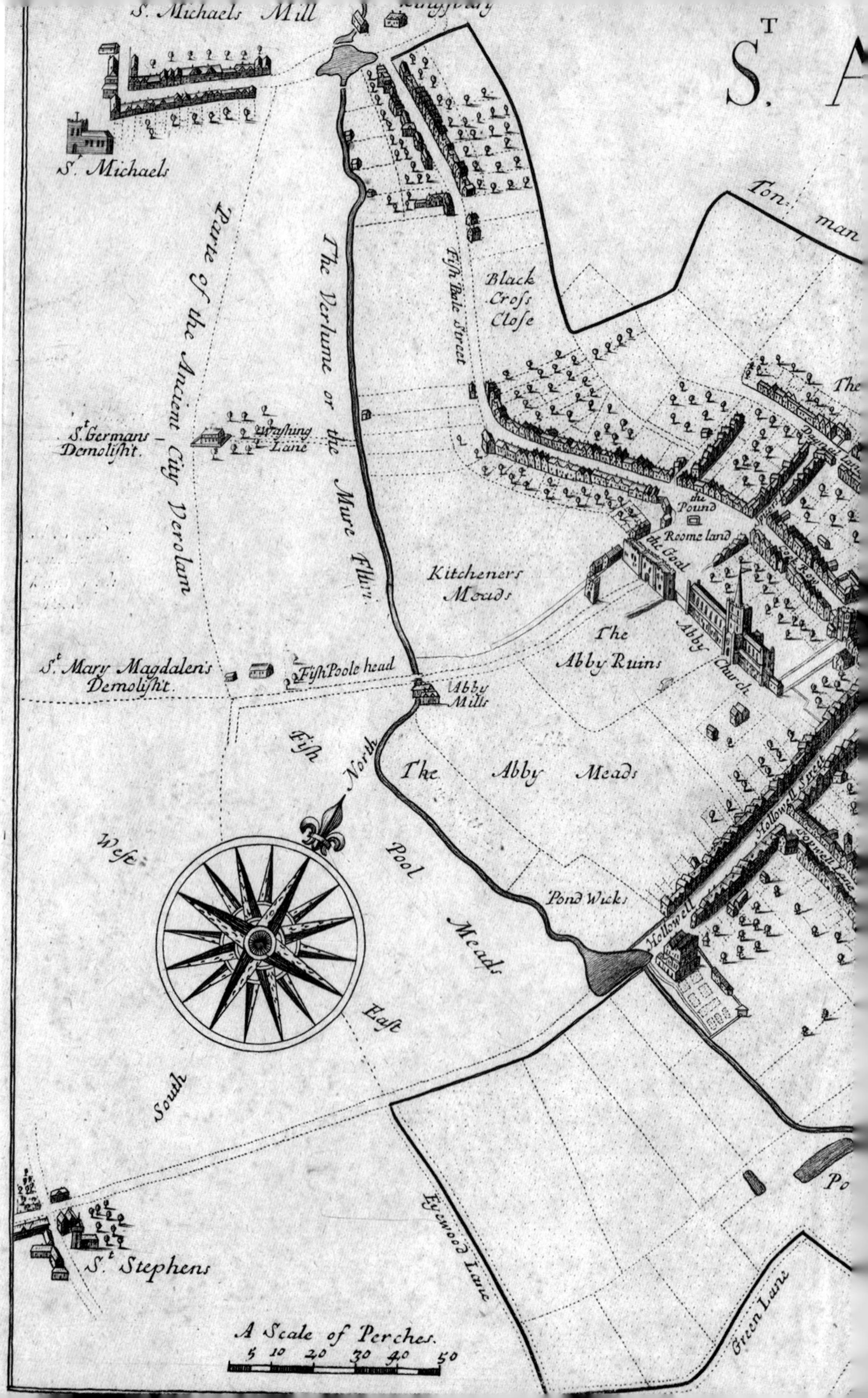

S. Michaels Mill

S.t A

St. Michaels

Parte of the Ancient City Verolam

The Verlame or the Muse Fluy

Fysh Poole street

Black Cross Close

Ton... man

The Pound

The Roome land

the Goal

St. Germans Demolisht

Wysling Lane

Kitcheners Meads

The Abby Ruins

Abby Church

St. Mary Magdalen's Demolisht.

FishPoole head

Abby Mills

The Abby Meads

Fysh

North

Pool

Meads

Pond Wicks

Hollowell street

Hollowell

West

South

East

Po

St. Stephens

Egewood Lane

Green Lane

A Scale of Perches.

5 10 20 30 40 50

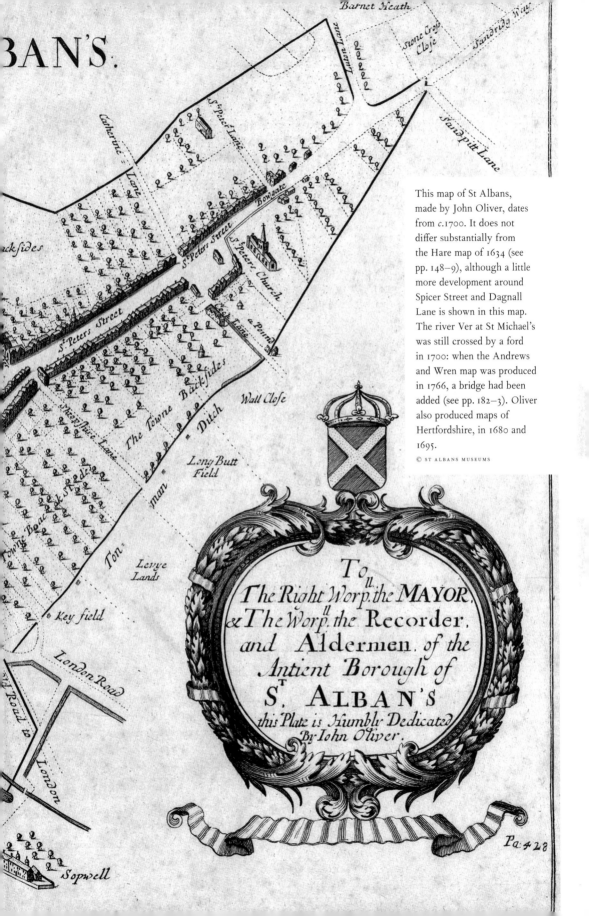

BAN'S.

Barnet Heath

Stone Cross Close

Sandridg Way

Stone Cross Close

Sandpitt Lane

Tuttin Lane

Catherine Lane

St Peter Lane

Bowgate

St Peters Street

St Peters Church

St Peters Street

a Pound

Cock Lane

Backsides

The Towne Backsides

Shropshire Lane

Ditch

Wall Close

Towne Beach Redd.

Ton

man

Long Butt Field

Levye Lands

Key field

London Road

Road to London

Sopwell

This map of St Albans, made by John Oliver, dates from *c*.1700. It does not differ substantially from the Hare map of 1634 (see pp. 148–9), although a little more development around Spicer Street and Dagnall Lane is shown in this map. The river Ver at St Michael's was still crossed by a ford in 1700: when the Andrews and Wren map was produced in 1766, a bridge had been added (see pp. 182–3). Oliver also produced maps of Hertfordshire, in 1680 and 1695.

© ST ALBANS MUSEUMS

To all
The Right Worp.ll the MAYOR,
& The Worp.ll the Recorder,
and Aldermen, of the
Antient Borough of
St ALBAN'S
this Plate is Humbly Dedicated
By Iohn Oliver.

Pa: 428

Michael's grew from 536 to 1,527 over the same period, an increase of 184.9 per cent, while the figures for St Peter's were 945 in 1668, 2,973 in 1831, and an increase of 214.6%.[9] The growth of St Albans rested on a number of economic foundations, in particular the continued expansion of trade and commerce in the eighteenth century, and the development of the straw industry.

As far as St Albans was concerned. the single most significant economic development in the eighteenth and early nineteenth centuries was the emergence of straw plaiting and straw hat manufacture. Straw came to dominate the counties of Hertfordshire, Bedfordshire and Buckinghamshire, which in turn dominated the industry itself. Straw plait was mostly produced in the countryside, and sold to straw merchants in towns. In this respect, it was similar to other proto-industrial developments – in textiles, for example – whereby, before the factory age, manufacturing took place in the countryside, usually in people's homes, organised by urban merchants. Proto-industrial manufacturing often gave employment to the families of men who worked in agriculture, and this was the case with straw plaiting. As the historian Laszlo Grof has explained, straw plaiting was 'ideally suited to the rural agricultural worker's family, as it required little or no capital outlay and used a widely available local material'.[10] Once plaited in the countryside, the straw was sold by the plaiters at urban markets, such as those as Luton and St Albans. Straw hat factories in these towns provided employment for local residents; again, these were generally women. The straw industry cemented the relationship between the town and the surrounding countryside: as one historian comments, 'the involvement of all these hamlets, villages and parishes in the plaiting of straw, producing a thriving cottage industry, tied them intimately to urban communities such as St Albans, for it was in the towns that [the] straw hat industry itself was established, and to which individual plaiters and straw factors would come to sell plait and straw'.[11]

One reason for the dominance of Bedfordshire, Hertfordshire and Buckinghamshire in straw plaiting and hat manufacture was the quality of local straw. To quote Thomas George Austin, author of *The Straw Plaitting, Straw Hat and Bonnet Trade* (1871), Bedfordshire 'became the chief seat of the Plait Manufacture, from the peculiar fineness of its wheat-straw, in which quality Herts participates'.[12] A second reason was the proximity of these counties to London. Not only was the capital by far the largest market for straw hats, but it also provided a crucial primary product: manure. The local historian Nigel Agar has explained,

Why … was straw plait so local? One explanation may lie in the relatively relaxed attitude of Bedfordshire and Hertfordshire farmers to straw gathering. In other parts of the country landlords looked askance at farmers who sold their straw … The reason was not far to seek. Selling the straw over a period of years would gradually remove nutrients from the land. Straw was to be used to feed and bed down the livestock but then the sweepings of the cow-shed and the stable must be ploughed back.

Wheat and barley were the dominant crops all over the eastern counties of England but only in the home counties within easy reach of London could landowners afford to take a relaxed attitude about straw. It was less essential to recycle the nutrients for the simple reason that … London produced such a vast quantity of animal manure – mostly from horses but also from humans. Wagon loads of London manure were conveyed from the capital every day to serve agriculture within about a thirty mile radius.[13]

At the same time, the de-industrialisation of London during this period allowed other areas in the South East to specialise in certain kinds of manufacturing: framework-knitting in Northamptonshire and food processing in Oxfordshire are other examples.[14] Straw-plaiting in Hertfordshire can be dated at least to the reign of Charles II (1660–85), when St Albans was known for what were later described as 'straw tankards and pots'.[15] In 1680 the parishes of St Albans entered into an agreement with John Hockley, a flax dresser from Ware, to set the poor to work at various tasks, including the manufacture of straw hats.[16] In 1689 a petition claimed that 14,000 or more people – probably an exaggeration – were dependent on straw plaiting, on an area centred on Luton, but extending as far south as Redbourn and Flamstead.[17] A subsequent petition of 1719 indicated that the straw plaiting area had expanded to include St Albans, and now stretched as far south as Watford.[18] In the following decade Daniel Defoe reported that 'the manufacture of straw work, especially straw hats … is wonderfully encreased within a few years past'.[19] In the eighteenth century the hat-making industry had to contend with a large increase in the imports of straw hats from Holland and Italy: the number imported grew from under 10,000 in 1721, to 34,063 in 1725, and then more than fourteenfold to a peak of 477,024 in 1760.[20] However, an even larger expansion of domestic demand meant that local hat manufacture survived, using locally plaited straw. When the Revolutionary and Napoleonic Wars (1792–1815) interrupted the supply of imported hats, the domestic industry – and the straw plaiting which supplied it – expanded further, especially after the introduction of heavy import duties in 1805.[21] The invention of the straw splitter around 1800 led to 'a major improvement in the quality of English plait', by allowing finer plait to be produced, using thinner straw.[22]

The steady return of imported hats, and plait, after the end of the war in 1815 diminished the earnings to be had from straw plaiting. Nevertheless, in the context of the very low wages paid to many male agricultural labourers in this period, any earnings from the work of women and children could enhance the family economy.[23] St Albans resident Solomon Shaw, writing in 1815, declared that 'the straw-plat sewing is a source of employment to many females in the town from which they may derive, and also from platting the straws, a respectable and comfortable livelihood'.[24] Even in Sandridge, where straw plaiting was less dominant than in some other rural parishes around St Albans, the village's local historian believes that plaiting was essential in 'keeping many poor families off parish relief'.[25] The poor law authorities themselves sometimes provided straw plaiting work for local paupers, which they would do in return for the provision of relief.[26] The work could be seasonal in character: one woman who had worked in the trade reported that 'the straw work is very bad, as a rule from July up to about Christmas'.[27] The historian Pamela Sharpe quotes an official report of 1843 in her description of the seasonality of the trade:

Single female workers moved into towns in the straw-plait areas to work for temporary high earnings, producing a mill-town atmosphere for a few weeks. Fancy straw weaving in … St Albans was described as work only carried on for two months: 'the people are paid by the piece, and as the season is brief, and called by the women their harvest, they work hard and earn good wages'.[28]

Straw-plaiters were also reliant on their ability to keep pace with the demands of the market. The rapidly changing urban fashions meant that the profitable plaiting of one year might be followed by poor earnings in the next.

Despite these disadvantages, straw plaiting was the most remunerative and easily available work for the women and children of St Albans and the surrounding area. The number of straw plaiters grew steadily in the first half of the nineteenth century. By 1841, there were 4,415 in Hertfordshire, a number which would increase significantly in subsequent decades.[29] An infrastructure of plait markets and plait schools grew up to service the industry. Plaiters might travel as far as 12 miles to attend the markets, which often started in the early hours of the morning.[30] Before the advent of compulsory elementary education in 1870, many children were given a rudimentary education at the plait schools. Plaiting became part of the social and cultural fabric of the region. It could be done by very young children, as Grof explains:

> The technique of plaiting straw was learned in early childhood. A small bundle of dampened straws, about nine inches in length, was held under the plaiter's left armpit and was pulled out one or two at the time with the mouth by bending the head. The straws were then kept moist in the mouth, ready for use. Plaiters used their thumbs and second finger of both hands to plait, leaving their forefingers for turning the splints. Setting in and pulling out new straws was a continuous process, giving a rhythmic motion to the plaiters.
>
> Plaits were made either from whole straws or straw which had been split into narrow 'splints'. Wholestraw plaits were rather cumbersome and produced a rather heavy straw hat. Much more favoured were plaits made from split straws, which could be used for the finer ladies' bonnets. Three main forms of plaits were produced: Plain, Pearl and Brilliant. Several types of plait in each of the three forms were developed, some by using coloured straws, others by plaiting two splints together to make 'improved' plaits. Seven-end plait was simple to make, usually attempted by children first learning to plait, while reciting the rhyme:

> > 'Under one, over two,
> > Pull it tight, and that will do!'[31]

Plait was produced in lengths of 20 yards, known as 'scores.'[32] Different places became synonymous with different styles of plaiting, and each town and its surrounding area specialised, at least to a degree. For example, Austin reported

Plaiting became part of the social and cultural fabric of the region.

that St Albans 'makes up Twists, Devons, and Improved Plaits of all qualities', contrasting with the 'Plain and Twist Whole-straw' plaits at the villages south-east of Luton (Breachwood Green, Lilley and Offley). Ivinghoe was known for 'narrow Twist ... and Rustic and mixed Colored Plaits', and Chesham for 'Devons and fine Split'.[33] In terms of the hats produced, St Albans became known for men's straw boaters, although this did not become a specialism until the nineteenth century.[34] There was also a brief flourishing of Brazilian hat manufacture in the mid-nineteenth century, using imported palm leaves: St Albans was the centre of this industry, which was introduced by T. G. Smith in the 1830s.[35]

With the exception of straw and hats, industrial development in St Albans was still relatively limited by the early nineteenth century. The main sectors were those which could serve the metropolitan market, and exchange the produce of a rural county like Hertfordshire for the luxuries produced in London. One historian explains that 'because they were nearby, the Home Counties were an excellent market for luxury goods and outlet for capital, and a source of supply not only of food but also of basic craft manufactures'.[36] Beer, straw, and agricultural produce found a ready market. The *Universal British Directory*, published in 1798, reported in its entry for St Albans that 'two common breweries, a cotton-manufactory, and an oil-mill, afford employ for several hands; and there are several good corn-mills both above and below the town' on the river Ver.[37] The directory recorded five traders who went under the designation of 'maltster', 'mealman', 'corn factor' or something similar.[38] There was a range of urban tradesmen and small manufacturers – a gunsmith, a handful of watchmakers and tallow chandlers, and a tanner – that one could find in most towns of a similar size; and there were several shoemakers, one of whom occupied the ground floor of the clock tower, a usefully prominent location for a retail outlet. The cotton manufacturer George Gill, an 'Oil-manufacturer' named Watts, and Samuel Hill, a 'Mop-yarn spinner' are the other entries in the directory that suggest a modest manufacturing sector. There was one cotton factory in St Albans, which lasted until the 1840s: its survival contrasted with the decline of the textile industries in some other towns in the south-east of England in this period, notably Canterbury and Colchester.[39] Similarly, although the silk industry at Canterbury 'had almost gone' by the start of the nineteenth century, in 1802 John Woollam established a silk mill in St Albans, which by 1815 was employing, according to Solomon Shaw, some 500 people, 'mostly children'.[40] The success of silk manufacture in St Albans may have been due to local demand for trimmings for straw hats,[41] although it is notable that the *Universal British Directory* listed only two milliners (Miss Cathrow and Miss Chambers) and no straw hat manufacturers, plait merchants or anyone else connected with the industry. The brick-making industry at St Albans continued and developed during the eighteenth century: on Bernard's Heath the industry existed in the seventeenth century,[42] and there is definite evidence of a kiln, mounds and pits from 1726. More brickmakers were digging on the Heath in the 1780s, and by the 1810s and 1820s Benjamin Fowler and his family were producing bricks on land that they had enclosed in 1813. The steady growth of St Albans would generate a demand for the materials of construction, and the *Universal British Directory* listed three bricklayers in St Albans in 1798, but no brick makers.[43]

Although there was an incipient manufacturing sector in the town, the

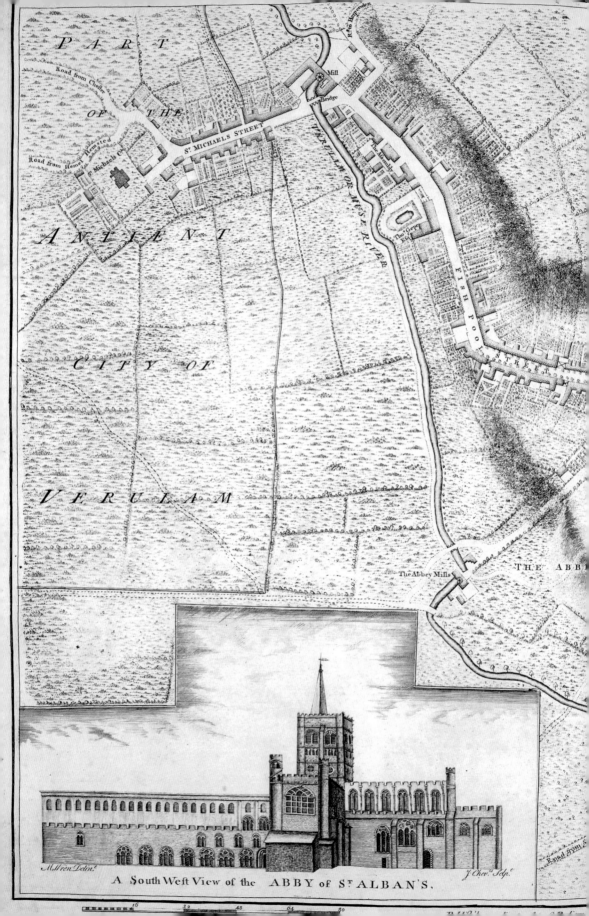

PART OF THE

Road from Chester

Road from Hemel Hemsted

St Michaels Ch.

St MICHAELS STREET

OF THE

ANTIENT

CITY OF

VERULAM

VERULAM OR WÆSE RIVER

Mill

Bridge

R. de Ingvenden

The Grinmill

Tho Gery Esq.

FISH POOL STREET

The Abbey Mills

THE ABB

Road from S.

M. Wren Delin.

J. Chev. Sculp.

A South West View of the ABBY of St ALBAN'S,

16   32   48   64   80

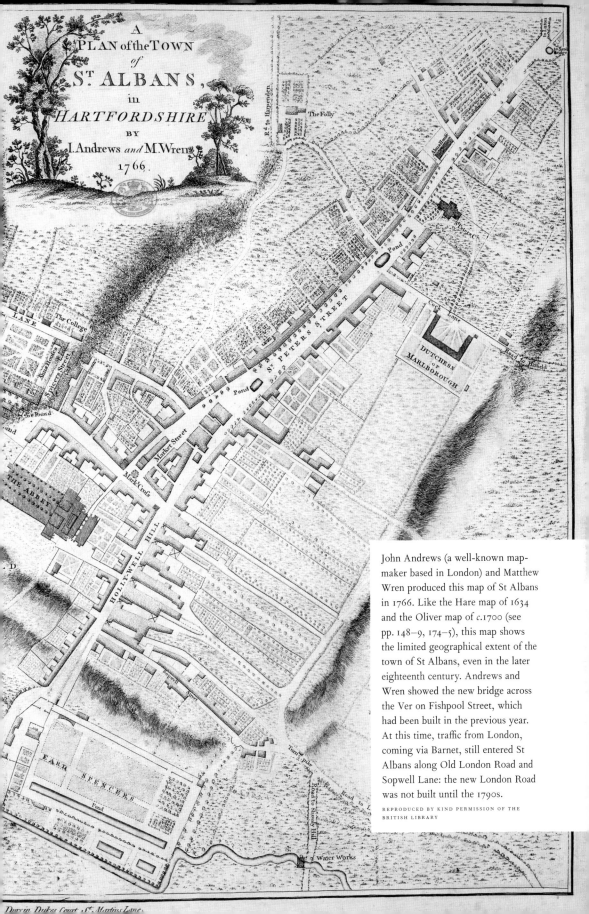

A
PLAN of the TOWN
of
St. ALBANS,
in
HARTFORDSHIRE
BY
I. Andrews and M. Wren
1766.

R.d to Harpenden

The Folly

Sleigate Ch.

LANE

The College

St. PETER'S STREET

Pond

Cock Lane

Annabaptists

Spicers Street

Road to Hatfield

The Pound

DUTCHESS OF MARLBOROUGH

Pond

Market Street

THE ABBEY

Mark.t Cross

HOLLYWELL HILL

D

EARL SPENCERS

Pond

Turnt. Pike

Road to Shady Hill

Road to L

Road to L

Water Works

Dwg in Dukes Court, S.t Martins Lane.

John Andrews (a well-known map-maker based in London) and Matthew Wren produced this map of St Albans in 1766. Like the Hare map of 1634 and the Oliver map of c.1700 (see pp. 148–9, 174–5), this map shows the limited geographical extent of the town of St Albans, even in the later eighteenth century. Andrews and Wren showed the new bridge across the Ver on Fishpool Street, which had been built in the previous year. At this time, traffic from London, coming via Barnet, still entered St Albans along Old London Road and Sopwell Lane: the new London Road was not built until the 1790s.

market was still at the heart of the life of St Albans. The *Universal British Directory* reported that, at St Albans, the market was still regulated by the corporation, as provided for in the town's charter from Charles II, although the two markets allowed for by charter had been reduced to one, held on a Saturday.[44] As the directory explained,

> Under this charter the corporation still acts, by which no higler, foreigner [i.e. non-freeman], &c., is to buy any commodity before the market bell rings, (generally at ten o'clock,) at which time the farmers untie their sacks of grain for the inspection of buyers, under a penalty, except the freeman and inhabitants, who may buy for their own use any article without regard to the bell. The market is well supplied with poultry, butter, eggs, &c.[45]

The old market bell is now housed in the clock tower. It dates from 1729, and was used until 1855. Non-freemen of the town were not allowed to trade before the ringing of the bell, which was rung at 10 a.m. in the market house. The market house was replaced by the corn exchange building, which still stands, in 1857. The bell is small, weighing just 30 kg; just a few seconds after this photograph was taken in August 2008 it was rung to announce the Saturday market.

PHOTOGRAPH: CARNEGIE

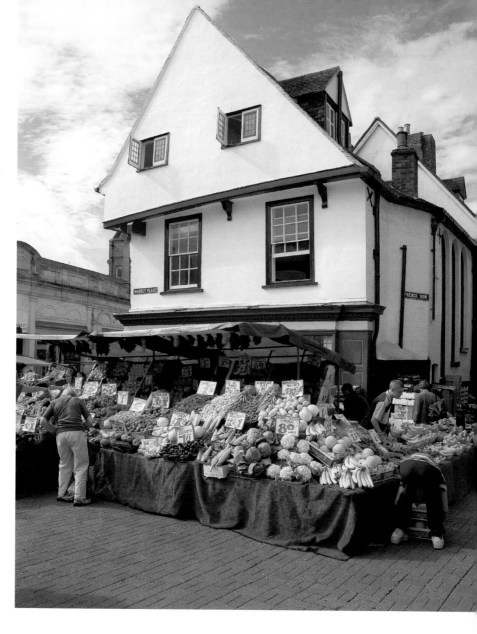

This vegetable stall stands in front of number 13, Market Place, known as 'the Gables', which was built in 1637. St Albans's sixteenth- and seventeenth-century borough charters confirmed its right to hold a market.

There was some discontent, at St Albans and elsewhere, about the monopoly privileges of the market, from the early eighteenth century onwards, although it appears that these were not always strictly enforced. Some indication of the strength of the market can be taken from the corporation's annual revenue from market tolls: these peaked at £326 in 1709–10, and declined thereafter, to around £100 in the mid-1730s and just £59 around 1750, although this was partly due to laxity of collection. Despite declining revenue, the market remained 'one of the greatest in England' in the 1750s.[46] Although the relative importance of the corn market appears to have diminished further by the end of the eighteenth century – the *Directory* remembered that, 'forty years ago, this was the first market for grain in the country', suggesting that by the 1790s this was no longer the case[47] – it survived and remained significant, in a period during which a number of markets disappeared. According to one estimate, there were around 700 markets in England and Wales in the eighteenth century, a slight decline from the number in the sixteenth and seventeenth; however, the number of markets that catered for trade and traffic beyond the very local declined more significantly.[48] The period saw, in P. J. Corfield's words, 'a rationalization of the market network … a period of consolidation and prosperous expansion for an array of strategically sited inland trading towns'; in this process, 'success depended on good transport services'.[49] St Albans was fortunate in this regard, and it held its own in a challenging period. In many other southern towns, markets were found to be in decay, and those at Shefford and Toddington in neighbouring Bedfordshire disappeared completely.[50]

> *'London operates much to the injury of the trading part of the town …'*

At St Albans, by the late eighteenth century the Saturday market had been supplemented by the plait market, described by Shaw in 1815 as 'one of the largest in England, which begins at the ringing of a bell by one of the beadles of the borough and terminates before the commencement of the corn market'.[51] In the 1790s were also 'pretty well attended' fairs, at Lady Day (25 March) and Old Michaelmas (10 October), at which clothes and toys were traded; and a statute fair for hiring farm servants, held at New Michaelmas (29 September), was held, but was 'sometimes but thinly attended' because other such fairs were held earlier in the year at other locations.[52] The decline of fairs mirrored the experience elsewhere.[53] These markets and fairs emphasise the importance of the surrounding countryside to the economy of the town: St Albans served as a market for an agricultural hinterland, trading in the core produce as well as the increasingly significant by-products of Hertfordshire agriculture. With the important exception of the innkeepers and victuallers, St Albans's local tradesmen tended to serve the town and its immediate neighbourhood: Shaw noted that 'there are many respectable and well-furnished shops, which supply the town with the necessaries and conveniences of life; but London operates much to the injury of the trading part of the town; and as there are no manufactories (except the silk and cotton mills), or other adventitious cause of increasing the trade, its chief dependence is upon its own population and that of the small towns and villages near'.[54]

This may have been true of the market, but St Albans still had a large number of temporary visitors because of its strategic position in the transport network. It remained a 'thoroughfare town', as it had been in the seventeenth century, and the amount of through traffic increased as local roads were improved. After around 1700 there was considerable development of turnpike roads close to London: the number of weekly carrier services from London to towns and villages across the south-east increased steadily, from 183 in 1681 to

247 in 1738.[55] Turnpike trusts were established to maintain and improve major roads, funding these activities through levying tolls, and relieving the parishes of their responsibility. The St Albans and South Mimms Turnpike Trust was established in 1715, with responsibility for the section of the main road between these places. As Daniel Defoe reported just a few years later,

> the road from St Albans to South Mimms, a village beyond Barnet ... is so well mended, the work so well done, and the materials so good, so plentifully furnished, and so faithfully applied ... here the bottom is not only repaired, but the narrow places are widened, hills levelled, bottoms raised, and the ascents and descents made easy, to the inexpressible ease and advantage of travellers, and especially of the carriers, who draw heavy goods and hard loads, who find the benefit in the health and strength of their cattle.[56]

The trade and commerce of St Albans benefited from its location at the junction of this road and Watling Street, itself a more than useful thoroughfare: Defoe was impressed that 'from Hyde-Park Corner, just where Tyburn stands, the road makes one straight line without any turning, even to the very town of St Albans'.[57] The turnpike trust erected tollgates to the north-west and south-east of St Albans, and made various improvements to the road during the eighteenth century, including a new bridge at St Michael's in 1765, replacing the

Holywell Hill, looking north, c.1850. The road was straightened following the demolition of Holywell House in 1837. The abbey church can be seen at the top of the hill, and the Duke of Marlborough pub, dating from c.1825, in the foreground.

shpool st., St Albans
Rvacustes A. Phipson, Jy 1902.

ford which previously stood at the end of Fishpool Street.[58] This can be seen on the Andrews and Wren map of St Albans, dating from 1766.[59] In 1794, an Act of Parliament was obtained 'for avoiding some dangerous turnings in the public road':[60] at this time, traffic from London travelled along what is now Old London Road, along Sopwell Lane, made a sharp right turn onto Holywell Hill, and then a left turn at the Peahen inn onto the High Street. This Act resulted in the construction of the new London Road, under the direction of Thomas Telford, which bypassed Sopwell Lane and Holywell Hill and ran straight to the Peahen, creating a crossroads where a T-junction had formerly stood. A tollgate was erected at the junction of the new and old London Roads.[61]

Despite these improvements, the St Albans turnpike at the beginning of the nineteenth century gave cause for concern. The road was built without foundation, using gravel, and on the clayey Hertfordshire soil this 'resulted in a glutinous road surface in wet weather'.[62] It was maintained by regularly scraping the surface and replacing it with fresh stone and flints, while the material scraped away was left at the side of the road. Over time, this reduced the level of the road to between four and eight feet below that of the land at either side, while the waste material left high banks, which coach travellers were sometimes unable to see over, and which prevented the sun from drying the road surface. Ridge Hill, between South Mimms and London Colney, was a particularly difficult section to maintain, and in 1807 the Trust spent £4,000 on this section alone.[63] In 1818 and 1819 a further £6,000 was borrowed from the Public Works Loan Commissioners to build a new section of road, again overseen by Telford. In St Albans itself, although the developments of 1794 had improved conditions for vehicles approaching the town from London, to leave the town this traffic still had to travel down George Street and Fishpool Street, cross the Ver, and then negotiate another winding stretch of road before rejoining the straight section of Watling Street. Some improvements were effected in 1814 and 1820, when George Street and Chequer Street were widened.[64] A house at the corner of George Street had formerly created 'a most dangerous turning'.[65] However, although the Commissioners of the Holyhead Road had been trying for some time to obtain parliamentary approval for a new road layout in St Albans, to bypass George Street and Fishpool Street, as Telford had recommended, opposition from within the town and from the earl of Verulam delayed the implementation of this until 1823, when an Act authorised the construction of a new road. More than £15,000 was spent on this road, which ran from the High Street to Pondyards, or Shafford, where Francis Bacon had constructed his fishponds two centuries earlier (see box 6). The new road was known as Verulam Street or Verulam Road. The old road beyond St Michael's was closed off by the earl of Verulam and used as part of a private drive leading to Gorhambury.[66] Further developments in the nineteenth century saw the construction of Hatfield Road, built by the Reading and Hatfield Turnpike Trust, running eastwards from St Peter's church, while in 1837 Holywell House, the former home of the Churchills and Spencers at the southern end of St Albans (see box 8), was demolished to allow the straightening of Holywell Hill, which had been diverted in the eighteenth century.[67]

St Albans continued to provide accommodation and services for a substantial amount of through traffic. In 1798 the *Universal British Directory* described some of this traffic:

> Two coaches go from the Woolpack-inn, to the Ram-inn, Smithfield, London, one or the other every day (sometimes both); one goes through Barnet, and the other through Edgeware; and returns the same day: sets out at eight in the morning from St Albans; and from London at two in the afternoon in winter, and three in summer. – Two waggons likewise pass from hence to London, twice a-week: Standbridge's, to the White Hart, St John's-street; and Weatherhead's, to the Horseshoe, Goswell-street: their regular days are, Monday and Thursday up, Tuesday and Friday down. Many other waggons go through this town and neighbourhood once or twice a-week; and, as the Chester road passes through this town, they have coaches and waggons going to and from London continually.[68]

'as the Chester road passes through this town, they have coaches and waggons going to and from London continually.'

By 1810, over 46,000 vehicles and 250,000 animals travelled annually along the section of road maintained by the St Albans and South Mimms Turnpike Trust.[69] The post was collected every evening except Saturday and delivered every morning except Monday to a post office at the clock tower.[70] Travel was not always pleasant or easy: in 1782 John Wesley noted in his journal that, at Luton, 'I could procure no other conveyance to St Albans but in an open chaise [a light carriage]; and hence (the frost being very sharp), I contracted a severe cold.'[71] However, travel was relatively quick between the main points on the road: on 31 November 1785 Wesley departed St Albans in a chaise at 1 p.m., arrived in Luton at 2 p.m.; and four days later he left St Albans in a chaise at 12.15 p.m., had dinner in Barnet at 2.45 p.m., and then took a coach from Barnet at 4 p.m., arriving home in London by 6.15 p.m.[72]

The accommodation and services available to travellers expanded to fill the buoyant demand that existed in the eighteenth century. In the second half of the century, before the main road was diverted away from its door, the Goat inn on Sopwell Lane alone could stable 72 horses,[73] and by 1815 Shaw estimated that over 1,000 people passed through St Albans every day.[74] In fact, by the early nineteenth century the amount (and the variety) of traffic had probably fallen from an earlier peak: Shaw certainly thought so, recalling that 'prior to the improvement of the public roads in England ... innumerable quantities of packhorses were constantly passing through St Albans, with the produce of the factories of Manchester, Nottingham, Stafford, Coventry, &c. and at which period the inns were more numerous than at present'.[75] Nevertheless, many inns remained. The *Universal British Directory* scratched the surface by naming the proprietors of ten,[76] as well as nine individuals who were styled 'Victualler'.[77] In 1815 Shaw named the White Hart and the Angel ('for families, and posting'); the Woolpack, Peahen and George, for commercial travellers; the Blue Boar, famous for its beer; the Great Red Lion, with 'accommodation for waggons'; the Crown, 'general resort of sportsmen particularly during the hunting season'; the Fleur-de-lis and White Horse, which let saddle horses and single-horse chaises; and the Chequers, Bell, King's Head and Swan, the last being 'for Hawkers, &c.'[78] Following the construction of the new Verulam Road the impressive Verulam Arms hotel was built, accommodating the wealthiest customers – including Princess Victoria and her mother for lunch in 1835 – although its location and the noise of the traffic ensured that it 'never flourished'.[79]

As provided for in the charters of the sixteenth and seventeenth centuries, the affairs of the borough of St Albans were in the hands of the corporation, in the persons of the mayor, aldermen and assistants; but, increasingly, other institutions also exercised power and influence within the town. In a survey of politics and government in urban Britain in the period 1700–1840, Joanna Innes and Nicholas Rogers identify four significant institutions of

'innumerable quantities of packhorses were constantly passing through St Albans, with the produce of the factories of Manchester, Nottingham, Stafford, Coventry, &c.'

urban governance: the corporation, the parish, voluntary societies, and the patronage of benevolent individuals (who provided services in the expectation of political advantage).[80] In addition, improvement commissions – established to oversee roads, paving, lighting, policing or other matters of concern to the population – were increasingly being used: these commissions were established by Act of Parliament, and often completely bypassed existing local government arrangements. In St Albans, all these institutions played a role in this period.

The role of urban corporations was coming under increasing criticism and challenge during the eighteenth century. They were usually unelected, and the 'oligarchic tendencies' in many corporations were thought to perpetuate a culture of secrecy and unaccountability, as well as inactivity.[81] In St Albans, according to the historian H. C. F. Lansberry, 'for most of the period 1685 to 1835 [the members of the corporation] showed a decreasing concern for the government of the borough, though they jealously guarded their rights to govern'.[82] During this 150-year period there were 118 different aldermen: as before, they held their office for life, as long as they lived in the town. They were mostly local tradesmen, attorneys or surgeons, and some were members of the local gentry, including the first and second Earls Spencer, who fulfilled the residency requirement through their ownership of Holywell House, although they did not live there most of the time. Some families, such as the Kinders (brewers and farmers) and Kentishes (wool staplers and corn dealers), provided many aldermen during this period, as did the Gapes of St Michael's.[83] Churchmen and Dissenters both served, although the former were in the majority. The aldermen were a self-perpetuating oligarchy of prominent families, not necessarily those best equipped to govern the town. In 1815, Solomon Shaw complained bitterly about them: some were too old for the job, others too young and inexperienced, while still others lacked 'a fair understanding and liberal education'. Sometimes incomers to the town had been chosen, before attaining the 'distinction' or 'respectability' (a quality with which Shaw was obsessed) that some longer-standing residents enjoyed.[84]

Below the aldermen was another layer of officials – the assistants, of whom Shaw was one.[85] As noted in the last chapter, these were originally elected by the guilds, but this responsibility had passed to the mayor and principal burgesses, and later the aldermen, in the seventeenth century.[86] The assistants were not remunerated for their work, and it was increasingly difficult to recruit people to the role; as a result there were usually vacancies. In Shaw's view, the assistants, who comprised mostly small tradespeople, did far more than the aldermen to promote the interests of the inhabitants of St Albans, but socially, a 'haughty distance' was always maintained between the two classes of official, another manifestation of the political and social elitism of urban governance in this period.[87] In the early nineteenth century Shaw and his

colleagues vigorously asserted their own interests, and pressed for reforms in the corporation's practices, especially in the enforcement of freemen's trading privileges, but they were unsuccessful.[88]

The finances of the corporation were in varying degrees of difficulty throughout the eighteenth century. Its revenue was small: apart from the market tolls, which, as noted above, were declining in the first half of the eighteenth century, the total revenue for a typical year early in the century was £117 15s. 6d., of which £40 was spent on the mayor's allowance.[89] Even this modest revenue was lower than it should have been, because some of the buildings owned by the corporation were let out on favourable terms to aldermen: in Lansberry's words, 'the corporation did not own much property and the administration of what little property they had was not such as to inspire further endowment'.[90] The result was that the corporation had to borrow money and to economise: for example, in 1715, £200 was borrowed, and in 1740 the costly mayoral feast was (temporarily) abandoned.[91] In the early 1720s a Commission of Charitable Uses was appointed by the Court of Chancery to investigate the affairs of the St Albans corporation. It revealed substantial debts to various charities, especially St Albans School; this in turn had helped to push the school itself into serious financial difficulties.[92] The Commission revealed that the total debts of the corporation and its members amounted to £3,024 6s. 6d., of which some was owed by individuals, including alderman Gape, who alone owed £495. As a body the corporation owed £2,273 1s. 6d.; after an appeal the sum was reduced to £997 4s. 3d., of which £808 12s. 9d. was to the school.[93] The corporation continued to contract more debt: for example, money was borrowed from Earl Spencer in the 1750s.[94]

Despite its financial difficulties, the corporation was involved in the provision of civic amenities during the eighteenth century, and acquired some new responsibilities. For example, in 1703 the corporation ordered that a market house be constructed on the site of the Eleanor Cross, which was demolished in or around 1701.[95] There had been a shelter at the cross in the seventeenth century;[96] and another structure, in the form of a lean-to against the clock tower, was built in 1720.[97] Other matters were of more fundamental importance to the inhabitants, as the urban historian Rosemary Sweet explains: 'The most pressing administrative need in any town was to keep the streets clean. Left unregulated, streets could rapidly degenerate into a quagmire of mud and potholes, awash with liquid manure and the detritus of urban life.'[98] In St Albans, the large number of horses that passed through the town made the problem especially pressing. Many towns already had scavengers – 'forerunners of our modern dustmen'[99] – and St Albans followed suit in 1735. Nevertheless, in many towns the services provided by scavengers were inadequate, and St Albans seems to have been one example, as there were frequent complaints about the dirtiness of the streets. Similar difficulties were encountered with the water supply. There were water works on the river Ver from the late seventeenth century, at Sopwell below Holywell House; these worked poorly in the early eighteenth century, although they were in use again from the early 1740s. They can be seen on the Andrews and Wren map from 1766.[100] In 1733 a water pump was built in St Peter's parish, over a well leased by the corporation from John Gape; but this was poorly maintained for many decades.[101] In 1815, Shaw complained that the pump was 'seldom in repair, therefore of very little service'.[102] In 1765 Earl Spencer built a new pump at the market cross; this was improved in 1781. The Spencers continued to maintain the pump until the second earl's abrupt withdrawal from St Albans politics in 1807 (see box 8).[103] By 1815 Shaw hoped for a return to the old ways of supplying water: 'Water was formerly, by means of water works, conveyed from the river near the town, for its use and which might doubtless be now effected, and prove a great acquisition to the inhabitants.'[104] The new works for which he hoped were built in the 1830s.

The corporation in the early nineteenth century was not in the dire straits of the 1720s, but it remained poorly financed, and its procedures were often tortuous. Even in the early 1840s the total annual income of the reformed corporation was only £412 17s. 6d., of which more than half was spent on policing.[105] Pressure on finances in the early nineteenth century led to a reduction in the expenses allowed for the mayoral feast; more importantly, expenditure on fire engines was also cut.[106] Payments to officials, most notably the mayor, did not keep pace with the expenses of the office: the mayor's allowance was £40 in 1688, and although this had risen steadily to £79 by 1835, it was thought that the expenses associated with the mayoralty were some £100 to £150 in excess of this allowance by this time.[107] Some mayors were reliant on patronage to meet the costs of the office: for example, Thomas Baker, mayor in 1795, was given £100 by Earl Spencer to cover his expenses, although he did not receive this money until 1797.[108] The corporation was bad at making decisions, and everything took time. As the local historian James Corbett has explained, the corporation's vacillation over the location of the various markets and the market cross was typical:

The corporation was bad at making decisions, and everything took time.

The council had decided in August 1804 that the plait market and poultry market should be held at the Market Cross; the council then had had second thoughts in October and moved the plait market to School Lane [Waxhouse Gate]. Having reminded themselves of the Market Cross, an open-sided octagonal structure near the Clock Tower, sheltering the pump, the city fathers resolved in December to think about removing the Market Cross 'for the purpose of rendering access to the market more easy and commodious to the public'. After thoughts lasting six years they reached the conclusion in January 1810 that the Market Cross was in a dangerous condition and should be taken down. Soon afterwards it was accidentally damaged by a waggon and in March 1810 the waggoner had to hand over £10 for repairs. A year later, as a result of the corporate mind undergoing another convulsion, the Market Cross was demolished.[109]

Some features of the corporation were becoming redundant in this period. The guilds or companies, of which only the Innholders and Mercers remained in St Albans after the 1660s,[110] declined further in power and influence, and were almost extinct by the early nineteenth century. The guilds each elected two wardens annually to collect the small quarterly dues that freemen were supposed to pay, but the collection had broken down by this time.[111] This followed the general pattern in urban England, whereby the supervisory functions of guilds were superseded by corporations or other bodies, and many guilds transformed themselves into administrators of charity or 'vehicles for ceremonial and festivities'.[112] Traditional routes into the freedom of boroughs were being undermined: one way into the freedom of St Albans, as with other towns, was by apprenticeship, but in practice the enforcement of apprenticeship statutes was not stringent, and 'after years of administrative leniency and legal uncertainty', the Elizabethan laws regulating to apprenticeships were repealed in 1814.[113] In St Albans, there remained after this reform the option of paying an entry fee for the freedom, and thereby joining one of the guilds; as noted above, this conferred certain privileges at the town's market, and also entitled the freeman to a parliamentary vote. By 1835, St Albans had 448 freemen, of whom 106 were resident in the borough and 81 were honorary; the non-resident freemen were the source of considerable political corruption (see box 8). The institution of the freedom was largely an anachronism by the 1830s, and was rendered meaningless by the Municipal Corporations Act of 1835. The association between the freedom and the parliamentary franchise was removed by the Reform Act in 1832.

The demise of the freedom and the privileges that went with it was the source of complaint in the early nineteenth century, from men such as Solomon Shaw, who felt that the corporation was not adequately protecting the interests of the inhabitants of the town or ensuring the enforcement of freemen's trading privileges. Shaw complained that, despite the very strict prohibition on trade within the borough by non-freemen, 'every innovation upon the trade is suffered with impunity, and the hawker (licensed or unlicensed) receives frequently more encouragement than the resident tradesmen'.[114] 'Hawkers' did not pay local taxes, and yet the members of the corporation, both as private individuals and in their corporate capacity, apparently 'conferred the favors' of their business on them. As for the regulation of weights and measures at the market court, which was overseen by the borough assistants, Shaw was ready with a sarcastic comment:

'... the hawker ... receives frequently more encouragement than the resident tradesmen.'

Dating from *c.*1810, this view shows the High Street, market cross and clock tower. There is a semaphore signal on the roof of the tower: this was installed in 1804, to transmit information during the Napoleonic Wars, and was taken down in 1814.

© ST ALBANS MUSEUMS

This court might be made productive of the best effects, was it conducted with policy, but it is much to be regretted that instead of being of any service to the public, it is rather injurious: – the mode of conducting it, the beadles give notice to the different inhabitants who use weights and measures, to assemble and bring them to be tried by the standard ones which are kept for that purpose in the Town-hall; so that, provided any person has other than honest ones, by giving him such notice, he would certainly be careful (if he was more fool than rogue) to bring the very same weights he used, and in such case would well deserve the heaviest fine they could impose upon him.[115]

In many English towns, municipal government in the late eighteenth and early nineteenth century was widely criticised because of the concentration of power among small cliques, secrecy in accounting practices and poor management.[116] These concerns were also voiced in St Albans. In 1815 Shaw

continued on page 202

THE small but intense theatre of St Albans borough politics in the eighteenth and early nineteenth centuries was dominated by three families who exercised considerable influence over the representation of the borough: the Marlboroughs, Spencers and Grimstons. St Albans returned two MPs – a right secured by the borough charter – and its electorate was highly susceptible to the persuasion and bribery of the great families. A detailed, but unpublished, study of politics and government in St Albans in the period 1685–1835 by H. C. F. Lansberry provides an excellent insight into borough politics.[1]

Sarah Churchill, the duchess of Marlborough, had been left a share in Holywell House, one of the largest properties in St Albans, by her father Richard Jennings. Following her marriage, aged 15, to John Churchill in 1675, the Churchill family acquired the whole house and the rest of the property of the manor of Sandridge. John Churchill was created duke of Marlborough in 1702. The Churchills were aligned with the Tories, although they moved closer to the Whigs in the later 1700s. Holywell House 'was retained largely for its political use as a base from which to influence elections in the borough', and gave its inhabitants 'a stranglehold for generations' on at least one of the borough's seats.[2] When the duchess died in 1744, her interest in St Albans passed to her grandson John Spencer, who himself died two years later, to be succeeded by his 11-year-old son, also John Spencer. This John Spencer was elected to Parliament as the MP for Warwick in 1756; unlike his Churchill ancestors, he was 'a member of the old Whig corps', and a supporter of the duke of Newcastle, prime minister 1754–56 and 1757–62. Spencer was given an earldom when Lord Rockingham became

prime minister in 1765.[3] He took the title Earl Spencer, and spent most of his time at the family home in Althorp, Northamptonshire. He was rarely seen in the House of Lords, partly because of ill health, and died in 1783; however, his family was able to exercise influence over borough seats in Northampton and St Albans. Spencer's son George John, second Earl Spencer, was much more active: conscious of his 'staunchly whig' family connections, he supported the Fox-North coalition government in the 1780s, but after the French Revolution he joined William Pitt's Tory government in 1794 as lord keeper of the privy seal, shortly afterwards becoming first lord of

---

[3] Richard Milward, 'Spencer, John, First Earl Spencer': *Oxford Dictionary of National Biography*.

Holywell House, at the bottom of Holywell Hill, was an important political base in St Albans in the eighteenth century. It was owned by the Churchills until 1744 and then the Spencers, and was demolished in 1837. This watercolour was painted by H.R. Wilton-Hall, a local historian and librarian of St Albans cathedral in the early twentieth century, and was copied from an original in the collection of Baron Dimsdale. This picture shows the house as it looked c.1800.

© ST ALBANS MUSEUMS

---

[1] Lansberry, 'Politics and Government'.

[2] Lawrence Stone and Jeanne C. Stone, *An Open Elite? England 1540–1880* (Oxford: Clarendon Press, 1984), pp. 113, 274.

William Luckyn Grimston (1683–1756) was elected as an MP for St Albans in 1710 and ennobled as the first Viscount Grimston in 1719. He was the great-nephew of Sir Samuel Grimston, and lived at Gorhambury House outside St Albans. His great-great-grandson, James Grimston (see pp. 248–9), was the second earl of Verulam. This engraving probably dates from after Grimston's death; the artist is unknown.

the admiralty.[1] However, in the early nineteenth century he returned to Whiggism and was home secretary in the Fox-Grenville government in 1806. Spencer's political strength in St Albans in the later eighteenth and early nineteenth century lay in his base at Holywell House, where his mother, the dowager countess Spencer, was able to manage the borough on his behalf.

The Grimston family was the other powerful political influence in St Albans. William Luckyn Grimston was the great-nephew and heir of Sir Samuel Grimston (see box 6), and was first elected as MP for St Albans on a Whig platform in 1710; he was ennobled as the first Viscount Grimston in 1719. His son James Grimston, like Spencer a supporter of the duke of Newcastle, was first elected for St Albans in 1754; based at Gorhambury House, the family interest in the borough lasted throughout the eighteenth century and well into the nineteenth. By the 1780s the Grimstons in Parliament supported Pitt; James presented an address of gratitude to king George III for his dismissal of the Fox-North coalition government in 1783, and he was created Baron Verulam in 1790.[2] The Grimston interest was firmly Tory by the nineteenth century (see box 9). Other important families in the borough included the Gapes of St Michael's Manor, 'pig-tail Tories of the old school',[3] and the Lomaxes, a Dissenting family based at Childwickbury, between St Albans and Harpenden. The Dissenting interest in St Albans tended to be aligned with the Grimstons, and given the size of the town's Dissenting congregations, it was important for parliamentary candidates to secure their support.

Corruption and bribery – at St Albans as elsewhere – were normal features of parliamentary elections. Petitions against the declared result were common, and dubious practices persisted. In particular, the creation of non-resident honorary freemen to swing the result of elections in St Albans caused considerable resentment. Creating honorary freemen required the intervention of the mayor of the time, on whom pressure could be exerted by the leading families of the borough. The strategy dated back to the later seventeenth century, but appeared to have been outlawed by a House of Commons ruling in 1705 that 'the franchise of St Albans should be in the freemen by birth, service and redemption and in the householders paying scot and lot' (scot and

---

[1] Malcolm Lester, 'Spencer, George John, Second Earl Spencer': *Oxford Dictionary of National Biography.*

[2] Lansberry, 'Whig Inheritance', p. 53.
[3] Lansberry, 'Politics and Government', pp. 205–6.

lot were obscure municipal taxes).[1] This franchise excluded honorary freemen, and as a result, the election in that year of John Gape – who owed his victory to the votes of non-resident freemen – was set aside and his opponent declared elected. However, following another disputed election in 1714, the Commons resolved more ambiguously that the franchise in St Albans was held by the mayor, the aldermen, householders who paid scot and lot, and freemen of the borough; this appeared to reverse the earlier ruling that only specific groups of freemen should be allowed to vote.[2] The duchess of Marlborough, having seen her candidate defeated in a by-election in 1717, determined to create honorary freemen to swing the result her way at the general election of 1722. The Marlboroughs were not popular in the borough: their association with Roman Catholicism, their control over troops stationed in or near St Albans, and the 'high-handed tactics' they employed in parliamentary and corporation politics all contributed to their unpopularity. This unpopularity was compounded in 1722, when a large number of honorary freemen were created in order to carry the election for the Tory candidates. This was done with the support of John Gape and the connivance of the mayor, William Carr, who by virtue of his office was also the returning officer for the borough.

When the election result was declared, the Tories William Clayton and William Gore each had 461 votes, and were elected, while the sitting MPs William Luckyn Grimston and Joshua Lomax had 325 and 258 respectively. However, in a petition the defeated candidates asserted that 192 'Foreigners' – honorary freemen – had voted for Clayton and 190 for Gore, as had various other unqualified voters, without whose votes Grimston and Lomax would have been elected. William Carr was criticised for his involvement in the enrolment of honorary freemen, especially as he had previously expressed his disapproval of

the practice, and sworn an oath not to engage in it. When a delegation of inhabitants, including Grimston himself, visited Carr after the election, Carr told them:

> I know what I have done is *wrong* and *unjust*; I am really *sorry* for it, and *ashamed* of it: nevertheless I *must go on* to make Foreigners Freemen, and poll them, *being under* the *Command* of a great Lady to do it. I am in hopes there will be a *Tory Parliament* that will bear me out: and she has promised to defend me, and bring me off if I am called to account ...[3]

The petition was withdrawn, and the result stood; as a result the participation of non-resident freemen remained a feature of parliamentary elections in St Albans until the Reform Act of 1832.

Ensuring the election of a candidate in St Albans was an expensive business – Sarah Churchill spent over £1,000 in 1722 – and, perhaps partly as a result, for much of the eighteenth century the two competing interests were willing to share the representation of the borough and to return one MP each. Only at by-elections. or when one interest attempted to return two MPs at a general election, as in 1722, did the borough became an ugly battleground. Sarah Churchill's own prickly personality was a cause of some unpleasantness – her personal dislike of William Luckyn Grimston resulted in a fractious campaign in 1734 after which she re-published an embarrassing play written by Grimston in his youth and which he had tried to suppress – but by the early 1740s she had given up on St Albans, and she died in 1744.[4]

[1] Ibid., pp. 86–7.

[2] Ibid., pp. 86–7, 210–11.

[3] *The Case of the Right Honourable William Lord Viscount Grimston and Joshua Lomax Esquire, Petitioners, against William Clayton and William Gore Esquires, Sitting Members* (1722): British Library, 748.c.6(2). Original emphases.

[4] Philip Carter, 'Grimston, William Luckyn, First Viscount Grimston': *Oxford Dictionary of National Biography*; Lansberry, 'Politics and Government', pp. 214–16.

The mid-eighteenth century was a period of some confusion in borough politics. In 1741 James West was elected, with support from the Grimstons and a large contingent of Dissenting votes: he supported the repeal of the Test Act (a statute of 1673 which required holders of civil and military office to take an oath of allegiance recognising the king as head of the Church of England, and to take the sacrament according to the practices of the established Church). In 1743, the Spencer candidate, Hans Stanley, defeated James Grimston (William's son) in a by-election, thanks to another large turnout of honorary freemen, which the mayor Joseph Handley had ensured: West, understandably, reacted badly to this. However, Handley soon transferred his support to West, and was followed by many of the honorary freemen, thus strengthening West's position. West remained MP for St Albans until 1768, when Handley switched sides again, taking the honorary freemen with him, and 'carefully nurtured' the out-of-town voters at a safe distance in London.[1] This improved the position of the Spencers in the politics of the borough, and West prudently found himself a safer seat elsewhere. By and large, after 1768, the Spencers and Grimstons were again willing and able to share the spoils of St Albans, and at the general election of 1784, managed to fight off a third interest, the Salisburys, who attempted without success to establish themselves in the borough.[2] In 1807 Earl Spencer abruptly abandoned both national politics and his interest in St Albans: he had made himself unpopular by supporting a bill to remove civil disabilities from Catholics, and as a result his candidate, Viscount Duncannon, came third in the election in St Albans. This caused Spencer immediately – and in Lansberry's view prematurely – to cut his ties with the borough.[3]

Although the Salisburys were seen off in the 1780s, in the next decade 'a permanent independent interest' was established in St Albans, which helped to break the Spencer-Grimston stranglehold, and in the longer term helped to ensure that St Albans would become particularly notorious for bribery and corruption (see box 9). In the wake of the St Albans food riots of 1795 and 1796,[4] Samuel Ferrand Waddington, a radical candidate, stood in the election of 1796. He stood on a platform of peace with France, lower taxes and support for manufacturing, and was supported, according to Lansberry, by 'the poorer classes' as well as notable local families such as the Kentishes.[5] Of course, most of the 'poorer classes' were not in a position to vote, but Waddington did manage to stir up resentment about the influence of the Spencers and Grimstons. Waddington lost the election – the Spencer candidate topped the poll with 378 votes, the Grimston man took 308 and Waddington came third with 208 – but he left behind an influential group of organised voters in St Albans. As Lansberry explains, this group 'was known as the "Independent Party" or the "Contest Party" or simply "The Party". Its existence threw doubt on the outcome of every election between 1802 and 1835.'[6] 'The Party' increased its strength after Spencer's withdrawal from the borough in 1807. Although it was not strong enough to return a candidate, it could affect the outcome of elections. Its main purpose appears to have been to ensure that as many elections as possible were contested, partly in order to maximise voters' gains from bribery. The strategy seems to have worked, because in 1832 the pro-Reform candidate H. G. Ward had to spend £2,500 on his election; he was elected second in the poll with 373 votes, which therefore cost some £6 14s. per vote.[7] The Reform

[1]   Lansberry, 'Whig Inheritance', pp. 49–50.
[2]   Lansberry, 'Politics and Government', pp. 237ff.
[3]   Ibid., p. 255.

[4]   See below, p. 203.
[5]   Lansberry, 'Politics and Government', pp. 243–4. Little is known of Waddington: see his brief entry by Stephen M. Lee, revised by E. I. Carlyle, in the *Oxford Dictionary of National Biography*.
[6]   Lansberry, 'Politics and Government', p. 246.
[7]   Ibid., p. 186; F. W. S. Craig, *British Parliamentary Election Results 1832–1885* (London: Macmillan and Co.,

This watercolour shows the declaration of the result in the borough of St Albans at the general election of 1835. It was painted by E.M. Brabant, probably the son of the mayor, Richard William Brabant, who is reading out the result. Even following the Reform Act of 1832, elections were colourful affairs, noted (especially in St Albans) for bribery and corruption. There was no secret ballot until 1872. In this election, E.H. Grimston (Tory) and H.G. Ward (Liberal) were elected, with 362 and 284 votes respectively, while Henry W. Beresford, a Conservative who was dubbed 'the poor man's friend' was defeated, gaining 237 votes. Even after the 1832 Reform Act, the total St Albans electorate numbered only 544.

Act of 1832, which Ward supported, disenfranchised the non-resident freemen, removing one source of corruption; however, it did not destroy 'The Party' in St Albans, and bribery remained widespread in the borough until St Albans itself was disenfranchised following the by-election of 1850 (see box 9).

1977), p. 261.

complained that the proceedings of the closed corporation were opaque and ill-understood: 'There is certainly a great deal of mystery and secrecy attached to the corporation affairs; and there are but very few who have any knowledge at all about them, although it would be reasonable to make, at least, all acquainted with them that are subject to their government.'[117] In general, Lansberry suggests that the inhabitants of St Albans 'showed an amused toleration of the corporation and its workings'.[118] It was increasingly bypassed in the provision of local services, and many other institutions did more to promote the well-being of the town. In 1835 the Municipal Corporations Act introduced popular elections to local government.

The parishes were a more open and democratic theatre of local government than the corporation, especially before legislation in 1818 and 1819 made it easier for the larger ratepayers in a parish to exercise more control. These statutes provided for the appointment of committees 'for the management of ... parochial concerns', and allowed wealthier ratepayers to cast multiple votes in the parish vestry, the governing body of the parish.[119] Arguably, eighteenth-century parishes were more effective in the provision of public services than municipal corporations: they were responsible for poor relief as well as for church matters, and as a result parochial budgets were often larger than those of corporations, especially as the power to levy rates was not universal among the latter.[120] As discussed in the last chapter, parishes had acquired greater responsibilities for the support of the poor after the Reformation;[121] and in 1723 the Workhouse Test Act permitted parishes to levy a rate to pay for the construction of a workhouse for the accommodation of the poor. The Abbey parish in St Albans had a workhouse even before this legislation, and by 1724 there were 20 adults and 14 children resident in it. According to a contemporaneous account, the adults, aged between 50 and 80, were 'employed in winding Cotton-Wick for the Tallow-Chandlers, at which they earn, one with another, about 2*d*. a Day; the Boys at making Horse-whips for Jockeys, &c. the Materials for which are found by a Sadler in the Neighbourhood; and the Girls at spinning both Linnen and Woollen'.[122] The regime was considerably more liberal than that which was later associated with the Victorian poor law, and which informs today's collective memories of workhouse life. Inmates at the St Albans workhouse ate meat on four days out of seven, and a barrel and a half of beer was consumed each week.[123] There was space for many more inmates:

> The House is an old Building, partly Brick, and partly Plaister, well repair'd for the purpose, and will accommodate 100 People: There is an Acre and an half of Ground belonging to it, and the whole cost the Town about £250 out of which they lett as much to a Gardener as yields £10 per Annum.[124]

The Abbey parish ... had a workhouse ... a barrel and a half of beer was consumed each week.

St Stephen's parish soon followed the Abbey parish's example:

> The Success of the Workhouse at St Alban's, has induced the Parish of
> St. Stephen's, within half a Mile of the Abbey Church, to agree upon the
> same Method as is used at St. Alban's, to employ their Poor; in order
> to which, the Vestry have already agreed to build a Brick-House, at the
> Charge of £120, adjoining to the Alms-house, which will receive all the
> Poor of the Parish; and 'tis hoped will accommodate them much better
> than now they live, as well as save Money to the Parish. We have paid
> four nine-peny Rates yearly, towards supporting the Poor there, and
> purpose to continue it, till the House, &c. are paid for, but then we hope
> to keep all our Poor for half what they used to cost.[125]

*There was
a complex
network of
parochial
charities for
the poor ...*

St Peter's parish workhouse opened in 1764, and St Michael's in the following
year.[126] The rural parish of Sandridge built a workhouse in 1777–78,[127] and
Redbourn followed in 1790. Sandridge workhouse cost the parish £128, and
the poor rate was temporarily increased to three shillings in the pound.[128] The
high costs of supporting the poor led to several parishes contracting out their
poor law services in the later eighteenth century.[129] By 1832, concerns about
the management of the Sandridge workhouse, the fabric of the buildings and
the behaviour of the inmates led to the parish borrowing a sum of almost £400
to carry out repairs and to support the large number of rural paupers for which
Sandridge had responsibility.[130] In a period when the total annual revenue of
the St Albans corporation was not much more than £500, this emphasises the
importance of parishes in local administration. It was especially important in
St Albans because of the high levels of pauperism in the town, which prevailed
in spite of the emergence of straw plaiting as an employment for women and
children. A higher proportion of the population was in workhouses than was
the case in neighbouring towns in the early nineteenth century, and local poor
rates were almost twice as high as those in Watford and Hertford.[131] Poverty
led to discontent: in the mid-1790s, in St Albans as in other towns, food riots
occurred, which centred on the market and involved the women who traded
poultry, eggs and plait. Local nervousness about these riots, intensified by the
political intervention of Samuel Ferrand Waddington in 1796 (see box 8), led
to the stationing of troops in the vicinity of the town.[132]

As in earlier periods, voluntary effort – by individuals and groups – was of
considerable importance in alleviating the problem of poverty and in providing
civic amenities in St Albans. There was a complex network of parochial
charities for the poor,[133] which caused widespread confusion, and generated
allegations of corruption. In the early eighteenth century, as we have seen,
the corporation's relationship with local charities was closely investigated by a
Commission on Charitable Uses.[134] Around twenty different bequests existed

The parish workhouse of St Peter's was built in 1764, following the successful construction of similar facilities in the Abbey parish and in St Stephen's. The small parish workhouses were replaced by the St Albans union workhouse in 1836–37.

PHOTOGRAPH: AUTHOR

for poor residents of the Abbey parish, while those for St Peter's were 'very numerous', although St Michael's and St Stephen's had rather fewer. By the early nineteenth century many of these bequests were not being managed in accordance with the wishes of those who had left them, and some investigation was being carried out at a local level in the parishes.[135] More generally, there was considerable scope for local philanthropy in this period, especially by those who wanted to gain politically from the borough. As we have seen, Earl Spencer filled some of the gaps in public service provision that were left by the corporation: he lent the corporation money, constructed a water pump, and provided various other amenities including a sedan chair for the ladies of St Albans.[136] This reflected a general tendency among towns like St Albans: Innes and Rogers remark that 'any (but especially small) parliamentary boroughs might benefit from the munificence of a current or would-be political patron, either in the form of cash gifts, for example to pay off corporate debts, or in the form of expenditure on public works'.[137] More voluntary institutional care was also being provided in the eighteenth century. For example, there was a private asylum, the 'Collegium Insanorum', which was run by a local doctor – Nathaniel Cotton – who also treated an outbreak of scarlet fever in St Albans in 1748.[138] In 1736 Sarah Churchill, the duchess of Marlborough, gave the Marlborough almshouses, on Hatfield Road, to the town. These housed 36 residents, 18 of each sex, and required them to live 'soberly, piously'.[139] In the late eighteenth and early nineteenth centuries the almshouses – also known as 'The Buildings' – were managed by the dowager countess Spencer, who died

RIGHT

The Marlborough
almshouses were
built by Sarah
Churchill, duchess
of Marlborough,
in 1736. They
addressed a
significant deficiency
in the charitable
landscape of St
Albans. Known as
'The Buildings',
they housed 36 poor
residents.

PHOTOGRAPH: AUTHOR

*The
inertia and
incompetence
of the
corporation
encouraged
would-be
improvers to
look to other
authorities ...*

in 1814. Solomon Shaw wrote warmly of 'her personal affectionate inquiries amongst them [the inhabitants of The Buildings] after their welfare, and her promptness to alleviate their various troubles and anxieties'.[140] The countess also supported educational charities, and taught in schools. She established the St Albans Female Friendly Society in 1802: this provided sickness and lying-in benefits for women, and pensions from the age of 60, in return for 'trifling' weekly payments of no more than 4*d*. It was managed by a 'committee of ladies'.[141] A similar society for men – the St Albans Benefit and Annuitant Society – was founded around 1810. Voluntary provision of education for children is explored further in box 7.

The statutory authority, or improvement commission, was another feature of the changing landscape of local government. The inertia and incompetence of the corporation encouraged would-be improvers to look to other authorities to provide urban improvements. Lansberry has written of 'the extraordinary growth of statutory authorities in England' in the century after 1750:[142] Acts of Parliament established new organs of local governance, with responsibility for specific areas of activity, and these bodies encroached on the powers of corporations and parishes. The St Albans and South Mimms Turnpike Trust, discussed above, was one example; others included a court of requests, established to allow for the recovery of small debts without recourse to more cumbersome legal processes.[143] Perhaps the best example is the Act of 1804 which appointed paving and lighting commissioners for St Albans, with wide powers: not only did the 125 commissioners oversee the pavements and lighting of the town, but they could also control the style in which new buildings were constructed, appoint watchmen, fine residents for failing to sweep the pavements, and levy a rate of up to 1s. 6d. in the pound on all householders who paid the poor rate. If the revenue from this rate was insufficient, they were allowed to borrow up to £4,000.[144] The new organs of local administration ensured that, in Lansberry's words, 'by the 19th century the corporation's deliberations were largely irrelevant to the government of the town'.[145] Indeed, the construction of the new town hall on St Peter's Street in 1831, at a cost of over £12,000, was itself carried out by commissioners under the authority of an Act of Parliament.

'the scene of the most profligate conduct on the part of women of the lowest description ...'

By the early years of the nineteenth century, St Albans was a fairly typical town of its size. It was large enough to be represented in Parliament – and to retain its right to return two MPs after the Reform Act of 1832 – but small enough to be passed through in just a few minutes, especially by vehicles using the new roads. Wealth and poverty lived close together. Shaw declared that St Albans was 'generally regarded as a healthy and respectable town'.[146] He reported that, to the traveller approaching St Albans from the new London road, the town 'bespeaks much respectability from the general appearance of the houses and shops' along the High Street; but on the other hand,

That part of the town in which the market-place is situated, is very confined, and, from thence to the bottom of St Peter's-street, are several very mean impoverished houses, with all the concomitants of poverty, filth and its nuisances, which a little public spirit would effect the removal of; and thereby render that part of the town much more healthy and respectable.[147]

Some of the lanes and passages in the town were 'but little calculated ... to reflect much credit upon those whose duty it is to keep them neat and clean'.[148] The behaviour of some of the poorer residents gave cause for concern: in 1833 the watchmen were put on duty at an earlier hour than usual because of what the *County Press* called 'the general complaint of the inhabitants of St Albans that the principle streets of that town, particularly the High Street, [have] become the scene of the most profligate conduct on the part of women of the lowest description'.[149] The social life of the town was 'very prescribed', which Shaw thought could be blamed on 'party – the bane of all neighbouring

Charles Marshall
(1806–90) drew
the scene on which
this engraving by
J. Henshall was
based. It dates
from the mid-
1830s, soon after
the construction
of the new town
hall in 1831–32.
The perspective is
foreshortened: the
Gables (number 13,
Market Place) and
the abbey church
look closer than they
really are. The town
hall was built by the
architect George
Smith.

© ST ALBANS MUSEUMS

fellowship' and on religious divisions.[150] However, there were some enjoyable social occasions. The Michaelmas fair, although its economic importance may have declined, was 'the resort of all the gaiety of the country for many miles round', hosting a popular travelling theatre, among other entertainments.[151] Horse racing was also a widely patronised local entertainment: the Chequers, one of the inns noted by Shaw and in the *Universal British Directory*, was renamed the Turf in 1820 and offered accommodation and a high standard of food, drink and comfort to sportsmen. It was, reputedly, following a dinner at the Turf that the St Albans steeplechase was conceived: this race was run for the first time on Nomansland Common, near Wheathampstead, in 1830. Other popular sporting events included shooting and prize-fighting, both at the same site.[152] Various civic events and rituals were enjoyed by many residents: for example, the annual celebrations of the king's birthday, the election and swearing-in of the mayor and the fairs and festivals of the town including St Alban's Day. Above all, inhabitants of St Albans could buy good food, drink and consumer goods more cheaply than in London. In Shaw's words,

> perhaps better butcher's meat is not to be purchased in any market in the kingdom; bread is always half an assize under that of London, and there are two common breweries, and also two very respectable inns, that brew

excellent home-brewed ale. Nor are the articles of grocery, drapery, &c. less excellent in their kind, or to be purchased on more moderate terms by consumers any where.[153]

Children could be educated at a number of schools (see box 7); there was reasonable charitable and parochial provision for the poor; and although the affairs of the civic leadership were subject to criticism from the inhabitants, St Albans was probably at least as pleasant as other towns that it resembled in size and function. Its economy remained relatively healthy, and although its social and cultural life may have been fairly restricted, London was only a short journey away. Although by no means all the inhabitants of St Albans shared the fruits of its economic success, and although extreme poverty was the lot of many, both in the town and in the surrounding countryside, the growth of the straw industry was ushering in a period of prosperity, during which the expansion of the town would accelerate significantly.

This engraving, based on a painting by James Pollard (1792–1867), shows the runners and riders in the St Albans steeplechase in 1832, leaving the Turf Hotel (known as the Chequers until 1820). The steeplechase itself took place on Nomansland Common.

Victorian and Edwardian St Albans

T HE STEADY BUT ACCELERATING GROWTH in the population of
St Albans in the eighteenth and early nineteenth centuries continued
after the 1830s. In common with most other towns and cities in Britain, St
Albans expanded considerably in the nineteenth century. The proportion of
the population of Britain living in urban areas expanded from just over 50 per
cent in 1851 to 77 per cent in 1901. Nineteenth-century urbanisation is usually
associated with the industrial revolution:[1] the cotton towns of Lancashire,
railway towns such as Crewe and Swindon, and above all with London and
the other major cities. However, the spectacular growth of these urban areas,
and the environmental and social problems that were associated with it, should
not obscure the considerable expansion of older, small towns such as St Albans,
which can be traced in the decennial census, first taken in 1801. The vitality
of the local economy, and associated urban expansion, has been questioned
by Asa Briggs, who has suggested that the growth of Victorian St Albans
was 'sleepy'.[2] Briggs's population figures are based on the flawed data in the
Victoria County History for Hertfordshire (see appendix). According to Briggs,
St Albans was 'off the map of the national economy'; he asserts that 'there was
never a great influx of young people into St Albans, never a great building
boom'.[3] Moreover, 'there was always very little industry – printing, there at the
beginning of the [nineteenth] century; silk mills which went; and straw plait ...
and brewing, two industries more closely related to domestic agriculture than
to carboniferous capitalism'.[4] This caricature of St Albans is flawed: there was
still a silk mill at the start of the twentieth century; the printing industry in the
city in the early twentieth century was on a completely different scale from its
counterpart a century earlier; and a whole range of new industries was located
in St Albans by 1914. With these new industries came new housing, bringing
in turn employment opportunities in the construction sector. Whereas Briggs
sees St Albans as experiencing particularly slow growth in the decade after 1871
– a flawed conclusion, as table 7.1 demonstrates – local historian James Corbett

characterises the last three decades of the nineteenth century as a time when 'St Albans underwent an enlargement faster and greater than for any similar length of time throughout the whole of its previous history'.[5]

Table 7.1   *The population of St Albans, 1801–1911*

Year	Census registration district of St Albans		Borough of St Albans	
	Population	growth (%)	Population	growth (%)
1801	9,834		3,038	
1811	11,214	14.0	3,653	20.2
1821	14,114	25.9	4,472	22.4
1831	15,833	12.2	4,772	6.7
1841	17,048	7.7	6,497	36.1*
1851	18,004	5.6	7,000	7.7
1861	18,926	5.1	7,675	9.6
1871	21,079	11.4	8,298	8.1
1881	23,296	10.5	10,931	31.7†
1891	26,872	15.4	12,898	18.0
1901	33,008	22.8	16,019	24.2
1911	43,768	32.6	18,133	13.2

* Boundaries extended 1835. See appendix for a detailed discussion of the figures for 1841.

† Boundaries extended 1879.

Census registration district: this included the town/city and a large surrounding area, embracing Harpenden, Redbourn, Sandridge, Wheathampstead and other places. It was co-extensive with the St Albans poor law union, created in 1835 under the terms of the Poor Law Amendment Act of 1834.

Borough of St Albans: for the period 1801–31 the figures are for the 'ancient' borough, whose boundaries dated to the medieval period. Its area was 320 acres. In 1835 the municipal borough was created, covering a larger area: 434 acres. The boundaries were significantly extended in 1879, after which the municipal borough covered 997 acres. The rates of growth shown for the decennia 1831–41 and 1871–81 therefore exaggerate the growth of population, although one reason for the extension of the boundaries in 1879 was the growth of the urban population beyond the area of the existing municipal borough.

See appendix for the sources used in compiling this table.

Table 7.1 shows the population of the borough of St Albans, the boundaries of which were extended in 1835 and 1879, and the census registration district, which included a substantial rural hinterland. Despite – or perhaps because of – its proximity to London, Hertfordshire was still a very rural county in the mid-nineteenth century: of 44 counties listed in the census report in 1851, Hertfordshire was the fifth most rural, with only 24 per cent of its population resident in towns.[6] St Albans was the largest town in Hertfordshire; the second largest was the county town of Hertford. In 1851 the borough of St Albans contained exactly 7,000 inhabitants, representing a substantial growth from previous years. The population expanded particularly quickly between 1831 and 1841, although this partly reflected an extension of the borough boundary in 1835. The population of the registration district was also growing, reaching 18,004 in 1851. As employment in straw plaiting had increased, some nearby villages also grew significantly: Redbourn had over 2,000 inhabitants in 1851 and Harpenden nearly as many. In the decade after 1851, the population of the municipal borough of St Albans increased by 9.6 per cent, and in the period 1861–71 it grew by 8.1 per cent. Boosted by another extension of the boundaries in 1879, the growth of population was 31.7 per cent in the decade 1871–81; and in the following three decades the growth rate was 18.0 per cent, 24.2 per cent and 13.2 per cent. It is difficult to see how this can be described as 'sleepy'. Although St Albans did not match the growth rates of some large industrial towns and major conurbations, it experienced steady and continuous growth throughout the nineteenth century, despite the decline of its largest industry – straw plaiting – in the second half of the century. This chapter examines the economic restructuring of St Albans, and the growth of new industries and new areas of housing development, in the Victorian and Edwardian period. It also discusses the growth of local government and public utilities and institutions, and the creation of an active culture of civic engagement and ritual, in which St Albans resembled many other towns of the period. Boxes 9 and 10 examine the political life of the borough and the establishment of the diocese of St Albans, two areas in which the experience of St Albans differed from those of other towns. St Albans became a city in 1877: this chapter uses 'town' when discussing the period before this, and 'city' for the period after 1877.

The economy of St Albans and its region was dominated by straw in the mid-nineteenth century. The last chapter examined the growth of the straw industry in the eighteenth and early nineteenth centuries. The report of the census of 1841 emphasises to what extent the straw trades were concentrated in Hertfordshire and a group of adjacent counties: in Hertfordshire there were 4,415 straw plaiters, in Bedfordshire 1,607, in Essex 431 (a number which would grow rapidly over the next decade) and in Buckinghamshire 1,181.[7] By contrast, the numbers in other counties were negligible, except for small pockets in Cornwall, Somerset and Lancashire. In the whole county of Oxfordshire, there were only 12 straw-plaiters; in Cambridgeshire, which bordered Hertfordshire, there were 14; and in Huntingdonshire there were just two.[8] Straw is a good example of regional specialisation in this period, and it was a distinctive feature of this part of Britain. Other industries flourished as a result of straw: it has been suggested that the demand for hat trimmings can explain St Albans's silk weaving industry (there was also a silk mill at Redbourn); and by the middle of the nineteenth century St Albans had a significant number of workers who made Brazilian hats, woven from imported palm leaves, an industry 'that can only have been inspired by the straw hat trade of the area'.[9] Despite the designation 'Brazilian', the palm leaves came mostly from Cuba. They were split into strips in the same way as straw. This industry was short-lived in St Albans, and by the early twentieth century was mostly carried on in France, although there were some attempts to reintroduce it to St Albans.[10]

Straw was an industry that employed mostly women; and as a result of these opportunities the population of St Albans and its surrounding villages exhibited a significant numerical superiority of females over males. In the St Albans census registration district in 1851, females made up 52.2 per cent of the population, a figure which reached 54.4 per cent in the urban parishes. To put it another way, whereas the sex ratio for England and Wales (the number of males per 100 females) was 96 and for Hertfordshire 99, for the St Albans registration district it was 91, and for the borough itself it was as low as 84 (see table 7.2).[11]

... the straw trades were concentrated in Hertfordshire and a group of adjacent counties ...

Table 7.2   *Sex ratios in St Albans (males per 100 females)*

Year	Census registration district	Borough of St Albans	England and Wales
1801	91	74	92
1811	86	81	92
1821	95	86	95
1831	95	89	95
1841	89	81	96
1851	91	84	96
1861	87	78	95
1871	88	78	95
1881	89	84	95
1891	90	84	94
1901	86	82	94
1911	85	81	94

Source: see appendix. Figures are given to the nearest whole number.

It seems clear that, in the words of the historian Nigel Goose, the availability of straw-plaiting and hat-making work for women 'served both to attract them into the region from further to the north and east of the county and to discourage those born here from moving away'.[12] Women took full advantage of the availability of employment. In 1851, some 46.7 per cent of the total female population of the St Albans registration district was in work;[13] a figure that reached 63 per cent for women aged 15 and over. In some parishes it was even higher: for example, in Harpenden 61.6 per cent of all females were in work, in Redbourn 55.3 per cent and in the urban part of St Michael's parish 50.3 per cent.

The silk mill at the bottom of Abbey Mill Lane was one of the largest employers of labour in St Albans in the late eighteenth and early nineteenth centuries. Even at the start of the twentieth century, more than 100 people, mostly women, worked in the mill. The mill closed in 1938, and the buildings have now been converted into housing.

PHOTOGRAPH: AUTHOR

In the parishes where straw was a less predominant employer – especially Sandridge and Wheathampstead – the female participation rates were lower.[14] The female participation rates recorded in the St Albans registration district were higher than in the Staffordshire Potteries, and in the cotton towns of Lancashire, which are better known known as centres of female employment during the industrial revolution.[15] Although later in the nineteenth century levels of employment in straw plaiting fell, the sex ratio of St Albans remained very low, standing at 82 in 1901 and 81 in 1911 for the municipal borough and 86 and 85 for the registration district (see table 7.2). These figures partly reflected levels of employment in domestic service, which are discussed in more detail below.

The work of women and children in straw plaiting occasioned considerable disquiet among observers. Victorian opinion was decidely opposed to the employment of women and children in many areas of the economy: legislation in the 1830s and 1840s restricted the employment of children in factories, and a campaign in the 1850s and 1860s focused on the immorality associated with women's and children's work in agriculture. Many of those who complained were clergymen, concerned that women's work fostered immoral behaviour, illegitimacy, and poor housekeeping and child-rearing practices. Echoing many of these complaints, one clerical observer of the straw industry (somewhat repetitiously) declared that plaiting

> is the certain ruin of the female character; they become bold, impudent, scandalmongers, hardened against religion, careless of their homes and children, most untidy, given to drink, caorseminded, debased, depravers of any virtuous girls who work with them, having no pride in their home or their children, and few home feelings. Their children are ragged and

quite untaught, and a dirty home often drives the husband to the public house.[16]

The diarist Arthur Munby, writing in 1863, remarked that 'the St Albans young women, who are all straw plaiters, have a very bad reputation'.[17] Although not all observers concurred – some thought plaiting less conducive to immorality than field work, for example, and certainly more remunerative and therefore useful than work in agriculture or the declining local lace industry – there was a widespread concern for the morality of straw plaiters. A more sober historical assessment would see plaiting as a 'mixed blessing': for example, there is no evidence that illegitimacy was much higher in plaiting communities than elsewhere;[18] but it was certainly the case that long hours spent plaiting, and the limited educational opportunities available in the plait schools, combined with the extreme youth of many straw-plaiters – there is evidence of children plaiting from the age of three[19] – made the benefits of plaiting debatable. It may, on the other hand, have been better for young girls than working in the fields or entering domestic service.[20]

One aspect of the straw industry that elicited almost universal condemnation was its impact on the education of the young. The environment in the plait schools, which survived well into the nineteenth century, was 'unbelievably squalid': overcrowding and illness were common. Young girls suffered from breathing difficulties and mouth ulcers caused by their occupation, and the schools were poorly regulated. The Workshops Act of 1867 applied to all premises employing fifty or fewer people that were not covered by factory legislation, but there was some doubt as to whether it applied to plait schools,

These decorated carts, outside St Albans Abbey station in 1908, were celebrating the 70th anniversary of the London and Birmingham Railway, which later became part of the London and North Western Railway. The line from Watford Junction to St Albans Abbey, on which trains still run, was a branch line of the London and North Western.

SCIENCE AND SOCIETY
PICTURE LIBRARY

and in any case it was not effectively enforced.[21] Apart from plaiting, little else was taught in the schools: Edwin Grey, from Harpenden, remembered that he 'never knew ... any of these plaiting schools where writing or arithmetic was taught, probably for the same reason that these old ladies [who taught in the schools] knew nothing of it themselves'.[22] Many children probably worked both at plaiting and at some other trade: 'Lucy Luck', born in 1848, later recalled that, at the age of nine, she had worked in a silk mill in Tring by day and was then expected to produce five yards of straw plait in the evening.[23] In a period when the educational opportunities available to all children, and especially girls, were very limited, straw-plaiters were particularly disadvantaged.

... the first ceremonial train was decorated with straw plait ...

The availability of employment in straw plaiting decreased sharply from the early 1870s, when the availability of cheap imported plait from China and Japan began to affect the industry. The situation for the plaiting communities in the countryside around St Albans was bleak. The number of plaiters in Hertfordshire declined from a peak of 12,089 in 1871 to 7,543 in 1881, 3,133 in 1891 and just 681 (out of a total in the four plaiting counties of 1,339) in 1901.[24] The earnings that could be made from plaiting fell: only the very poorest women in the rural communities of Hertfordshire would take plaiting work by the beginning of the twentieth century, and the term 'plaiter' became synonymous with 'skivvy' in some people's folk memories.[25] Nevertheless, the manufacture of hats, using imported plait, survived in the city of St Albans, although the numbers employed were relatively small.

The decline of straw meant that the economy of St Albans needed to diversify in the last third of the nineteenth century. This was an experience common to many other small towns in Britain, although not all were successful. As one urban historian has explained, 'manufacturing towns whose industry was not modernised declined ... by the end of the nineteenth century if a small town could not adapt to change it faced decline'.[26] Examples of decline include wool towns such as Diss in Norfolk, and agricultural small towns such as Swaffham in Norfolk and Bungay in Suffolk, and Marlborough in Wiltshire; St Albans did not share their fate. In the period 1870–1914, St Albans experienced a growing population and an influx of new industries, as well as acquiring a new significance as a religious and cultural centre.

The single most significant industrial development in St Albans was the coming of the railway, which arrived somewhat later than in some other towns. St Albans already enjoyed relatively good road links with London, and the direct Midland Railway link to the capital was the third and last of the town's railways. The first station in St Albans, the Abbey Station, at the end of a branch line to Watford Junction operated by the London and North Western Railway, opened in 1858. This was followed by a Great Northern Railway branch line to Hatfield in 1865, and then the Midland Railway station – the City Station – in 1868. When the City Station was opened, the first ceremonial train was decorated with straw plait, to symbolise the still dominant industry of the town and its surrounding area.[27] The railway brought employment to the town, and encouraged the development of other industries in areas close to the stations. As early as 1872, the official report of the 1871 census explained that, 'by the opening of the Midland Railway, St Albans now possesses stations connected with three of the great railways of the country, and houses are in great demand, especially in the hamlet of Tittenhanger, which contains two of the railway stations'.[28] (By Tittenhanger the authors of the report meant the area containing the Midland and Great Northern stations; this comment emphasises the limited geographical extent of the town of St Albans.) Encouraged by the railway and other factors, a range of small industrial concerns came to St Albans in the second half of the nineteenth century, many in the new areas of Fleetville and the Camp; as one of the contributors to the *Victoria County History* of Hertfordshire explained in the early twentieth century, recent years had seen 'the creation … of a factory industry, distributed among various trades, and drawn to the county by cheaper labour and greater opportunities of expansion than crowded cities can afford'.[29] Factories were not the only new arrivals. Perhaps the most distinctive newcomer was Sander's orchid nursery, established

LEFT

A bridge carrying the Midland Railway line, opened in 1868, crossed the Great Northern branch line, opened three years earlier. The Great Northern line, which closed in 1964, is now a public footpath, and National Cycle Network Route number 61.

PHOTOGRAPH: AUTHOR

In Allotment or Garden

Ryders' SEEDS score every time!

To grow bigger and better Vegetable Crops and more beautiful Flowers sow RYDERS'— the Seeds for results!
RYDER & SON (1920) LTD., ST. ALBANS

on Camp Road in 1886, which continued in operation until the Second World War. Frederick Sander, from Bremen in Germany, took over Josling's seed business in George Street in 1876, and expanded onto land behind the premises before buying a larger site at the Camp in 1882.[30] The scale of operations at the Camp was impressive. In March 1884, the *Gardener's Chronicle* reported:

> Where the spread of this extraordinary Orchid establishment will end it is impossible to say, so fast do the houses range themselves up one after the other. Already twelve fine structures are up, having an aggregate length of nearly 3,000 feet and varying in width from 14 feet to 31 feet … Such a vast establishment, backed by the resources and great facilities which Messrs Frederick Sander and Company possess for importing good and new things, cannot fail to assist in giving stability to the trade in the future … [31]

Despite this endorsement, Sander's experienced almost continual difficulties: the company had to contend with high fuel and labour costs, and was 'always on the verge of insolvency'.[32] Sander was a notoriously unenlightened employer, who demanded long working hours – 6 a.m. to 6 p.m. 'with minimal breaks for meals'[33] – and paid very low wages. According to his biographer, 'the fact that the men were … miserably poor and not far above subsistence level were no concern of his … his views on labour could be very harsh and rigid indeed.'[34]

An employer with a better reputation among his employees was Samuel Ryder, best known as the founder of golf's Ryder Cup. A seed merchant whose family ran a market garden business in Lancashire, Ryder established a mail-order seed company in St Albans in the mid-1890s, beginning above a hatter's shop on the High Street. Ryder marketed his wares under the slogan 'All seeds in penny packets from orchids to mustard and cress', hoping to profit from the growing hobby of gardening, which was popular on the new housing estates of St Albans, and elsewhere.[35] The low cost of Ryder's products meant that the business did not really compete with Sander's, which aimed at the top end of the market, and Ryder's successes meant a series of moves, to Lower Dagnall Street in 1897, Upper Dagnall Street in 1902, and finally to a large site of some 50,000 square feet on Holywell Hill in 1903. Whereas Sander's employed mostly men, Ryder's employees, some 80 or 90 of them by 1906, were mainly female.[36] Further extensions to the premises, and the construction of new office buildings, took place in 1910 and 1911. According to his reverential biographer, Ryder's 'generosity and ingenuity left gardens transformed … and

continued on page 224

BELOW
The Fleet Works was the home of Smith's Printing Agency from 1898 until 1923, and then Howard Grubb and Sons, astronomical instrument makers. In 1926 the works were taken over by the company that became Ballito, and turned over to the production of silk stockings. The factory closed in 1967, and Morrison's supermarket now stands on the site. This postcard dates from *c*.1910.

REPRODUCED BY KIND PERMISSION OF ST ALBANS CENTRAL LIBRARY

SMITHS PRINTING AGENCY, FLEETVILLE.

A s DISCUSSED in box 8 (pages 197–201), St Albans was known for bribery and corruption in parliamentary elections in the eighteenth and early nineteenth centuries, and this reputation persisted, with good reason, even after the Reform Act of 1832. The size of the St Albans electorate was not greatly affected by the Act, which gave the vote to male householders in the borough (including non-freemen) whose properties were assessed at £10 or more, but

Local artist John Henry Buckingham (1800–81) depicts the election as mayor, for an unprecedented third successive year, of W. Balcombe Simpson in November 1862. Simpson was a solicitor: a 'smart polished solicitor', according to this cartoon. The 'very high and indignant' Alderman R.G. Lowe, who opposed Simpson's re-election at this meeting, felt that the mayor's profession conflicted with his duties as presiding magistrate of St Albans. In the cartoon, Simpson is standing to address the council, and to his right sits councillor Joseph Russell ('little Joey Bustle'), who proposed his re-election. Opposite Simpson sits councillor Thomas Bowman: Buckingham felt that Simpson's re-election had been fixed behind the scenes by Bowman and himself.

This cartoon by John Henry Buckingham depicts the
proceedings of the special commission of inquiry into
bribery at the St Albans by-election of 1850. Meeting in
the town hall, the commission heard evidence of corrupt
practices on behalf of the Liberal candidate Jacob Bell, and
as a result the town was disenfranchised.

disenfranchised the non-resident freemen, as a
result of which the number of voters remained
steady at around 550.[1] St Albans continued to
elect two MPs; and in the general elections of
1835, 1837, 1841 and 1847 one Conservative and
one Liberal were elected. Bribery – encouraged
by 'The Party' (see box 8) – remained rife: for
example, petitions were submitted against the
results of by-elections in 1841 and 1846.[2] The local
historian James Corbett attributes the proneness
of St Albans to bribery and corruption to its
nearness to London: 'seats within easy reach of
Westminster were proving attractive to wealthy
candidates prepared to pay extravagantly for the
privilege of proximity'.[3] At municipal elections,
too, there was evidence of corruption: following
the elections of 1846, legal proceedings following
an incorrect declaration resulted in the outcome
of one contest being reversed.[4] St Albans was
known as a borough where elections could be

[1] Lansberry, 'Politics and Government', p. 260.
According to F. W. S. Craig, *British Parliamentary Election
Results 1832–1885* (London: Macmillan and Co., 1977), p.
261, there were 657 electors in 1832 and 544 in 1835.

[2] Craig, *British Parliamentary Election Results 1832–
1885*, p. 261.
[3] Corbett, *History of St Albans*, p. 94.
[4] Ibid., pp. 91–2.

bought; and this was dramatically proved at a by-election in 1850, fought between Jacob Bell and Robert Carden.[1]

Jacob Bell (1810–59) was the first editor of the *Pharmaceutical Journal* and a founding member of the Royal Pharmaceutical Society. He ran a pharmacy business with Thomas Hyde Hills, who was to serve as his election agent. Bell was brought up as a Quaker, and shared the Liberal politics that were closely associated with religious Nonconformity in Victorian England. Bell had long campaigned for a Pharmacy Act, which it was hoped would regulate the pharmaceutical profession and restrict its practice to those who were registered and had passed professional examinations. To promote this reform, Bell had decided to stand for Parliament, and was selected to fight the vacant seat of St Albans following the death of the sitting Liberal MP Alexander Raphael in 1850. As the borough was solidly Conservative in municipal politics, and the last by-election, in 1846, had resulted in a Conservative victory by 264 votes to 149, it was clear that Bell faced a difficult campaign.

Bell's Conservative opponent in the by-election was Alderman Sir Robert Carden (1801–88), a London banker and stockbroker. Carden had recently been chosen, unopposed, as alderman for the Dowgate ward of the City of London. Both candidates would have been aware that St Albans was a borough noted for corruption and bribery, and Carden stood on an explicitly anti-bribery programme under the slogan 'purity of election'. In the by-election, held on Christmas Eve 1850, Bell defeated Carden by 276 votes to 147. Almost immediately, allegations of bribery by Bell's supporters were aired, and *The Times* reprinted an address signed by 10 members of the 16-man corporation of St Albans, which was presented to Carden. The address thanked him for his insistence on 'purity of election', and

called for the injustices of the by-election to be addressed and overturned.[2]

As a result of these complaints, a select committee of the House of Commons was appointed to investigate the events at the by-election. This committee met with obstructiveness in the form of the refusal of some witnesses to answer questions, while others were 'clandestinely carried away'. As a result, the serjeant-at-arms, Lord Charles Russell, was forced to travel to France to ascertain the whereabouts of witnesses who had absconded; some were in Boulogne and at least one in Paris by May 1851. One of the witnesses, George Sealey Waggett, was given a copy of the writ of the speaker of House of Commons summoning him to attend the committee, but he sarcastically told the police inspector who accompanied Russell that 'he understood the Speaker's warrant was of no avail at Boulogne', and that he intended to travel further into 'the interior of France'.[3] Two other witnesses – James Skegg and Thomas Burchmore – were approached by Russell on the beach, but, rather predictably, declined to talk to him. The result of this failed inquiry was that the select committee, although able to draw inferences from the behaviour of some its witnesses, could find no evidence that any of Bell's votes had been given in return for bribes, nor that Bell had played any part in removing the potential witnesses to France.[4] However, the select committee recommended the appointment of a special commission of inquiry, which came to a more definite conclusion.

The commission of inquiry found clear evidence of bribery of voters by Bell's supporters. It emerged that in November 1850 Bell had spoken to two men who had suggested that it would cost him between £2,000 and £2,500 to fight the election at St Albans. Bell knew about

[1] Peter M. Claus, 'Carden, Sir Robert Walter, first baronet (1801–1888)', and Juanita Burnby, 'Bell, Jacob (1810–1859)', *Oxford Dictionary of National Biography*.

[2] *The Times*, 1 January 1851.
[3] *The Times*, 13 June 1851; reprinting a letter from Russell dated 19 May 1851.
[4] *The Times*, 6 November 1851; *Pharmaceutical Journal*, vol. 212 (1974), p. 175.

St Albans's reputation and mentioned it, but the men told him that no bribery would take place. At subsequent meetings with various agents Bell was 'particular' on three matters: 'First, there should be no bribery; secondly, no treating; and thirdly no intimidation.'[1] Bell's election agent promised that these conditions would be adhered to, and Bell agreed to stand. The money required for election 'expenses' was advanced by Bell's business partner Hills, who, according to the commission's report, deliberately obscured the issue of how he had raised the money, in order to frustrate any subsequent inquiry. Hills conveyed the money in separate instalments of £500 in gold sovereigns, in a packet carried by a man using a false name. The money, of course, was used by Bell's agent in St Albans to bribe voters, usually with the sum of £5 each. Although Hills insisted that Bell was unaware of the bribery, it was clear to the commission that this explanation was implausible, especially given Bell's known belief that all elections in Britain were corrupt, and given the particular and long-standing notoriety of St Albans. Embarrassingly for Bell's opponent, the commission also found that some of Carden's election expenses had been used to bribe voters, although in Carden's case the commission was satisfied that the 'purity of election' candidate had no knowledge of the bribery. Bell later admitted, in a letter to a friend, that he knew what was being done in his name in St Albans, and that he wanted to withdraw:

I am aware that I made a mistake in going to St Albans. I found this out when it was too late to retract. I have never from that time had any opportunity of doing so for I was like a person who has taken his seat on a train and is unable to stop it.[2]

The verdict of *The Times* on Bell's conduct was unforgiving:

Mr Bell terms himself 'the victim of a system'. We should have rather looked upon him as the peck of the fancy. St Albans has done a good deal for many people but for none so much as for him. The electors not only placed him at the top of the poll, but they defied all the efforts of Parliament to elucidate the bargain. He paid his money and he became their choice. He was asked for £2,500 and he purchased it.[3]

More important than the outcome of this single by-election, however, was the official confirmation that bribery and corruption were endemic in St Albans, and that as many as 200 or 300 voters, from an electoral roll of 483,[4] were in the pay of one of the Liberal agents in the borough.[5]

Bell's election was declared invalid – although not before a Pharmacy Act had been passed, as Bell and the Pharmaceutical Society wanted – and St Albans was disenfranchised for a period of 60 years by an Act passed in 1852. Its voters were incorporated into the Hertfordshire county constituency. The same had happened in the case of Sudbury, which was disenfranchised for similar reasons in 1844 and incorporated into the Suffolk county constituency.[6] Some commentators thought the decision harsh, seeing the two boroughs as scapegoats for a more widespread absuses of the system that occurred in many, if not most, boroughs.[7] Others thought that it highlighted

[1] *Pharmaceutical Journal*, vol. 212 (1974), pp. 175–6. Most of the account below is based on this summary of the commission's report.

[2] Quoted in ibid., p. 177.

[3] *The Times*, 14 November 1851.

[4] Craig, *British Parliamentary Election Results 1832– 1885*, p. 261. *The Times*, 6 November 1851, suggested that the roll was 530 or 540.

[5] *The Times*, 6 November 1851.

[6] Craig, *British Parliamentary Election Results 1832– 1885*, p. 294.

[7] *The Times*, 6 November 1851, dismissed this argument in an editorial: 'No doubt bribery is more prevalent than it should be, but the bribery now before the Court is something quite unique. It is not simply that candidates spent money at St Albans, or that electors got the benefit

wider problems in Britain's political representation. The prominent Radical campaigner Richard Cobden, speaking at Bradford in January 1851, told his audience: 'Take, for instance, the West Riding of Yorkshire, which returns two members. It contains ... a million and a half of people. I have the honour to sit for this Riding, yet I am outvoted by the member who sits for a small corrupt borough like St Albans, who gets into Parliament by bribery and corruption.'[1] In St Albans, feelings were mixed. One observer suggested that 'the disfranchisement was a source of satisfaction rather than of regret to the inhabitants who had kept aloof from the corrupt practices which prevailed, and even many of those who had not kept aloof from them were glad to be quit of them forever, though at the cost of disfranchisement'.[2]

The corrupt practices highlighted by the St Albans case were restricted (though certainly not eliminated) by the introduction of the secret ballot at elections in 1872 and the Corrupt Practices Act of 1883, which limited election spending and prohibited specific kinds of bribery such as the provision of free food and drink for voters. Two years after the passage of the Corrupt Practices Act, as part of the reformed distribution of parliamentary seats in 1885, St Albans regained its MP, 33 years into its original 60-year period of disenfranchisement. The redistribution of 1885 changed the old system of separate borough and county representation, and the municipal borough of St Albans became part of a 'grotesquely enlarged' constituency, known as the Mid-Herts or St Albans division, which elected just one MP.[3] By this time, following the Reform Acts of 1867 and 1884, electorates in both urban and rural districts had been substantially increased: the St Albans/Mid-Herts electoral roll in 1885 numbered 8,741. The reform of 1885 ushered in an age of Conservative dominance of parliamentary representation of St Albans. At the general election of 1885, Viscount Grimston won the new seat for the Conservatives by 4,108 votes to his Liberal opponent John Coles's 3,037, and the Liberals did not bother to contest the seat in 1886. In 1892, in a three-cornered contest featuring an 'Independent Conservative', who won 20.9% of the vote, the Tory candidate, the prominent businessman and banker Vicary Gibbs, was elected with 3,417 votes, 45.1% of the total cast, and a majority of 844. He was re-elected unopposed in the general elections of 1895 and 1900, both of which returned Conservative governments.[4] The only interruption to the Conservative dominance of the seat came in 1904, when Gibbs was forced to seek re-election, because the business he ran with his brother Alan (who was also an MP) had taken a contract with the Commissioners of the Admiralty.[5] In a tightly fought contest, marred by violence and rowdiness at the candidates' meetings, the Liberal J. Bamford Slack was narrowly elected by 4,757 votes to 4,625.[6] The Liberal victory was celebrated with a torchlight procession; and the momentum was sustained in the following year when the Liberal party took control of the city council, with Samuel Ryder becoming mayor.[7] However, despite the landslide Liberal victory in the general election of 1906, Slack lost the St Albans seat to the Conservative Hildred Carlile, by a margin of 552 votes. From then until 1945, St Albans always elected a Conservative MP.

of the outlay, but that every election on every occasion was always carried on wholly and solely by purchase, and that the seat for the borough was as absolutely a subject of bargain and sale as a place in a railway carriage.'
[1]   *The Times*, 29 January 1851.
[2]   Mason, *Gibbs' Illustrated Handbook to St Albans*, p. 41.
[3]   Corbett, *Secret City*, p. 42.

[4]   F. W. S. Craig, *British Parliamentary Election Results 1885–1918* (London: Macmillan and Co., 1974), p. 297; see also Cox, *St Albans News of 1889*, pp. 22–3.
[5]   P. W. Hammond, 'Gibbs, Vicary (1853–1932)', *Oxford Dictionary of National Biography*.
[6]   Craig, *British Parliamentary Election Results 1885–1918*, p. 297.
[7]   Fry, *Samuel Ryder*, pp. 44–6.

St Albans refreshed with his years of noble service';[37] he was certainly popular enough to be elected to the city council as a Liberal in a generally Conservative borough, and to serve a term as mayor. Ryder's continued as a large employer in the city into the interwar period.

The printing industry was another notable growth in later nineteenth-century St Albans. The origins of printing in the city lay in the late medieval period (see box 4); but modern printing can be said to have begun in St Albans when Richard Gibbs's press was established in the 1820s. Gibbs expanded quickly, moving into the old town hall in 1837.[38] From the 1880s onwards printing expanded rapidly, to the extent that, in the early twentieth century it could be described as 'the chief industry of St Albans, in that more hands are employed in it than in any other business'.[39] The Campfield Press, next to the Great Northern Railway branch line, opened in 1889, first housing Orford Smith Limited, and then the Salvation Army Printing Works.[40] A railway siding was built at the press in 1902.[41] Nearby Watford also saw development in the printing industry in this period: John Peacock established a printing works in Watford High Street in 1893, which took over the printing of the *Watford Observer*. In St Albans, 1896 saw the opening of the Dangerfield Printing Company works in Inkerman Road, which housed 'the most up-to-

These houses on Woodstock Road South were built by Smith's Printing Agency, owners of the nearby Fleet Works, in the early twentieth century. Although Smith's did not stay very long in St Albans, the company had a considerable impact on local housing. The decoration on the front of each pair of houses shows a casket with fruit.
PHOTOGRAPH: AUTHOR

date lithographic printing works in England';[42] and the Priory Press, built on Grosvenor Road in 1902, housed Robert Taylor and Company, fine art printers.[43] Most important of all was the establishment of Smith's Printing Agency's Fleet Works on the corner of Hatfield Road and Sutton Road: the name of the surrounding area, Fleetville, comes from the Fleet Works, which were established in 1898 and produced 'mainly horticultural literature'.[44] The Fleet Works stimulated further housing development in the area, the result of substantial investment by Smith's. The company built houses on Hatfield Road, Woodstock Road South and Arthur Road, as well as the Fleetville Club and Institute.[45] Although the association of Smith's with St Albans was short-lived, ending in the 1920s, the houses built by the company remained.

... industrial companies were keen to take advantage of the city's proximity to London ...

Like the Fleet Works, new industrial concerns were increasingly likely to be located on the edges of St Albans, although some smaller enterprises such as Charles Gentle and Sons Limited, iron and brass founders (1863), and John Freshwater and Company Limited, shoemakers (1880s), were in the city centre, on French Row and Lower Dagnall Street respectively.[46] In 1862, H. Rose and Sons, brush manufacturers, appeared on the corner of Grosvenor and Ridgmont Roads; they became Brushes Limited in 1902. In 1893, Grosvenor Road was also the location for Edwin Lee and Sons, shoe manufacturers, and the St Albans Mineral Water Company was established on nearby Alma Road in 1906, although this company moved back into the city centre, again to Lower Dagnall Street, in 1912. In the south of St Albans, on Prospect Road, Mercer's Chronometers established a small factory in 1874, moving to larger premises on Eywood Road in 1912; Mercer's had commenced business in Clerkenwell in 1858. There were 30 employees, many highly skilled, in 1913.[47] To the north of the city, St Albans Cardboard Box Company established a short-lived factory on Grange Street in 1903; and the new Verulam Industrial Estate was developed on London Road, served by the Great Northern Railway branch line, in the 1900s. Vickers built an experimental tank on London Road in 1910, and the St Albans Rubber Company was established there in 1909, but in this case the premises were soon moved to Camp Road. The Beaumont Works, built on Sutton Road in 1900, housed the coat manufacturers Nicholson and Company and their forty employees; like Ryder's, this company had come from Lancashire. In 1905 a siding from the Great Northern line was built at the Beaumont Works. The Sphere Works, built on Campfield Road in 1909, belonged to Arc Lamps Limited, which made Davy and enclosed arc lamps. In 1901 the Campfield Musical Instrument Works opened, serving the Salvation Army; this was sold to Boosey and Hawkes in 1972. Nearer the Midland station, on Hatfield Road between Granville and Stanhope Roads, W. O. Peake coat manufacturers' factory was built in 1911: by 1916, this employed over 300 workers. The development of light industry in St Albans reflected similar trends in other small southern towns: industrial companies were keen to take

BEAUMONT WORKS, FLEETVILLE.

ALPHA S⊢ALL

The Beaumont Works were built on Sutton Road in 1910 for Nicholson and Company, coat manufacturers. This was one of many new industrial premises established on the edge of the city in the late Victorian and Edwardian period, and was served by a siding from the Great Northern branch line, which crossed Sutton Road at or near the place from where this picture was taken in *c*.1910. The Beaumont Works building still stands, decorated with the company logo (see p. 313).

ST ALBANS CENTRAL LIBRARY

advantage of the city's proximity to London and its large market for a range of consumer goods, as well as the cheaper land prices and a more pleasant urban environment than could be found in the capital itself.

At the same time, more traditional forms of economic activity continued. The silk mill on the river Ver, at the bottom of Abbey Mill Lane, employed some 130 people at the beginning of the twentieth century; as in earlier times, these were mostly female.[48] The construction boom of the period stimulated the growth of the local brick-making industry, which was a long-standing feature of Bernard's Heath, to the north of St Albans, going back to the fifteenth century.[49] In the eighteenth and early nineteenth centuries, Benjamin Fowler's brick works was on the site; and in 1864 G. F. Arnold's brick works opened, served by several large clay pits. In 1888 a fatal accident occurred in one of the clay pits, and by 1890 Arnold's site had been taken over by Wiles and Lewis's tallow works. The smells from Wiles and Lewis's city centre premises had prompted complaints in the 1880s, and they had been forced to relocate. A fire destroyed the Bernard's Heath tallow works in 1911, but another new factory was built, and stook on the site until the 1960s. There was another brick works on the other side of Sandridge Road, to the north of Sandpit Lane. Straw was another industry that survived in some form in St Albans. Although the manufacture of Brazilian hats fell off rapidly from around 1870, straw hat manufacture declined much more slowly. In 1901, of 4,583 occupied

Victoria Street
from the Midland
Railway bridge,
looking towards
the city centre. The
cathedral tower
can just be seen
at the left-hand
side of the picture,
and closer, on the
right-hand side, is
the tower of the
Congregationalist
Trinity Church,
which opened in
1903. This area of
St Albans expanded
rapidly following
the arrival of
the railway in
the 1860s, after
which many new
industrial premises,
as well as housing
developments, were
situated here.

FROM THE COLLECTION OF
TONY BAXTER

males in the St Albans municipal borough, 227 worked in the manufacture of
headwear, while 256 females worked in the tailoring and dressmaking trades,
which included hat manufacture.[50] Straw hat factories included Scotts, Slades
and H. P. Smith's on Victoria Street; Johnsons of Lower Dagnall Street;
Webdale's on Fishpool Street; Sheldrake's on Holywell Hill; and Munt, Brown
and Company, established in the 1860s, also on Fishpool Street, which became
Dunham and Martin, closed in 1937, and was demolished in 1973.[51] Between
1910 and 1923 Vyse, Sons and Company Limited had a straw hat factory on
Ridgmont Road. To serve factories like this, between the 1870s and the Second
World War, Hitchcock's straw dying and bleaching works were in operation on
Grange Street.[52] The decline of local straw plaiting meant that these factories
were increasingly likely to use imported plait: although of a lower quality than
English plait, this was more suited to machine stitching.[53] Hat manufacture
– particularly St Albans's speciality, the men's straw boater – remained a
distinctive feature of the city's economy well into the twentieth century.[54]

The industrial development of St Albans stimulated the growth of new
housing, especially in the vicinity of the Midland Railway station. In the
1870s, new housing was built on Alma Road, Alexandra Road, Bedford
Road and Inkerman Road; the 1880s saw the development of Oswald Road,
Stanhope Road, Granville Road and Camp Road. Workers' cottages were built
in the mid-1880s in Albion Road, Cavendish Road and numbers 1–35 Camp

Road, housing mostly railway workers and prison staff.[55] These developments were described, as early as 1872, as 'almost a second St Albans', in a *Herts Advertiser* editorial which complained about the lack of drainage, even in these modern homes.[56] At around the same time, development began to the north of St Albans, to the east of Bernard's Heath, in a district that was known as Sandridge New Town. Houses on Sandridge Road, Culver Road and Heath Road were built in the 1880s, Warwick Road was developed in the 1890s and 1900s, and there were 16 houses on Boundary Road by 1901.[57] There was a development of larger houses at St Peter's Park, including Hall Place Gardens and Townsend Avenue (then known as Townsend Place). The bricks for many of these houses may have come from the local brickworks. A guidebook published in 1884 held out great hopes for the new suburban community:

> Of late years the city, and especially the north-eastern part of it, lying between Bernard's Heath and the Midland Railway Station has very much increased, and is still increasing. A considerable portion of land, known as St Peter's Park, has been planted and laid out for the erection of villas, and new roads have been made, and these will form a pleasant addition to the suburbs of the city. Other estates in the same quarter have been sold for building purposes. Altogether a prosperous future appears to lie before the good city of St Albans.[58]

Sandridge Road from Bernard's Heath. These houses, part of a large development known as Sandridge New Town, were built in the 1880s. The area was notorious in the late nineteenth and early twentieth centuries for unemployment, distress, gambling, drinking and immorality. The smell from the nearby Wiles and Lewis tallow works was frequently unpleasant, and refuse from St Albans was deposited on Bernard's Heath into the twentieth century.

PHOTOGRAPH: AUTHOR

In Fleetville, the arrival of printing and other industry in the 1900s led to further residential development: from 1903, housing was built in Camp View Road, and in the following years on Castle, Hedley, Cape, Sutton, Cambridge, Royston, College, Ely, Wellington, Beresford and Maxwell Roads.[59] The building of houses – as well as the many new industrial premises, and public institutions (which are discussed below) – brought more employment to the city. Despite Asa Briggs's assertion that there was 'never a great building boom' in St Albans, in 1901 there were 885 construction workers in the municipal borough, representing 19.3 per cent of the occupied male population.[60] The population of the surrounding rural district of St Albans grew by 58.7 per cent, from 12,264 to 19,463, between 1901 and 1911 (see table 8.1), demonstrating in part the continuing tendency for the city to expand beyond its borders.

'homes of men which were blots on the beauty of Nature'

Although the decline of straw plait helped to weaken the intimate relationship between St Albans and the surrounding countryside, the city remained a commercial centre for local agriculture. As the historian Stephen Royle has commented, 'at mid-century there remained hundreds of towns performing traditional roles as agricultural service centres and central places, part of the traditional symbiosis between town and country'.[61] Although this symbiosis became less crucial to the economy of St Albans over time, the numbers employed in agriculture in the census registration district did not decrease much, in absolute terms, in the nineteenth century: there were 1,870 men aged aged 20 and over working in agriculture in the census registration district in 1841, and as late as 1931 there were 1,793 men working in agriculture in the municipal borough and rural district of St Albans.[62] Of course, as a *percentage* of total employment in the registration district agriculture declined considerably; and at the same time some rural parishes in the area lost population, especially as straw-plaiting employment opportunities for women disappeared from the 1870s.

The social and environmental conditions of the surrounding villages were probably worse than those within St Albans itself. The rural housing of Hertfordshire was notorious, especially in Harpenden, Redbourn, Wheathampstead and 'the environs of St Albans'.[63] A series of official investigations of rural housing conditions drew attention to these areas: for example, in 1867 the agricultural improver Sir John Lawes told the Royal Commission on the Employment of Children, Young Persons and Women in Agriculture that cottages in the vicinity of Harpenden were 'bad and insufficient for the labourers'.[64] At House Lane in Sandridge in 1861,

> There were 31 cottages with only 11 privvies between them, some had one between 2, others one between 3, and in one case 5 families shared just one. 12 cottages had no privy at all, and disposal was 'into the high road'. There was also insufficient sleeping accommodation.[65]

The situation had not greatly improved in the early twentieth century, when a local barrister and housing reformer, Hugh Aronson, described 'homes of men which were blots on the beauty of Nature', and asked: 'Must one always find in the most perfect corners of this most beauteous countryside that which deprives these places of half their glory?'[66] Aronson explained how the tied cottage system (whereby labourers and their families lived in houses owned by their employers) deterred agricultural workers from complaining about conditions for fear of eviction. Although in fact only a small minority of rural homes in Hertfordshire were tied,[67] there is ample evidence of insanitary conditions. At Sandridge, for example, the regular flooding of the High Street earned the village the nickname 'Sandridge Docks'.[68] The poverty of agricultural labourers in the area encouraged an attempt in 1872 to establish a branch of the National Agricultural Labourers' Union, led by a Sandridge carpenter, William Paul.[69] The union branch, which held open-air meetings on Nomansland Common, appears to have had some local success, although here, as nationally, it was short-lived. The most effective response to the poor pay and conditions in agricultural employment was to move to the towns: the depopulation of some Hertfordshire villages in this period reflects the increasing availability of industrial employment in towns such as St Albans, as well as the pull of London.

... the railway also allowed people to commute from St Albans to London ...

Although the expansion of local industries created work for many people in St Albans, the service sector, as always, was also a significant employer. Historically, St Albans had been reliant for centuries on services, providing lodging, stabling and board to large numbers of travellers. This function declined with the arrival of the railway, but in Victorian St Albans, as elsewhere, service occupations were increasingly pursued in domestic locations. By far the largest occupational group among women in St Albans, and in Hertfordshire, and England as a whole, was domestic service: in 1901 there were 873 female domestic servants in St Albans, representing 30.6 per cent of the occupied female population. This helps to explain the low sex ratio (males per 100 females) in the municipal borough – somewhat lower, as table 7.2 (on page 212) shows, than that of the St Albans registration district as a whole. There were 20 (female) domestic servants for every 100 families in St Albans in 1901, higher than the 18.5 per 100 in Watford but lower than the 25.5 per 100 in Hertford.[70]

These figures suggest that there was an expanding middle class which could afford domestic servants, but that this middle class was, proportionately, larger in the county town of Hertford. This would reflect the higher numbers of local government employees in Hertford, especially after the establishment of county councils in 1888. It is not possible to obtain exact numbers of males engaged in the professions or business in St Albans in 1901, but numbers were certainly expanding. There were 148 male commercial or business clerks in the city, reflecting the opportunities in trade, commerce, banking and insurance. For middle-class women, teaching was a growing occupation: there were 103 female teachers in 1901.[71] Not only were there increasing opportunities to pursue professional careers in St Albans itself, but the railway also allowed people to commute from St Albans to London (and elsewhere) to pursue their employment. The spread of the commuting habit was particularly noticeable on Hertfordshire's metropolitan fringe in the later nineteenth century. Londoners were moving to Watford in very large numbers: the population of the town increased from 7,461 in 1871 to 29,327 in 1901, far outstripping the growth of St Albans.[72] One observer in 1884 remarked of Watford that 'many members of the great trading community of the metropolis, who at one time saw the country and breathed its pure air only on the occasions of their journeys on business or periodical holidays, have of late years deemed it necessary to the health of themselves and their families to reside out of town; the head of the family going to London each morning to business, and returning to the country in the evening ... The facilities offered by railways have greatly encouraged this exodus'.[73] St Albans and Harpenden also participated in this development, but more slowly; and a guide to St Albans published in 1903 emphasised to prospective residents that

'... one of the healthiest towns around London ... there is civic and social life in abundance ...'

> St Albans in one of the healthiest towns around London and as a place of residence or as a health resort it is difficult to find its superior in the Home Counties ... There are frequent trains to London ... and the Metropolis can, by the majority of trains on the Midland system, be reached in half an hour. Compared with the slow suburban trains this to the business man is most favourable ... [moreover,] as a residential suburb for London, [St Albans] has claims which cannot be conceded to ordinary suburban London for there is civic and social life in abundance, and its rural surroundings and splendid train service make it an ideal place of residence for the city man.[74]

Within St Albans, another area that offered employment was local institutions: in 1911, 721 individuals, almost 3 per cent of the population of the municipal borough, lived in 'institutions' or 'large establishments', which in turn provided employment for many living in the city.[75] The growth of urban institutions was associated with new organs of local government and the democratisation (within certain limits) of political structures. The Municipal Corporations Act of 1835 restructured the government of boroughs across England and Wales, and revitalised local politics, at least in the short term. According to Barry Doyle, the reform 'injected party politics into municipal elections' – with the result that the Liberals won landslide victories in the larger cities, and in many smaller places – although by the 1840s 'municipal

politics in most places had settled into inactive one-party rule', and by the 1850s 'party battles' were rare.[76] St Albans largely followed this pattern, but without the early Liberal landslide that was seen elsewhere. The reformed St Albans corporation consisted of four aldermen and 12 councillors; two of the aldermen were rotated every three years, giving a six-year term, and four of the councillors every year, giving them a three-year term. At the first election in 1835, in St Albans as elsewhere, all 12 councillors were elected at once: a Liberal, Richard Webster, was elected at the top of the poll, with 318 votes, but the other 11 councillors elected were all Conservative.[77] The council remained Tory-dominated for most of the nineteenth century, although the Liberals fared a little better in parliamentary elections (see box 9). Following extensions of the municipal borough boundaries in 1879 and 1913, the number of aldermen was increased to seven and the councillors to 18. Councillors represented three wards: North, South and East. The roles and responsibilities of local government expanded steadily in the nineteenth century, and St Albans had its share of local government professionals, as a new class of officers grew up in British towns. As early as the 1870s urban local authorities were required to appoint a medical officer of health, a surveyor, an inspector of nuisances, a town clerk and a treasurer, and most appointed a large – and diverse – range of other officials.[78] Local government was further reformed – and extended – in

This cartoon by local artist John Henry Buckingham (1800–81) depicted a disturbance at the corn exchange in December 1859. To the fury of market traders, the corporation had attempted to force the closure of business at 3 p.m. A number of those involved were fined. A boycott of the corn exchange followed, as a result of which, in March 1859, the council reversed its decision, and agreed that the exchange could stay open as long as the traders wished.

1888, when county councils were created; these institutions gradually acquired more power in the following decades. In 1894, two more new bodies were created: parish councils, which democratised parochial government, and rural district councils, which acquired some functions that were exercised in towns by municipal boroughs. The St Albans rural district council was responsible for an area of almost 40,000 acres surrounding the city itself.

Other institutions of local government were created in the nineteenth century that had significant implications for St Albans. As explained in the last chapter, the unit of poor law administration in the eighteenth century was the parish, and some parishes in and around St Albans provided workhouse accommodation for the poor. As described in the last chapter, a workhouse had opened in St Albans in the early eighteenth century, and by the end of the century there were workhouses in St Stephen's, St Peter's, St Michael's, Sandridge and Redbourn.[79] These institutions, in common with most parish workhouses across the country, catered for small numbers of paupers. The Poor Law Amendment Act in 1834 reorganised the parishes into larger poor law unions, combining several parishes to promote administrative efficiency. The St Albans poor law union, which came into existence in May 1835, comprised eight parishes in total: all the urban parishes of St Albans, the rural parts of St Michael's, St Peter's and St Stephen's, as well as Harpenden, Wheathampstead, Redbourn and Sandridge. The union was co-extensive with the census registration district, and was run by a board of 17 poor law guardians representing the eight parishes.[80] Although the workhouse and other poor law facilities were provided by the union, funding was still organised at a parish level, so each parish was responsible for the upkeep of its own paupers, and for contributions to the common fund of the union based on the number of paupers it had. Across England and Wales, parish workhouses were replaced

continued on page 239

RIGHT
The St Albans poor law union workhouse, on Normandy Road (originally called Union Lane). The workhouse replaced a number of smaller parish workhouses following the Poor Law Amendment Act of 1834, which consolidated parishes in larger poor law unions. The design is fairly typical of the workhouses of the period, which were designed to deter people from claiming poor relief. Built in 1836–37, the workhouse now forms part of St Albans City Hospital.

PHOTOGRAPH: AUTHOR

Box 10: Church and town, cathedral and city: the restoration of the abbey church and the creation of the diocese of St Albans

FOR MANY DECADES the condition of the abbey church in St Albans gave great cause for concern. In February 1832 a large section of wall fell through the roof of the south aisle, as a result of which it became clear that 'fundamental repairs were urgent if the building was to continue to stand'.[1] The churchwardens and vestry

---
[1] Roberts, *Hill of the Martyr*, p. 195.

ABOVE

Edmund Beckett Denison (1816–1905), first Baron Grimthorpe from 1886, lived at Batchwood, and oversaw the restoration of the cathedral in the late nineteenth century. He was a successful barrister, specialising in railway law, but his interests ranged widely, and he had largely retired from the bar by 1880. He spent large sums of his own money on the work, much of which was controversial. The new west front of the cathedral, completed in 1883, was built to his own design.

commissioned a survey of the church, which was carried out by the architect L. N. Cottingham, and which proposed a substantial series of repairs to the fabric of the building which would cost some £14,000.[2] Subscriptions were opened, but failed to raise anything like the sum required, and although the most urgent work was done, it was not until the 1840s that the necessary impetus towards major repair came about in the form of the establishment of the St Albans Architectural Society.[3] The Society drew attention to the state of the abbey: seven of the nine members of its first committee were clergymen, including Henry Nicholson, rector of the abbey church from 1835, who from 1846 began to charge for admission to the building, both to raise money for the repairs and 'to impress upon the public that the abbey was something worth seeing'.[4] A Restoration Committee, under the chairmanship of the earl of Verulam, pushed forward ambitious schemes of reconstruction.[5] In 1856 George Gilbert Scott was appointed as the architect, in which capacity he served until his death in 1878. Scott also carried out repairs to the St Albans clock tower in 1865.

Despite the work of the Restoration Committee, in 1870 the state of the abbey remained 'desperate'.[6] Scott estimated that the necessary repairs would cost over £40,000.[7] Emergency work was carried out, this time to the tower, in 1871, and Scott oversaw some repaving in 1872, along with the creation of new stained glass windows. In 1871 the school moved out of the crowded Lady Chapel and into the abbey gatehouse, which had been

---
[2] Ibid., p. 197.
[3] See below, p. 249.
[4] Roberts, *Hill of the Martyr*, p. 199.
[5] Moody, *Light of Other Days*, pp. 5–6.
[6] Toms, *Story of St Albans*, p. 162.
[7] Owen Chadwick, 'The Victorian Diocese of St Albans', in Runcie, *Cathedral and City*, pp. 89–90.

replaced as the town jail by the new building
at the end of Victoria Street near the Midland
Railway station.[1] At about the same time the
Restoration Committee was joined by Edmund
Beckett Denison, who became Sir Edmund
Beckett on inheriting a baronetcy in 1874 and
Lord Grimthorpe in 1886. Grimthorpe lived at
Batchwood, and had distinctive ideas on church
architecture, which were not always shared by
members of the St Albans Architectural and
Archaeological Society, which he conspicuously

failed to join.[2] According to one historian,
Grimthorpe 'ruled the restoration like a
dictator'.[3] His power lay in his wealth, much

---

[1] See below, pp. 240–1.

[2] Roberts, *Hill of the Martyr*, pp. 212–14; Moody, *Light
of Other Days*, p. 6.
[3] Chadwick, 'Victorian Diocese', p. 91.

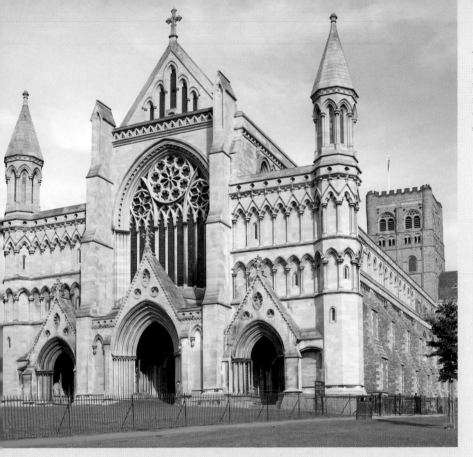

of which was spent on the restoration – the new west front cost him £20,000 and the restoration of the nave £50,000[1] – and in the support he enjoyed from some prominent members of the Restoration Committee, notably the earl of Verulam. Grimthorpe's divisive impact was reflected in the fact that, at one point, the Architectural and Archaeological Society, beset by controversy, did not meet for 2½ years.[2] Grimthorpe's influence can be seen in many of the internal features of the abbey, and most spectacularly in the west front, designed by him in 1880 and completed in 1883. He also designed the rose window in the north transept, tiled the presbytery and redecorated the Lady Chapel. None of his projects in the abbey was uncontroversial.[3] Grimthorpe died in 1905; and his influence has been much debated. During his lifetime, he was praised for saving the abbey from ruin, but politely criticised for the way in which this was done: one report in 1895 asserted that 'although there may be differences of opinion as to the character and style of some of the restoration, it cannot be denied that his lordship has at immense expenditure of time and money now placed this ancient building in a thoroughly sound condition'.[4] In the early 1960s, the historian (and former mayor of St Albans) Elsie Toms agreed with this assessment:

[1] Roberts, *Hill of the Martyr*, pp. 219, 221.
[2] Moody, *Light of Other Days*, p. 6.
[3] For a detailed examination of Grimthorpe's work on the abbey, see Roberts, *Hill of the Martyr*, chapter 18.
[4] Quoted in Corbett, *History of St Albans*, p. 107.

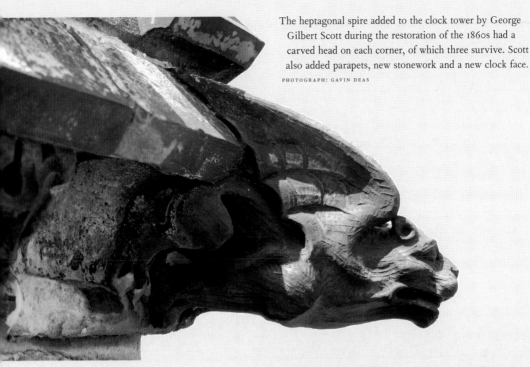

The heptagonal spire added to the clock tower by George Gilbert Scott during the restoration of the 1860s had a carved head on each corner, of which three survive. Scott also added parapets, new stonework and a new clock face.

PHOTOGRAPH: GAVIN DEAS

'had he not poured out his money, as he did on his new toy, we should have no Abbey to-day, for within a short time it would assuredly have been completely beyond rescue'.[1] The architectural historian Eileen Roberts praises Grimthorpe's 'exemplary ideals: know what you are doing, build well, be bold, be strong', but deprecates his 'arrogance, bad taste, and a lack of historical sense'.[2]

As the mid-nineteenth-century campaign to restore the fabric of the abbey church got under way, another series of developments, not unconnected with the progress of the repairs, resulted in the elevation of the abbey church into a cathedral and in the creation of the diocese of St Albans. The origins of this lay in urban demography and church politics, a long way from the architectural convulsions of the Restoration Committee and the Architectural and Archaeological Society.

In 1852 a Church Commissioners' report had suggested that it would be 'desirable' to establish new dioceses at St Albans, and also at Newcastle, Liverpool, Brecon, Derby, Chelmsford or Colchester, Coventry, Ipswich and Bath. (The immediate creation of a diocese of Cornwall was also recommended.)[3] These proposals were the result of the growing population of the large urban centres of the north of England, and of the expansion of London, which put considerable pressure on the metropolitan bishop. Although these recommendations were not immediately heeded, they must have struck a chord with many in Hertfordshire. Recent reorganisations – before which St Albans had been in the diocese of London and part of the county in the diocese of distant Lincoln – had transferred most of the county to the see of Rochester, part of a series of boundary changes by which Rochester lost much of south London to the metropolitan diocese. Because of these changes, the diocese of

[1] Toms, *Story of St Albans*, p. 163.
[2] Roberts, *Hill of the Martyr*, p. 228.
[3] Francis Warre Cornish, *The English Church in the Nineteenth Century* (2 vols, London: Macmillan and Co.,), vol. 2, p. 53.

Rochester now consisted of part of Kent and a large swathe of territory north of the Thames; as a result the bishop, who at Rochester was cut off from most of his diocese, moved to a new palace near Chelmsford, in Essex. As Owen Chadwick has commented, 'The commissioners who made this arrangement do not seem to have asked how the inhabitants of Boreham Wood were to be expected to feel loyalty to Rochester; nor how the dilapidated cathedral at Rochester could be any use to the parishes of Baldock or Hemel Hempstead. The surroundings of London were sacrificed for the sake of London.'[1]

The commissioners' report of 1852 recognised the difficulties of the situation in the diocese of Rochester; and in 1856 another commission was appointed to examine the question of the diocese of London, which was becoming increasingly unwieldy as the city grew in population. A delegation of representatives from Hertfordshire asked this commission for a new diocese of St Albans, but this was rejected.[2] It is possible that the poor condition of the abbey church influenced the decision of the commissioners, who would have been aware that Rochester cathedral was also in a state of disrepair.[3] The problem of London remained, however, becoming more acute as the population, and the number of churches in the capital, continued to expand.[4] A consensus was emerging in favour of the creation of new sees; but the commissioners of 1852 had been careful to recommend that none should be established unless enough money was available to provide a residence for the bishop and to endow the prospective diocese with a sufficient income.[5] In the case of St Albans, it would also be necessary to compensate the diocese of Rochester for the territory it would lose: this was eventually done by giving Rochester some parishes belonging to the diocese of Winchester. St Albans was endowed

by the sale, for £45,000, of Winchester House in London, under the terms of the Bishopric of St Albans Act (1875).[6] The diocese was established in 1877, consisting of Hertfordshire and Essex; its first bishop was Thomas Legh Claughton, who moved from Rochester, having begun the restoration of the cathedral there. Claughton continued to live in his Essex palace until his death in 1892.

The creation of the new diocese did not solve all the problems it was intended to. As Chadwick remarks, the size of the see of St Albans did not give it much more geographical coherence than the old diocese of Rochester: Essex parishes 'saw hardly more connexion with a cathedral in St Albans than a cathedral in Rochester'.[7] At the same time, the growth of east London, much of which lay in the county of Essex, outside the jurisdiction of metropolitan political or diocesan authorities, created a lot of work for the new St Albans diocese. Although ministering to the poor in East London was a 'pastoral mission' that 'gave a meaning to the St Albans diocese which otherwise it would have lacked', the diocese was too large and diverse to be coherent.[8] In 1914 the diocese of Chelmsford was created to serve Essex, and most of Bedfordshire was removed from the diocese of Ely and placed in the diocese of St Albans, where it remains today.

Although the day-to-day implications of the creation of the new diocese of St Albans may have been minimal in St Albans itself, it resulted in the elevation of the town to the status of a city. This was confirmed in letters patent issued by the Crown, and read publicly by the mayor of St Albans to large crowds, in September 1877.[9] This was another example of a civic event which enabled the municipal leadership to engage in the ritual proclamation of the prestige of the borough.[10]

[1] Chadwick, 'Victorian Diocese', pp. 74–5.
[2] Ibid., p. 76.
[3] Ibid., p. 75; Toms, *Story of St Albans*, pp. 164–5.
[4] Cornish, *English Church*, vol. 2, pp. 57–8.
[5] Ibid., p. 53.
[6] Chadwick, 'Victorian Diocese', pp. 78–83.
[7] Ibid., p. 84.
[8] Ibid., pp. 95–6.
[9] Dunk, *Around St Albans*, p. 34.
[10] See below, p. 245.

RIGHT

Sir John Blundell Maple (1845–1903), owner of a
London furniture and drapery business, was elected as
Conservative MP for St Pancras in 1885, and for Dulwich
in 1887. He represented Dulwich until his death. A
baronet, Maple lived at Childwickbury, between St Albans
and Harpenden, and owned and bred many successful
racehorses. He donated the Sisters' Hospital to the city
of St Albans in 1893, and Clarence Park in 1894. He also
supported the rebuilding of University College Hospital in
London, which was completed after he died.

REPRODUCED BY KIND PERMISSION OF THE NATIONAL LIBRARY OF
SCOTLAND

LEFT

Thomas Legh Claughton (1802–92) was the first bishop
of St Albans, serving from 1877 until 1890. Prior to this,
Claughton had been vicar of Kidderminster from 1841 to
1867, and bishop of Rochester from 1867 to 1877. He never
lived in St Albans, staying instead at Danbury Palace in
Essex, where he had lived as bishop of Rochester. Essex
was removed from the jurisdiction of Rochester and placed
in the new diocese of St Albans, but transferred to the
diocese of Chelmsford in 1914.

AUTHOR COLLECTION

by larger union workhouses. The St Albans union workhouse, on Union
Lane (later renamed Normandy Road), was built in 1836–37 to a design by
the architect John Griffin. In 1851 it housed 233 paupers, and fifty years later
there were 191 pauper inmates.[81] At both dates 10 other people – members of
staff and their families – were also inhabitants of the site. There was considerable development of the workhouse in the nineteenth century. As early as
1841, St Michael's parish voted a sum to spend on improvements to the union
workhouse, including a casual ward (for the accommodation of tramps), a 'foul
ward' and an infirmary.[82] By the end of the nineteenth century a chapel had
been added, paid for with money collected by the Reverend Canon Edward
Liddell, an experienced philanthropist who had moved to St Albans from
Jarrow.[83] Paupers were also sometimes housed in the city lodging house on
Sopwell Lane.

The non-pauper sick in St Albans were cared for by various other institutions. The St Albans General Dispensary was established in 1844 on Holywell Hill, funded by public subscriptions; this was replaced by a hospital on the same site in 1870; and in 1887 this was relocated to Verulam Road, on the corner of Church Crescent, where it was known as the St Albans and Mid-Herts Hospital and Dispensary, or the 'Cottage Hospital'.[84] In 1893 a fever hospital, known as the Sisters' Hospital, was added to the workhouse infirmary site. This was donated by Sir John Blundell Maple, a Conservative MP (for Dulwich) and racehorse owner who lived at Childwickbury, where he bred a succession of victorious horses. (Maple was a well-known philanthropist, who also supported the rebuilding of University College Hospital in London.)[85] In 1901 there was a handful of permanent residents at both the fever hospital and Verulam Road. However, by far the largest institution in St Albans at this time was the Hertfordshire County Lunatic Asylum at Hill End, which was established just two years earlier, in 1899. In 1901 there were 522 inmates, 226 male and 296 female, as well as 79 other residents, officials and their families.[86] By 1913 the asylum had acquired two new blocks (in 1908) and could accommodate 820 patients on its 214-acre site.[87] The Hertfordshire facility at St Albans was one of many lunatic asylums founded, or taken over, by the new county councils, which were established in 1888. Another institution for which the county acquired responsibility was the prison, which was built in 1867 at the end of Sweetbriar Lane (later Victoria Street) as a city jail. The jail was interesting enough to feature in an illustrated guide book to St Albans in 1884, when it was described as 'rather imposing in its proportions'; the author explained that the

Hatfield Road elementary school for boys was opened by the St Albans School Board in 1881, one of a number of new educational establishments built under the terms of the Education Act of 1870, which made elementary education compulsory. The school was enlarged in 1885 and 1898, and by 1911 had an average attendance of 440 boys. This photograph was taken in the early twentieth century.

These terraced houses, on Folly Lane to the north-west of the town, were built in 1886. This area lay outside the boundaries of the old borough of St Albans, but these were extended in 1879 and 1913 to take new built-up areas into the municipal jurisdiction. This side of St Albans saw relatively little industrial development, most of which took place to east of the city, stimulated by the Midland and Great Northern Railways.

PHOTOGRAPH: AUTHOR

prison 'has not been made unnecessarily grim or ugly. It is castellated … The principal feature of the prison is the complete and extensive arrangements for carrying out the separate systems of prison discipline.'[88] By this it was meant that males and females could be accommodated in separate prisons (there were 85 male and 14 female cells, of which 69 and 5 respectively were occupied in 1901),[89] and that executions could be carried out. Men, and at least one woman, were executed at the jail, which ceased to be a civilian prison in 1915 and was taken out of use completely in the 1920s.[90]

Another impetus to the development of public institutions was provided by the Education Act of 1870: under the provisions of this Act, St Albans School Board was established in 1878, building rate-financed elementary schools in various parts of the city, including Alma Road (girls and infants), Hatfield Road (boys), and the new school at Bernard's Heath.[91] In 1889 a census of children in the public elementary schools showed that a total of 2,171 children were on school rolls in the city. The average daily attendance was 1,740, a little over 80 per cent of the roll, reflecting a level of truancy which is likely to have concerned the School Board's attendance officer. A further difficulty for the School Board in 1889 was the recent flight of Thomas Littlejohn Brash, headmaster of the Hatfield Road school, who had apparently embezzled a large sum of money.[92] In 1902 school boards were abolished, and their responsibilities passed to local education authorities: in St Albans, the authority was Hertfordshire County Council. St Albans School itself – also known as the Grammar School – was expanding in this period: it moved out of the cramped Lady Chapel and into the abbey gatehouse in 1871, and the next forty years saw considerable development. There were 42 boys on the roll in 1880, and 92 by 1888, and the number of masters also increased, to four by 1886.[93] Although the financial position of the school was not always secure, even with the increasing number of pupils, heavy investment was made in buildings and facilities in this period, helped by large loans from various benefactors. By 1893, the science laboratory at the school was reported as being 'well fitted with the most modern appliances'.[94] Further expansion took place in the 1900s, under a new headmaster, Edgar Montague Jones, who oversaw the construction of a new building, linked to the abbey gatehouse by a cloister. The foundation stone was laid 'with masonic ritual' by the Provincial Grand Master of Hertfordshire (who was also chairman of the county council) in 1907, and the building was opened by the mayor in 1908.[95] There were now more than 150 pupils, and seven masters; and School House was constructed for the use of the headmaster.[96]

'practically no system of drainage, save into cesspools ... there is nowhere else to which the sewage can be conducted ...'

As well as custodial and educational institutions, the Victorian and Edwardian period was notable for the development of public utilities and civic amenities. This was led by the large municipalities, where 'progressive' local authorities pursued ambitious schemes of improvement; and many smaller towns followed their example. As Royle has remarked, improvement and municipalism was 'not reserved to the great cities': many, if not most, small towns developed their water and sewage provision, and built town halls, public baths and other amenities.[97] In St Albans, gas mains were laid in 1824 by the General Gas Company, and the St Albans Gas Company was established in 1852.[98] However, in the provision of water and sewage, small towns in the south of England often lagged behind the large conurbations and the new industrial centres of the north. In P. J. Waller's words, in this respect 'the most conspicuously negligent were older established towns', such as Exeter, Salisbury and Guildford, as well as St Albans and neighbouring Hitchin.[99] The first water works in St Albans were opened in 1833, and were followed by the Sandridge Road pumping station in 1865; the latter was enhanced by the addition of a wrought iron water tank in 1873.[100] These improvements did not extend to drainage, and a public health problem that arose in the form of a smallpox outbreak in the early 1870s caused the *Herts Advertiser* to hope that the town council and the ratepayers 'may not learn too late the value of pure water and effective drainage'.[101] At this time, according to one observer, the town had 'practically no system of drainage, save into cesspools, some of which are actually dug underneath the parlour-floors, because, from lack of main drains and of unbuilt-upon ground, there is nowhere else to which the sewage can be conducted except into the soil on which the houses stand'.[102] The supply of water remained problematic in the 1880s, and as late as 1901 well water in the rural part of St Stephen's parish was condemned as unsafe.[103] Mains sewerage was not available until the 1880s: sewage pipes were laid in Victoria Street in 1882, and the Park Street sewage works were opened in 1883.[104]

Although these developments improved the urban environment, there was still a problem of smell, and the phrase 'manhole Nuisance' was used in St Albans to describe 'the stench of sewage and actual leakage of sewage from the system under certain conditions'.[105] The smells were worsened by the emissions from some of the industrial sites in the city, notably the tallow works, which were served with notice to abate their foul smells in 1885, and which – as noted above – later relocated from the city centre to Bernard's Heath.[106] As residential development had been happening next to the Heath, this relocation did not solve the problem of the smell, which in any case could be blown on the wind back to St Albans. The *St Albans Lantern*, a short-lived local newspaper, proclaimed in its final issue in 1893 that 'there are many things required to make St Albans presentable': 'For years past we have patiently endured stenches which no other city, borough or town in the kingdom would have submitted to for a week.'[107] The collection of refuse was also felt to be inadequate. In 1905, a letter in the *Herts Advertiser* complained in stark terms:

> 'The winds blow strong on Bernard's Heath' – very strong. Day by day the refuse of the city of some 18,000 inhabitants is carted up to the Heath to the detriment of our Garden City; and what is naturally the finest and healthiest part of the city is made a frowsey, vile-smelling, dusty, microbe-laden vermin-haunted district. Monday by Monday the refuse is collected from the back premises of the Heath houses and deposited just over the road, immediately opposite the County Council School. This accumulation of many years is a standing menace to the health and well-being of the district. His Majesty's liege subjects, passing to and fro along the King's highway ... have frequently to encounter a considerable belt of sound, solid STINK – I write the plain English word in capital letters without a blush. Often we, who dwell here, wake at night and find our bedrooms filled with the reek from this St Albans Gehenna.[108]

Moreover, despite the development of new housing estates around the light industrial sites of Fleetville, the Camp and Bernard's Heath, some of the city's housing was notorious: even in the early 1920s, as one observer recalled, 'the poorer parts of the town were dire slums, a disgrace to any decent community'.[109] Another series of smallpox outbreaks in 1901–02, although effectively contained with minimal loss of life, created some local panic.[110]

St Albans was more successful in the provision of civic amenities, paid for by a mixture of donations, subscriptions and rates, although by the time the *St Albans Lantern* fired its parting shot at the city authorities in 1893 the rate

'the poorer parts of the town were dire slums, a disgrace to any decent community'

burden had reached almost seven shillings in the pound.[111] The new town hall had opened in 1831, and other public buildings included new police cells in Chequer Street in 1861 as well as the new prison later in the same decade.[112] In 1857 the corn exchange on Market Place was erected, at a cost of £1,470, much of it raised by public subscription: the straw plait market was held there.[113] In 1880 the corner stone was laid for a new public library on the south side of Victoria Street: £2,500 of public subscriptions had been raised, and this was augmented by a penny rate under the provisions of the Public Libraries Act of 1850.[114] The library was replaced by one donated by the philanthropist Andrew Carnegie in 1911, standing on the opposite side of Victoria Street. There were open air baths on the site of the old cotton mill from 1883, and public baths were opened in 1887. There was also a sanitary laundry on Belmont Hill.[115] The clock tower was restored in 1865, public subscriptions to the amount of £309 having been raised, and a rate was levied to pay for a new clock.[116] Before the 1890s St Albans had little in the way of public recreational spaces – Bernard's Heath was the only one, and, as discussed above, beset with smells and other public health problems – but Sir John Blundell Maple, who had donated the fever hospital to the city in 1893, also gave Clarence Park in 1894.[117] Verulamium Park was used for civic events, but was in the hands of the earl of Verulam until acquired by the city council in 1929. An example of an amenity provided through private endeavour was the cinema. The first in St Albans, and in Hertfordshire, was the Alpha, on London Road, opened by the photographer and animator Arthur Melbourne-Cooper in 1908; the St Albans Cinema on Chequer Street followed in 1912.[118]

The corn exchange on Market Place was built in 1857, and replaced an earlier building on the same site. Attempts by the corporation to regulate trading at the corn exchange met with resistance in 1859–60 (see above, p. 232).

above, p. 232).

PHOTOGRAPH: CARNEGIE

The late nineteenth and early twentieth centuries were remarkable for a flowering of social life and civic pride across urban Britain. For Royle, the Edwardian years were, 'in many ways ... the apogee of British small-town life', when clubs and associations, and other institutions of civil society, generated a distinctive and powerful urban culture.[119] This reflected the political strength of the urban middle classes, who occupied positions of power in town and city councils and other organs of local government, and who could also exercise local social leadership through a range of voluntary associations. As R. H. Trainor has explained, by the end of the nineteenth century,

Ritual events ... helped to reinforce a popular sense of the urban community.

the urban scene ... featured the huge range of institutions – and positions of leadership – which British towns and cities had spawned from the 1780s: municipal corporations, boards of poor law guardians, health commissioners, school boards and panels of borough JPs; Mechanics' Institutes, reform societies and voluntary hospitals; churches, chapels, synagogues and their affiliated social and cultural organisations; associations and clubs attached to political parties; Chambers of Commerce and trade.[120]

In St Albans local politicians actively promoted pride in the city. When the boundaries of the borough were extended as a result of legislation in 1879, a ceremony was organised for 'beating the bounds' of the new city. The boundary was marked by 18 new iron posts, and the ceremonial walk around the boundary was a major civic occasion, for which a general closing day was declared and public entertainments staged by the municipality, which also hosted a mayoral banquet.[121] When the boundaries were further extended in 1913, another 'beating the bounds' ceremony was staged, during which some 500 people, led by the mayor and corporation, travelled between the boundary posts, decorating the first with a straw hat. Although these festivities were marred by rowdiness, the evening was rounded off with a mayoral banquet, a concert and a dance.[122] Ritual events such as the laying of ceremonial stones helped to reinforce a popular sense of the urban community. Other examples in St Albans were the unveiling of the ornamental drinking fountain in Market Place in 1872, which served a decorative and a practical function in a town whose water supply had been a long-standing cause for concern;[123] the repair and embellishment of the clock tower; the official declaration of St Albans's new status as a city in 1877 (see box 10); and the laying of the first stone at the new museum, 'amid scenes of great public rejoicing', in 1898.[124] These municipal events were mirrored by public rituals commemorating the construction of private buildings: for example, the opening of the London and North Western Railway station in 1858 was marked by a civic procession, a fair, horse racing and a ball.[125] Similarly, the first train at the Midland Railway station a decade later, and the opening of Ryder's new offices in 1911, were accompanied by ceremony and festivity. Other major events, such as the funeral in 1883 of Isabella Worley of Sopwell House, straddled a boundary between public and private ritual: Worley had donated the ornamental drinking fountain, endowed places of worship for the Church of England and for Nonconformists, and supported local schools and charities. Her funeral in St Peter's attracted a crowd of 2,000 or more to the churchyard, and shops in the city closed in honour of the occasion.[126]

Worley was one of the many members of Victorian and Edwardian civic elites who exercised social leadership through the support and patronage of religious bodies. This was particularly important in a long-standing religious centre such as St Albans. St Albans was served by the abbey church itself, and by the Anglo-Saxon parish churches of St Peter, St Stephen and St Michael. As discussed earlier, a strong Dissenting tradition had also emerged in the town (see box 7). By contrast, there was only a minimal Roman Catholic presence.

Christ Church, Verulam Road, was a copy of St Raphael's church in Surbiton, Surrey, designed by the same architect, Charles Parker. Although originally intended as a Catholic church, it was completed by the local philanthropist Isabella Worley, and consecrated as a Church of England place of worship in 1859. It closed in 1974 and is now used as offices.

PHOTOGRAPH: AUTHOR

In the religious census taken on 30 March 1851, a total of 13,497 attendances at church services were recorded in the St Albans census registration district: of these, 7,064 (52.3 per cent) were at Church of England places of worship, 2,389 (17.7 per cent) were Wesleyan Methodist, 1,776 (13.2 per cent) were Independent/Congregationalist, 1,651 (12.2 per cent) were Baptist and just 76 (0.6 per cent) were Catholic.[127] There was no Catholic church in St Albans at the time: a room in the White Hart Inn on Holywell Hill was used, from 1840, as a place of worship. In 1848, the recently elected MP for the borough, Alexander Raphael, a Catholic, bought some land on Verulam Road which he gave to build a church. His death in 1850, which precipitated a controversial by-election (see box 9), stopped the construction of the church, which was not finished until Isabella Worley bought the site in 1856 and finished the project. However, she gave the building, known as Christ Church, to the Church of England: it was consecrated in 1859, the first consecration in St Albans since the reconsecration of the abbey church in the early twelfth century.[128] Worley also paid for the construction of the Wooden Room (1865), a Nonconformist meeting house in Lattimore Road.[129]

The other denominations also expanded their premises, and their wider social activities, in the nineteenth and early twentieth centuries. The Baptist church on Upper Dagnall Street, which dated from c.1720, was altered and enlarged on various occasions in the nineteenth century, and completely rebuilt (on the same site) in 1884. A school was established in 1846, and later transferred to the jurisdiction of the School Board.[130] A Methodist church was built on Upper Dagnall Street in 1841, and replaced by the larger church on Marlborough Road in 1898.[131] The Congregationalist community, based at the Spicer Street Independent Chapel since 1811, also expanded: a Sunday school building was opened in the 1860s and extended in 1888, and in 1903 Trinity Church on Victoria Street was opened to house the growing congregation, of which Samuel Ryder was a prominent member.[132] The Catholics, frustrated by the whims of Isabella Worley in the 1850s, were given a small church on London Road by Major James Gape; this was dedicated in 1878. A larger church, built with subscriptions of £6,000, was built on Beaconsfield Road and dedicated in 1905, like its predecessor, to SS Alban and Stephen.[133] The various denominations were energetic in their promotion of religious education. The religious census of 1851 recorded 22 Sunday schools in the St Albans registration district, 9 of them Church of England, with a total of 2,726 pupils in membership.[134] In 1889, the total number of pupils at Sunday schools in the city of St Albans, as reported in the *Herts Advertiser*, was more than 2,639, well in excess of the total elementary school roll.[135]

Active participation in religious activity was only one way of ensuring a high civic profile in the Victorian period. In St Albans, an active organisational culture embraced a range of political, intellectual, philanthropic, cultural and sporting activity. Political clubs flourished: even in Conservative-dominated St Albans, the Liberal Club had 400 members at its Victoria Street site, which opened in 1886, and moved to new premises on Hatfield Road in 1899.[136] (The size of the club rarely translated into political success, as discussed in box 9.) The new urban medical and charitable institutions offered further scope for activity. An example of the range of public associational activities open to prominent local individuals is provided by H. J. (Harry) Toulmin, one of the first members of the new Hertfordshire County Council, elected in 1889, in which year he was also mayor of St Albans.[137] Toulmin was born in 1837, and had lived at Childwickbury House, on the road between St Albans and Harpenden, and at the Pré, a house on the Gorhambury estate.[138] According the *Herts Advertiser*, which carried a profile of Toulmin following his election, this energetic individual was honorary secretary of the Hertfordshire Children's Convalescent Home, treasurer of the St Albans Church Choral Union, churchwarden at St Michael's, member of the St Albans Diocesan Endowment Fund, lay representative on the St Albans Diocesan Conference for the Archdeaconry of St Albans, vice-president of the Hertfordshire Discharged Prisoners' Aid Society, a committee member of the Hertfordshire Seaside Convalescent Home and treasurer of the St Albans Hospital and Dispensary.[139]

Sport was another outlet for the energies of the population in the nineteenth century. Cricket was played on Bernard's Heath in the 1840s and 1850s, but there was some difficulty in raising the necessary subscriptions to establish a permanent club. A more successful effort was made in 1865, when a ground on Verulam Road was used, but despite the large attendances at matches – one three-day match attracted 3,000 spectators, each paying a 6d. admission charge – the new ground did not prove profitable, and the club returned to Bernard's Heath.[140] According to R. G. Simons, the historian of Hertfordshire cricket, the St Albans club was the cause of considerable social tension in the 1860s and 1870s, exhibiting, in contrast to other clubs in Hertfordshire, 'less deference to the gentry and a willingness to ignore the accepted social conventions of the game': the club appointed a professional to act as captain for a match against Cambridge, and the second earl of Verulam was pointedly dropped from the titular presidency of the club having failed to subscribe for a number of years.[141] By the 1890s, although the quality of the cricket played had declined, the club was in better shape, having moved to Clarence Park when it was given to the city in 1894, and the earl of Verulam's son took on

the captaincy.[142] Strengthened by its revived aristocratic associations, and enjoying good facilities, the club merged with the Hertfordshire county club in 1898, when a new club was established to represent the city. County matches played at Clarence Park attracted local interest and large crowds. Football and hockey were also played in the park: St Albans City Football Club was founded in 1908.

The intellectual life of St Albans was also well provided for. The St Albans Literary Institute had a long history, dating back to 1823, while in the later nineteenth century the library housed a 'very Victorian' School of Science and Art.[143] Under the auspices of the library and school, an annual 'conversazione' was held, at which prints depicting the history of St Albans were exhibited, a musical entertainment staged and refreshments served. An eclectic lecture series was also staged: lectures in 1889 ranged from the vicar of Hemel Hempstead on 'Peter the Great' to Frederick Kinneir Tarte on 'The Progress, Art and Mystery of Woodcarving'.[144] Tarte was a member of one especially prominent organisation, the St Albans Architectural Society, which was established in 1845 and played a key role in the restoration of the clock tower and the abbey church in the nineteenth century (see box 10). Under the long presidency of the second earl of Verulam, James Grimston – who exhibited considerably more enthusiasm for architecture than for sport, and who held the office from 1846 to 1895 – the Society hosted lectures and discussions, and carried out archaeological digs; its annual meeting, in the words of its historian, 'became one of the social events of the year'.[145] Like other Victorian learned societies, the Society published a series of *Transactions*, beginning in 1883; by 1895 it had about 120 members.[146] Two name changes – to the St Albans Architectural and Archaeological Society in 1850 and the St Albans and Hertfordshire Architectural and Archaeological Society in 1897 – reflected its broadening intellectual and geographical scope. In the 1890s and early 1900s William Page, who served as joint honorary secretary of the society, edited – and contributed to – the four volumes of the *Victoria County History* for Hertfordshire, as well many volumes covering other counties.

The Society was involved in one particularly notable arena of civic display: the urban pageant, a heavily promoted feature of the lives of several towns in the Edwardian period. Pageants with a historical theme, popular in places with long and distinguished histories such as St Albans, were especially colourful, and embodied a distinctive conception of national and local history. As Waller explains, at St Albans, Bury St Edmunds, Colchester and elsewhere, 'citizens re-enacted ancient battles and royal visits, and melodramatised key episodes in their civic past ... These pageants ... emphasized the continuing honour and fulfilment of civic life.'[147] At St Albans, the pageant held in July 1907 involved six days of festivities with a historical theme, scripted by Charles Ashdown, a science master at St Albans School, secretary of the Architectural and Archaeological Society and author of *St Albans Historical and Picturesque*, published in 1893.[148] Ashdown's pageant involved the 'dramatic representation' of eight historical episodes;[149] the large board of patrons and ten organising committees (for example, the costumes committee, the casting committee and the horse committee) were assisted by Herbert Jarman and Philip Carr from the Lyric Theatre in London. Ashdown's wife was given the title 'Chief Mistress of the Robes'. The eight episodes were Julius Caesar's first invasion of Britain; Boudicca's revolt; the martyrdom of St Alban; Offa's foundation of the abbey; the funeral procession of Queen Eleanor; the peasants' revolt; the second battle of St Albans; and the visit of Elizabeth I to Gorhambury in 1572.[150] Each required a large cast: for example, the last scene involved 27 main actors, plus a chorus of 9 aldermen and 16 burgesses.[151] In total, there were 3,000 performers at the St Albans pageant, and the temporary grandstands that were erected in Verulamium Park had a capacity of 4,000.[152] The Elizabethan scene ended with morris dancing, masquing and 'Old English Sports', reflecting the popularity of nostalgic displays of folk culture in the late nineteenth and early twentieth centuries.[153] The pageant concluded with an 'Ode to Verulam and St Albans' and 'Apotheosis of St Albans', followed by the national anthem. A brief extract from the 'Apotheosis' gives a flavour of the mingled pride in Englishness, and in the city itself (still referred to as a 'Town'), that was in evidence at the pageant:

'So many visitors came, especially Americans ... there were many amusing and incongruous sights ...'

> O fain would we sing of St Alban's town,
> Its history rare and its bright renown
> That is written in song and in story;
> Its sons stand proudly in niches of fame,
> And its daughters fair have honoured the name
> And have shared in its life and its glory.
>
> ...
>
> For centuries long have your highways rung
> With the sibilant sound of the Saxon tongue
> Resounding in song or in ditty;
> And the sturdy race with its thews of steel
> Have striven and fought, for woe or for weal,
> For Lady-love blithesome and witty.[154]

The pageant embodied a mixture of professionalism and amateurishness, in both organisation and performance. Elsie Toms, who became mayor of St

Albans in the 1960s and wrote a history of the city, attended the pageant as a child and remembered the occasion as

a huge success. So many visitors came, especially Americans wishing to take back a souvenir, that they started to take away bits of the Roman wall, and the Earl of Verulam, then the owner, was forced to put up an unclimbable fence along the length … There were many amusing and incongruous sights in the streets. Since there were no extensive dressing-rooms on the site for the very large cast, the performers dressed at home and walked or drove to the pageant ground, and one laughed to see a Roman soldier strolling along smoking a pipe, and a Briton in skins riding a bicycle. One saw an Elizabethan lady in brocade (probably the drawing-room curtains cut up), walking arm-in-arm with a cross-gartered Saxon in a yellow wig and long drooping moustache. It all added to the fun, and it brought trade to the shops and warmed the hearts of the shopkeepers. The ordinary citizen began to comprehend that there was something special about his city and something worth preserving.[155]

A second pageant, in 1909, centred on Clarence Park, was a smaller affair, resulting from an exchange between St Albans and Caen in Normandy.[156] 'Pageant fever' gripped many English towns in the Edwardian period, stimulating local history and generating substantial sales for the lavish souvenir programmes that were produced for the occasions.[157] One historian has recently seen the historical pageants of the period as having 'embodied the perceived significance of individual localities in the broader tapestry of English history'.[158]

Pageants were one aspect of a historical or preservationist consciousness that was awakened in English towns in these years, epitomised in St Albans by a bitterly fought, and successful, campaign to prevent the Post Office from installing telegraph poles in St Peter's Street in 1906, and a less successful attempt in the previous year, led by Charles Ashdown, to stop the demolition of Hall Place, the house in which Henry VI had reputedly stayed prior to the first battle of St Albans in 1455 (see box 3).[159] Writing to the *Herts Advertiser*, Ashdown complained that 'in losing Hall Place we lose a connecting link with the past history of our city which is nothing short of a misfortune for the town … yet, perhaps, good may ensue by directing the attention of the citizens to the existing

The St Albans pageant of 1907 was one of a number of similar civic occasions that took place in Edwardian urban England. This poster features an illustration by Robert Groves, head of St Albans School of Art, showing a knight in armour with a trumpet from which is hanging a St Albans flag.

© ST ALBANS MUSEUMS

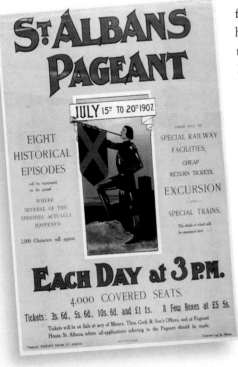

treasures in our midst still remaining to us, and which may be at some future time threatened with similar destruction'.[160]

There was a growing interest in St Albans as a tourist destination in this period, as demonstrated by Toms's remarks about visitors coming from as far as the USA, which Ashdown also mentioned in his letter about Hall Place.[161] A letter in the *Herts Advertiser* in 1889 remarked on the visitors 'who come to St Albans, to enjoy its fine air and pretty scenery', and complained about the lack of seats available in and around the city for their use.[162] At the August bank holiday of the same year, the paper reported that some 3,500 visitors, mostly from London, had visited the city on Midland trains, and a further 1,050 using the Great Northern railway. (On the same day, 2,790 residents of St Albans took advantage of bank holiday excursion trains to travel elsewhere.)[163] A series of histories and guidebooks was published for use by both natives and visitors. One example, a guidebook by Charles Ashdown, published in 1907, told the familiar history of St Albans, and described the abbey and the places of interest in the city centre. Ashdown also recommended a visit to St Michael's church – 'The church is locked, but the verger lives close by, half-way between the churchyard gate and the bridge, No. 13, St Michael's Cottages'[164] – and to the Roman theatre and Gorhambury. Unsurprisingly, as secretary of the Architectural and Archaeological Society, Ashdown deemed the Hertfordshire County Museum on Hatfield Road 'thoroughly worthy of a visit'.[165] The museum contained a natural history collection, the Lewis Evans collection of Hertfordshire books and prints, the library of the Architectural and Archaeological Society, a large range of antiquities from St Albans and other sites in Hertfordshire and beyond, and a series of more modern exhibits such as old local banknotes, fifteenth-century consumer goods from London and a trimming loom for bonnets dating from the early nineteenth century.[166] Ashdown's guidebook gave practical advice on how to reach St Albans from London – by rail, or by any one of five road routes from the capital, including the line of Watling Street. St Albans's proximity to London meant that it was accessible by bicycle.[167]

By the time of the First World War, St Albans was a flourishing small cathedral city, with a range of light industry and a fairly diverse economy, which would stand it in good stead during the economic upheavals of the interwar years. Horticulture, printing, clothing and a fledgeling electrical sector were the most striking newcomers; but the largest sectors of employment were construction, for men, and domestic service, for women. The former was the result of the continuing growth of the city and its surrounding area – houses, schools, churches, factories and offices were all under construction – and the latter reflected the continued importance of domestic service in the economic structure of Britain in the early twentieth century. In common with other towns, St Albans suffered from the fluctuating fortunes of the

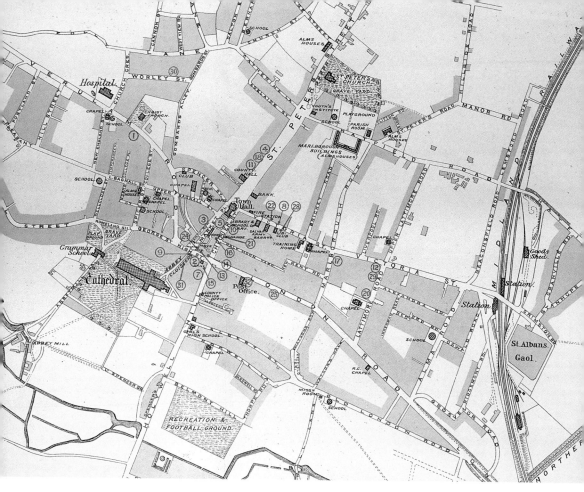

This map, dating from the 1900s, was produced by Borough and County Advertisers, and shows many of the businesses of St Albans. The eastward expansion of the city in the Victorian period is clearly visible on this map, and the Midland Railway station is shown, next to the city jail.

construction sector. St Albans was no longer an important service point for road traffic as it had been well into the first half of the nineteenth century; and it was no longer at the centre of a flourishing straw industry, although some straw hat manufacture still took place. There was still a preponderance of females in the population, exceeding that of most other places in Britain. Economically, the arrival of the railway had re-established the importance of St Albans's closeness to London: by the early twentieth century, although St Albans retained some importance as a service centre for its surrounding agricultural communities, its main economic links were with the capital. Culturally, in common with other towns and cities in this period, St Albans had developed a network of organised activities and a sense of civic pride that bore tangible results in the form of institutions such as the museum and the library, as well as events such as the pageant of 1907. The reforms of the parliamentary and local government electoral franchises in the nineteenth century, together with the establishment of new municipal and county authorities, meant that the political culture of St Albans in 1914 was very different from that of the 'small corrupt borough' which had been disenfranchised due to bribery and corruption in the by-election campaign of 1850 (see box 9). The associational life of the city was active and engaged, contrasting with the 'very prescribed' social life of which Solomon Shaw had complained in 1815.[168] Moreover, although insanitary conditions and poverty had certainly not disappeared, St Albans was probably a much more pleasant environment in which to live by the early twentieth century.

CHAPTER EIGHT

An expanding manufacturing centre, 1914–1945

THE social historian John Stevenson has explained that 'the dominating impression of the [1914–45] era is of economic dislocation and instability: two world wars and a severe and persistent depression marked one of the most chequered periods for economic life at both national and local levels'. However, Stevenson goes on:

> alongside this catalogue of disruption and deprivation has to be placed the fact of major economic growth in Britain between these years. In spite of war and depression, economic growth permitted a rise in living standards for the majority of the population over the period as a whole. Whether measured in terms of real incomes, mass consumption or standards of health and welfare, side by side with the suvival of large areas of poverty and deprivation the period witnessed a rise in material standards of living …[1]

Whereas the old 'staple' industries of iron and steel, coal, cotton and shipbuilding suffered from a combination of longer-term decline and the depression of the early 1930s, new and growing industries – car and aircraft manufacture, light engineering, food processing, chemicals, electricity generation and consumer durables such as irons, vacuum cleaners and radios – prospered. Mass production of consumer goods, together with the earnings available from employment in these industries, sparked a 'retailing revolution'.[2] Mail order – aggressively promoted in St Albans before the First World War by Samuel Ryder[3] – hire purchase, high street chain stores and mass advertising campaigns were all features of the period. At the same time, salaried employment in the service sector increased; house-building accelerated (2.7 million new homes were built in England and Wales in the 1930s alone);[4] and the provision of social services, especially healthcare and education, was steadily improved, at least in the places that shared in the new industrial and commercial prosperity. These developments were concentrated in the south of England: car manufacture was associated with Coventry, Oxford, Dagenham and Luton, aircraft manufacture with Hatfield – and so on. A shift in the economic balance of power within Britain was in evidence, so that from 1925 onwards unemployment was lower in London and the south-east than in the rest of the country.[5]

St Albans benefited from the changing economic climate, attracting new industries and inhabitants during the interwar years. The population of the municipal borough (see table 8.1, opposite) grew from 18,133 in 1911 to 25,593 in 1921, an increase of 41.1 per cent. Much of this expansion was due to the extension of the boundaries in 1913; however, by 1931, with no further boundary changes the population had grown to 28,624, an increase of 11.8 per cent on 1921. The St Albans rural district was also increasing in population, by 34.7 per cent in the period 1921–31. The continued expansion of St Albans resulted in a further extension of the boundaries in 1935, with the result that the borough population on the eve of the Second World War was estimated at 42,450, well over twice its size in 1911. Between 1921 and 1939 the combined population of the municipal borough and rural district grew from 40,126 to 68,608, or more than 70 per cent in 18 years (see table 8.1). This chapter explores the economic and social changes associated with the growth of the city. However, it is necessary to start with an examination of the impact of war.

... the city rapidly filled with troops ... Some 8,000 territorials arrived ...

The initial impact of the First World War on St Albans was comparatively modest. When it began in August 1914, a recruiting office was set up in St Peter's Street, but, despite widespread pressure to enlist, including sermons preached by local clergymen, recruitment to the armed forces in St Albans was slow: not until eight months had elapsed since the start of the war did the number reach 1,000.[6] The relative slowness of the 'rush to the colours' in the city – after the initial enthusiasm, recruitment became a 'trickle' of four or five a week – can be explained by the relatively buoyant economy, and the low pay of soldiers, coupled with a widespread uncertainty about whether jobs would be kept open for those who enlisted.[7] In addition, some workers' ordinary jobs were important to the war effort, such as the skilled employees of Mercer's Chronometers, who were required to increase production to equip ships during the war.[8] However, the city rapidly filled with troops, being a training centre for the London territorial regiments, and later regiments from further afield, who were billeted in private houses and in schools.[9] Within a few days of the outbreak of war, some 8,000 territorials arrived in St Albans.[10] According to the historian William Page, writing in 1920, the arrival of these troops for training

Table 8.1 Population of St Albans, 1901–1971

	Municipal Borough of St Albans		St Albans Rural District	
	Population	Growth (%)	Population	Growth (%)
1901	16,019	24.2	12,264	
1911	18,133	13.2	19,463	58.7
1921	25,593	41.1*	14,533	−25.3†
1931	28,624	11.8	19,578	34.7
1939	42,450	48.3‡	26,158	33.6§
1951	44,098	3.9	28,608	9.4
1961	50,293	14.0	38,947	36.1
1971	52,174	3.7	45,350	16.4

* Boundaries extended 1913.

† Boundaries reduced 1913.

‡ Boundaries extended 1935.

§ Boundaries reduced 1935.

The boundaries of the borough were extended in 1913 and 1935. In 1913 the area of the borough increased from 997 acres to 2,703 acres, and in 1935 it was increased to 5,125 acres, an area over 16 times larger than the medieval borough. On the same occasions, reductions occurred in the area of the rural district, although, because of other alterations, these did not exactly correspond to the increases in the acreage of the borough. In 1911 the rural district consisted of 38,772 acres; this was reduced in 1913 to 37,066 acres; and in 1935 it was further reduced to 31,783 acres. The expansion of the population of the rural district in the 1930s therefore looks particularly impressive.

In 1945 the population of the 'city' of St Albans was estimated at 47,088: the 'normal' population was swollen by troops and evacuees.

See appendix for the sources used in compiling this table.

'the tramp of soldiers soon became too familiar to attract attention.'

changed the whole aspect of the town. Soldiers were billeted in every available house or other building, every hotel was crowded with officers, and every vacant house was commandeered for headquarters or other military purposes. The streets were filled with khaki-clad men, and the sound of the bugle, the sharp words of military command, the rumbling of the transport lorries and the tramp of soldiers soon became too familiar to attract attention.[11]

The influx of troops necessitated emergency public health measures, as the sewage disposal facilities in the buildings used for billeting soldiers were 'quite inadequate'.[12] Buckets were used as makeshift lavatories, and the disposal of excreta carried out carefully under the direction of the medical officer of health; at the same time an increased frequency of household refuse collection was required. Collaboration between civil and military authorities was essential, and, at least in the early years of the war, it appears to have worked in St Albans.[13]

Under the Defence of the Realm (Consolidated) Regulations of 1914, a blackout was imposed across the city from one hour after sunset to one hour before sunrise.[14] A warning hooter was placed on the town hall roof, but there were no air raids on St Albans during the First World War, although the headquarters of the Anti-Aircraft Defence for London (Northern Command) were established in the city.[15] German airships fell at nearby Cuffley and Potter's Bar, and were visible from St Albans; but in 1918 the *Herts Advertiser* reported a 'sense of immunity from, at any rate immediate danger' that seemed to prevail in the city.[16] On a day-to-day level, the disruption caused to the city was considerable, and needed to be managed with care: for example, the use of schools to billet soldiers in the early months of the war caused concern, and a Board of Education inspector was appointed to oversee the transition back from military to educational use.[17] Medical services in St Albans and nearby were turned over to military use, notably the asylum at Napsbury, which was used as a military hospital that could accommodate 2,000 men; a Voluntary Aid Detachment Hospital was also established, at Bricket House.[18] Local men volunteered for duties as special constables; and a 'National Kitchen' was established at the corn exchange.[19] The cinemas showed films depicting the events of the war, and the people of the city collected chocolate to send to the troops at the front line, who in turn sent letters of thanks to the local press when it arrived.[20]

The men who volunteered were likely to find themselves in the Hertfordshire Regiment, although over time they were increasingly likely to be drafted

A postcard dating from 1914, showing soldiers marching on Hatfield Road in Fleetville. As an important training centre in the First World War, St Albans experienced a considerable influx of troops, with which the urban infrastructure was not easily able to cope.

into other regiments, including the Bedfordshire Regiment, which served at Gallipoli.[21] Following the introduction of conscription in 1916, many served with the 7th (Service) Battalion of the Bedfordshire Regiment at the Somme.[22]

A street war memorial on Fishpool Street, one of 10 in St Albans erected, along with the main memorial on St Peter's Street, after the First World War. More than 100 names are recorded on these street memorials, which are believed to be unique in Britain.
PHOTOGRAPH: AUTHOR

The *Herts Advertiser* also reported the involvement of local men at Jutland, Mons, Ypres (where 110 men of the Hertfordshire Regiment were killed in a single day), Italy, Iraq and Palestine.[23] In total, 640 are named on the war memorial in front of St Peter's church, almost all of whom were in the Army. It is difficult to estimate the impact of this loss on the general population trends in St Albans, but the number of recorded deaths is about 15 per cent of the total male population aged 20–44 in 1921. The loss of these young men had little impact on the sex ratio in the municipal borough, which stood at 81 in 1911 and 80 in 1921.[24] As well as this memorial, there were ten street memorials, a memorial at St Albans School, and a book of remembrance in the cathedral.[25]

After the war, a widely articulated desire to return to 'normalcy' was echoed in St Albans, where many of the developments of the pre-war decades continued. Already home to a range of industrial premises, many dating from the Edwardian period, as described in the last chapter, the city continued to attract new businesses in the years after the war. In the 1920s, St Albans was a flourishing place. In 1922, *Kelly's Directory* for St Albans announced: 'Here is a silk mill, employing a number of hands; the manufacture of straw trimmings also gives employment to a large number of persons, and straw plaiting is carried on, straw hats being the staple manufacture; there are two breweries, maltings, two boot factories, chromo-lithographic printing works, a brush factory and a clothing factory.'[26] In 1924, there were 82 factories, 110 workshops and 27 other workplaces in St Albans, a total of 219; of these, 29 employed more than 40 people.[27] The next fifteen years would see significant industrial expansion. The one area in which decline was evident was straw hat manufacture. Although *Kelly's Directory* could still, optimistically, call it 'the staple manufacture' of St Albans in 1922, this was certainly not the case at the outbreak of the Second World War. Even in 1920, according to John G. Dony, there were 'only three or four firms left' in St Albans making straw hats.[28] The industry was increasingly concentrated in Luton, which by the time of the Second World War was 'the biggest centre for the manufacture of women's hats', and had about 270 'hat manufacturing units'.[29] In St Albans, E. Day (St Albans) Limited, hat manufacturers on Marlborough Road, went bankrupt in 1923, and Dunham and Martin on Fishpool Street closed in 1937 (they occupied the former premises of Munt, Brown and Company).[30] Other hat manufacturers diversified their operations: as early as 1916, stimulated by wartime demand, Webdale and Day's factory, at the corner of Oswald Road and Alma Road, moved into the manufacture of 'tropical helmets', becoming Helmets Limited in 1923; and Horace Slade and Company Limited on Victoria Street increasingly concentrated on cardboard boxes rather than straw hats.[31] The underlying 'tendency for women to go hatless', which was also found among men, further restricted demand for the products of hat factories.[32] Another casualty of the interwar period was the silk mill at the end of Abbey Mill Lane, which closed in 1938; the Holywell brewery near the Peahen closed in 1918, when its owners merged with Adey and White, operators of

The main St Albans war memorial, in front of St Peter's church. The memorial was unveiled in 1921, and contains the names of 640 men who fell in the First World War. After the Second World War the names of a further 162 were added to the memorial.

PHOTOGRAPH: CARNEGIE

the St Albans Brewery on Chequer Street. In turn, Adey and White ceased production in 1936.[33]

However, in many other manufacturing industries, St Albans saw considerable growth in this period. Not only did some older firms flourish and expand, but many companies established new premises in the city, encouraged by a promotional campaign undertaken by the city council, and supported by the local chamber of commerce. The city's propaganda emphasised its 'modernity': in 1919, the official guide to St Albans proclaimed,

'a large percentage of the population consists of the artisan and working class'

St Albans is a historic city, but its claim to notice in the twentieth century is not based simply upon its ancient greatness or its relics of yester-year. These things, while they give to it dignity and romantic attraction, have yet made way for progress, expansion, enterprise and modernity. St Albans has not lagged behind in the race of the years: it is as close abreast of the twentieth century as it was of the tenth.[34]

By 1928, the tone of the official guide was even more confident: 'In the manufacturing world, St Albans is securely winning a position of importance, while the advantages it offers to those interested in the selection of sites for new factories or works, particularly in connection with light industries, are such as to merit special attention.'[35] The city's 'commercial advantages' included 'cheap, healthy available sites; proximity to the Metropolis; low rates; progressive local administration; a plentiful supply of labour; and excellent housing accommodation'.[36] The point about labour was emphasised again: 'Labour is plentiful – a large percentage of the population consists of the artisan and working class.'[37] Of course, not all the skills required by employers were available locally: for example, the demand for chronometers in the First World War was more than could be met by the skilled workers available to Mercer's, and chronometer parts had to be sought from elsewhere.[38]

Some industrial and commercial ventures in St Albans in the 1920s reflected the specialisms that had developed in the city before the First World War; others were representative of the new industrial sectors of the interwar period. The New Barnes flour mill on the river Ver, which had been in use since the late nineteenth century (and stood on the site of a much older mill), was operated by the British Flour Research Committee from the 1920s, and taken over by the Co-operative Wholesale Society in the 1930s.[39] Cardboard box manufacture had been carried out briefly in the 1900s,[40] and in 1922 the British Cardboard Box Company acquired the site of the old sanitary laundry on Belmont Hill. This establishment, known as the Belmont Works, employed 150 people at its peak.[41] As we have seen, Horace Slade also moved into cardboard box production. There were also new printing ventures, such as J. W. Vernon and Company, who took over the Fleetville Club and Institute in 1925, turning it into a printing press.[42] Meanwhile, Smith's closed in 1923, and the Fleet Works were occupied, for a short period, by Sir Howard Grubb and Sons, who manufactured astronomical instruments.[43] In 1926, the premises were taken over by St Albans Hosiery Mills Limited, later known as Ballito, which manufactured silk stockings, and employed as many as 1,000 workers, even during the depression of the 1930s.[44] The spread of electricity in domestic and industrial use in the interwar period was reflected in St Albans by the establishment of a factory on Mile House Lane in 1919 by the Electrical Apparatus Company, which was previously based in Battersea.[45] Although no cars were made at St Albans – unlike nearby Luton which became one of the centres of the industry – the arrival of Handley Page at Park Street in 1928, and the opening of Radlett Aerodrome in 1930, heralded the importance, for much of the twentieth century, of aircraft manufacture in the area.[46] At Hatfield, de Havilland's aircraft factory was constructed in the early 1930s: 900 employees worked there in 1934, when the DH–88 Comet aircraft was built.[47] Food processing was another developing sector, represented in St Albans by Avery's Vermicelli Limited, which took over the the premises occupied by Helmets Limited in 1923.[48] Another example of new interwar developments was Heath and Heather Limited, established by Samuel Ryder and his brother James (a retired schoolmaster). This herb company started on Albert Street in 1920, moved to a former hat factory in Dagnall Street in 1922, and then to another old hat manufacturer's premises – Vyse, Sons and Company Limited – on Ridgmont Road two years later. By 1925 Heath and Heather proclaimed itself 'the largest retail herb warehouse in the world', and employed 120 people.[49] Continued expansion throughout the interwar period and beyond saw the company grow to a strength of 46 shops across the country by 1946.[50]

Existing industrial companies were expanding their premises, workforces and ranges of products in interwar St Albans. From 1921 onwards, the city council's official guide included details of 'Representative Firms', most of which had long associations with the city. In 1923, six companies were featured, including A. E. Massey, timber merchants on London Road, who also operated a steam sawmill until the late 1920s,[51] as well as Horace Slade's and Ryder's. Another was Wiles and Lewis Limited, established 'in the reign of George III [1760–1820]', whose modern factory on Bernard's Heath had been rebuilt after the fire of 1911 and expanded to meet the worldwide demand for Ariston suet.[52] Wiles and Lewis were increasingly concentrating on edible, rather than commercial fats: they

This advertisement for Heath and Heather dates from 1948. The company was established by Samuel and James Ryder in 1920, and grew rapidly thereafter. The company had its head office on Ridgmont Road, and retail outlets across the country, including the one advertised on St Albans High Street.

AUTHOR COLLECTION

Advertisements dating from 1948 for three local products and services. Rose's lime juice cordial, along with lime marmalade, was produced at St Albans from 1939. L. Rose and Company Limited was acquired by Schweppes in 1957, although production continued in St Albans thereafter. The Waterend Barn was in fact two barns: one dating from the seventeenth century, taken from Water End near Sandridge, and one from the sixteenth century, from Great Hormead in east Hertfordshire. Adams Bakers survived until the mid-1950s.

AUTHOR COLLECTION

had previously specialised in tallow. The other two firms featured in the 1923 guide were John Freshwater and Company Limited and Edwin Lee and Sons Limited, both boot and shoe manufacturers. Freshwater's, on Lower Dagnall Street, specialised in ladies' footwear 'designed for moderate purses'; they were acquired by H. E. Joyner and Company Limited two years later, moving to the production of children's shoes in the mid-1930s.[53] The official guide declared that St Albans, 'if not the Metropolis of the boot-making industry, is at least one of its most important centres'.[54] Other companies that expanded during the interwar period included W. O. Peake Limited, which launched Rodex, 'the aristocrat of coats', in the 1920s, and grew steadily from the 300 employees of 1916 to around 500 in the early 1950s.[55] The St Albans Rubber Company was also growing, and Brushes Limited, which became Kra Brushes in 1933, continued in production to 1939, when its factory was taken over by L. Rose and Company Limited, producing lime juice cordial and lime marmalade.[56] There was also various small-scale industrial production – wigs, mats, wire and ribbons – at Heath Road in Sandridge New Town;[57] and Mercer's Chronometers, stimulated by the additional demand of the First World War, expanded, and diversified into a range of products, including survey chronometers, chronometer-controlled electric clocks, and dial gauges, in the 1920s and 1930s.[58]

All this industrial expansion generated employment in and around St Albans, and the economy, along with those of other towns in the south-east of England, remained relatively buoyant during the difficult economic circumstances of the 1930s. According to Elsie Toms, 'St Albans largely escaped [the depression], and there was almost no unemployment'.[59] This was a slight exaggeration, as according to the manager of the St Albans labour exchange in 1930, cited in

James Corbett's history of the city, there were about 300 unemployed; the manager blamed local unemployment partly on the depression and partly on the decline of industries such as ribbon-making.[60] However, in most respects, St Albans was one of the more fortunate places in the country in the 1930s: in 1934, just 3.9 per cent of insured workers in St Albans were unemployed, an even lower rate than the prosperous car manufacturing towns of Luton (7.7 per cent), Oxford and Coventry (both 5.1 per cent). These compare with rates of well over 50 per cent in some manufacturing towns in the north of England, Wales and Scotland.[61] In terms of health, measured crudely by the death rate, St Albans out-performed the rest of the country during the interwar period: in 1924 the death rate was 11.4 per thousand, compared with 12.2 in England and Wales as a whole, and in 1938 it stood at 10.1, against 11.6 for England and Wales.[62] Although the infant mortality rate (deaths of children under 1 year of age per 1,000 live births) in St Albans was 84 in 1924 compared with 75 for England and Wales as a whole, the St Albans figure was inflated by several deaths from pneumonia; and in 1938 the rate was 42, against 53 for England and Wales.[63]

In terms of social welfare provision, the interwar period is often characterised as one of steady but not spectacular improvement; sometimes as a 'missed opportunity', compared with the periods of intense welfare legislation before the First World War and again after 1945.[64] It was a time of considerable regional

Warwick's crisps were made for a local family, who ran a chain of fish and chip shops in the city, from the 1920s to the 1980s. This packet dates from the 1930s.

© ST ALBANS MUSEUMS

The Sisters' Hospital was a fever hospital built in 1893 and donated to the city by Sir John Blundell Maple. It was on the poor law infirmary site, where the St Albans City Hospital now stands. In 1936 it became part of the St Albans Joint Hospital. This picture shows part of the hospital, now called Sisters' Lodge and converted into housing.

PHOTOGRAPH: AUTHOR

inequalities in healthcare and other welfare services, when local authorities had certain statutory duties, but when much legislation was permissive, and unadopted by many authorities. Healthcare, in St Albans as elsewhere, was made available through a mixture of private and public hospitals and services. In 1924, the medical officer of health, Richard R. K. Paton, described eight institutions in the city. Four of these were hospitals, all dating from before the First World War: the St Albans and Mid-Herts Hospital and Dispensary, a private institution with about 50 beds, which treated 389 in-patients and 1,756 out-patients in 1924; the Sisters' Hospital, with 36 beds, which treated scarlet fever and diphtheria; the Cherry Tree Hospital near Redbourn, for smallpox cases; and the Union Infirmary, with 140 beds, an operating theatre, a lying-in ward and three isolation wards.[65] By 1938, the Union Infirmary had been restyled the Public Assistance Institution and Infirmary, and was in the hands of the Hertfordshire County Council; its capacity had expanded to 192 beds. The Sisters' Hospital, rebuilt in 1936, was renamed the St Albans Joint Hospital; and the St Albans and Mid-Herts Hospital and Dispensary remained, still financed by 'Endowments, Voluntary Contributions, [and] Fees from or in respect of Patients'.[66] An x-ray wing had opened in 1929.[67] The other four institutions in 1924, all of which survived, largely unchanged, in 1938, were the St Albans District Nursing Association, based in Bricket House and supported by voluntary contributions and grants from the county council; the Herts

The artist Louis William Wain (1860–1939) was a patient at Napsbury mental hospital near St Albans from 1930 until his death. He was known for his paintings of cats. This painting is entitled 'A Teaparty at Napsbury'

County Nursing Association, Massage and Orthopaedic Centre, also at Bricket House and supported by the Red Cross, ex-servicemen's charities, and fees paid by civilian patients; the Tuberculosis Dispensary on Victoria Street; and an ambulance service – one Red Cross motor ambulance in 1924 and two, owned by the city council, in 1938.[68] The medical officer of health reports did not mention the Hertfordshire County Mental Hospital (formerly Lunatic Asylum) at Hill End, which by 1922 had grounds comprising 352.5 acres and, following the construction of a new block in 1917, could accommodate 920 patients.[69] Further extensions to the site and the buildings were made in 1934, and by 1938 the hospital could accommodate 1,232 patients on a 589-acre estate.[70]

One area of healthcare provision in which local authorities were increasingly involved in the interwar period was maternal and child welfare, and St Albans city council participated in this development. A circular from the Local Government Board in 1914 suggested that local authorities should take upon themselves the organisation of a midwife service, the provision of advice to pregnant women and 'arrangements for efficient and skilled attendance at childbirth', as well as health services for infants and young children. As a result, Hertfordshire County Council appointed eight health visitors, who would work with the medical officers of health in different parts of the county; one of these, a Miss Ransom, was appointed for St Albans.[71] The Maternity and Child Welfare Act (1918) gave statutory authority to the 1914 circular, although the legislation was still only permissive; it also required local authorities which made provision to establish a committee for the purpose, which must have at least two female members.[72] The St Albans committee, established in 1915, consisted of five members of the council 'and 3 ladies'.[73] By 1924, the St Albans Maternity and Child Welfare Centre – organised under county council auspices – had 12 pregnant women and 343 children under the age of five on its register. The children made a total of 2,981 attendances during the year.[74] By 1938 the numbers had risen to 148 pregnant women and 722 children, with a total of 5,232 attendances.[75] In the case of maternal and child welfare, as in other areas of healthcare, provision in St Albans was relatively good: as one historian has pointed out, 'the services provided by local government ... tended to be least well developed in the areas of greatest need', and the relative affluence of St Albans, and Hertfordshire as a whole, ensured that a range of services could be provided.[76] The same was true for education (see box 11).

The interwar period saw the expansion of municipal utilities and local transport services, which in turn provided more employment in St Albans and enhanced the facilities available to the inhabitants. Gas continued to be supplied by the St Albans Gas Company, as had been the case before the war, but this 'very well managed undertaking' merged with its Watford counterpart to form the Watford and St Albans Gas Company in 1930.[77] Meanwhile, the North Metropolitan Electric Power Supply Company Limited offered special rates

... material and child welfare ... provision in St Albans was relatively good ...

continued on page 271

THE EXPANSION of educational provision was another significant but uneven development in the interwar period, and assumed particular importance in a growing city such as St Albans. As noted in the last chapter, the expansion of elementary education on the new housing estates following the requirements of the Education Act of 1870 was a feature of the late nineteenth century,[1] and further changes followed the First World War. The expansion of St Albans necessitated a significant investment in education, although the birth rate in the city was somewhat lower than in the nation as a whole: 14.1 per thousand people versus a national rate of 18.8 in 1924, and 14.4 against 15.1 for England and Wales in 1938.[2]

Since 1902, the local education authority (LEA) had been Hertfordshire County Council, but direct responsibility for St Albans was devolved to a Local Education Sub-Committee, which included representatives of the city council. In 1922 the Sub-Committee controlled seven infants' and elementary schools: Alma Road, Bernard's Heath, Camp, Fleetville, Garden Fields, Hatfield Road and Priory Park, all of which dated from before the First World War.[3] There were also several 'maintained schools', in the voluntary sector but in receipt of some LEA and Board of Education Grants, including Christ Church, SS Alban and Stephen Roman Catholic school and St Peter's.[4] The national school leaving age was 14, as provided for by the Education Act of 1918; and in 1926 the Hadow Committee report recommended that elementary schools be divided into primary and post-primary, or senior, schools, with the change coming at age 11. In Hertfordshire, the policy of the county council, in one historian's words,

was founded upon the conviction of most county councillors and education committee members that elementary education should be practically based and vocationally orientated, and would best serve the needs of employers and the children attending these schools by providing a rurally based education in the country and a technically based education in the towns.[5]

There was little enthusiasm for the expansion of more 'academic' secondary education in Hertfordshire. In the case of rural schools, the county's focus was part of an integrated rural educational structure, at the apex of which stood the Hertfordshire Institute of Agriculture at Oaklands, just outside the municipal boundaries of St Albans, which was established in 1921, the site having been purchased by the county council in the previous year for over £34,000.[6] Meanwhile, in towns such as St Albans, expanding employment opportunities in the manufacturing sector made a focus on technical education seem appropriate. This was not fundamentally challenged in the interwar period, and although there were significant institutional changes, most notably the construction of new schools, the curriculum was altered rather less.

The rapid growth of the population of interwar Hertfordshire gave a particular urgency to the question of educational provision. In the 1920s, the population of the county grew faster than that of any other, except Middlesex and Surrey, and in the 1930s its rate of growth was the highest of all.[7] The rapid in-migration of population was not

---

[1] See above, p. 241.

[2] *MOH Report 1924*, p. 5; *MOH Report 1938*, p. 4.

[3] Some of these schools were divided into separate infants' and juniors', or boys' and girls', sections; the total number given was 10.

[4] *Kelly's 1922*, pp. A65-A67.

[5] David Parker, '"This Gift from the Gods": Hertfordshire and the 1936 Education Act', *History of Education*, vol. 25 (1996), p. 167.

[6] Pelham, *Oaklands Story*, pp. 9, 13.

[7] Parker, 'Gift from the Gods', p. 170.

met by a correspondingly rapid school-building
programme in the 1920s or early 1930s, when a
combination of financial stringency during the
depression, and the opposition of the diocese of
St Albans, restricted the expansion of educational
facilities. In Hertfordshire, the role of the diocese
was crucial. Across England, during the interwar
period, Church of England schools were being
handed over to local education authorities, as
the Church found it increasingly difficult to find
the pupils and the money to support them. This
trend was not matched in Hertfordshire, where
under the leadership of Bishop Michael Furse,
the diocese of St Albans took part in 'a relentless
campaign to promote parish missions, rejuvenate
church-based social life, restore crumbling parish
churches, retain church schools, and revive
voluntary giving to pay for it all'.[1] Furse despised
the non-denominational religious education
provided in the LEA schools, and resisted the
surrender of parochial educational establishments
to the 'atheistic predator' that he identified in the

---

[1] David Parker, '"Stand Therefore!": Bishop Michael
Bolton Furse, the Diocese of St Albans, and the Church
Schools Controversy 1919–1939', *History of Education
Quarterly*, vol. 39 (1999), p. 171.

guise of the LEA.[1] As expanding populations and the evident unsuitability of school buildings in several Hertfordshire towns in the mid-1920s made educational reorganisation an urgent necessity, the diocese fought hard to maintain its powerful influence in secondary education. This prompted Nonconformist congregations to unite in opposition to the role of the established church, echoing the bitter confrontations of the Victorian and Edwardian period.[2] In Hertfordshire, the division took a political form, as Conservative MPs and county councillors supported the claims of the diocese, while the Liberals on the county council, and the growing number of Labour councillors in the 1930s, were more hostile.[3]

In 1928, following the recommendations of the Hadow Committee, the council established a Schools Reorganisation Committee, which repeatedly bypassed bishop Furse, who had asked to be consulted on the proposed reorganisation. The diocese was struggling to maintain its schools by the mid-1930s, and Furse inveighed against the spirit of surrender that seemed to have arisen in the parishes. The Education Act (1936) made

Board of Education grants available for LEA school-building programmes, and this 'altered substantially the balance of negotiating power in favour of LEAs'.[4] The Hertfordshire LEA was enabled to take control of the construction of new voluntary schools, by making large capital grants available and insisting on the highest standards of facilities. The result was a large programme of construction of secondary and senior elementary schools, the latter 'indistinguishable from secondary schools', which most of them would soon become, and 'a steady stream of gymnasia, assembly halls, laboratories, workshops and Domestic Science rooms'.[5] In St Albans, Beaumont senior boys' and girls' schools (which became Beaumont Secondary Modern school), the County Grammar School for boys (later Verulam school) and the County Grammar School for girls (later St Albans Girls School), were all built in 1938.[6]

This is not to suggest that voluntary sector provision of education was eclipsed in interwar St Albans. Indeed, the construction of Townsend Church of England Secondary Modern school,

1 Parker, 'Gift from the Gods', p. 169.
2 Parker, 'Stand Therefore!', pp. 174–5.
3 Ibid., p. 169.
4 Parker, 'Gift from the Gods', p. 171.
5 Ibid., pp. 178, 174.
6 Corbett, History of St Albans, p. 134.

which opened in 1936, demonstrated the vitality of diocesan education.[1] There was also a notable expansion of Roman Catholic education. Loreto school for girls opened in January 1922 with seven pupils, and expanded rapidly, purchasing Samuel Ryder's home, Marlborough House, in 1923.[2] A classroom and dormitory were added in 1924, a gymnasium in 1929, a 'science room' in 1934 and a chapel and library in 1937.[3] In 1934, SS Alban and Stephen elementary school moved from Beaconsfield Road to a new site at Vanda Crescent; this debt-financed building cost £7,100 and could accommodate 168 children.[4] Senior girls could be educated at St Albans High School for girls, which dated from the nineteenth century. Control of the school had passed from the Church Schools Company to a private limited company in 1907, and by 1933 the school could accommodate 300 pupils, including day girls and boarders.[5] In September 1939 St Columba's boys' school, owned

and headed by the flamboyant Philip O'Neill and focusing on 'character-building', opened on Beaconsfield Road, moving in the following year to Camp Road, and eventually to King Harry Lane.[6] Other private education was provided by St Albans School – the word 'Grammar' was dropped from its name in 1930 – which had 300 pupils (including 45 boarders) in 1919, and was undergoing what its historian has called a 'great expansion' under the headship of Edgar Montague Jones (1902–31). The number of boys reached 400 in 1928, and new classrooms were built in 1929.[7] The school received more than half of its income from fees, but around a third came from LEA and Board of Education grants.[8] From 1927, the school participated in the new Direct Grant scheme, which required it to offer a quarter of its places free, mostly funded by the county council. This funding was cut following the opening of the county council's new secondary schools in the second half of the 1930s.[9] Nevertheless, there were 463 pupils at the school in July 1939.[10]

[1]   Parker, 'Gift from the Gods', p. 170; Corbett, *History of St Albans*, p. 134. J. H. Brett, *St Albans: The City and Its People* (St Albans: St Albans City Council, 1974), pp. 72–3 gives the date as 1934.
[2]   Fry, *Samuel Ryder*, p. 65.
[3]   Corbett, *Celebration*, pp. 40–1.
[4]   Ibid., pp. 44–5.
[5]   *St Albans Annual and Who's Who 1933*, p. 26.

[6]   Corbett, *Celebration*, pp. 51–2.
[7]   Kilvington, *Short History of St Albans School*, chapter 9.
[8]   Ibid., p. 88.
[9]   Ibid., pp. 97–8.
[10]   Ibid., p. 102.

Beaumont senior boys' and girls' schools (now Beaumont secondary school), on Oakwood Drive were among a number of schools built in 1938, in a period of significant development of secondary and senior elementary education under the auspices of Hertfordshire County Council.

PHOTOGRAPH: AUTHOR

'designed to encourage the use of electricity for domestic purposes in addition to lighting'.[78] The city's streets were lit by electricity from 1933, also by the North Metropolitan company, rather later than in some other places – some urban electric street lighting was in place in the early 1880s and improvements in the 1890s and 1900s led to its increasing adoption in many towns and cities[79] – although the market stalls in St Albans had electric lights as early as 1923. There had a been a power station on Campfield Road from 1908, generating electricity from the city's refuse, and connected to 482 houses by 1914, but this project ran into political difficulties in the 1920s and the city reverted to a more conventional electricity supply in 1929.[80] Meanwhile, some of the surrounding rural districts still lacked gas lighting: for example, Sandridge acquired gas only in 1929.[81]

Transport developments also played a significant part in the life of the city in the interwar period. St Albans was still served by three railway stations, and the lines were heavily used by passengers and freight: the Great Northern Railway line enjoyed its 'heyday' in the early 1920s.[82] However, goods trains were losing out to competition from road hauliers, and passenger trains to bus services, in the post-First World War years, as former military vehicles were pressed into civilian service.[83] Bus services gave another opportunity for passenger travel: as early as 1909 a service between the city centre and Fleetville was started, followed by a bus link to Dunstable. Then, as Elsie Toms remembered,

> the London and General Omnibus Company took a hand, and we had a bus, open-topped of course, to Golders Green. To go up to Golders Green on the bus, stay on top, and return with the next journey, was an exciting excursion until the novelty wore off and we took buses for granted.[84]

By 1922, *Kelly's Directory* could report that 'motor omnibuses run at frequent intervals to & from the Market place to Golders Green, Luton, Watford, Dunstable, Radlett & Wheathampstead';[85] and although exactly the same summary was given by the directory until the Second World War,[86] it is clear from the official guide to St Albans that, by 1928, the range of destinations had increased to include Welwyn Garden City, Hitchin, Bedford, Leighton

This picture, dating from 1943, shows the entrance to St Albans city station, on the Midland Railway. The roof over the driveway was made of glass and iron.

Chequer Street is one of the oldest streets in St Albans: some historians believe that it was occupied before the Norman conquest. This view, looking north from the Peahen crossroads, dates from *c*.1910. On the right-hand side of the photograph is the Cross Keys pub, which then stood on the corner of Chequer Street and London Road. The sign shows that the Cross Keys sold ales and stout produced by Adey and White's brewery, which was further up the street on the right.

Buzzard, Bishop's Stortford and Harpenden (the last was, in any case, on the way to Luton). In addition, there were summer services (and restricted winter services) to Sandridge, Colney Heath, Tyttenhanger Green, Hemel Hempstead, Leverstock Green and Redbourn.[87] Within St Albans, several companies began to operate services running from the city centre along Camp Road from the mid-1920s.[88] A bus garage was opened on St Peter's Street, north of St Peter's Church, in 1936;[89] and in 1931 there were 487 male 'road transport workers' in the St Albans municipal borough, compared with 164 who worked on the railways.[90] (Figures for females are not available.) Private car ownership also increased significantly in the interwar period – in Britain, there were just over half a million cars in use in 1924, and over 2 million by 1938[91] – and St Albans, at a major road junction, experienced difficulties in accommodating traffic. Hatfield Road was widened in the early 1920s, a project which entailed the rehousing of some residents;[92] and traffic lights at the Peahen junction were introduced in the 1930s, to the bewilderment of some inhabitants and the amusement of others.[93] In 1928, the city council informed visitors that car parking was available in St Peter's Street, and there was 'ample' garage accommodation: two on London Road, one on Hatfield Road, one on Verulam Road and one at the Red Lion on the High Street.[94]

The improvement of local transport facilities enhanced St Albans's status as a commercial centre, and the number and variety of shops and services expanded, to meet demand both from the growing population of the city itself,

AN EXPANDING MANUFACTURING CENTRE | 273

and from the surrounding area. Not only would shoppers from nearby villages go to St Albans, but trains from the London suburbs, as well as the new bus service from Golders Green, opened up the shopping facilities of St Albans to inhabitants of north London. New stores in the interwar period included branches of Marks and Spencer (called a 'bazaar' in the trade directory),[95] Woolworth's and Sainsbury's, and various shoe shops.[96] Large numbers found employment in the retail sector: 717 men and 360 women in the municipal borough in 1931, and a further 247 men and 120 women in the St Albans rural district.[97] The city advertised itself as a place where shopping could be an enjoyable experience in many ways, especially to women, whose role as consumers was being increasingly appreciated in this period. In 1919, the city's official guide rather patronisingly claimed: 'The streets are so clean and bright, the shop windows so well dressed and attractive, and the service so prompt and careful that the feminine mind at least cannot fail to take pleasure in a shopping expedition in the old Cathedral city.'[98] By 1928 the city's self-promotion was even more effusive:

> St Albans is naturally the shopping centre for a considerable area. It is the shopping town for the county far more than is the county town [Hertford]. Its streets are wide and pleasant, well kept and cheerful, flanked in the chief business quarters by shops of every description, including many

flourishing modern establishments. The large shops are equal to all the demands of fashion and luxury; likewise they can supply everything required in the domestic ménage and in the furnishing and adornment of the home. Both the prices and the quality of goods compare very favourably with those of the big London houses.[99]

There were various 'refreshment houses', both chains and independents: the Pilgrim's Rest, Dolphin and Black Cat tea rooms, all on Holywell Hill; Slater's and Lyon's on the High Street; the Creamery on Chequer Street; and the Mecca and Bugler's on Market Place. There were also branches of Barclay's, Lloyd's, the Midland and the Westminster banks.[100] There were three cinemas in the city, two of which dated from before the First World War.[101] The Alpha on London Road was renamed the Poly in 1918 and the Regent in 1926; it was destroyed by fire in 1927, and replaced in 1931 by the Capitol, which had 1,620 seats. Only a little smaller was the Grand Cinema Palace on Stanhope Road, built with 1,408 seats in 1922; and although the St Albans Cinema on Chequer Street, renamed the Chequers in 1927, was smaller with only 799, it was claimed that 12,791 people had watched *Ben Hur* at the cinema in one week in 1928.[102]

Allied to the promotion of St Albans's advantages to the shopper was a growing exploitation of the potential for tourism. The pageant of 1907,[103] and the increasing opportunities available to Londoners – and those from further afield – to travel to places like St Albans, had heightened public, and official, awareness of the history and antiquities of the city. Not only were annual official guides to St Albans produced, serving a number of purposes, including attracting residents and business to the city, but there were unofficial publications as well, and the ongoing activities of bodies like the St Albans and Hertfordshire Architectural and Archaeological Society drew residents' attention to places of interest within the city. Sisley's *What to See in St Albans and Verulamium* is one example, in which three tea rooms and the Blacksmith's Arms pub were advertised.[104] The official guides included brief histories of, and guides to, the cathedral and other places of interest. The recent economic history of St Albans was not ignored: as early as 1919, Sander's orchid nursery had become a 'notable building', a designation that may have been encouraged by its proximity to the Midland railway station.[105] Although the interwar period has been seen as the 'nadir of local urban history' in some parts of the country, in St Albans there was a widespread popular consciousness of the past, reflected in the growing membership of the St Albans and Hertfordshire Architectural and Archaeological Society, which reached 270 on the eve of the Second World War.[106]

An urban conservationist movement arose in St Albans in this period, as old buildings were destroyed and replaced by examples of unattractive modernity.

The town hall and market stalls are shown in this picture, dating from *c*.1911.

Urban conservation societies existed in Britain before the First World War, and there was conflict about urban development in St Albans,[107] but fears about the impact of modernity were intensified in the interwar period, as conservationists assessed the impact of suburbanisation and the expansion of towns like St Albans. These concerns were closely associated with the development of tourism. For example, R. L. P. Jowitt, author of a guide to St Albans published in 1935, regretted that 'featureless suburbs are stretching out from the old city in most directions', and was relieved that none was visible from Verulamium.[108] Like many twentieth-century observers, Jowitt excoriated the style in which the cathedral had been restored by Lord Grimthorpe (see box 10), believing that 'public opinion would not now tolerate such vandalism'.[109] But in general, Jowitt thought that:

> Of all the places within a twenty-mile radius of London it is hard to find the equal of St Albans for beauty and intense historical interest. Its charm survives the inevitable intrusion that modern vulgarity has made here and there, and it still retains in a great measure the bright and happy air of the typical English market-town and cathedral city.[110]

The inhabitants of St Albans were increasingly campaigning against developments that, they felt, epitomised Jowitt's 'modern vulgarity'. However, although the opponents of telegraph poles in St Peter's Street in 1906 had been victorious,[111] campaigners in the 1920s and 1930s met with limited success. Opposition to the demolition of a Georgian house to construct the bus garage further up St Peter's Street in 1936 was unsuccessful;[112] and Elsie Toms regretted the interwar 'demolition of many of our fine old Georgian houses in St Peter's Street, which, especially on the west side, lost its dignified aspect and assumed the non-descript look it now has', as new shops were built.[113] A contemporaneous observer also felt that 'wide St Peter's Street is fast changing for the worse, Georgian work making way for plate-glass'.[114] A more sensitive piece of building work was the restoration in 1930 of the White Hart inn on Holywell Hill, where the brick front was removed and the wooden frame exposed.[115] On the whole, there was little scope for civic intervention in private developments such as this until the planning legislation of the 1940s.

The apogee of civic interest in the history of St Albans was the excavation of Verulamium, a large part of which (104 acres) had been purchased from the earl of Verulam in 1929.[116] From 1930, the site was extensively excavated by Mortimer Wheeler, together with his wife Tessa.[117] The city council asked the Society of Antiquaries to oversee the excavations, and the Verulamium Excavation Committee was formed to raise funds in aid of the proposed work. The Committee was chaired by Sir Charles Peers, president of the Society of Antiquaries, and included the earl of Verulam, Alderman W. S. Green and the mayor for 1929–30, I. H. Ironmonger, as its vice-chairmen. Succeeding mayors, together with the president of the St Albans and Hertfordshire Architectural and Archaeological Society, were *ex officio* members of the committee; Margaret Wix, who had been the first female mayor of the city in 1924, was also a member.[118] Mortimer Wheeler was keeper of the London Museum, and 'did not hesitate to use any popularizing means available' to spread news of his excavations, and thereby to raise funds.[119] Members of the Architectural and Archaeological Society contributed a total of £237 towards the costs of the work in the first year, but, as the Society's historian explains, 'the project became partly self-financing, with considerable sums raised by visitors' donations and the sale of booklets and postcards'.[120]

The Verulamium Museum, on St Michael's Street, was opened in 1939, displaying many of the artefacts discovered by the Wheelers; there was also a Verulamium Tea Room.[121] The museum was greatly enlarged, with financial support from the Heritage Lottery Fund and the Verulamium Museum Trust, in 1998.[122] When the excavations of the early 1930s were over, an artificial lake was constructed alongside the Ver, using the labour of unemployed men from Wales and the north of England, financed by the Public Works Loan Board.[123] Cricket, football and hockey pitches were laid out. The acquisition and development of Verulamium by the local authority was part of a wider trend towards civic involvement in the promotion of leisure, and the provision of playing fields and open spaces, in this period. In the capital, parks, playing fields, tennis courts and other facilities were provided by the London County Council in increasing numbers in the 1920s and 1930s, and other towns and cities were doing the same, although demand in many areas

... an artificial lake was constructed alongside the Ver, using the labour of unemployed men ...

The Verulamium museum, pictured around the time of its opening in 1939. The museum was built to house some of the items unearthed in the excavations led by Mortimer Wheeler in the 1930s. The building now forms part of a much larger museum, opened in 1998.

This picture shows the excavations of Verulamium carried out under the direction of Mortimer Wheeler in the 1930s. A floor mosaic is shown being carefully uncovered.

remained unsatisfied.[124] In St Albans, the city council purchased land at Watson Avenue in 1928 and Cunningham Hill in 1930; Bell Meadow in 1934; and the Sandridge Road wastes from Earl Spencer in 1936. Although these were all relatively small, just a few acres each, the 138-acre Batchwood Hall estate was purchased in 1934, and a public golf course laid out.[125] This development paralleled a nationwide expansion of municipal golfing facilities.[126] The city of St Albans also received gifts of land: the Sandpit Lane playing field was given by Sir A. Copson Peake and Lady Peake in 1929, and Beech Bottom by Earl Spencer in 1932.[127]

'a social conscience was arising in the city'

The biggest problem faced by the local authority in the interwar period was housing. St Albans's expanding industrial and commercial workforce generated demand for new homes, and housing had been a cornerstone of the national post-war reconstruction programme, encapsulated in the slogan 'Homes for Heroes'. Housing Acts in 1919, 1923 and 1924 enabled local authorities to construct council houses, and provided subsidies to assist them. Nationally, local authority homes had formed less than 1 per cent of the British housing stock in 1914, but would expand to around 10 per cent of the total by 1939.[128] In St Albans, the presence of 'dire slums' seemed to necessitate urgent action.[129] As early as December 1918, a meeting was held in the town hall to discuss the issue, at which local trade unions, friendly societies, the St Albans and District Trades Council and various voluntary bodies were represented. By March 1919, pressure from these groups had resulted in a council resolution to build 100 houses in the Townsend area, although this was subject to long delays and occasioned considerable local frustration.[130] Elsie Toms remembered that 'a social conscience was arising in the city', which manifested itself in the establishment of the St Albans Housing Enquiry Committee, a voluntary body established by Michael Furse, the bishop of St Albans. The committee drew up a damning report on the state of local housing, identifying a need for at least 600 new houses just to meet the demands of local homelessness, and showing that 'many more were needed to deal with overcrowding, and still more were unfit for habitation by any decent standards'.[131] Despite this pressure, the public house-building programme remained slow throughout the interwar period in St Albans. A total of 734 council homes were constructed before the Second World War, including 93 on the Townsend estate, 132 at the Camp, 160 at Dellfield (off Camp Road), 126 on the Doggetts Way estate, 56 on Cottonmill Lane and 111 on the Sandridge Road estate.[132] Council housing was also built in the villages, including Sandridge, where ongoing problems of sanitation were in evidence: the 18 semi-detached council houses built on Spencer Place in 1920–21 were the first in the village to have running water and sewage disposal.[133]

As in many towns and cities in interwar Britain, private developments were more successful at meeting housing needs in St Albans. Nationally, the decline

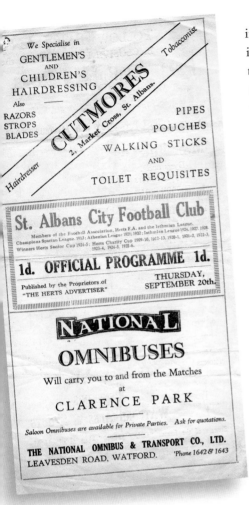

in the cost of building materials, falling interest rates from the early 1930s, and the demise of wartime and post-war rent controls all helped to stimulate the private construction of houses for sale and for rent. Across the period 1920–39, 1.1 million council houses were built in England and Wales, compared with 2.9 million built by private enterprise.[134] Some towns in Hertfordshire expanded very rapidly, mostly due to private enterprise: the population of Welwyn Garden City grew from 430 to 13,500 in the period 1920–37, and Letchworth, the first garden city, grew from 400 in 1903 to 14,545 in 1931.[135] In much longer-established St Albans, the total number of houses expanded from 5,000 in 1914 to 6,084 in 1924 ('of which about 3,690 are for the working classes', according to the medical officer of health), 6,650 in 1928 and 8,347 in 1934, prior to the extension of the municipal boundaries in 1935.[136] Only a minority of the new houses were built by the council. In the 1930s new privately owned housing was built on Batchwood Drive, Beech Road, Marshalswick Lane and Beechwood Avenue, creating the 'ring road' (although this was probably not the intended function of those streets).[137] Further development took place in the Camp, including Campfield Road in 1933.[138] The 'Park' area, comprising Homewood Road, Marshal's Drive, Charmouth Road and Gurney Court Road, was also built up in the 1930s.[139] At the very end of the 1930s, and considerably delayed by the Second World War, the Marshalswick estate was commenced: in 1939 Kingshill Avenue, Queen's Crescent, Pondfield Crescent and the Ridgeway were under construction, and shopping facilities and a cinema were planned.[140] A concerted effort was made, by private builders and the city council, to attract residents to St Albans. Reflecting the interest in preservation and conservation, a common theme was an insistence that industrial development had not spoiled the city. Whereas 'modernity' was the key theme of the 1919 official guide, which seems to have been aimed more at businesses than visitors, by 1928 it was made clear that local industries, 'being conducted on modern lines do not mar the residential amenities of the place'.[141] Successive official guides pointed to the low death rate in St Albans, which 'testifies to the healthfulness of the district'.[142]

As a result of the substantial programme of house-building, problems of poor sanitation and overcrowding were eased during the interwar period, but not entirely solved. As the complaints of 'dire slums' testified, there were serious problems in many of the city's houses. In 1924 the medical officer of health was able to report that, 'with the exception of a very few earth closets which are still in existence, and are emptied by the occupiers, the whole of the City has water closet accommodation'.[143] However, during the same year a total of 585 houses were inspected under the terms of the Public Health and Housing Acts, and another 232 under the Housing (Inspection of District) Regulations (1910), and although none of these was deemed 'so dangerous or injurious to health as to be unfit for human habitation', 425 were 'found not to be in all respects reasonably fit for human habitation'. All the defects were, apparently, remedied without formal action being taken.[144] Fourteen years later, in 1938, a larger number of houses were inspected under various legislation and regulations: 1,410 in total, of which 867 were 'found not to be in all respects reasonably fit for human habitation', an even higher proportion than in 1924. Following investigations carried out under the terms of the Housing Act (1936), a more optimistic picture was presented in 1938 as regards overcrowding: only 33 dwellings in St Albans were deemed to be overcrowded, accommodating 257 people.[145] There was also cause for optimism regarding the sanitary accommodation in workplaces. In 1924, sanitary inspectors made 233 inspections, and found 20 sanitary defects in workplaces, all of which were quickly remedied, and in 1938, 262 inspections found 45 defects, mostly relating to 'want of cleanliness'.[146]

The increasing oversight of housing and industrial premises reflected the steady expansion of local government in the interwar period. The city or borough council, with its seven aldermen and 18 councillors representing three wards, was responsible for the municipal government of St Albans; it sat both as a full council and as the Urban Authority and General Purposes Committee. By 1933, there were 13 additional committees, responsible for issues ranging from finance to town planning to the market. There was also an 'Emergency Sub-Committee for dealing with Epidemics of Infectious Diseases'.[147] A whole range of officials policed particular aspects of the life of St Albans, and an even larger number of officers appointed by the county council had some responsibilities in the city. The size of the local government workforce of interwar St Albans is not clear, but it was certainly growing, as the arm of the local state reached into more and more areas of civic life. In 1935 the boundaries of the borough of St Albans were once more extended, increasing the area under municipal control from 2,703 acres to 5,125 acres, although the size of the council and the division

The ... local government workforce ... was certainly growing ...

into wards was not altered. The surrounding areas were under the government of the St Albans rural district council, established in 1894. The rural district council met in the St Albans council chamber, and consisted of 12 councillors, representing Harpenden Rural, Redbourn, St Michael Rural, St Peter Rural, London Colney, St Stephen, Sandridge Rural and Wheathampstead wards. The size of the rural district was reduced in 1935, as more areas surrounding St Albans were brought into the municipal borough. There was also a lower level of government – parish councils – who exercised some responsibilities in these areas. Local government in this period was usually in Conservative hands, and the dominance of the Conservatives in the parliamentary politics of St Albans was further entrenched by the inclusion of a large surrounding rural area in the constituency. The Tories held the parliamentary seat from 1906 to 1945. Following a by-election in 1919, and until his death in 1943, the MP was F. E. Fremantle, who only just won in 1919, but who achieved comfortable majorities thereafter, peaking in 1931 when he took 78.1 per cent of the vote in a two-cornered contest.[148]

... the growth of voluntary organisations and a flourishing of the associational culture of the city.

The wide spectrum of voluntary bodies that characterised St Albans and other towns and cities in the Victorian and Edwardian period was also apparent in the years after the First World War; indeed, the increasing leisure time available to many in the interwar years stimulated the growth of voluntary organisations and a flourishing of the associational culture of the city. Perhaps the most prominent voluntary organisations were the churches, which struggled hard to maintain their profile in the interwar period, but some of which experienced notable success. By 1938, there were eight Church of England places of worship in addition to the cathedral, and four Baptist churches, three Methodist, two Congregationalist, a Roman Catholic, a Christian Scientist, a Salvation Army, a Brethren and a Quaker meeting house. There were also 16 mission halls and similar venues, including a men's and a women's adult school.[149] The adult schools – which in St Albans dated to before the First World War – were associated with the Society of Friends, or Quakers, who had long maintained a small but active presence in St Albans. They had a modest but expanding 47 members in the mid-1930s, and maintained a higher profile than these numbers would suggest through their pacifist responses to the two world wars and involvement in relief work both nationally and internationally.[150] One Quaker, Cyril Dumpleton, was mayor of St Albans in 1943, and was elected as the constituency's first Labour MP in 1945.[151] The Methodist church at Marlborough Road was considerably improved after the First World War, with electric lighting installed; membership of the local Methodist Circuit was 'holding fairly steady' at 454 in 1920, and success of services aimed at young people was reported. The number had increased slightly to 469 by 1930, and reached 548 in 1937, following the 'Reunion' of the Wesleyan and Primitive Methodist churches.[152] Roman Catholicism, a

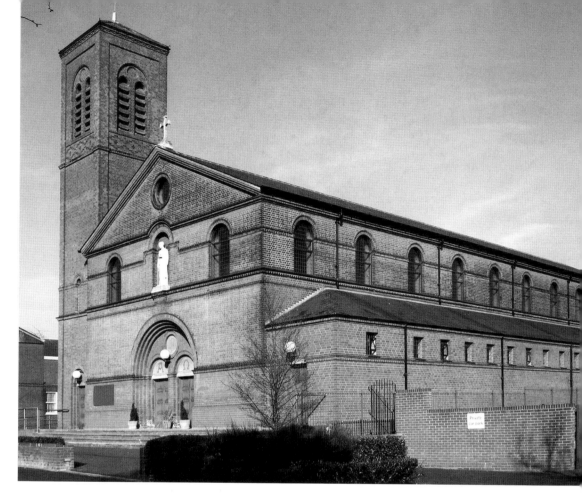

The Roman
Catholic church on
Beaconsfield Road,
dedicated in 1905
to SS Alban and
Stephen, replaced
an earlier church on
London Road.

PHOTOGRAPH: AUTHOR

negligible presence in the nineteenth century, was boosted by high attendances at mass among soldiers billeted in St Albans during the First World War, and through in-migration, especially from Ireland. Catholics numbered 500 adults and 100 children in 1930. There was a high rate of church attendance among the Catholic population; Catholic schools were developed in the period (see box 11); and a branch of the Society of St Vincent de Paul (a national Catholic charitable society founded in 1833) was established in St Albans in 1923.[153] Other churches were less successful: for example, the Congregationalist chapel at Spicer Street was 're-organised' in 1919, having 62 members, and was led by a series of pastors whose tenure was short. Although its membership had been increased slightly by 1950, its pastor in that year wrote that the older members of the church would be able to 'recall, no doubt, churches which were full in the early years of the present century but which are now almost empty or closed'.[154] In the case of the Baptist church on Dagnall Street, the interwar years were 'difficult'. It had 284 members in 1938, some of whom came from the surrounding villages, and its historian later recalled that:

The records of the twenty or so years between the two World Wars give the impression of a Church doing its best to maintain itself as a purposeful Christian community while at the same time trying to come to terms with the rapidly changing world around it ... after the war, with the increasing secularisation of society, churchgoing was becoming a minority interest.[155]

Other voluntary societies were flourishing. *Kelly's Directory* for 1922 listed 60 'Societies, Institutes, &c.', some with more than one branch: these included sporting and political clubs. There were branches of the Freemasons, Oddfellows and Ancient Order of Foresters; and the National British Women's Temperance Association was one of at least four temperance societies represented in St Albans, including the Band of Hope Union.[156] In 1933 the *St Albans Annual and Who's Who* carried the details of 120 societies and associations for adults, not counting youth organisations.[157] Exactly half of this number were sports clubs, several of which were associated with workplaces, such as the Hosiery Mills, Postals and Sphere Works Football Clubs, and the Rubber Works Sports Club. As well as the predictable football, cricket, rugby and tennis, other sports were represented, including table tennis, cycling, rifle shooting and netball. Musical clubs included orchestral, change ringing, choral, light orchestra and plainsong organisations, as well as the St Albans British Legion Band. In addition to the Legion, there were three ex-servicemen's associations. St Albans Chess Club, dating from 1870, met on Tuesday evenings at the Pilgrim's Rest

These urinals at St Albans city station, on the Midland Railway, were made of cast iron. The picture dates from 1943. The advertisement on the lamppost proclaims that St Albans is the 'home town of Ryders' seeds'.

tea rooms.[158] Among youth organisations, there were 10 Scout troops in St Albans and more in the surrounding villages, 9 companies of Girl Guides, and many Wolf Cub and Brownie packs.[159] By 1938, more new organisations were listed in *Kelly's*, such as the St Albans League of Nations Union (the Union was one of the largest voluntary societies in interwar Britain, claiming 400,000 members at its peak in 1931).[160] The English Folk Song and Dance Society (Hertfordshire branch) represented another facet of the historical consciousness of the period, which was also reflected in the growth of the St Albans and Hertfordshire Architectural and Archaeological Society, while the National Union of Boot and Shoe Operatives (St Albans section, London Metropolitan branch), demonstrated the advance of labour organisation in an industrial sector in which St Albans was important.

The Second World War provided further opportunities for voluntary action in St Albans. Prior to the outbreak of war St Albans, along with the rest of the country, was in an increasing state of preparedness. In 1938 gas masks were issued and emergency mortuaries established, while the city fire brigade acquired additional supplies of protective clothing and ladders in 1939.[161] Public air raid shelters were constructed in several locations: Belmont Hill, New England Street, Bernard's Heath and Clarence Park, while more primitive shelter was available in St Peter's Street; and the new lake at Verulamium was drained so that it did not reflect the moonlight.[162] As in the previous war, but this time even more promptly, blackout regulations were in force, and strictly policed, so that over 300 people were fined during the war for breaching them.[163] The dangerous conditions resulting from the blackouts created safety problems: in St Albans, 15 people died from blackout-related road accidents, whereas only 10 were killed by air raids.[164] Some bombs did fall, especially in November 1940, causing deaths in Camp Road and Beaumont Avenue. However, the comparatively light bombing of St Albans, compared with nearby locations such as Hatfield and Garston, justified the optimism that led to the designation of the city as a major evacuee reception centre. In the first week of the war, 6,000 evacuees arrived in St Albans, and a total of 12,000 were accommodated during the course of the war, large influxes arriving during the blitz of 1940 and the flying bomb attacks of 1944.[165] Other nearby towns also took large numbers of evacuees: for example, the population of Welwyn Garden City grew by 20,000 during the war years.[166] Not all the evacuees came from London: Hastings Grammar School, for example, was evacuated to St Albans, as was the junior department of Northampton Polytechnic. St Bartholomew's hospital and its staff also moved to the city, as did a number of London businesses.[167]

The arrival of evacuees placed considerable strain on the infrastructure of St Albans, in terms of housing, sanitation and education, and necessitated the mobilisation of official and voluntary effort. The number of attendances by

... evacuees placed considerable strain on the infrastructure of St Albans ...

children at the maternal and child welfare clinic increased from 5,232 in 1938 to 8,735 in 1940.[168] Despite the scarcity of resources, Elsie Toms recalled that 'the citizens treated [the evacuees] well and in such a friendly fashion that many of them fell in love with the place, and became adopted sons and daughters who are still with us [in 1962]'.[169] This optimistic assessment overlooks some 'friction' between natives and evacuees,[170] but in general the accommodation of the newcomers was undertaken successfully. It stimulated new forms of welfare provision: an Evacuees Welfare Committee was formed, at first with the Dean, Cuthbert Thicknesse, in the chair, and later Cyril Dumpleton.[171] The Committee urged the establishment of a nursery school and a citizens' advice bureau. The Muriel Green nursery school was opened in 1940, and the citizens' advice bureau in the following year; both were important resources for evacuees and natives, and are examples of the war hastening the onset of changes that had first been proposed in the 1930s.

Civil defence precautions in St Albans included branches of the 'Home Guard' and the Air Raid Precautions (ARP) services: although the city escaped with relatively little damage from air raids, the local ARP was 'a complex organisation', with 216 full-time employees, not to mention voluntary assistance, at its peak.[172] Conscientious objectors offered an additional 'Fire Watching Service', based at the Quaker meeting house.[173] The cathedral was protected by a fire pump and dry risers, installed on the outbreak of war, and the bells were removed from the tower; a special fire watch was initiated for the building.[174] Some of the manufacturing capacity in the city was turned over to war production: the Ballito factory at Fleetville produced ammunition shells in place of silk stockings, and aircraft production was intensified at nearby Hatfield and Radlett.[175] On a more modest scale, the workforce at Mercer's Chronometers made its contribution to the war effort, producing over 2,000 chronometers during the war.[176] The Hertfordshire College of Agriculture and Horticulture at Oaklands was taken over by the Agricultural Executive Committee (from the county council), and employed conscientious objectors, as well as members of the Women's Land Army.[177] Later in the war, Italian and German prisoners were accommodated at several locations in the vicinity of St Albans, and as many as 1,000 evacuees remained, even in 1945.[178] The memorial on St Peter's Street contains the names of 162 inhabitants of St Albans who were killed in action during the war: a much lower death toll than during the First World War, but still a significant loss to the city. However, the accommodation of refugees from London and elsewhere was the most significant contribution made by St Albans to the war effort, and emphasises the crucial importance of proximity and access to London that has characterised the modern, as well as the ancient and medieval, history of the city. As the next chapter shows, the relationship with London would remain a key determinant of the experiences of the people of St Albans after the war.

The memorial on St Peter's Street contains the names of 162 inhabitants ... who were killed in action ...

CHAPTER NINE

'A terribly smug place':
St Albans since 1945

D ESPITE the dislocations of the war years, and leaving aside the (mostly) temporary influx of evacuees, the population of St Albans, which was growing in the 1930s, continued to expand in the 1940s and 1950s. A study of the city and its surroundings carried out in 1946 by the Association for Planning and Regional Reconstruction found that 'as soon as "evacuation" finally ceased the population reverted to a position that was in a direct line with its pre-war trends'.[1] The population of St Albans expanded by 3.9 per cent from an estimated 42,450 in 1939 to 44,098 in 1951, although in 1945, swelled by evacuees and troops, it was estimated at 47,088, an increase of 10.9 per cent on 1939 (see table 8.1 on page 257). By 1961, it had reached 50,293, a growth of 14.0 per cent on 1951 and 18.5 per cent on 1939. Some of the early post-war expansion was planned: the Greater London Plan, prepared by Patrick Abercrombie in 1944, proposed the extension of the 'green belt' around London, which had been shaped by local authorities in the 1930s, and designated an 'outer country ring' of satellite towns.[2] After the war, St Albans was designated an 'expansion town', to accommodate London overspill.[3] Other Hertfordshire towns – Hemel Hempstead, Stevenage, Welwyn Garden City and Hatfield – were 'new towns', selected for more dramatic development, often amid local opposition, which was particularly fierce in the case of Stevenage.[4] As had been the case in the 1930s, the population of Hertfordshire grew more quickly than that of any other county in the 1950s, and the growth of the 'new towns' exceeded even that which was originally planned.[5] St Albans also expanded beyond what was forecast. In the case of St Albans, rapid post-war development and associated changes – industry, housing, commerce and traffic – intruding into a city with a powerful sense of history and tradition, sometimes provoked opposition from the local community. The second half of the twentieth century in St Albans was a story of 'the mediation of urban change in a historic townscape'.[6] In many respects the history of St Albans resembles that of other English towns, embracing rapid post-war housing developments, the flourishing and then decline of the local manufacturing sector, and the gradual dominance of the service sector in the economy; however, more so than in some other towns and cities, the historic importance of the city, and the strength of local conservationist movements, have made recent changes in the urban environment especially problematic.

Well into the second half of the twentieth century, St Albans remained a manufacturing centre. As charts 9.1(a)–(c) show (see pages 296–7), almost a third of occupied men and 16.3 per cent of occupied women in the municipal borough worked in the manufacturing sector; these numbered over 5,500 in total, and represented 26.6 per cent of employed inhabitants of St Albans. During the Second World War itself, manufacturing industry had expanded 'at approximately the same pace as during the early thirties', and this expansion was carried into the second half of the 1940s and the 1950s.[7] Both small and larger enterprises were present. An official guide to St Albans published in 1950 discussed the industry of the city in these terms:

> variety is the most noteworthy feature; the smith, the carpenter, the painter and the mason represent still those industries which are literally the work of men's hands; but mechanical power produced from coal and oil, and distributed as electricity, renders St Albans, a city in the country, ideal for general manufacture ... the industry of St Albans itself is large and important.[8]

There were 261 factories in the city in 1956, many of which were small, although the largest employer in St Albans, Marconi Instruments Limited, had two sites (at Longacres and on Hatfield Road) and employed 'thousands'.[9] Other industries that had been established before the First World War, or in the interwar period, prospered and generated much local employment. For example, in the early 1950s, the Electrical Apparatus Company employed 800 people, Peake's coat manufacturers around 500, the Engineering and Lighting Equipment Company Limited (formerly Arc Lamps) about 300, Ryder's seed company 250, Nicholson's coat manufacturers and Brushes Limited around 200 each, Edwin Lee and Sons shoe manufacturers around 100, Wiles and Lewis's suet factory 90, and Avery's Vermicelli 50. Meanwhile, the St Albans Rubber Company continued to expand, employing 240 people in 1958;[10] while Mercer's Chronometers, which produced 465 chronometers in 1962, 'perhaps the greatest year for chronometer production', had around 500 employees by this time, many of them very highly skilled.[11] Printing also remained an important sector of the local economy, employing 792 men (5.6 per cent of St Albans's male workforce) and 186 women in 1951.[12]

The manufacturing sector in St Albans did not produce much pollution, something which had been noted in the interwar period, and which was

RIGHT
This map shows the position of St Albans in relation to the railway network before the Beeching cuts of the 1960s. The remains of some disused stations can still be seen alongside the footpath that runs along the line of the Great Northern Railway branch line. Napsbury station, shown on the Midland Railway line, was built in 1905 to serve the local mental asylum, and closed in 1959.

REDRAWN BY CARNEGIE FROM AN ORIGINAL BY BRIAN BUTLER IN CHILTERN RAILWAYS (1991)

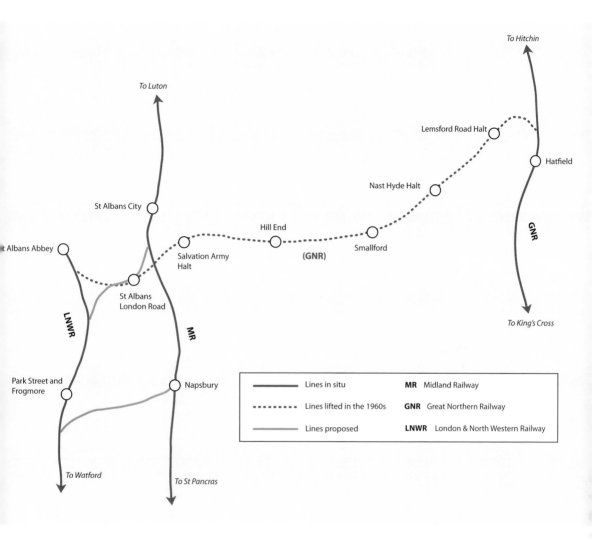

To Hitchin

To Luton

Lemsford Road Halt

Hatfield

Nast Hyde Halt

St Albans City

Hill End

GNR

Albans Abbey

Salvation Army
Halt

Smallford

(GNR)

St Albans
London Road

LNWR

MR

To King's Cross

Park Street and
Frogmore

Napsbury

―――――	Lines in situ	**MR**	Midland Railway
•••••••••••	Lines lifted in the 1960s	**GNR**	Great Northern Railway
―――――	Lines proposed	**LNWR**	London & North Western Railway

To Watford

To St Pancras

also emphasised in the civic propaganda of the 1950s. The official guide in 1950 announced that 'the factories of St Albans do not produce smoke, dust or noise'.[13] A complaint by 'a firm of precision instrument manufacturers', presumably Mercer's Chronometers, about atmospheric pollution from the nearby gas works, was atypical.[14] Some industrial premises still produced unpleasant smells: for example, Wiles and Lewis's Ariston suet factory, which was in operation at Bernard's Heath until 1960.[15] However, in the years before the Clean Air Act (1956), when London's industrial and other emissions were notorious, an advantage of St Albans's relatively clean manufacturing sector was that factories could be located close to housing areas. According to one contributor to the official guide, this was beneficial to the city and its inhabitants in a number of ways:

The factories are remarkably unobtrusive; they are tucked away in the outskirts, or scattered among the dwelling houses. This runs counter to the idea now fashionable, that factories should be located in a special factory area, but … has very great advantages for the ordinary worker, and still more so for the woman and the part-timer. With all the modern developments of transport, travelling is always a time-consumer. On many days in the British climate it is demonstrably unpleasant and, whenever waiting for a bus is involved, unhealthy for all those not abounding in youth and vitality.[16]

*'no longer …
a dormitory
town for
London'*

The fashion for concentrated industrial sites was followed in some parts of post-war St Albans: for example, an industrial estate was established at Porter's Wood, off Valley Road, in the 1950s.[17] Nevertheless, the official guide for 1950 noted that the town planner Sir Patrick Abercrombie, author of the Greater London Plan of 1944, had praised the 'dispersal of industry' in St Albans;[18] and when sanitary inspectors visited the factories in St Albans, they found few defects.[19]

For the writer of the official guide of 1950, the effect of the industrial development of St Albans was that it 'should no longer be regarded, as it once was, as a dormitory town for London'.[20] Commuting remained significant, not only to London but also to Hatfield, where many residents of St Albans worked, at de Havilland's and elsewhere. Overall, the incidence of commuting declined in the 1930s and 1940s: whereas around 40 per cent of the occupied population of St Albans travelled outside the city to work in 1931, this figure had fallen to 30 per cent by 1946, although at this date some 40 per cent of St Albans's *industrial* workers travelled outside the borough to work, mostly to Hatfield.[21] (The war had greatly increased the size of the workforce at de Havilland's.) In St Albans itself, the industries were staffed mainly by residents of the city and areas 'within a very few miles of the town'.[22] The only exception to this generalisation was the Handley Page aircraft factory at Park Street, where half the employees commuted from London. The surrounding rural district also had small manufacturing industries, employing around 1,500 people in 1946.[23] There were, of course, other significant areas of employment in St Albans: the official guide of 1950, although focusing on the manufacturing sector, also spoke warmly of

those classes of workers who are common to every city, such as the transport people, the shop and distributive people, the municipal staffs, those who work in offices, professional men and women, those on the farms round the city, the teachers and the housewives: their work is essential to the life of the community, and they take their honoured place in St Albans at work.[24]

Among men living in St Albans in 1951, there were just under 1,000 working in construction (including painting and decorating) and just over 1,000 in transport, together making up some 15 per cent of the occupied male population. Meanwhile, 1,658 women and 1,210 men worked as typists or in other clerical employment, comprising in total some 13.6 per cent of the total occupied population of the borough. Retail was also a significant employer: there were 909 salesmen and women and shop assistants in St Albans in 1951.[25] Green's department store on the High Street was later remembered for 'the elite ranks of young ladies who served at this posh outfitters'.[26] There was a substantial group of professionals, as well as a total of 2,340 employees in the commercial and financial sectors resident in St Albans. (For a full breakdown of occupations, see charts 9.1(a)–(c) on pages 296–7.) We cannot tell how many of these white-collar workers travelled outside St Albans to work, but wherever they found their employment, their residence in the city contributed to the pressing demands for housing, education and social services that arose in the 1940s and 1950s.

In 1946, it was felt that the industries of St Albans 'are interspersed with rather second class development of commerce and housing'.[27] As an 'expansion town', St Albans's housing stock was of key concern in the early post-war period: the improvement of existing homes and the construction of new ones was the most pressing issue facing the municipal authorities. After the war, it was estimated that 1,300 new homes were needed 'immediately' and that a further 4,500 would be needed in the near future, to accommodate the expected increase in population. Early post-war development, in St Albans and elsewhere, was dominated by council housing. Post-war town planners disliked the 'wasteful sprawl' that had resulted from the unco-ordinated efforts of private builders in the interwar period.[28] In St Albans, the 1,000th post-war council house was completed as early as 1950; there were 2,000 by 1953; and the 3,000th (in Frobisher Road, off Drakes Drive) was finished in 1959.[29] In total, between 1945 and 1968 the city council built 3,268 houses and flats, many of them in large purpose-built estates around the edges of St Albans, such as New Greens (530 homes), St Julian's (497) and the London Road estate (715). Other notable developments included more housing on the Cottonmill estate (319 to add to the 56 built before the Second World War), the Everlasting Lane estate (289) and Marshalswick, where 181 council homes were constructed in addition to the large private development that had been delayed by the war.[30] A small amount of temporary post-war housing accommodation was built at Tavistock Avenue, and there were caravan sites at Drakes Drive and Cell Barnes Lane. In 1968, the council also owned a total of 997 permanent and 49 temporary allotments, about one for every 17 households in St Albans.[31] Council tenants were subject to strict conditions: among other things, the tenants' handbook for 1953 explained that rent was due weekly in advance on

... between 1945 and 1968 the city council built 3,268 houses and flats ...

The 3,000th council home in post-war St Albans was completed, on Frobisher Road, in 1959. A further 2,000 were built in the surrounding rural district in the 20 years after the end of the Second World War. Today only around a tenth of the housing stock of St Albans is in council hands.

PHOTOGRAPH: AUTHOR

Mondays; that tenants were not to take lodgers or sub-let, or keep pets (except for one cat and one dog); that they could not remove trees or shrubs, or drive nails into walls or woodwork, or erect any outdoor aerial or shed or outhouse or greenhouse, or tolerate vermin; that they must keep their house and gardens clean, sweep chimneys every six months, inform the medical officer of health of any contagious disease, replace broken glass and other fittings promptly, and allow entry to council inspectors and workmen 'at all reasonable hours of the day'.[32] These regulations appear to have caused some resentment among tenants.[33] The council house building programme in St Albans itself was matched in the surrounding rural districts. For example, in Sandridge, council housing on Woodcock Hill, St Leonard's Crescent and Langley Grove was built between 1946 and 1953.[34] In total, over 2,000 council houses were built in the St Albans rural district in the twenty years after the war.[35]

The pre-war boom in construction of houses for private sale continued after the war. The most notable private housing development was at Marshalswick, where the Ridgeway, Woodfield Way and neighbouring streets were built up in the 1950s.[36] The housing association flats at the Quadrant were completed in 1961, and Barnfield Road and the closes off it were built in the 1960s, as was Windmill Avenue, a mixture of private and council houses.[37] Other developments included some very early post-war housing in the roads between Hatfield Road and Sandpit Lane.[38] The total number of households in the municipal borough grew from 13,500 in 1951 to 16,133 in 1961. Meanwhile, the surrounding rural areas saw intensive private house-building activity: Sandridge, Wheathampstead, Colney Heath and Sleapshyde all expanded considerably in the 1950s.[39] House-building, as well as other projects, helped to boost levels of employment in the construction industry in St Albans, which, together with painting and decorating, represented 7 per cent of the occupied male population in 1951 (see chart 9.1(a) on page 296). In the rural district, private construction outstripped council house building, with 3,400 private-sector houses being built in the first twenty years after the war.[40] House prices grew steadily in the 1950s: a typical three-bedroom semi-detached property in the city cost £2,675 in 1950 and £3,925 in 1959.[41] In 1962 Elsie Toms remarked that 'so much building has gone on since the war that the city is bursting at the seams, and built right out to its boundaries, where it is restrained by the green belt'.[42] Further developments in the 1960s included the houses to the south-west of King Harry Lane, a further extension of the urban area into the ancient rural parish of St Stephen's; these houses became known as the 'Verulam estate'.

The new estates of post-war St Albans were served by new schools. Between 1945 and 1974, over 5,000 extra places were provided in primary schools in St Albans and the surrounding area.[43] Although Alma Road and Hatfield Road schools closed, many more were constructed. Aboyne Lodge school opened in 1951, New Greens infant school in 1959, Skyswood school on the

LEFT
Windmill Avenue was one of the last roads to be added to the Marshalswick estate. A mixture of private and local authority homes was built c.1965.
PHOTOGRAPH: AUTHOR

Marshalswick estate in 1960, and Wheatfields school, also in Marshalswick, in 1963. Skyswood started with 173 pupils and Wheatfields with 175.[44] Across the road from Skyswood, St John Fisher Roman Catholic JMI school opened in 1965.[45] Elsewhere in the city, Windermere school on the London Road estate opened in 1957, Cunningham Hill junior school in 1962 and its infants' school in 1967; Maple school in Hall Place Gardens dates from 1969, and the Abbey Church of England school acquired a new building in 1970.[46] Prae Wood school opened to serve the Verulam estate in 1971. The Education Act of 1944 also required local education authorities to provide secondary schooling for all from ages 11 to 15, and subsequent guidance from central government encouraged the tripartite division of secondary education into grammar, secondary modern and technical schools. In St Albans, the pre-war senior elementary schools, which were virtually the same as secondary schools (see box 11), were expanded and improved after the war, 'bringing existing buildings up to a standard consistent with the developing concept of secondary education by the provision of such necessary facilities as workshops, housecraft rooms, laboratories, libraries, gymnasia and the like'.[47] The new Marshalswick secondary modern school for boys was opened in 1959; it became co-educational in 1972. With 450 pupils at the outset, Marshalswick school expanded in the 1970s when Sandfield and Redbourn secondary schools closed; and in 1988 it was merged with Wheathampstead school and renamed Sandringham. St Julian's boys' school was founded in 1953, Francis Bacon school in 1960, and St Julian's girls' school in 1965, later merging with its boys' namesake and neighbour to create Marlborough school. Meanwhile, Nicholas Breakspear Roman Catholic secondary school opened in 1963, and Loreto school, which had been in the independent sector, became voluntary-aided in the early 1970s.[48] By 1992, Hertfordshire County Council was responsible for three nursery schools, 48 primary schools and 11 secondary schools in the expanded St Albans district (these numbers had fallen slightly from a peak in the 1980s due to mergers). There were also four special schools, including Heathlands (for the deaf) and Mentmore ('for senior maladjusted girls'), and 10 independent schools of various kinds.[49]

'bringing existing buildings up to a standard consistent with the development concept of secondary education ...'

The leading independent school in the city was St Albans High School for Girls, which was under the management of a limited company dedicated to the purpose. One pupil, who started at the High School in 1952, recalled its rather old-fashioned atmosphere: 'Most of our teachers were elderly spinsters, some of whom had been there during my mother's time at the school.'[50] Meanwhile, St Albans School, having operated under the Direct Grant scheme from 1927 (see box 11), found itself in financial difficulties in the late 1940s as county council funding per free pupil fell in real terms, but pupil numbers expanded from 508 in 1949 to 654 in 1955. Sports facilities, including a gymnasium, were developed in the same period, under the headship of W. T. Marsh. The school achieved 'a high intellectual standard': when its most famous twentieth-century alumnus, Stephen Hawking, started at the school in 1952, there were three applicants for every place, and the fees were 51 guineas per term.[51] By 1964, when Marsh was replaced as headmaster by F. I. Kilvington, the school's pupils were enjoying 'record-breaking' levels of success in obtaining places at Oxford or Cambridge.[52] Under the direction of L. G. Walker and subsequently Geoffrey Pryke, who reached the rank of Colonel and was also the Freemasons' Deputy Provincial Grand Master of Hertfordshire, the school's Combined Cadet Force (compulsory in the 1950s for all boys except the handful whose parents were conscientious objectors) achieved a formidable reputation, although many boys, including Hawking, hated it.[53] When the Direct Grant scheme was abolished in 1976, St Albans School became fully independent, although it offered places to pupils under the assisted places scheme, which was introduced by the incoming Conservative government in 1979.[54] The High School also participated in this scheme, as well as offering its own scholarships to daughters of members of the clergy.[55] Both St Albans School and the High School faced competition from Haberdashers Aske's, which moved from Cricklewood to Elstree in 1961 and became one of the leading independent schools in the country.[56]

As well as reforming secondary education in Britain, the Education Act of 1944 also made the provision of adult and further education a statutory duty of local education authorities. Each was required 'to secure the provision for its area of adequate facilities for further education', which explicitly included 'leisure-time occupation'.[57] To address the local need for these facilities, the St Albans College of Further Education opened in 1949 on Hatfield Road, and 'expanded continuously' into the 1970s.[58] Its new building opened in 1960, and has been called 'the city's most successful modern structure'.[59] The college had a full-time teaching staff of over 100 in the early 1970s, offering a range of formal and recreational classes, and also hosted the Hertfordshire College of Building from the latter's inception in 1959 until it obtained its own premises ten years later. According to the official guide to St Albans in 1971, the College of Further Education 'serves the local area in the fields of engineering, business studies, home economics and general education by providing day and evening courses', including A-levels, as well as offering 'cultural and recreational' adult education classes and sponsoring musical and artistic activity, through which 'it makes a major contribution to the cultural life of the City'.[60] Some of the college premises are now used by the University of Hertfordshire's Faculty of Law. At Oaklands, the Hertfordshire College of Agriculture and Horticulture had accommodation for over 100 students by 1974, and more than 300 part-time students were enrolled every year.[61] The local education authority also had responsibility for 'the fostering, development and co-ordination' of youth work in St Albans, and offered assistance and funds to youth clubs and other voluntary organisations.[62]

... the College of Further Education ... 'makes a major contribution to the cultural life of the City'.

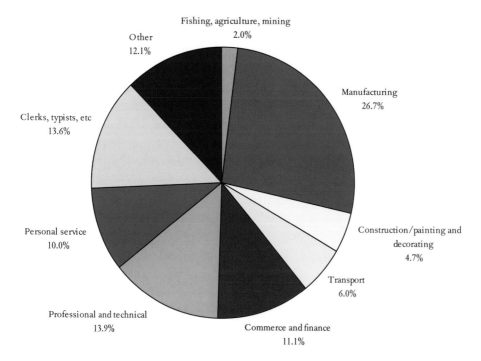

Chart 9.1(a) *Occupational profile of occupied inhabitants, St Albans municipal borough, 1951*
Occupations given as percentage of total occupied (N=21,085). *Source:* see appendix.

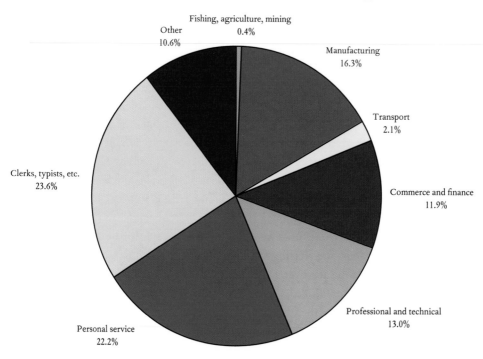

Chart 9.1(b) *Occupational profile of females aged 15 and over, St Albans municipal borough, 1951*
Occupations given as percent of total occupied (N=7,039). Source: see appendix.

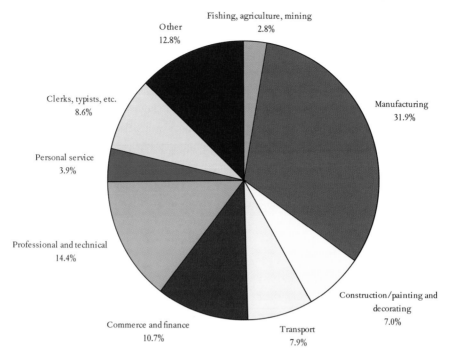

Chart 9.1(c) *Occupational profile of males aged 15 and over, St Albans municipal borough, 1951*
Occupations given as percent of total occupied (N=14,046). *Source:* see appendix.

Fishing, agriculture, mining
2.8%

Other
12.8%

Clerks, typists, etc.
8.6%

Manufacturing
31.9%

Personal service
3.9%

Professional and technical
14.4%

Construction/painting and
decorating
7.0%

Commerce and finance
10.7%

Transport
7.9%

Chart 9.2 *Occupational profile of occupied inhabitants, City and District of St Albans, 1991*
Occupations given as percentage of total occupied population.
Based on a 10 per cent sample: number in sample = 6,038. Source: see appendix.

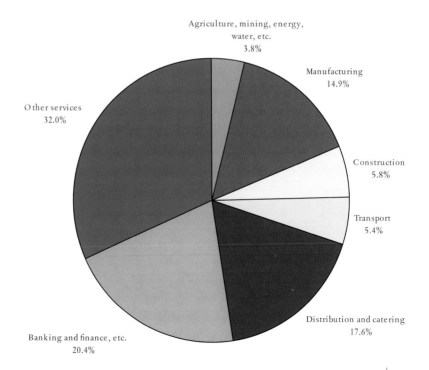

Agriculture, mining, energy,
water, etc.
3.8%

Other services
32.0%

Manufacturing
14.9%

Construction
5.8%

Transport
5.4%

Distribution and catering
17.6%

Banking and finance, etc.
20.4%

The increased involvement of the state and local authorities in social welfare provision during and after the Second World War had considerable implications for St Albans. The last chapter examined the structure of healthcare provision in the city during the interwar years. Although services were expanded, they remained inadequate to meet the needs of the population, and additional strain was inevitably thrown on to services during and after the war. In 1946 it was apparent that 'St Albans has a great shortage of hospital beds for the acute sick'; the Ministry of Health had recommended in the previous year that additional hospital accommodation be provided. There were also insufficient clinics and a shortage of around 20 doctors.[63] There were 448 hospital beds in the city, 236 of them in Oster House, as the former Union Infirmary and Public Assistance Institution and Infirmary was known.[64] When the National Health Service was created in 1948, responsibility for hospital provision in St Albans passed to the Mid-Herts Group Hospital Management Committee, and Oster House became St Albans City Hospital.[65] Improvements and additions in the following decade increased the size of the hospital to 384 beds (ten of them in a private wing).[66] A physiotherapy department and a chest clinic were opened, existing wards were refurbished and operating theatres and x-ray facilities added; however, power cuts caused problems for some of the new facilities in the early 1950s.[67] The general health of the population was good: in 1956, the medical officer of health gave a very positive report on standards of health in St Albans, and on the range of hospital and community care facilities that were available. The school medical service, for example, 'continues to work very smoothly, due largely to the help and co-operation received from Head Teachers', while school meals and milk were 'of a very high standard and a well worth while investment'.[68] The infant mortality rate in St Albans was almost exactly the national average: 23.8 per 1,000 live births compared with 24 for England and Wales as a whole. The overall death rate was rather more favourable – 11.0 per 1,000 people against 11.7 for England and Wales – but this could be attributed partly to demographic factors as well as the environment and health services. In the St Albans rural district, the death rate was considerably higher than in the borough, at 19.3, but infant mortality was lower, at 15.3 per 1,000 live births.[69]

The structure of the government of St Albans in the 1950s and 1960s was essentially the same as before the war, with some responsibilities taken by the county council and others by the municipal borough itself. There was a municipal reorganisation in the mid-1950s, when the North, South and East wards were replaced by the new Abbey, Cunningham, Fleetville, Heath, Marlborough, Marshalswick and St Julian's wards, each of which elected three councillors, increasing the total number from 18 to 21. The number of aldermen remained unchanged at seven.[70] St Albans was not a county borough, and therefore Hertfordshire County Council retained responsibility for education, policing, the fire service and many other services, but the city council was responsible

... school meals and milk were 'of a very high standard and a well worth-while investment'.

for all roads except trunk roads, and for housing, the market, weights and measures, leisure, parks and a whole range of public health services. Although the county council was the planning authority for St Albans, its responsibilities in this area were delegated to the borough.[71] By the early 1970s, in St Albans as in many other places, the existing local government arrangements were felt to be out of date, and it was clear that a major reorganisation was imminent. The town clerk, Betty Entwhistle, explained,

Now it seems likely that the present system of local government will not continue for long … It is clear that the pace of life has quickened since the present pattern of local government was established, to the extent that radical change is needed. Town and country are interlinked as never before. Country dwellers work in towns and townspeople spend much of their leisure in the country. Local authorities provide many more services.[72]

A royal commission had recommended 'brutal' changes to the structure of local government; and the resulting reorganisation in 1974 created the City and District of St Albans, bringing a larger surrounding area into the control of a new district council. As Table 9.1 shows, the population of the area covered by the new district had grown by 12.9 per cent between 1961 and 1971.

Table 9.1   *Population of the City and District of St Albans, 1961–2001*

	Population	Growth (%)
1961	107,458	
1971	121,359	12.9
1981	125,124	3.1
1991	126,202	0.9
2001	128,982	2.2

The City and District of St Albans was created in 1974 as part of the local government reorganisation. It comprised the former municipal borough and rural district of St Albans, as well as the urban district of Harpenden. The figures given for 1961 and 1971 are for the area covered by the new district.

See appendix for the sources used in compiling this table.

The City and District was a merger of the St Albans municipal borough, most of the St Albans rural district (some of this became part of the neighbouring Dacorum district) and the Harpenden urban district. There were 54 councillors, increased to 57 in 1979, and the office of alderman was abolished; there were ten main committees, each with 12 councillors, and a total of 17 sub-committees. The transfer to the new authority was 'a difficult one for public and staff alike':

the district council had around 900 staff based in nine different buildings.[73] It was difficult to generate a sense of identity and common interest within the district – Entwhistle had remarked in advance of the change that St Albans would not lose its 'essential identity'[74] – and among local politicians in St Albans resentment was aroused by the activities of the so-called 'Harpenden Mafia', which was well represented on the council.[75] One result of the strength of Harpenden, in the short term, was to enhance the Conservative stranglehold on local politics. Although there had been a Labour presence on the city council for many decades – indeed, the Labour Party provided one of the most prominent post-war mayors, Elsie Toms – the Conservative Party was comfortably the strongest for most of the three decades after the war. It was even more invincible in parliamentary elections, where a large rural hinterland was included in the St Albans constituency. Following Labour's success in 1945, every general election from 1950 to 1992 inclusive saw the return of a Tory MP for St Albans: John Grimston from 1950, when he defeated the Labour incumbent Cyril Dumpleton; Victor Goodhew from 1959; and Peter Lilley from 1983. The incorporation of much of the rural hinterland in the City and District ensured that, while St Albans itself might flirt with centre-left politics, the larger administrative unit stayed firmly in the Tory fold. In 1976 there were 45 Conservative councillors, 6 Labour, 2 Independent and 1 Liberal. In the next few years the Conservative

St Albans town hall was built in 1831. It is now used as a coffee shop and tourist information centre. This photograph shows market stalls on St Peter's Street. The building with dormer windows to the right of the town hall, next to the tree, can also be seen in the drawing on page 150.

PHOTOGRAPH: CARNEGIE

The civic centre of St Albans was completely redeveloped in the 1960s. The City Hall, now the Alban Arena, was the heart of this seven-acre development, which also included Hertfordshire House, Forrester House and Lockey House. The building in this picture is somewhat newer, and contains district council offices. It is connected by a bridge to the Alban Arena.

hegemony was weakened, partly because of the so-called 'Chequer Street affair',[76] but the party still had an overall majority in 1983, with 30 councillors, against 16 for the Liberal/SDP Alliance, 9 for Labour and 2 Independents.[77] By the early 1990s – when the threatened (and actual) closure of some hospital services helped to further reduce Conservative representation – the composition of the council was more politically balanced: by 1994, there were 23 Tories, 9 Labour councillors and 24 Liberal Democrats.[78] The Liberal Democrats had overall control of the council from 1994 to 1999, and took control again in 2006. They lost control the following year, but won the council back in 2008. Following boundary changes in the mid-1990s, the Conservatives also lost their hold on the parliamentary constituency: Kerry Pollard was elected for Labour in the landslide victories of 1997 and 2001, although Anne Main won the seat back for the Tories in 2005.

Even before the creation of the City and District of St Albans, the expanding role of the city council was increasing the size of the local government workforce. To accommodate this workforce, and to provide other local services, a new civic centre was developed on a seven-acre site behind the east side of St Peter's Street. This was one of the major public projects of the post-war years. The first building to be completed was Forrester House, in 1960, which housed commercial premises; and Lockey House in 1966, which is now home to the Royal Bank of Scotland. In the same year the new police headquarters were opened on Victoria Street, together with a new 200-space car park. Hertfordshire House was built to house various county council services. A new library building was projected, but this was not built.[79] The centrepiece of the development was the City Hall – now known as the Alban Arena – which opened in 1968, described as 'a major landmark in providing entertainment in St Albans'.[80] The auditorium could seat 1,000, and the hall was also used, along with the neighbouring Waterend Barn, for social events. The City Hall was designed by Sir Frederick Gibberd, the chief planner of the new town of Harlow, who was also responsible for the earliest terminal buildings at Heathrow airport, two power stations and the Roman Catholic cathedral in Liverpool.[81] One observer described the City Hall as 'less comfortable and agreeable, though larger and more expensive, than the Abbey Theatre', which opened on Holywell Hill, also in 1968.[82] The city council took over the museum on Hatfield Road in 1955, extending it in 1961, and the Verulamium museum was expanded in the following year.[83] Local library provision was extended in 1959, when the first branch library, at Fleetville was opened;[84] this was followed by branch libraries on the Marshalswick estate and Cell Barnes Lane. Other developments, not under public auspices, included the opening of the organ museum in 1961, 'a fine collection of fairground and dance organs'.[85]

... local government ... increased the availability of playing fields and public open spaces.

Another example of the active involvement of local government in areas of the social and cultural life of the city is in the provision of leisure facilities. After the war the city council, and later the district council, increased the availability of playing fields and public open spaces. Most of the council's purchases were of small open spaces, such as the Vesta Avenue playing field in 1958, Causeway Field in the same year, Orchard House open space in 1960, Longacres playing field in 1964 and St Stephen's Hill open space in 1965. All these spaces comprised just a few acres and required little in the way of modification, but a more ambitious project was the purchase, in 1961, and subsequent development of Westminster Lodge.[86] This estate of 53.4 acres became the site of a running track and a new swimming pool, designed to replace the old pool at Cottonmill Lane, which Elsie Toms described as 'a pitifully inadequate bath', the replacement of which was long overdue.[87] There were some delays at central government level in approving the plans for Westminster Lodge, and the facilities did not open until 1971. In the meantime, water heating was installed at the old swimming pool in 1964, and although it was open only in the summer months, it accommodated almost 63,000 bathers during 1967–68.[88] From 1974, recreation services were overseen by a single department of the new St Albans district council, which in 1978 controlled over 700 acres of open space, 54 football pitches, 29 tennis courts, 9 cricket pitches, the golf course at Batchwood, Westminster Lodge itself and a range of other facilities in St Albans and Harpenden.[89] The local authority worked in partnership with the voluntary sector in the provision of recreational opportunities, a partnership that was given institutional form by the St Albans District Sports Council. As the council's *Leisure Handbook* in 1978 explained:

> The aims of the St Albans District Sports Council are to assess the needs for sport in the district for all ages. In this the Council consults

continued on page 306

Box 12: 'Remember, if you will, your ancient past': civic pageantry, history and festivals

A S HAD HAPPENED in 1907,[1] civic pride in St Albans was promoted in the post-war years through pageantry. There were two historical pageants in this period: a millennary pageant in 1948 – marking the millennium of the traditional date of foundation of abbot Ulsinus's three churches, the market and the school – and another in 1953, which commemorated the coronation of queen Elizabeth II. On both occasions the 'pageant-master' was Cyril Swinson, a former pupil of St Albans School and a prominent resident of the city. In 1948, the cast numbered 1,000 and the choir 200,[2] and there was a large staff of committees and officers. Swinson's script depicted nine historical scenes, only three of which were the same as in 1907: the martyrdom of St Alban, Offa's foundation of the abbey, and the visit of Elizabeth I to Gorhambury in 1572.[3] The other six were the establishment of the churches, market and school in 948, under the title 'Ulsinus Has a Plan'; 'Holy Day' (a visit to the abbey by Henry VI in 1440); a visit of Charles I to the school in 1626; a Civil War scene in 1643; 'Whigs Versus Tories: An Election Scene', depicting the contest of 1722; and the declaration of St Albans's city status in 1877. Thus, whereas the 1907 pageant had taken the story of St Albans only to 1572, the event of 1948 included historical events much closer in time. However, it did not mention the controversial by-election of 1850, and the disenfranchisement of the borough (see box 9), preferring to depict the more distant events of 1722. (Elsie Toms's *Story of St Albans*, published in 1962, also overlooked the disenfranchisement.) There was an epilogue to the pageant, in which the chorus referred to more recent events:

Remember, if you will, your ancient past,
Remember all those men, and women too,
Who three times in this century
Have left their homes to fight,
And three times have returned
To build their lives anew
Here in their native town.
And be reminded, that our youth to-day,
Will be the guardians of our heritage
    tomorrow.[4]

The destruction wrought by the war – albeit less severe in St Albans than in many neighbouring places – emphasised the sentiment of preservation. Swinson's concern for the guardianship of the heritage of St Albans was timely in the context of widespread concerns about the threats posed by commercial and residential development to the historical environment of the city.

The pageant of 1953, prompted by the coronation of Elizabeth II, was, as Elsie Toms recalled nine years later, 'a tremendous success and attracted thousands of visitors to the city, and had a very great effect on the growing sense of pride in the history of their home which was becoming a feature of civic life'.[5] Interest in local history had been awakened in the Edwardian period, and intensified in the interwar years, and these early post-war pageants can be seen as the apotheosis of civic historical consciousness in St Albans. There was 'a cast of hundreds' in 1953, and 'hundreds of volunteers' worked on the costumes and scenery.[6] The historical scenes portrayed in this pageant were all on the theme of 'The Masque of the Queens': each scene re-enacted the visit of a queen to St Albans, beginning with Boudicca, played by Brenda Swinson, the

---

[1] See above, pp. 249–51.
[2] Corbett, *History of St Albans*, p. 140.
[3] *St Albans Millenary Pageant*, p. 13, for the contents of the pageant, and subsequent pages for the text.
[4] Ibid., p. 57.
[5] Toms, *Story of St Albans*, p. 191.
[6] Corbett, *History of St Albans*, p. 141.

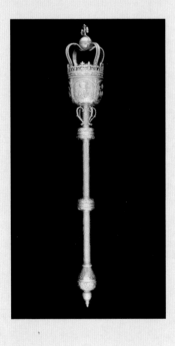

St Albans. There was no consideration of the economic and social development of the city: not even straw plaiting, which had featured at the opening of the Midland Railway station almost a century earlier.[3] These pageants marked the gradual emergence of St Albans – and Britain – from post-war austerity, although in the case of 1948 there was a reminder of contemporary difficulties when the *Herts Advertiser* asked the Board of Trade for permission to exceed its paper ration in order to produce additional copies of its special pageant edition, but permission was refused.[4]

Other showpiece events in St Albans in the 1950s included two visits by the new queen, Elizabeth II: in 1952 to mark the 75th anniversary of the diocese of St Albans, and in 1957 to distribute the Royal Maundy.[5] In 1961, the quatercentenary of Francis Bacon's birth was marked by a memorial service, in St Michael's church, and an exhibition. The Lord Chancellor attended in full regalia, and the Regius Professor of History at the University of Oxford, Hugh Trevor-Roper, gave what Elsie

pageant-master's wife.[1] Other queens who had visited the city included Eleanor, Elizabeth I and Anne Boleyn.[2] In both 1948 and 1953, the scenes depicted military and political history, and the involvment of national elites in the history of

---

[1] 'St Albans in the Fifties', pp. 16–17.
[2] *St Albans Pageant 1953: A Masque of the Queens: Souvenir Programme*: St Albans Central Library, LOC.791.624.

[3] See above, pp. 215–16.
[4] *St Albans Millenary Pageant*, advertisement for *Herts Advertiser* on p. 8.
[5] Brett, *St Albans*, p. 10; 'St Albans in the Fifties', pp. 8–11.

Folk dance and
song have been
popular in St Albans
in the twentieth
and twenty-first
centuries. The
Hertfordshire branch
of the English Folk
Song and Dance
Society was formed
in the 1930s. These
morris dancers
were photographed
in Verulamium in
2007.

PHOTOGRAPH: GAVIN DEAS

Toms described as 'a brilliant address'.[1] Twenty
years later, another historical showpiece generated
considerable local enthusiasm and controversy: the
six hundredth anniversary of the peasants' revolt
of 1381.[2] This 'unprecedented popular commemo-
ration' involved a series of events from March
to July 1981, organised by a range of groups
including the St Albans Folk Music Club and the
Architectural and Archaeological Society. Trade
union and Labour Party involvement gave some
of the events a more explicitly political dimension,
and the Leader of the Opposition, Michael Foot,
addressed a rally in the abbey orchard, which
was disrupted by protesters against British
troops in Northern Ireland. Meanwhile, the city's
Conservative mayor, Kenneth Jenkins, having
been invited to present the prizes in a children's
art competition associated with the commemo-
rations, refused to do so, on the grounds that
there was 'enough conflict in the world today
... without encouraging children to spend their
leisure time depicting the theme of revolt'. On
the whole, however, the celebrations of 1981 were
popular among the residents of St Albans, which
had been one of the main centres of the peasants'

revolt (see chapter 4). In the following year,
1982, there was another royal visit, when the new
cathedral chapter house was opened by queen
Elizabeth II.

The cover of the programme for Festalban in 1977 showed
a map of the diocese of St Albans. This series of events
celebrated the centenary of the diocese, although these
boundaries date only from 1914.

AUTHOR COLLECTION

---

[1] Toms, *Story of St Albans*, p. 195.
[2] The account below is based on Corbett, *Secret History*,
chapter 10.

Five years earlier, in 1977, the centenary of the diocese of St Albans, and of the elevation of St Albans to city status, was celebrated, alongside the queen's silver jubilee. The celebrations were styled 'Festalban', and the programme featured a series of 'celebrity lectures' organised by bishop Robert Runcie, which were collected together in a book entitled *Cathedral and City*. Contributors included the historians Asa Briggs and Owen Chadwick, the archaeologists Sheppard Frere and Martin Biddle, and Runcie himself. Religious, musical and artistic events were held at St Albans cathedral and at many of the deaneries within the diocese. Some events featured morris dancing and folk song, as had the civic pageants of earlier years, and the programme ran from March to December.[1] At the heart of FestAlban was the centenary carnival procession, organised by the St Albans Round Table, held on 29 August; this became an annual event, raising a total of £300,000 in the next 15 years.[2] The carnival procession's route was from Bernard's Heath, through the city and centre and on to Verulamium. In 2005 the carnival was moved from its previous date, at the August bank holiday weekend, to 26 June, close to St Alban's Day, and the procession followed a new route, from Bernard's Heath to Clarence Park.

---

[1] *FestAlban 77: A Celebration in the Hundredth Year of the Cathedral City and Diocese of St Albans*, pp. 17–19: copy in the author's possession.
[2] Corbett, *History of St Albans*, p. 146.

with such local bodies as Sport clubs, educational organisations, county and regional Sports Councils and associations. The Council compiles and maintains records of all existing sports facilities in the district whether publicly or privately owned. It also keeps a schedule of additions and improvements to sports facilities and it recommends priorities for District Council expenditure on such matters. It encourages the fullest possible use of all local sports facilities including those belonging to local schools. It promotes, organises and co-ordinates such essential services to sport as coaching courses. Above all, it provides information on sports organisations, facilities and services in the district to all sections of the community and, in particular, to newcomers to the area.'[90]

'there are few opportunities for surfing or winter sports in St Albans'

The official guide to the city for 1974 noted only two sports for which, unsurprisingly, provision was deficient: 'there are few opportunities for surfing or winter sports in St Albans'.[91]

The wide range of voluntary associations involved in sporting activity reflected an associational culture that continued to thrive, as it had done in the pre-war years. This culture was showcased in the St Albans pageants of 1948 and 1953, the 'Festalban' celebrations of 1977 and the carnival, which became an annual event thereafter (see box 12). In 1948 the very large cast of non-speaking extras in the pageant included groups representing the British Legion, the Townswomen's Guild, the Company of Ten theatre group and the

English Folk Song and Dance Society, as well as local schools.[92] This wide involvement reflected the social life of the city, which, according to several observers, was dynamic. In 1946 the St Albans and District Council of Social Service had records of 217 voluntary organisations in the city, 68 of which were youth clubs, although it was noted that youth and sports clubs were 'unevenly distributed over the town'.[93] As in other towns and cities, the new housing estates of the interwar years were relatively poorly provided with social amenities, and in St Albans a demand had been 'voiced' by a number of voluntary organisations – including the Women's Co-operative Guild and the Women's Voluntary Service – for community centres to be established. It was thought that four would be needed in St Albans.[94] Centres were eventually built at Marshalswick and Fleetville within the city of St Albans, and also at London Colney in the rural district; of course, many villages already had village halls, which performed the same functions as community centres. Much later, a community centre was also built on the Jersey Farm estate. The centres served the organised social and cultural life of the city. In 1950 Cyril Swinson, chairman of the Council of Social Service (and also St Albans's post-war pageant-master – see box 12), explained that 'the value of living in a comparatively small community such as St Albans is reflected the wide variety of societies, cultural, educational and otherwise, that may be joined'.[95] Swinson gave lots of examples: cultural societies including the St Albans Orchestral Society, the Company of Ten and various choirs; women's groups such as the Mothers' Union, Young Wives' Groups, Inner Wheel and Townswomen's

The Farrier's Arms, on Lower Dagnall Street, was in existence from at least the mid-nineteenth century. It was the first meeting place of the Campaign for Real Ale, which now has its national headquarters on Hatfield Road.

PHOTOGRAPH: AUTHOR

Guild; the Debating Society and Baconian Club, which 'provide a forum for discussion of all matters of intellectual interest'; societies devoted to natural history, architecture, archaeology and horticulture; the Film Society, 'which provides throughout the winter a programme of films – foreign, documentary and classic – which do not usually form part of the commercial cinema programmes' – and a large collection of sporting clubs.[96]

In 1964 the St Albans District Arts Council was established: this carried out similar functions to the Sports Council, co-ordinating the activities of local voluntary organisations, promoting various activities and, in some cases, offering sponsorship. It was supported by grants from the city, and later the district, council, as well as Hertfordshire County Council; and member organisations paid an annual subscription.[97] The pursuit of local history by amateur enthusiasts accelerated in the decades after the war: after faltering in the 1940s, the St Albans and Hertfordshire Architectural and Archaeological Society recovered to a level of over 200 members by the early 1950s, and was involved in excavations led by Sir Mortimer Wheeler in 1949. From 1958 to 1967 the Society's director of excavations was also the director of St Albans Museums,

Dr Ilid Anthony.[98] Although the last volume of the Society's *Transactions* was published in 1961, it participated in the launch of a new periodical, *Hertfordshire Archaeology*, in 1968.[99]

The St Albans Association of Honorary Guides was formed in 1964: its members led guided walks around familiar locations, and also along more esoteric routes, such as the medieval borough boundary.[100] Elsie Toms dated the revival of interest in local history to the pageant of 1953 (see box 12), and remarked, in 1962, that 'since that time all sorts of voluntary societies want lectures on the history of old St Albans, and anybody who knows about it is in constant demand'.[101] The interest in history fed the conservationist spirit that emerged in St Albans in this period, and which will be discussed further below. Other examples of powerful voluntary activity in St Albans included the Campaign for Real Ale (CAMRA), which first met at the Farrier's Arms in 1971, establishing premises on Victoria Street, and later on Alma Road (the organisation moved

to Hatfield Road in 1995).[102] Large areas of urban parkland, 70 or more pubs, and three cinemas added to the attractiveness of the city. Although local newspapers throughout the 1950s reported incidents of violent disorder among teenagers, including Teddy Boys, juvenile crime rates were lower in St Albans than in many other places.[103] Not everyone appreciated the advantages of St Albans: one former resident remembered the city in the 1950s as 'a terribly smug place, upwardly mobile, but so awfully suffocating'.[104]

The churches retained an important role in the cultural life of St Albans in the second half of the twentieth century, which was characterised by a 'deepening ecumenical awareness' among the Christian churches.[105] This ecumenism may have been partly defensive, in the face of a decline in religious observance, but it can also be seen as embodying a genuine desire to shape the civil society of the period. The St Albans Council of Churches had a high profile in the city, and the bishop of St Albans from 1970 to 1980, Robert Runcie, participated enthusiastically in ecumenical events, such as a service in 1979 that also involved Cardinal Basil Hume.[106] Meanwhile, at the cathedral, various improvements were made to the internal fabric of the building. The medieval murals and the organ were restored in the 1950s and 1960s respectively, work was carried out on the high altar and other features in the 1960s and 1970s, and the nave was reordered in 1972.[107] In subsequent years the nave was more fully restored, and the west front strengthened. The nave restoration, completed in 1984, cost £1.75 million, most of which was raised by collections.[108] The centenary of the diocese of St Albans was celebrated in 1977 with a series of events (see box 12). The most significant development was the construction of the new chapter house beside the south transept of the cathedral, following archaeological excavations of the site led by Martin Biddle. The chapter house opened in 1982, and houses a refectory, shop and library.[109] The shrine of St Alban was restored in the 1990s, and in 2002 a supposed relic of the martyr was placed in the shrine by a delegation from Cologne (see box 2). The diocese courted controversy in 2004 when Jeffrey John, a gay man, was installed as dean, provoking protests from the

St Albans Diocesan Evangelical Fellowship, which represented 37 parishes, many of whom threatened to withhold the 'quotas' they paid to central diocesan funds.[110] John caused further distress to conservatives in the Anglican communion when he entered a same-sex civil partnership with a Church of England chaplain in 2006.[111]

The established, Roman Catholic and Nonconformist churches all worked hard to establish a presence on the new housing estates. At Marshalswick, St Mary's was consecrated as a parish church by Robert Runcie in 1972, although it was founded as a place of worship as early as 1943.[112] The Marshalswick Baptist Free Church opened in 1968, while after the war the Baptists had also started a Sunday school on the Cottonmill estate.[113] Methodist congregations declined in the 1950s, and Methodists comprised an insignificant 1 per cent of the population of St Albans by 1967, but there were still 244 members of the Marlborough Road church in 1998.[114] The Roman Catholic church remained buoyant after the war, boosted by its role in the provision of education. In 1947, a hurling club was established in the parish of SS Alban and Stephen, 'the only organisation in the area to cater specifically for Irish people'. In 1952, a St Albans section of the Catholic Women's League was formed.[115] The Quakers in St Albans extended their meeting house in the 1950s, and again in the 1990s, and membership remained steady at around 70 in the last quarter of the twentieth century. Involvement in the peace movement ensured a higher profile for Quakers, especially in the political climate of the early 1980s, and again following the invasion of Iraq in 2003, than their numbers alone may have warranted.[116] Quakers and other denominations were involved in voluntary social activity stemming from ecumenical organisations: one example was the St Albans Good Neighbour Scheme, which emanated from the St Albans Council of Churches in 1980, and another was the St Albans Churches Housing Association, which was established by Richard Stagg, a Quaker and Liberal councillor. The Association built accommodation for the elderly, the homeless, and young single people, at Perrycoste Court, at the west end of the new Jersey Farm estate, in 1987.[117]

By this time, the foundations of the economy of St Albans had changed fundamentally from the 1950s. The confident spirit of early post-war St Albans rested on a mixture of manufacturing prosperity and the pleasant surroundings offered by the city. However, between the 1950s and 1990s, the economic structure of St Albans was radically reshaped, and although the environment remained more pleasant than in many comparable towns, some features came under threat from new buildings and the expansion of road traffic. In the second half of the twentieth century, the industrial sector shrank, at least in relative terms, while the service sector expanded, and in this respect St Albans reflected wider British trends. Total employment in manufacturing industry in Britain fell from 8.7 million in 1964 to 4.2 million in 1993, although

The former London Road station, on the Great Northern Railway branch line between St Albans and Hatfield. This line was opened in 1865 and closed to passenger traffic in 1951 and to goods trains in 1964.

PHOTOGRAPH: AUTHOR

increasing productivity meant that actual output did not fall. Within the manufacturing sector, employment in textiles, footwear and clothing fell from 1.4 to 0.4 million, and in food, drink and tobacco production from 0.8 million to less than 0.5 million. Other areas of employment were also in decline: for example, in the construction sector, total employment halved between 1964 and 1993, from 1.6 million to 0.8 million. Meanwhile, the service sector saw a corresponding increase in employment, of some 4 million jobs between 1959 and 1993, employing 15.2 million at the latter date. The decline of manufacturing was especially sharp in the 1980s, when manufacturing fell from 31 per cent to 22.5 per cent of total employment.[118] The shift to services has often been seen in terms of the declining competitiveness of British manufacturing, which was hampered by managerial conservatism and poor industrial relations. As early as the 1950s, there were indications of industrial decline in St Albans. For example, Bill Murgatroyd, the town clerk in the 1950s, later recalled that Marconi Instruments 'were always inventing new things, but they never seemed to get them into production. They were the pioneers, but someone else always beat them to it.' He also recalled visiting de Havilland's at Hatfield, where many inhabitants of St Albans were employed, and remembered: 'I suddenly realised all the staff were pretending to work – they had nothing to do'.[119] De

RIGHT
The distinctive blue-glass Ziggurat building on Grosvenor Road was built by Michael Sassoon Associates in 1990, on the site of the former Edwin Lee and Sons shoe factory. It houses the offices of several companies.

PHOTOGRAPH: AUTHOR

The Nicholson and Company (Beaumont) works on Sutton Road are still standing today, and still feature the distinctive Nicholson logo, although the premises are now occupied by other companies. There is an older picture of the works on page 226.

PHOTOGRAPH: AUTHOR

Havilland's was taken over by Hawker Siddeley in 1963; Hawker Siddeley in turn became part of British Aerospace in 1977; and the Hatfield airfield finally closed, after a long period of decline, in 1993, a victim of increasing competition in aircraft manufacturing. Improved processes and techniques made many industries less labour-intensive, and this led to industrial conflict, for example at the Handley Page factory in 1959. The printing industry, one of the most important in St Albans, was beset by conflict between management and trade unions in this period: as a study of printing explained in 1970, 'the unions have placed considerable emphasis on protecting their members' employment opportunities in the face of technological changes'.[120] Eventually, technological change seriously diminished employment opportunities in printing, and although three of the largest employers in St Albans in 1992 were still printing companies – Ambassador Press Limited (at Colney Street), Eversheds (on Alma Road) and Home Counties Newspapers (on Campfield Road) – only around 490 inhabitants of the St Albans district worked in printing and related occupations in 1991, compared with almost 1,000 in the borough alone forty years earlier.[121]

... industrial and other concerns ... disappeared after the industrial heyday of the city in the 1950s.

Many of the industrial and other concerns that had been established in St Albans in the nineteenth and early twentieth centuries disappeared after the industrial heyday of the city in the 1950s.[122] The 1950s themselves saw the disappearance of some well known names. Sander's orchid nurseries, after decades of difficulty, finally closed in 1953; they were followed by New Barnes mill in 1957, Freshwater's shoe factory at about the same time, and J. W. Vernon and Company's printing press in 1960. Ryder's closed in the 1960s; and Wiles and Lewis's suet factory stopped production in 1960. Another casualty of the 1960s was Horace Slade and Company, who had moved to the industrial estate at Porter's Wood, to the north of St Albans, in 1954, but who ceased production of cardboard boxes in 1966. The last goods trains on the Great Northern Railway branch line ran in 1964, although passenger trains had been discontinued as early as 1951. Acquisitions and mergers also characterised the 1960s, but these delayed rather than prevented the decline of local industries. For example, in 1962 Aquascutum acquired Peake's coat manufacturing business, and production continued in St Albans until the 1980s, when it was moved to Hemel Hempstead. Avery's Vermicelli merged with the Record Bread Company in 1964 to form Pasta Foods Limited, which continued production in St Albans, but eventually relocated to Great Yarmouth. In 1970 Handley Page's aircraft factory at Park Street closed, and this was followed three years later by another large employer of the mid-twentieth century, the Electrical Apparatus Company. The Ballito stocking factory ceased production in 1967, and the gas works closed in 1971; there is now a retail development on the site, although two gasholders remain. Nicholson and Company continued to manufacture coats at the Beaumont works, and lighting was still produced on the Sphere estate, until around the same time. The Vickers experimental tank closed in 1980, and was followed in subsequent years by A. J. Dixon and Company's flour mills, H. Punford and Company's embroidery works on Watson's Walk, and the St Albans Rubber Company, which lasted until 1990. Mercer's Chronometers, who were still producing 300 to 400 chronometers per annum in the mid-1970s, found their products subject to competition from 'increasingly sophisticated electronic instruments', and later from satellite navigation techniques. Chronometer production was moved to Gloucestershire in 1982; the dial gauge side of the business was acquired by Brown and Sharpe in 1984; and the St Albans factory was closed and sold for housing development.[123] There were some exceptions to these trends: in the St Albans rural district, light engineering remained a significant employer, and in St Michael Rural parish in the late 1960s, the large and later notorious Buncefield oil depot had been constructed, connected by a pipeline to Shellhaven.[124] Buncefield was destroyed in a spectacular fire in 2005.

St Albans 'suffered far less from recession than most other parts of the country'.

By 1984, it was clear to the authors of the official guide to St Albans that the district 'could never rank as a major industrial or commercial centre'. However, it noted 'the variety of work [St Albans] offers to the local population' and the low unemployment rate, which at 6.7 per cent was much lower than the national average.[125] In the early 1980s, St Albans 'suffered far less from the recession than most other parts of the country',[126] partly because its economic restructuring was already progressing rapidly. Manufacturing employment among residents of the St Albans district remained high, at 24.7 per cent of the occupied population, but more than half of these worked outside the district. Of those who both lived and worked in St Albans, the proportion working in manufacturing was only 20.1 per cent.[127] By 1991, only 14.9 per cent of the occupied population worked in manufacturing (see chart 9.2 on page 297), although the proportion was rather higher, at 19.2 per cent, among males. The St Albans percentage was considerably lower than the national figure of 22.5 per cent.[128] Much of the manufacturing employment in the district was concentrated in industrial estates on the edge of St Albans, such as Porter's Wood to the north of the city, Napsbury Lane to the south-east and Lyon Way near Smallford. In a similar development, wholesale warehousing sites were constructed in the 1980s at London Colney and Colney Street, together employing up to 1,000 people.[129] However, by the 1980s the planning authorities were rejecting many applications by companies from outside Hertfordshire to establish new industrial premises, in line with central government policy, which urged restrictions on industrial expansion in the region.[130] As a result, the service sector became predominant in St Albans and the surrounding area. In 1991, as chart 9.2 on page 297 shows, banking, finance and related occupations employed 20.4 per cent of the occupied population, while 'other services' employed 32.0 per cent. There were still some large manufacturing employers, most notably Marconi, which was the only employer of over 500 people in St Albans in 1992, but which ceased production in the city soon afterwards.[131] However, the increasing specialisation in services was noted with concern by one analyst in 1990:

> The District ... has a very narrow economic base. The heavy reliance on the service sector has led to an abundance of professional and managerial positions, whilst the decline in industry has led to the loss of important unskilled and semi-skilled work.[132]

Overall, distribution and catering, banking and finance, and other services, not including transport, accounted for 70 per cent of the jobs held by residents of the St Albans district, and an even higher proportion, around 80 per cent, of employment within the district itself.[133] There were certain idiosyncrasies in local employment patterns: for example, Hertfordshire has been noted for having 'a liberal sprinkling of mental hospitals'. In 1971, almost 10,000 patients lived in mental hospitals in the county, half of them in the vicinity of St Albans.[134] These generated considerable employment, and although changing healthcare policies would see residential care for the mentally ill decline after this date, the official guide to St Albans for 1984 claimed that hospitals 'in the area' employed around 4,000 people.[135] In 1991, at least 4,300 people in the district worked in healthcare, not including clerical and secretarial staff.[136] The number remains high, despite the closure of some of the facilities at the city hospital, including maternity and accident and emergency, in the 1990s. There were also around 3,260 'teaching professionals' in 1991; these included many who worked for the new University of Hertfordshire, created in 1992, the main campus of which is in Hatfield but which also uses some of the former premises of the St Albans College of Further Education.[137] Local government and the services it provided were responsible for the employment of a large share of the population: the district council had 626 employees in 1984.[138] In the 1980s, the rapid expansion of office space in the city centre brought many companies, especially in the financial sector, to St Albans: by 1992, Barclay's, KPMG Peat Marwick and General Accident all had more than 100 employees in St Albans, and Nationwide Anglia had over 200.[139] Examples of office developments in the 1980s included Bricket House, previously used as a hospital which closed in the mid-1970s: after a long delay during which the district council refused permission for a change of use for the site, Bricket House was demolished and replaced by a 26,000-square-foot office development.[140] Finally, the retail sector has grown. Although St Albans 'was late in the procession of towns that followed the fashion for new shopping centre schemes in the sixties and seventies',[141] more recent expansion of shopping facilities, in purpose-built centres such as Christopher Place and the Maltings, and in out-of-town developments such as the Sainsbury's Savacentre in London Colney, has

'late in the procession of towns that followed the fashion for new shopping centre schemes'

generated employment on a large scale. There were about 2,300 'sales assistants and check-out operators' living in the district in 1991, of whom almost three-quarters were female.[142] Marks and Spencer and Sainsbury's both had over 200 employees in St Albans in 1992.[143]

These large employers were atypical, and by 2003 St Albans was remarkable for the small size of its firms. The average firm in the district employed 7.1 people, compared with a national average of 11.2. In neighbouring Welwyn Hatfield, the average was 14.9 employees, while in Watford it was 14.2. In terms of average business size St Albans ranked 387th out of 407 districts in the country. Of 7,644 businesses in the district, 6,829 (88.2 per cent) employed 10 people or fewer, and only 26 (0.3 per cent) employed 200 or more.[144] Concerns were raised about rising unemployment in the early 2000s, but the district was still able to attract new companies, many in new and dynamic sectors of the economy. A report prepared for the district council noted that 'the Knowledge sector, seen by the EU and UK Government as a major source of future employment and wealth, is strong in St Albans', in common with other districts to the north and east of London.[145]

> 'the knowledge sector … a major source of future employment and wealth, is strong in St Albans'

By 2003, a majority – 51 per cent – of the occupied population of the St Albans district worked outside its boundaries, and although it is not clear exactly what proportion of these worked in London, it was certainly high.[146] In 1981, about 20 per cent of the working population of the district worked in London, and this seems to have increased in the following years: according to one correspondent to a local newspaper, the 1980s was the decade when St Albans changed 'from a county town to a commuter town'.[147] Transport improvements assisted in this development, notably the electrification of the Midland line in 1985, and the re-opening of the Thameslink tunnel in 1987, which allowed trains to run directly from St Albans to the City of London.[148] In 1986 the section of the M25 motorway from Bricket Wood to London Colney was opened.[149] The attraction of commuting in the early twenty-first century is partly explained by the available earnings: in 2003 the average weekly pay for jobs based in London was £637.19, while for jobs in St Albans it was just £525.68. However, the average weekly earnings among *residents* of St Albans were £736.30.[150] At the same time, the good reputation of local schools, and the favourable property prices compared with London, exerted a powerful attraction. Meanwhile, St Albans itself continued to provide employment for large numbers of people: 42 per cent of the jobs in the district were done by in-commuters in 2003.[151]

Changes in the employment structure and government of St Albans have been accompanied by changes in the housing of the population. The most notable change has been the decline in the number of proportion of homes that are publicly owned. In 1976, there were 4,337 council homes in the city of St Albans, and a further 4,336 in the rest of the district, making 8,673 in total, and the waiting list for these properties numbered 2,000.[152] Much of this housing stock was in urgent need of repair: already the new district council had improved 400 houses, mostly dating from before the Second World War, and improvements to a further 1,000 were planned.[153] In 1981 there were 8,509 households living in council properties in the St Albans district, 19.8 per cent of the total.[154] Under the terms of the Housing Act (1980), local authorities were required to give tenants the right to buy their council homes, and as a result, by 2003, the number had been reduced to 5,528, around 10 per cent of the housing stock of the district.[155] Of these properties, 3,096 were houses and bungalows, 2,381 were flats and 51 were 'dwellings in multi-occupied dwellings' [sic].[156]

As the number of council houses fell, housing developments in the private sector have expanded the number of homes in the St Albans district. Although, as table 9.1 on page 299 shows, the population of the district increased only very slowly, between 1981 and 2003 the number of households grew by around 28 per cent.[157] This reflected a wider national trend towards smaller household size. A large majority of homes – 78 per cent in 2003 – in the district were owner-occupied.[158] Major private-sector developments towards the end of the twentieth century included the Jersey Farm estate, begun in 1977 and completed in the 1980s. The estate comprised a total of 1,350 properties, of which just 120 (in Newgate Close) were council houses; the remainder were built by private developers.[159] There was a property boom in the late 1970s, one observer reporting with disbelief that 'Victorian terraced houses in the back streets, which would almost qualify as slum property in some towns, change hands for £12,000' in St Albans.[160] Since the 1980s, conversions of industrial and commercial premises, and newly built developments, have seen a significant increase in the proportion of the housing stock of St Albans that consists of flats: 17.4 per cent of private-sector housing units in 2003.[161] One example among many is the development at Chime Square, on the site of the bus garage on St Peter's Street, which closed in the 1980s.[162] The buoyancy of the local housing sector in the early twenty-first century was reflected in the large growth of employment in the construction sector in the district, which increased by 106 per cent, from 1,800 in 1993 to 3,700 in 2001.[163] The strong housing market in St Albans since the recession of the early 1990s has created difficulties for many sections of the population. As in most parts of Britain, housing costs in the private sector soared in St Albans in the second half of the 1990s and the early twenty-first century, with many first-time buyers being priced out of entry to the housing market. In June 2002, the average price of a one-bedroom flat in the district was £118,254; the average semi-detached house cost £290,137, compared with £237,449 in the county of Hertfordshire as a whole and £191,566 in the south-east of England.[164] In 2002, a first-time buyer would need an annual income of £35,000 to buy a one-bedroom property, and at least £18,000 to afford the rent for a one-bedroom flat in the private rented sector.[165] Recent

'Victorian terraced houses in the back streets, which would almost qualify as slum property in some towns, change hands for £12,000 …'

pressures on the housing market have not significantly improved the prospects for those who are trying to climb the 'property ladder'. The need for affordable housing amounted to 1,173 homes per annum, and as an annual average of only 67.5 affordable housing units were completed in the period 1994–2002, it has been admitted that 'it is not expected that the Council will be able to achieve this scale of supply within the timescale'.[166] Ninety-three properties for 'key workers' were under development, and due for completion in 2004.[167]

Housing and other building projects in St Albans in the second half of the twentieth century caused widespread discontent, as a burgeoning urban conservationist movement organised opposition to a range of developments. As noted in the last chapter, some concerns had been voiced in the 1920s and 1930s about the impact of urban change on the historic environment, and these were intensified when St Albans became an 'expansion town'. When the town clerk sought opinions on post-war reconstruction from local interest groups in 1945, the St Albans trades council urged that 'the ancient character of such streets as St Peter's Street should be preserved' in any plan for St Albans.[168] Similarly, the planning report of 1946 expressed the fear that developers 'might, unthinkingly, advocate measures that would entirely destroy the beauties of St Peter's Street, French Row and Fishpool Street'.[169] Although the manufacturing industries of St Albans were relatively unobtrusive, some developments caused concern: for example, there was widespread local opposition to the expansion of the gas works, which commenced in 1955.[170] In the later 1950s, the Luton Water Company was proposing to take 5 million gallons of water per day from the river Ver, and a public inquiry in 1958 reduced the amount to 2 million in the face of a concerted campaign by residents of St Albans.[171] Protection of the urban environment took institutional form in 1961, when the St Albans Civic Society was formed, numbering Elsie Toms and pageant-master Cyril Swinson (see box 12) among its founder members. Under pressure from the Civic Society and individuals such as Toms, the city council paid increasing regard to conservationism: for example, French Row and the Pemberton almshouses were sensitively restored, as were some buildings in Fishpool Street. According to Toms, 'the plans committee of the City Council is one of the principal agents in such good work, for by refusing permission to develop in a way that is unsuitable, such buildings which would spoil our city are in many cases avoided, although the powers in this direction are not as great as could be wished'.[172] Nevertheless, the mobilisation of local sentiment could achieve results, as in the case of the Civic Society's successful campaign against a proposed inner ring road in 1964, a scheme which, according to local historian James Corbett, 'would have meant the demolition of hundreds of houses and the ravaging of the city's appearance'.[173]

The radical inner ring road proposal, although considered unsuitable and never carried out, was a response to difficulties encountered by the municipality

'the ancient character of such streets as St Peter's Street should be preserved'

French Row, looking towards High Street, with the back of the clock tower to the left. At the end of the road, on the right-hand side, was the Red Lion pub, one of two with that name in St Albans. The Lower Red Lion still exists, on Fishpool Street.

FROM THE COLLECTION OF TONY BAXTER

in controlling road traffic, which have beset St Albans in the post-war period. Road safety campaigns in the 1960s called for pedestrian crossings at notorious accident blackspots – notably the Ancient Briton junction, where Harpenden Road meets Batchwood Drive and Beech Road – and for reduced speed limits on some stretches of road, such as the Watford Road in Chiswell Green.[174] Safety was not the only concern: the traffic problem in St Albans had deleterious effects on the urban environment. A bypass route was opened in the 1950s along King Harry Lane and Bluehouse Hill.[175] The A414, between St Albans and Hemel Hempstead, was linked to this bypass, and was widened in the early 1960s. The new M1 motorway opened in 1959; and increasing volumes of traffic were carried by the A5 and A6 from London, which met at the Peahen crossroads. This crossroads was widely, and probably erroneously, believed to be the busiest in Britain, or even the world.[176] In 1978, the author Brian Bailey commented:

'the city's
historic core
has gradually
been eroded
by piecemeal
office
development'

> When the M1 motorway was opened, it was anticipated that it would take a lot of the traffic away from what had been described, with wild exaggeration, as the busiest crossroads in the country. It failed to do so, however, and the town centre is certainly, at times, a nightmare for old people wanting to cross the streets, and an infuriating bottleneck for drivers ... short of some major and very expensive scheme to divert traffic away from it, it is difficult to see how further deterioration of this very old city can be avoided.[177]

The 'major and very expensive scheme' that was eventually drawn up, a one-way system imposed in 1988 at a cost of £775,000, proved unworkable and unpopular, and was dropped early in the following year.[178] By this time, the district council had become so anxious about the traffic problem that a moratorium was instigated on all office development in St Albans 'which generates excess traffic'.[179]

Traffic congestion was just one of the problems that the planning authorities faced in the late twentieth century. In both the 'historic core' of St Albans, and on the periphery, a careful balance needed to be struck between the interests of development and conservation. On the edges of St Albans, there was 'understandably much opposition' among residents of the Marshalswick estate and the village of Sandridge to the construction of the Jersey Farm estate, which was permitted following a three-week public enquiry held by the Department of the Environment in 1973. Once the estate had been built, its own residents, together with many in Marshalswick, opposed the large supermarket which had been planned for the site, and a smaller retail development was built instead.[180] On the other side of St Albans, permission to build the 204,000-square-foot retail park at London Colney, featuring the Sainsbury's Savacentre, was initially rejected in the face of opposition, although given on appeal in 1988.[181] Meanwhile, in the city centre, 'excessive office development' in the 1980s was felt to be damaging the heart of St Albans: as one investigator, Christina Todd, explained in 1990,

> the city's historic core has gradually been eroded by piecemeal office development which has led to the loss of many cherished local buildings

and to deterioration in the general environment. Since 1984 six large office developments have been constructed within the central office core, four allowed on appeal to the Secretary of State [for the Environment].[182]

Although part of St Albans was designated a conservation area in 1969, and this was extended in 1981, many important buildings remained unlisted.[183] Todd blamed the environmental deterioration of the city on the impact of national political decisions on the local planning process – epitomised by the role of the Department of the Environment in the planning process – but blame could also, to an extent, be laid at the door of the local authority itself. Some years earlier, Brian Bailey saw the problem in these terms:

In some ways, St Albans is an epitome of the so-called advance of civilization and the state of England at present, in which chaos and stress take the place of style and dignity, and pride precedes the fall. The place seems to have a schizoid personality. Uncertain of its identity in the modern world, indecisive as to whether it wants to present itself as an historic town or a progressive community, it makes no decisions at all and loses on both counts, criticized by shoppers and traders for not being up to date, on the one hand, and by conservationists for not being sufficiently out of date, on the other.[184]

The view northwards from the top of the clock tower. French Row and Christopher Place shopping centre can be seen to the left, and Market Place to the right. The Corn Exchange stands on the right-hand side of Market Place, and in the distance is St Peter's church. When this photograph was taken, in 2007, the town hall was being refurbished; as the scaffolding shows. When St Albans was first laid out, most of the area to the right-hand side of French Row was open ground, where the markets were held.

PHOTOGRAPH: GAVIN DEAS

The civic uncertainty detected by Bailey in St Albans was highlighted in the long-running 'Chequer Street affair', which dominated local politics in the late 1970s and early 1980s. As Ralph Glasser – the author of *Town Hall*, a study of the St Albans district council in this period – melodramatically explained,

> Chequer Street ... cast a heavy shadow. Whoever I talked to seemed drawn to speak of it; as if an irritant substance were deeply implanted, the unsettling influence erupted again and again. The very words Chequer Street triggered powerful responses. As with some great family drama, no facet of life was free of it ...[185]

A proposal to develop a site, of just over six acres, bounded by Chequer Street, Victoria Street, London Road and Upper Marlborough Road, was first put forward in the 1960s.[186] The site was run-down – the Chequers cinema had closed in 1962 – and appeared suitable to be turned into a shopping centre. The various plans drawn up for the site were opposed by traders in St Albans who feared the competition from the shopping centre, and by the St Albans Civic Society and the newly established Chequer Street Action Group, which had the high-profile local support of the *Review* newspaper. The ruling Conservative group on the district council favoured a development in the private sector, but the organised opposition – the Chequer Street Action Group came close to winning a council by-election in 1978 – forced adjustments to the plans. An opinion poll was commissioned in 1979, finding that 'a substantial public

majority favoured a reduced size development, with greater emphasis on restoration of existing buildings and introduction of some leisure and housing facilities'.[187] The controversy was featured on a BBC *Tonight* documentary in 1978. The council had to reach an out-of-court settlement with the original developers of the site, and entered into an agreement with Bredero Consulting Limited, of Epsom, who eventually carried out the work at a cost of £20 million. The new shopping centre, named The Maltings, finally opened in 1988, although without the department store that was originally planned. As the campaigners had wanted, there were leisure facilities in the development, including the new St Albans central library and an arts centre. There is no sign of an end to the ongoing conflict between development and conservation in the St Albans district: in 2006 plans for a rail-freight depot employing 3,000 people on the airfield site at Park Street encountered opposition from local residents, who were concerned about the significant increase in lorry traffic that would result.[188]

'a visit to St Albans for shopping is a unique and varied experience'

In the early twenty-first century, the reputation of St Albans is generally high, for a variety of reasons. In an edited collection of 'personal views' of the city, published locally in 2004, selected authors gave their brief, and overwhelmingly positive, impressions. St Albans was variously styled 'City of Pubs' (by Roger Protz, editor of CAMRA's *Good Beer Guide*), 'City of Ecumenism' (by the Revered Noel Pepper, a former chaplain to the cathedral), 'City of Humour', 'City of Mystery', 'City of Trade and Market', 'City of Quaint Streets' and 'City of Special People'.[189] Schools, shopping facilities and civic life were particularly highly praised in this document. The then MP Kerry Pollard, a member of the Education and Skills Committee, announced himself 'the more convinced that we in St Albans can feel privileged to be surrounded by top quality schools, with experienced and totally professional staff led by exceptional head teachers'.[190] Meanwhile, Melvyn Teare, 'City Centre Manager', adopted the long-standing theme of the intermingling of past and present to describe the shopping 'experience' in St Albans:

> In marked contrast to the dull uniformity of most modern indoor shopping malls, a visit to St Albans for shopping is a unique and varied experience. The city's historic ambience, the vibrant street market and many high street names give shoppers the best of the old with the best of the new.[191]

According to this book, the lively associational life of St Albans survived into the new century: as Jenny Stroud, a former mayor, remarked in her foreword, 'quietly and without fuss, there are hundreds (or could be thousands) of St Albans people engaging in the variety of activities which make a thriving civic society'.[192] Not all inhabitants of St Albans subscribed to this image of the city, which in 2003 was described in *The Idler Book of Crap Towns* as one of 'the fifty worst places to live in the UK'. One long-standing resident complained:

> Having lived in St Albans since 1975 I have witnessed many changes to this historical and frankly suffocating satellite town. We have no cinema and more importantly no hospital ... You can either drink with nauseating Morris-dancing CAMRA members or with drunken, violent polo-shirt wearing Neanderthals and their vacuous harridans. You have to be careful if you're black or gay or look a bit weird, because the lace curtains will be twitching and we don't like strangers who talk funny.[193]

... it might be conceded that there is some justification for smugness ...

Another described a St Albans street scene: 'The (catastrophically bored) teenagers ... pave the streets with their prone bodies after attempting to drink themselves out of their middle England hell ... they long to die. A perfectly reasonable reaction to life in St Albans.'[194] Of course, most residents and observers of St Albans would probably disagree with this portrait of their city, and in its defence could point to the relatively low crime rate – although car crime rates are the highest in Hertfordshire, and in 2006 there was widespread public concern about drive-by shootings[195] – high standards of education, low unemployment, high average earnings, and good range of pubs and shops, along with the theatrical, sporting and cultural opportunities. In 2004 the *Independent* described St Albans as a 'well-heeled commuter town', with 'Georgian homes and neat tea rooms'.[196] The neatness and outward prosperity masks some social problems: increasing unemployment in the early 2000s, insufficient access to housing, especially for the low-paid, and the troubled relationship between progress and tradition, to name just three. However, there are many worse places in which to live than St Albans. As noted above, one memory of the 1950s is that St Albans was 'a terribly smug place'. In an indication of this smugness, in September 2007 St Albans easily won an online poll initiated by the games company Hasbro, in which visitors to a website voted for which town or city they would like to see on the new Monopoly board, featuring towns and cities from across the UK in place of London streets. With over 10 per cent of the votes, which in total numbered more than a million, St Albans won the right to the space traditionally occupied by Mayfair.[197] St Albans is 'a terribly smug place' even today, and it might be conceded that there is some justification for smugness, not least because of the interesting and varied history that has been traced in this book. The length and richness of this history contribute to a widespread sense among the people of St Albans of what one commentator has called 'the unique feeling and style of the venerable city, the sense of an intricate inheritance'.[198]

Notes and references

Notes to Chapter 1: Verlamion and Verulamium: the Iron Age and Roman town

1. R. E. M. Wheeler, 'A Prehistoric Metropolis: The First Verulamium', in Gillian Carr and Simon Stoddart (eds), *Celts from Antiquity* (Cambridge: Antiquity Publications, 2002), p. 161. The summary of Wheeler's findings below is based on the same article, which originally appeared in *Antiquity*, vol. 6 (1932).
2. *The St Albans Mapguide* (St Albans: Michael Middleditch, 2003 [1st edn, 1988]), pp. 3–4; Rosalind Niblett, *Verulamium: The Roman City of St Albans* (Stroud: Tempus Publishing, 2001), p. 33; see below, pp. 58, 60, 98, 99.
3. Barry Cunliffe, *Iron Age Communities in Britain: An Account of England, Scotland and Wales from the Seventh Century* BC *until the Roman Conquest* (London: Routledge, 2005 [1st edn, 1974]), p. 163.
4. Keith Branigan, *The Catuvellauni* (Gloucester: Alan Sutton, 1987), p. 1.
5. Ibid., pp. 5–7.
6. Julius Caesar, *Seven Commentaries on the Gallic War* (Oxford: Oxford University Press, ed. Carolyn Hammond, 1996), v.14.
7. Charles H. Ashdown, *St Albans Historical and Picturesque, with an Account of the Roman City of Verulamium* (London: Elliot Stock, 1893), pp. 3, 5.
8. Carolyn Hammond, notes on Caesar, *Seven Commentaries*, v.14.
9. Rosalind Niblett, *Roman Hertfordshire* (Wimborne: Dovecote Press, 1995), p. 10.
10. Niblett, *Verulamium*, p. 34.
11. Ibid., pp. 46–7.
12. Cunliffe, *Iron Age Communities*, pp. 402–6.
13. Ibid., p. 406.
14. Branigan, *The Catuvellauni*, p. 38.
15. Niblett, *Verulamium*, pp. 50–1.
16. Ian Stead and Valery Rigby, *Verulamium: The King Harry Lane Site* (London: English Heritage, 1989), pp. 80–6.
17. Niblett, *Roman Hertfordshire*, pp. 18–19; Niblett, *Verulamium*, pp. 46–8.
18. Wheeler, 'Prehistoric Metropolis', p. 164.
19. Ibid.
20. Niblett, *Roman Hertfordshire*, p. 17.
21. Branigan, *The Catuvellauni*, p. 14.
22. Niblett, *Verulamium*, pp. 42–3; Branigan, *The Catuvellauni*, pp. 16–18.
23. Branigan, *The Catuvellauni*, p. 14; see above, pp. 8, 11.
24. Niblett, *Verulamium*, p. 47.
25. Rosalind Niblett, 'A Catuvellauni Chieftain's Burial from St Albans', in Carr and Stoddart, *Celts from Antiquity*, pp. 259–72. Niblett's article was first published in *Antiquity*, vol. 66 (1992).
26. Branigan, *The Catuvellauni*, pp. 34, 38.
27. Tacitus, *Annals of Tacitus, Translated into English with Notes and Maps*, trans. Alfred John Church and William Jackson Brodribb (London: Macmillan, 1876), xiv.33: Tacitus reported that Boudicca's rebels 'passed by the fortresses with military garrisons'. See below, pp. 15–17.
28. Tacitus, *Annals*, xiv.31.
29. Niblett, *Verulamium*, pp. 61–2.
30. Ibid., pp. 62–4.
31. Branigan, *The Catuvellauni*, p. 38.
32. Tacitus, *Annals*, xiv., 29–38.
33. Ibid., xiv. 33.
34. Ibid., xiv. 38.
35. Niblett, *Verulamium*, p. 67.
36. David S. Neal, Angela Wardle and Jonathan Hunn, *Excavation of the Iron Age, Roman and Medieval Settlement at Gorhambury, St Albans* (London: Historic Buildings and Monuments Commission for England, 1990), p. 55.
37. See above, p. 15.
38. Niblett, *Verulamium*, pp. 59–60.
39. Ibid., p. 60.

40. Peter Salway, *Roman Britain* (Oxford: Clarendon Press, 1981), p. 573.

41. Ibid., p. 575.

42. John Wacher, *The Towns of Roman Britain* (London: Routledge, 1997 [1st edn, 1975]), p. 21.

43. Ibid., p. 34.

44. Ibid., p. 36.

45. Martin Henig, 'Religion and Art in St Alban's City', in Martin Henig and Phillip Lindley (eds), *Alban and St Albans: Roman and Medieval Architecture, Art and Archaeology* (Leeds: British Archaeological Association and Maney Publishing, 2001), p. 15.

46. Sheppard Frere, 'Verulamium', in Robert Runcie (ed.), *Cathedral and City: St Albans Ancient and Modern* (London: Martyn Associates, 1977), p. 11.

47. Wacher, *Towns of Roman Britain*, pp. 42–3, instancing Exeter and Silchester.

48. Niblett, *Verulamium*, p. 75.

49. 'The Basilica Inscription', display panel in the Verulamium Museum, 2006.

50. Ibid.

51. Niblett, *Verulamium*, p. 78; St Albans Museums, 'Roman Verulamium' (1998: film shown in Verulamium Museum).

52. Wacher, *Towns of Roman Britain*, p. 227.

53. Niblett, *Verulamium*, p. 78.

54. There has been considerable discussion of the dating and purposes of the first ditch (excavated by Sheppard Frere and known as the '1955 ditch') and the Fosse. This will not be explored in detail here. See Niblett, *Verulamium*, pp. 71–3.

55. Niblett, *Verulamium*, p. 81.

56. Ibid., p. 69.

57. Rosalind Niblett and Isobel Thompson, *Alban's Buried Towns: An Assessment of St Albans Archaeology up to AD 1600* (Oxford: Oxbow Books, 2005), pp. 11, 88.

58. 'The Verulamium Region Pottery Industry': display panel, Verulamium Museum, 2006.

59. Niblett and Thompson, *Alban's Buried Towns*, p. 43.

60. Niblett, *Verulamium*, p. 108.

61. This description of insula XXI, building 3 is based on Sheppard Frere, *Verulamium Excavations* (3 vols, London: Society of Antiquaries of London, 1983), vol. 2, pp. 157–76.

62. Ibid., p. 163 n. 2.

63. Henig, 'Religion and Art', p. 21.

64. Ibid., p. 22.

65. St Albans Museums, 'Roman Verulamium'.

66. Neal *et al.*, *Excavation … at Gorhambury*, p. 44.

67. Ibid., pp. 45–9, 55.

68. Ibid., p. 94.

69. 'The Verulamium Region Pottery Industry', display panel.

70. Neal *et al.*, *Excavation … at Gorhambury*, p. 94.

71. Niblett, *Verulamium*, pp. 113–14.

72. Ibid., p. 115.

73. 'Changing Burial Practices': display panel, Verulamium Museum, 2006.

74. 'A Face from the Past': display panel, Verulamium Museum, 2006; St Albans Museums, 'Lifting the Lid' (1994: film shown in Verulamium Museum).

75. 'Food for the Journey': display panel, Verulamium Museum, 2006.

76. Niblett and Thompson, *Alban's Buried Towns*, p. 71.

77. Ibid., p. 75.

78. Niblett, *Verulamium*, p. 124.

79. Neal *et al.*, *Excavation … at Gorhambury*, p. 98.

80. Ibid., pp. 94–5.

81. Wacher, *Towns of Roman Britain*, p. 235.

82. Salway, *Roman Britain*, pp. 575–8.

83. Niblett, *Verulamium*, pp. 125–6.

84. Quoted in ibid., p. 132.

85. See the map in ibid., p. 129, and Niblett's comments on pp. 130–1.

86. Ibid., p. 135.

87. Quoted in D. M. Palliser, 'The Origins of British Towns', in D. M. Palliser (ed.), *The Cambridge Urban History of Britain, Volume I: 600–1540* (Cambridge: Cambridge University Press, 2000), pp. 22–3.

88. Wacher, *Towns of Roman Britain*, pp. 411ff.

89. Ibid., p. 414.

90. Niblett, 'Catuvellauni Chieftain's Burial', p. 270.

91. Niblett, *Verulamium*, p. 108.

92. Rosalind Niblett, 'Why Verulamium?', in Henig and Lindley, *Alban and St Albans*, p. 5.

93. Ibid., p. 5.

94. Niblett and Thompson, *Alban's Buried Towns*, p. 40.

95. Henig, 'Religion and Art', p. 22.

96. Ibid., pp. 22–4.

97. 'Shrine': display panel at the Verulamium Museum, 2006.

98. Niblett, 'Why Verulamium?', p. 6.

99. Henig, 'Religion and Art', p. 26.

1. J. N. L. Myres, *The English Settlements* (Oxford: Clarendon Press, 1986), p. 1.
2. David Wilson, *The Anglo-Saxons* (Harmondsworth: Penguin Books, 1971), p. 25.
3. Stephen Johnson, *Later Roman Britain* (London: Routledge and Kegan Paul, 1980), p. 105.
4. Ibid., p. 110.
5. Ibid., p. 116.
6. Ibid., p. 123.
7. Ibid., p. 145.
8. Niblett and Thompson, *Alban's Buried Towns*, p. 191; Bede, *Ecclesiastical History*, book I, chapter 7; Bailey, *Portrait of Hertfordshire*, p. 83.
9. Quoted in Myres, *English Settlements*, p. 210.
10. Neal *et al.*, *Excavation ... at Gorhambury*, p. 82.
11. Martin Welch, *Anglo-Saxon England* (London: B. T. Batsford/English Heritage, 1992), p. 107.
12. Ibid.
13. Wilson, *Anglo-Saxons*, p. 77; Niblett and Thompson, *Alban's Buried Towns*, p. 266.
14. Wilson, *Anglo-Saxons*, p. 63.
15. Robert Lacey and Danny Danziger, *The Year 1000: What Life Was Like at the Turn of the First Millennium* (London: Little, Brown and Company, 1999), p. 87; James Tait, quoted in D. M. Palliser, 'Introduction', in Palliser, *Cambridge Urban History of Britain, Volume I*, p. 4.
16. Jeremy Haslam, 'Introduction', in *Anglo-Saxon Towns in Southern England* (Chichester: Phillimore, 1984), pp. xvi, xiv.
17. Wilson, *Anglo-Saxons*, pp. 81–2.
18. Myres, *English Settlements*, pp. 129–30.
19. See above, p. 24.
20. Myres, *English Settlements*, p. 23 n.
21. Martin Biddle, 'Alban and the Anglo-Saxon Church', in Runcie, *Cathedral and City*, p. 35.
22. Reginald A. Smith, 'Anglo-Saxon Remains', in William Page (ed.), *The Victoria History of the County of Hertford* (4 vols, London: Constable, 1902–14; hereafter *VCH Herts*), vol. 4, p. 253.
23. Ibid., p. 256.
24. Biddle, 'Alban and the Anglo-Saxon Church', p. 35.
25. This account is based on William Page, 'Abbey of St Albans – Before the Conquest', *VCH Herts*, vol. 4, p. 367.
26. Ibid.
27. Elsie Toms, *The Story of St Albans* (St Albans: Abbey Mill Press, 1962), p. 12.
28. Biddle, 'Alban and the Anglo-Saxon Church', p. 30.
29. Ibid., p. 29.
30. Dom David Knowles, *The Monastic Order in England: A History of Its Development from the Times of St Dunstan to the Fourth Lateran Council* (Cambridge: Cambridge University Press, 1940), p. 4. The above account of the Benedictine Rule is based on Knowles, *Monastic Order*, pp. 3–25, and Danziger and Lacey, *Year 1000*, pp. 103–9, 135–6.
31. Knowles, *Monastic Order*, p. 10.
32. Danziger and Lacey, *Year 1000*, p. 109.
33. Page, 'Abbey of St Albans', pp. 367–8.
34. Danziger and Lacey, *Year 1000*, p. 103; Knowles, *Monastic Order*, p. 19.
35. Page, 'Abbey of St Albans', pp. 367–8.
36. Ibid., pp. 368–9.
37. Knowles, *Monastic Order*, pp. 34–5.
38. H. R. Loyn, *The Vikings in Britain* (London: Batsford, 1977), p. 59, map on p. 119.
39. Ibid., p. 120.
40. M. E. Simkins, 'Political History', *VCH Herts*, vol. 2, p. 2.
41. Page, 'Abbey of St Albans', pp. 371–2.
42. Danziger and Lacey, *Year 1000*, p. 87.
43. William Page, quoted in Niblett and Thompson, *Alban's Buried Towns*, p. 179.
44. Niblett and Thompson, *Alban's Buried Towns*, pp. 178–84.
45. Ibid., pp. 184–94.
46. Ibid., pp. 191–2.
47. Matthew Paris, translated in Niblett and Thompson, *Alban's Buried Towns*, p. 363.
48. Knowles, *Monastic Order*, p. 51.
49. Ibid., p. 47.
50. Ibid., pp. 42ff; Danziger and Lacey, *Year 1000*, pp. 108–9.
51. Knowles, *Monastic Order*, p. 100.
52. Niblett and Thompson, *Alban's Buried Towns*, p. 363; William Page *et al.*, 'St Michael's', *VCH Herts*, vol. 2, p. 400.
53. Ibid., pp. 187–8.
54. F. I. Kilvington, *A Short History of St Albans School* (no publisher given, 1986 [1st edn, 1970]), p. 3.
55. Niblett and Thompson, *Alban's Buried Towns*, 178, 194.
56. Ibid., pp. 194, 366; see below, p. 90.
57. Ibid., p. 194.
58. Ibid.
59. Matthew Paris, translated in Niblett and Thompson, *Alban's Buried Towns*, p. 363.
60. Pamela Taylor, 'The Early St Albans Endowment and Its Chroniclers', *Historical Research*, vol. 68

(1995), pp. 127–8.

61. D. M. Palliser, T. R. Slater and E. Patricia Dennison, 'The Topography of Towns 600–1300', in Palliser, *Cambridge Urban History of Britain, Volume I*, pp. 171–2.

62. Grenville Astill, 'General Survey 600–1300', in Palliser, *Cambridge Urban History of Britain, Volume I*, pp. 35–6; Richard Holt, 'Society and Population 600–1300', in Palliser, *Cambridge Urban History of Britain, Volume I*, p. 81.

63. Astill, 'General Survey', p. 42.

64. Holt, 'Society and Population', p. 81.

65. James Campbell, 'Power and Authority 600–1300', in Palliser, *Cambridge Urban History of Britain, Volume I*, p. 55.

66. Richard Britnell, 'The Economy of British Towns 600–1300', in Palliser, *Cambridge Urban History of Britain, Volume I*, p. 123.

67. James Campbell, *Essays in Anglo-Saxon History* (London: Hambledon Press, 1986), p. 143.

68. T. R. Slater, 'Benedictine Town Planning in Medieval England: Evidence from St Albans', in T. R. Slater and Gervase Rosser (eds), *The Church in the Medieval Town* (Aldershot: Ashgate, 1998), pp. 158–9.

69. Ibid., pp. 159, 166.

70. Ibid., pp. 165–6, 171–2.

71. Ibid., pp. 167–8.

72. Ibid., p. 172.

73. Niblett and Thompson, *Alban's Buried Towns*, pp. 300–1.

74. Ibid., pp. 286–7.

75. Ibid., p. 195.

76. Page, 'Abbey of St Albans', pp. 369–70.

77. Ibid., pp. 371–2.

78. Knowles, *Monastic Order*, p. 102.

79. Ibid., pp. 100–2.

80. Taylor, 'Early St Albans Endowment', p. 128.

81. F. M. Stenton, *Anglo-Saxon England* (Oxford: Oxford University Press, 1971 [1st edn, 1943]), p. 635.

82. Quoted in Page, 'Abbey of St Albans', p. 372. Some sources give Leofstan's date of death as 1064 or 1065.

Notes to Chapter 3: Norman Conquest to Black Death

1. N. M. Trenholme, *The English Monastic Boroughs: A Study in Medieval History* (Columbia: University of Missouri, 1927), p. 28.

2. James Corbett, *A History of St Albans* (Chichester: Phillimore, 1997), p. 20; Niblett and Thompson, *Alban's Buried Towns*, p. 263.

3. Wilson, *Anglo-Saxons*, p. 85.

4. M. W. Beresford and H. P. R. Finberg, *English Medieval Boroughs: A Hand-List* (Newton Abbot: David and Charles, 1973), p. 125.

5. J. Horace Round, 'Introduction to the Hertfordshire Domesday Survey', *VCH Herts*, vol. 1, p. 292.

6. Alan Dyer, 'Ranking Lists of English Medieval Towns', in Palliser, *Cambridge Urban History of Britain, Volume I*, pp. 752–4.

7. Colin Platt, *The Abbeys and Priories of Medieval England* (London: Chancellor Press, 1995 [1st edn, 1984]), p. 62.

8. Emma Cownie, *Religious Patronage in Anglo-Norman England 1066–1135* (Woodbridge: Boydell and Brewer, 1998), pp. 1, 26.

9. Platt, *Abbeys and Priories*, p. 57.

10. Judith A. Green, *The Aristocracy of Norman England* (Cambridge: Cambridge University Press, 1997), pp. 393–6.

11. Cownie, *Religious Patronage*, pp. 81–2.

12. Ibid., p. 80.

13. Ibid., pp. 82ff.

14. Ibid., p. 83.

15. J. Horace Round, 'Introduction to the Hertfordshire Domesday Survey', *VCH Herts*, vol. 1, pp. 282, 299.

16. Cownie, *Religious Patronage*, p. 85.

17. Green, *Aristocracy of Norman England*, pp. 396–7.

18. Christopher Brooke, 'St Albans: The Great Abbey', in Runcie, *Cathedral and City*, pp. 45–6.

19. Platt, *Abbeys and Priories*, pp. 15–16.

20. Michelle Still, *The Abbot and the Rule: Religious Life at St Alban's 1290–1349* (Aldershot: Ashgate, 2002), p. 2.

21. Ibid., p. 20.

22. Ibid., pp. 23–4.

23. Ibid.; see Still's map on p. 263.

24. Ibid., pp. 25–6.

25. Platt, *Abbeys and Priories*, p. 21.

26. Eileen Roberts, *The Hill of the Martyr: An Architectural History of St Albans Abbey* (Dunstable: The Book Castle, 1993), p. 35.

27. Ibid., p. 45.

28. Ibid., p. 53.

29. Still, *Abbot and the Rule*, pp. 1, 14–15; Still gives the date as 28 December 1115, while other historians give the date as 1116 (Cownie, *Religious Patronage*, p. 90).

30. W. Page *et al.*, 'City of St Alban', *VCH Herts*, vol. 2, p. 510.

31. Roberts, *Hill of the Martyr*, p. 35.

32. Brooke, 'St Albans', p. 59.

33. See Malcolm Thurlby, 'The Place of St Albans in Regional Sculpture and Architecture in the Second Half of the Twelfth Century', in Henig and Lindley, *Alban and St Albans*, pp. 162–75.

34. Cownie, *Religious Patronage*, p. 94; Still, *Abbot and the Rule*, pp. 27–8; Platt, *Abbeys and Priories*, pp. 89–90.

35. William Page, *The Story of the English Towns: St Albans* (London: Society for Promoting Christian Knowledge, 1920), pp. 23–4: Hudson Memorial Library, St Albans, Beardsmore collection (hereafter Beardsmore) DA690.S13.P32.

36. Page *et al.*, 'City of St Alban', p. 510.

37. Platt, *Abbeys and Priories*, p. 91.

38. Quoted in ibid., p. 91; see also Roberts, *Hill of the Martyr*, p. 77; Corbett, *History of St Albans*, p. 26.

39. Roberts, *Hill of the Martyr*, chapter 9.

40. Platt, *Abbeys and Priories*, pp. 117–19.

41. Niblett and Thompson, *Alban's Buried Towns*, pp. 295–6.

42. Roberts, *Hill of the Martyr*, p. 15; Still, *Abbot and the Rule*, pp. 18–19.

43. Quoted in Platt, *Abbeys and Priories*, p. 82.

44. *Matthew Paris's English History: From the Year 1235 to 1273* (trans. J. A. Giles, 3 vols, London: Bohn, 1852–54), vol. 3, p. 242.

45. See also above, pp. 48–9, 54.

46. *Matthew Paris's English History*, vol. 2, pp. 260–1.

47. Brooke, 'St Albans', pp. 51–2; Paolo Squatriti, 'Offa's Dyke between Nature and Culture', *Environmental History*, vol. 9 (2004), p. 27.

48. *Matthew Paris's English History*, vol. 3, pp. 175–6.

49. Still, *Abbot and the Rule*, pp. 32, 78–80.

50. Ibid., pp. 87–8.

51. Minne Reddan, 'Abbey of St Albans – After the Conquest', *VCH Herts*, vol. 4, p. 385.

52. Still, *Abbot and the Rule*, pp. 102–3.

53. Lawrence Hoey, 'The Gothic Reconstruction of the Nave and Presbytery of St Albans Abbey', in Henig, *Alban and St Albans*, pp. 182–203 (p. 182 quoted).

54. Still, *Abbot and the Rule*, pp. 94–5.

55. Ibid., p. 51.

56. Ibid., p. 43; Platt, *Abbeys and Priories*, pp. 26–7, 31–2, 51–7, 59ff, 124ff.

57. Still, *Abbot and the Rule*, pp. 61–3, 67.

58. Toms, *Story of St Albans*, pp. 49–50, suggests that this is unlikely: 'some form of eczema' seems more probable.

59. Still, *Abbot and the Rule*, pp. 68–71.

60. Niblett and Thompson, *Alban's Buried Towns*, pp. 263–4.

61. Ibid., pp. 300–1.

62. Ibid., p. 301.

63. Slater, 'Benedictine Town Planning'.

64. Niblett and Thompson, *Alban's Buried Towns*, pp. 276–8.

65. Ibid., p. 278; see above, p. 64.

66. Niblett and Thompson, *Alban's Buried Towns*, p. 272.

67. Corbett, *History of St Albans*, p. 22.

68. Niblett and Thompson, *Alban's Buried Towns*, p. 285.

69. Ibid., p. 287.

70. Corbett, *History of St Albans*, pp. 24–5.

71. Niblett and Thompson, *Alban's Buried Towns*, p. 291, and map on p. 274.

72. L. F. Salzmann, 'Textiles', *VCH Herts*, vol. 4, p. 248.

73. Mark Bailey, 'Introduction', in Janice Brooker and Susan Flood (eds), *Hertfordshire Lay Subsidy Rolls 1307 and 1334* (no place given: Hertfordshire Record Society, 1998), p. xxv.

74. *Hertfordshire Lay Subsidy Rolls 1307 and 1334*, pp. 126–8.

75. Susan Flood, 'Wealth and Piety in St Albans in the Late Fifteenth and Early Sixteenth Centuries', unpublished MSt thesis, University of Cambridge (1997; copy in St Albans Central Library, LOC.942.585.05), p. 12.

76. St Albans and Hertfordshire Architectural and Archaeological Society (hereafter SAHAAS), *St Albans 1650–1700: A Thoroughfare Town and Its People* (ed. J. T. Smith and M. A. North, Hertford: Hertfordshire Publications, 2003).

77. Niblett and Thompson, *Alban's Buried Towns*, p. 286.

78. Ibid., p. 302.

79. Still, *Abbot and the Rule*, pp. 30–1.

80. Ibid., p. 31; Niblett and Thompson, *Alban's Buried Towns*, p. 281.

81. Colin Platt, *The English Medieval Town* (London: Secker and Warburg, 1976), p. 30.

82. Ibid., pp. 23–5.

83. Ibid., p. 15.

84. Bailey, 'Introduction', pp. xxiii–xxiv.

85. Toms, *Story of St Albans*, pp. 71–2.

86. Platt, *English Medieval Town*, pp. 45–7.

87. Page *et al.*, 'City of St Alban', p. 477.

88. Dyer, 'Ranking Lists of English Medieval Towns', pp. 755–7. This list of towns excludes the Cinque ports and a number of counties: Cheshire, Durham,

and parts of Shropshire, Cornwall, Devon and Kent. Some towns in these counties would certainly have been wealthier than St Albans. In an earlier ranking list compiled by Dyer, Bury was 25th and St Albans 47th: Alan Dyer, *Decline and Growth in English Towns 1400–1640* (Cambridge: Cambridge University Press, 1995 [1st edn, 1991]), pp. 62–3 (the rankings were 24th and 46th, but the lists exclude London).

89. Bailey, 'Introduction', p. xxv.
90. Niblett and Thompson, *Alban's Buried Towns*, p. 268; Frank Barlow, *The Feudal Kingdom of England 1042–1216* (London: Longman, 1988 [1st edn, 1955]), p. 222.
91. Simkins, 'Political History', p. 5.
92. Corbett, *History of St Albans*, p. 22; see Niblett and Thompson, *Alban's Buried Towns*, pp. 268–72.
93. Corbett, *History of St Albans*, pp. 26–7.
94. Simkins, 'Political History', p. 8.
95. Toms, *Story of St Albans*, p. 40.
96. Ibid., p. 29; Niblett and Thompson, *Alban's Buried Towns*, p. 302. The date of construction of the Tonman Ditch is uncertain, but it was 'well established' by 1271.
97. Corbett, *History of St Albans*, p. 31.
98. Simkins, 'Political History', pp. 10–11.
99. Trenholme, *English Monastic Boroughs*, p. 2.
100. Rosmund Faith, 'The Class Struggle in Fourteenth-Century England', in Raphael Samuel (ed.), *People's History and Socialist Theory* (London: Routledge and Kegan Paul, 1981), p. 52.
101. Adolphus Ballard, *The English Borough in the Twelfth Century* (Cambridge: Cambridge University Press, 1914), pp. 2–3.
102. Edward Miller and John Hatcher, *Medieval England: Rural Society and Economic Change 1086–1348* (London: Longman, 1978), pp. 150, 142.
103. Ibid., p. 116.
104. Bailey, 'Introduction', p. xxv.
105. Faith, 'Class Struggle', p. 51.
106. Ibid., pp. 53–4.
107. Ibid., p. 56. See below, pp. 91–3, 99–100, 105–15.
108. Niblett and Thompson, *Alban's Buried Towns*, p. 263.
109. *Matthew Paris's English History*, vol. 1, pp. 291–5.
110. Corbett, *History of St Albans*, p. 29.
111. Ibid., vol. 3, pp. 261–5.
112. Miller and Hatcher, *Medieval England*, p. 205.
113. Trenholme, *English Monastic Boroughs*, p. 1.
114. Ibid.
115. Still, *Abbot and the Rule*, p. 109.
116. Ballard, *English Borough*, pp. 3–4.
117. Ibid., pp. 6–9.
118. Ibid., pp. 13–14.
119. Platt, *English Medieval Town*, p. 21.
120. Trenholme, *English Monastic Boroughs*, p. 2.
121. Beresford and Finberg, *English Medieval Boroughs*, pp. 21, 125.
122. Ibid., p. 125.
123. Ballard, *English Borough*, pp. 25–6.
124. Ibid., pp. 26–7.
125. Simkins, 'Political History', pp. 10–11, 11 n. 1.
126. Ibid., p. 11.
127. Bailey, 'Introduction', pp. x, xv.
128. The account below is based on Page *et al.*, 'City of St Alban', pp. 477–9.
129. Ibid., p. 478.
130. Ibid., p. 469.
131. Ibid., p. 478.
132. See below, pp. 145–6.
133. Faith, 'Class Struggle', p. 54; Trenholme, *English Monastic Boroughs*, p. 29.
134. Trenholme, *English Monastic Boroughs*, pp. 29–30.
135. Page, *Story of the English Towns*, pp. 28–9; see below, pp. 145, 193.
136. Trenholme, *English Monastic Boroughs*, p. 19.
137. Ibid., pp. 2–11.
138. Ibid., pp. 12–18; Campbell, 'Power and Authority', p. 74.
139. The account below is largely based on Still, *Abbot and the Rule*, pp. 111–13, and Faith, 'Class Struggle', pp. 55–6.
140. Simkins, 'Political History', p. 13.
141. Page *et al.*, 'City of St Alban', p. 478.
142. Toms, *Story of St Albans*, p. 48.
143. See above, pp. 79–80.
144. Toms, *Story of St Albans*, p. 49; Still, *Abbot and the Rule*, pp. 113–15.
145. Toms, *Story of St Albans*, p. 49.
146. Faith, 'Class Struggle', p. 56.
147. See below, p. 110.
148. Still, *Abbot and the Rule*, pp. 115, 70.
149. Faith, 'Class Struggle', p. 54.

Notes to Chapter 4: From the Black Death to the dissolution of the monasteries

1. Asa Briggs, *A Social History of England* (London: Book Club Associates, 1984 [1st edn, 1983]), p. 114; Toms, *Story of St Albans*, p. 50.
2. Toms, *Story of St Albans*, pp. 50–1.

3. Corbett, *History of St Albans*, p. 37; Niblett and Thompson, *Alban's Buried Towns*, p. 263.

4. Briggs, *Social History of England*, pp. 120–1.

5. Rodney Hilton, *Bond Men Made Free: Medieval Peasant Movements and the English Rising of 1381* (London: Methuen and Co., 1973), pp. 169–70.

6. Niblett and Thompson, *Alban's Buried Towns*, p. 254.

7. Bailey, *Portrait of Hertfordshire*, pp. 91–2.

8. See above, pp. 89–90.

9. Hilton, *Bond Men*, pp. 198–9; Dyer, 'Ranking Lists of English Medieval Towns', pp. 758–60; Dyer, *Decline and Growth*, p. 65.

10. See above, p. 67.

11. Corbett, *History of St Albans*, p. 37. The number of weavers is given as 12 in Salzmann, 'Textiles', p. 249; Salzmann, 'Textiles', p. 244 n. 41a, gives the number of brewers in 1355 as 79, making the point that many also worked in other industries. Flood, 'Wealth and Piety', pp. 9–10, gives a very similar list dated to 1360.

12. Niblett and Thompson, *Alban's Buried Towns*, map on p. 273.

13. Hilton, *Bond Men*, p. 201.

14. Simkins, 'Political History', p. 13.

15. Taylor, Childs and Watkiss, 'Introduction', pp. xviii–xxvii.

16. Ibid., pp. 447–9, 451–3, 561–3.

17. Hilton, *Bond Men*, pp. 198–9.

18. Ibid., pp. 138–9; *St Albans Chronicle*, pp. 411–15. Page references to the *Chronicle* are to the recto pages, which are in English.

19. *St Albans Chronicle*, p. 421.

20. Ibid., pp. 443–5.

21. Ibid., p. 445.

22. Ibid., p. 447.

23. Ibid.

24. Ibid., pp. 447–9.

25. Ibid., p. 451.

26. Ibid.

27. Ibid., pp. 453–5.

28. Faith, 'Class Struggle', p. 57.

29. See above, pp. 77–8.

30. Faith, 'Class Struggle', p. 57.

31. Ibid.

32. *St Albans Chronicle*, p. 456 n. 527.

33. Ibid., pp. 457–9; see Faith, 'Class Struggle', p. 59, and above, p. 99.

34. *St Albans Chronicle*, p. 461.

35. Ibid., pp. 467–9.

36. Ibid., pp. 471–3.

37. Ibid., p. 473.

38. Ibid., p. 479.

39. Hilton, *Bond Men*, p. 186.

40. Ibid., pp. 198–9.

41. Ibid., p. 203.

42. Faith, 'Class Struggle', p. 54.

43. *St Albans Chronicle*, pp. 519–23.

44. Ibid., p. 525.

45. Ibid., pp. 529–31.

46. Ibid., pp. 533–5, 539.

47. Ibid., p. 541.

48. Ibid., p. 543.

49. Ibid., pp. 543–53.

50. Ibid., pp. 557–9.

51. Ibid., p. 563.

52. Christopher Dyer, *Making a Living in the Middle Ages: The People of Britain 850–1520* (New Haven, Conn.: Yale University Press, 2002), p. 291.

53. Corbett, *History of St Albans*, p. 43. John A. F. Thomson, 'Oldcastle, John, Baron Cobham (d. 1417)', *Oxford Dictionary of National Biography*, does not mention St Albans as a hiding place.

54. Niblett and Thompson, *Alban's Buried Towns*, p. 284. See F. G. Kitton, *The Clock Tower, St Albans: Its Origin and History* (St Albans: H. A. Richardson, 1956).

55. Gervase Rosser, 'Urban Culture and the Church 1300–1540', in Palliser, *Cambridge Urban History of Britain, Volume I*, p. 345.

56. The clock tower at Morpeth in Northumberland is the only similar structure in the country.

57. Rosser, 'Urban Culture', p. 345.

58. Toms, *Story of St Albans*, pp. 56–7. See also Corbett, *History of St Albans*, p. 43.

59. Toms, *Story of St Albans*, p. 58.

60. Corbett, *History of St Albans*, p. 46.

61. Antonia Gransden, 'Letter of Recommendation from John Whethamstede for a Poor Pilgrim 1453/4', *English Historical Review*, vol. 106 (1991), p. 937.

62. Toms, *Story of St Albans*, pp. 57–9.

63. G. H. Cook, *Portrait of St Albans Cathedral* (London: Phoenix House, 1951), p. 25.

64. Roberts, *Hill of the Martyr*, chapter 12.

65. John Goodall and Linda Monckton, 'The Chantry of Humphrey, Duke of Gloucester', in Henig, *Alban and St Albans*, pp. 231–55.

66. See G. L. Harriss, 'Humphrey, Duke of Gloucester (1390–1447)', *Oxford Dictionary of National Biography*.

67. Christine Carpenter, *The Wars of the Roses: Politics and the Constitution in England c.1437–1509* (Cambridge: Cambridge University Press, 1997), pp. 76–9.

68. Ibid., p. 92.

69. Ibid., p. 97.

70. Goodall and Monckton, 'Chantry of Humphrey', p. 248.

71. G. L. Harriss, 'Humphrey, Duke of Gloucester (1390–1447)', *Oxford Dictionary of National Biography*.

72. Goodall and Monckton, 'Chantry of Humphrey', p. 249.

73. Ibid.

74. Harriss, 'Humphrey, Duke of Gloucester'.

75. Corbett, *History of St Albans*, p. 46.

76. Heather Swanson, *Medieval British Towns* (Basingstoke: Macmillan, 1999), p. 109.

77. R. B. Dobson, 'Urban Decline in Late Medieval England', *Transactions of the Royal Historical Society*, 5th series, vol. 27 (1977), pp. 11–13; D. M. Palliser, 'Urban Decay Revisited', in John A. F. Thomson (ed.), *Towns and Townspeople in the Fifteenth Century* (Gloucester: Alan Sutton, 1988), pp. 4–5.

78. A. R. Bridbury, 'English Provincial Towns in the Later Middle Ages', *Economic History Review*, vol. 34 (1981), pp. 6–7.

79. Quoted in Dobson, 'Urban Decline', p. 3.

80. Dyer, *Decline and Growth*, pp. 64–6.

81. Thomas Starkey, *Dialogue between Reginald Pole and Thomas Lupset*, quoted in Robert Tittler, 'The Emergence of Urban Policy 1536–1558', in Jennifer Loach and Robert Tittler (eds), *The Mid-Tudor Polity c.1540–1560* (London: Macmillan, 1980), p. 79.

82. Palliser, 'Urban Decay Revisited', p. 11.

83. Bridbury, 'English Provincial Towns', pp. 3–4.

84. Palliser, 'Urban Decay Revisited', p. 11.

85. Dyer, *Decline and Growth*, p. 64.

86. Palliser, 'Urban Decay Revisited', p. 9.

87. Dyer, *Decline and Growth*, pp. 58–9, places St Albans 14th in a list that excludes London. The rank for St Albans is given as 13th, but there are 13 towns above St Albans in the list, which is based on the number of taxpayers in 1524–25. A more recent list in Dyer, 'Ranking Lists of English Medieval Towns', pp. 761–4, places St Albans 16th, in a list that includes London but excludes Ludlow, the Cinque Ports, and the counties of Durham, Cheshire, Northumberland, Cumberland and Westmorland.

88. Dyer, *Decline and Growth*, pp. 64–6.

89. Palliser, 'Urban Decay Revisited', p. 17.

90. Dyer, *Decline and Growth*, pp. 17–18.

91. Ibid., p. 25.

92. Palliser, 'Urban Decay Revisited', p. 12.

93. Dyer, *Making a Living*, p. 307.

94. See above, pp. 89–90.

95. Dyer, *Decline and Growth*, pp. 62–3.

96. C. G. A. Clay, *Economic Expansion and Social Change: England 1500–1700, Volume I: People, Land and Towns* (Cambridge: Cambridge University Press, 1984), p. 182. The larger town of Northampton had 60 inns, which would be able to accommodate 4,000 horses. See below, p. 165.

97. Niblett and Thompson, *Alban's Buried Towns*, pp. 258, 282.

98. Ibid., p. 282.

99. James G. Clark, 'Reformation and Reaction at St Albans Abbey 1530–1538', *English Historical Review*, vol. 115 (2000), p. 317.

100. G. R. Owst, *Every-Day Life in Mediaeval St Albans: Some Notes on a Fifteenth-Century Register of Wills* (no publisher given; reprinted from SAHAAS *Transactions*, 1926), p. 6.

101. Corbett, *History of St Albans*, p. 47; Toms, *Story of St Albans*, p. 64; Page *et al.*, 'City of St Alban', p. 481.

102. Kitton, *Clock Tower*, p. 5.

103. Corbett, *History of St Albans*, p. 47; on guilds, see Swanson, *Medieval British Towns*, pp. 91–102.

104. Page *et al.*, 'City of St Alban', p. 480.

105. Page, *Story of the English Towns*, p. 52.

106. SAHAAS, *St Albans*, p. 31.

107. See below, p. 145–6.

108. Flood, 'Wealth and Piety', pp. 40–1.

109. Swanson, *Medieval British Towns*, p. 129. In the first part of this quotation, Swanson is referring specifically to the guild at Ashburton in Devon.

110. Ibid., pp. 129–30.

111. Page *et al.*, 'City of St Alban', p. 480; Flood, 'Wealth and Piety', p. 39.

112. Page *et al.*, 'City of St Alban', pp. 480–1.

113. See below, pp. 137–41.

114. Page *et al.*, 'City of St Alban', p. 481.

115. Flood, 'Wealth and Piety', p. 41.

116. Page, *Story of the English Towns*, p. 54.

117. Flood, 'Wealth and Piety', pp. 10–11, 84.

118. Page, *Story of the English Towns*, p. 54.

119. Ibid., p. 54. Page's spelling 'gildsmen' has been altered.

120. W. J. Sheils, *The English Reformation 1530–1570* (London: Longman, 1989), chapter 1.

121. Briggs, *Social History of England*, p. 163.

122. Sheils, *English Reformation*, pp. 4–5.

123. Gilbert Burnet, *The History of the Reformation of the Church of England* (ed. Nicholas Pocock, 7 vols, Oxford: Clarendon Press, 1865), vol. 1, pp. 302–3.

124. Sheils, *English Reformation*, pp. 29–30.

125. Ibid., p. 303.

126. Niblett and Thompson, *Alban's Buried Towns*,

127. Geoff Egan, 'Pilgrims' Souvenir Badges of St Alban', in Henig, *Alban and St Albans*, pp. 215–16.
128. Brooke, 'St Albans', p. 55.
129. Clark, 'Reformation and Reaction', p. 299.
130. Ibid.
131. Sybil M. Jack, 'Wolsey, Thomas (1470/71–1530)', *Oxford Dictionary of National Biography*.
132. Sheils, *English Reformation*, p. 19.
133. Clark, 'Reformation and Reaction', p. 300.
134. Sheils, *English Reformation*, p. 7.
135. Briggs, *Social History of England*, p. 163.
136. Sheils, *English Reformation*, p. 28.
137. Ibid., pp. 28–9.
138. Clark, 'Reformation and Reaction', p. 297.
139. Ibid., p. 298; Toms, *Story of St Albans*, p. 67.
140. Clark, 'Reformation and Reaction', p. 300.
141. Ibid., pp. 301–4.

142. Ibid., pp. 304–8.
143. Ibid., p. 310.
144. Ibid., pp. 310–14.
145. Sheils, *English Reformation*, p. 29.
146. Burnet, *History of the Reformation*, vol. 1, p. 376.
147. Corbett, *History of St Albans*, pp. 49–50; Toms, *Story of St Albans*, p. 68.
148. Richard Watson Dixon, *History of the Church of England from the Abolition of the Roman Jurisdiction* (6 vols, Oxford: Oxford University Press, 1891–1902), vol. 2, pp. 221–3. I am grateful to Alan Crosby for drawing my attention to this scheme of new dioceses.
149. Roberts, *Hill of the Martyr*, p. 153.
150. Ibid., p. 155; James G. Clark, 'Boreman, Richard (c.1485x90–c.1558)', *Oxford Dictionary of National Biography*.

Notes to Chapter 5: Chartered borough and 'thoroughfare town', 1539–1700

1. Marcus Merriman, 'Lee, Sir Richard (1501/2–1575)', *Oxford Dictionary of National Biography*.
2. Toms, *Story of St Albans*, p. 68; Clark, 'Boreman, Richard'.
3. See above, p. 131.
4. Toms, *Story of St Albans*, pp. 78–9; William Page et al., 'St Peter's', *VCH Herts*, vol. 2, pp. 412–13.
5. Ibid., p. 80; Page et al., 'St Michael's', pp. 401–2.
6. James Corbett, *Secret City: Hidden History of St Albans* (St Albans: McDermott Marketing, 1993), chapter 1.
7. Corbett, *History of St Albans*, pp. 51–2.
8. Robert Tittler, *The Reformation and the Towns in England: Politics and Political Culture c.1540–1640* (Oxford: Clarendon Press, 1998), p. 91.
9. Ibid., p. 153.
10. Ken Powell and Chris Cook, *English Historical Facts 1485–1603* (London: Macmillan and Co., 1977), p. 199.
11. SAHAAS, *St Albans*, p. 44, and chapter 3 passim.
12. See above, pp. 125–6.
13. See above, pp. 125–6, 135–6.
14. SAHAAS, *St Albans*, p. 50.
15. Ibid., p. 31. See above, p. 125.
16. Ibid., p. 47.
17. See above, pp. 71, 78.
18. Gerald Sanctuary, *Tudor St Albans* (St Albans: no publisher or ISBN given, 1985), p. 7; for the fifteenth-century Court of Pie Powder, see C. H. Vellacott, 'Industries: Introduction', *VCH Herts*, vol. 4, p. 242.

19. SAHAAS, *St Albans*, pp. 52–3.
20. Ibid., p. 59.
21. Corbett, *History of St Albans*, pp. 51–2.
22. Sanctuary, *Tudor St Albans*, p. 8; Kilvington, *Short History of St Albans School*, p. 8.
23. Tittler, *Reformation and the Towns*, p. 94.
24. There is a brief description of the charter, and of St Albans at the time when it was granted, in SAHAAS, *St Albans 1553* (St Albans: SAHAAS, 2003).
25. The following account is based on SAHAAS, *St Albans*, pp. 51ff.
26. Sanctuary, *Tudor St Albans*, p. 10.
27. Kilvington, *Short History of St Albans School*, p. 9.
28. Tittler, *Reformation and the Towns*, p. 230.
29. Ibid., p. 232.
30. SAHAAS, *St Albans*, p. 44.
31. Ibid., p. 49.
32. Ibid., p. 50.
33. Ibid., pp. 44–5.
34. See above, pp. 125–6.
35. Page et al., 'City of St Alban', p. 481.
36. Page, *Story of the English Towns*, p. 65.
37. Page et al., 'City of St Alban', p. 481.
38. SAHAAS, *St Albans*, pp. 49–50.
39. Page et al., 'City of St Alban', p. 481.
40. For the division of St Albans into wards, see above, p. 96.
41. SAHAAS, *St Albans*, pp. 48–9.
42. Tittler, *Reformation and the Towns*, pp. 104–5.
43. SAHAAS, *St Albans*, pp. 69–70.

44. Toms, *Story of St Albans*, pp. 91–2.
45. See for example, SAHAAS, *St Albans*, pp. 68–9.
46. Roberts, *Hill of the Martyr*, p. 156; Page, *Story of the English Towns*, pp. 75–6.
47. SAHAAS, *St Albans*, pp. 34–5.
48. Ibid., p. 31.
49. Michael Reed, 'The Urban Landscape 1540–1700', in Peter Clark (ed.), *The Cambridge Urban History of Britain, Volume II: 1540–1840* (Cambridge: Cambridge University Press, 2000), p. 300.
50. Paul Glennie and Ian Whyte, 'Towns in an Agrarian Economy 1540–1700', in Clark, *Cambridge Urban History of Britain, Volume II*, p. 187.
51. Cook, *Portrait of St Albans Cathedral*, pp. 25, 48. Roberts, *Hill of the Martyr*, p. 154, suggests that the chapel was 'allowed to tumble into disrepair'. See above, pp. 72–3, 116, 125, 126.
52. Cook, *Portrait of St Albans Cathedral*, p. 48.
53. Roberts, *Hill of the Martyr*, p. 156.
54. Ibid., pp. 161–2.
55. Ibid., p. 177.
56. Sanctuary, *Tudor St Albans*, p. 11.
57. Toms, *Story of St Albans*, p. 94.
58. SAHAAS, *St Albans*, pp. 41–2.
59. Sanctuary, *Tudor St Albans*, p. 20; see also Toms, *Story of St Albans*, p. 90.
60. SAHAAS, *St Albans*, pp. 7–10.
61. Ibid., p. 10.
62. Ibid., pp. 93–4.
63. Quoted in Corbett, *History of St Albans*, pp. 58–9.
64. Quoted in Toms, *Story of St Albans*, p. 106.
65. SAHAAS, *St Albans*, p. 62.
66. Ibid., pp. 53, 65.
67. Ibid., pp. 20–1.
68. Corbett, *History of St Albans*, pp. 64–6.
69. Sanctuary, *Tudor St Albans*, p. 3.
70. Toms, *Story of St Albans*, p. 81.
71. SAHAAS, *St Albans*, p. 148.
72. Corbett, *History of St Albans*, pp. 54–6.
73. SAHAAS, *St Albans*, p. 7.
74. Ibid., p. 33.
75. Ursula R. Q. Henriques, *Before the Welfare State: Social Administration in Early Industrial Britain* (London: Longman, 1979), p. 156.
76. Corbett, *History of St Albans*, p. 61.
77. SAHAAS, *St Albans*, p. 60.
78. *Oxford English Dictionary*: 'pillory'.
79. Briggs, *Social History of England*, p. 168.
80. Corbett, *History of St Albans*, p. 55; A. E. Gibbs, *The Corporation Records of St Albans* (St Albans: Gibbs and Bamforth, 1890), p. 282; see below, p. 159.
81. Briggs, *Social History of England*, pp. 156, 164.
82. Janet R. Rose (ed.), *Historic Sandridge Revisited* (Sandridge: St Leonard's Publishing, 1999), pp. 17–18. Rose's book is an updated version of a history of Sandridge written in the 1950s by Edward Giles and Richard W. Thrale.
83. SAHAAS, *St Albans*, pp. 89–93.
84. Ibid., p. 90, fig. 4.2.
85. Ibid., pp. 87–8.
86. Ibid., pp. 88–9.
87. Rose, *Historic Sandridge Revisited*, pp. 21–3.
88. A. F. H. Niemeyer, 'Social and Economic History', *VCH Herts*, vol. 4, p. 219.
89. SAHAAS, *St Albans*, p. 94; see below, pp. 203–4.
90. Page et al., 'City of St Alban', p. 512.
91. Page et al., 'St Peter's', pp. 421–2.
92. SAHAAS, *St Albans*, pp. 94–6; see below, pp. 204–5.
93. Page et al., 'St Peter's', p. 422.
94. Page et al., 'City of St Alban', p. 512.
95. Ibid., p. 513.
96. Ibid., p. 514; SAHAAS, *St Albans*, p. 95.
97. SAHAAS, *St Albans*, chapter 6.
98. Norman Alvey, 'Growth in the Population of St Albans from the Seventeenth to the Nineteenth Centuries', *Local Historian*, vol. 30 (2000), esp. p. 156, table 3; SAHAAS, *St Albans*, p. 116.
99. See above, p. 123.
100. Niemeyer, 'Social and Economic History', p. 211.
101. SAHAAS, *St Albans*, p. 115.
102. John Langton, 'Urban Growth and Economic Change c.1688–1841', in Clark, *Cambridge Urban History of Britain, Volume II*, pp. 473–4; this list includes four Scottish cities. See above, p. 123.
103. SAHAAS, *St Albans*, p. 14.
104. Ibid.
105. Simkins, 'Political History', pp. 35–6.
106. Ibid., p. 39.
107. SAHAAS, *St Albans*, p. 71.
108. This account is based on ibid., pp. 54–8, 68–71.
109. Ibid., pp. 241–2: list of mayors with indications of political leanings.
110. Page, *Story of the English Towns*, pp. 89–90.
111. Ibid., pp. 90–1.
112. SAHAAS, *St Albans*, p. 71.
113. Roberts, *Hill of the Martyr*, p. 165.
114. SAHAAS, *St Albans*, p. 103.
115. Ibid., p. 108.
116. See also below, p. 162.
117. Rose, *Historic Sandridge Revisited*, p. 19; William Lamont, 'Clarkson, Laurence (1615–1667)', *Oxford Dictionary of National Biography*.
118. SAHAAS, *St Albans*, pp. 103–4.

119. Ibid., pp. 104–6; Page *et al.*, 'St Peter's', p. 421.
120. SAHAAS, *St Albans*, p. 97.
121. D. G. Turner, 'The Origins of the St Albans Baptists', *Baptist Quarterly*, vol. 37 (1998), p. 404.
122. Ibid., pp. 402, 405.
123. SAHAAS, *St Albans*, p. 107.
124. Niemeyer, 'Social and Economic History', p. 210.
125. Glennie and Whyte, 'Towns in an Agrarian Economy', p. 181.
126. Niemeyer, 'Social and Economic History', p. 208.
127. Salzmann, 'Textiles', pp. 249–50; Gibbs, *Corporation Records*, p. 282; see above, p. 151.
128. Gibbs, *Corporation Records*, p. 282.
129. SAHAAS, *St Albans*, pp. 201–3.
130. Chris Reynolds, *A Short History of Bernard's Heath* (Tring: Codil Language Systems Ltd, 2000), section 'Early Brickmaking on Bernard's Heath' (pamphlet has no page numbers); SAHAAS, *St Albans*, pp. 18ff.
131. SAHAAS, *St Albans*, pp. 143 (map), 155.
132. L. F. Salzmann, 'Pottery, Tiles and Bricks', *VCH Herts*, vol. 4, p. 266.
133. Ibid.
134. See below, p. 188. The list of inns given here is based on Sanctuary, *Tudor St Albans*, pp. 12–21.
135. Sanctuary, *Tudor St Albans*, pp. 16–17.
136. SAHAAS, *St Albans*, pp. 137, 142.
137. Toms, *Story of St Albans*, pp. 77–8; Vellacott, 'Industries: Introduction', p. 239.
138. See above, p. 124.
139. SAHAAS, *St Albans*, pp. 137–8.
140. T. C. Barker and C. I. Savage, *An Economic History of Transport in Britain* (London: Hutchinson, 1974 [1st edn, 1959]), pp. 25ff.
141. Clay, *Economic Expansion*, p. 182.
142. SAHAAS, *St Albans*, pp. 139–45.
143. Ibid., p. 138.
144. Ibid., p. 147–57.
145. Ibid., pp. 167–8.
146. See above, pp. 87, 103–4.
147. SAHAAS, *St Albans*, p. 169.
148. Ibid., pp. 171, 175–6.
149. Niemeyer, 'Social and Economic History', p. 210.
150. Page *et al.*, 'St Michael's', p. 393.
151. Paul Glennie, 'Continuity and Change in Hertfordshire Agriculture 1550–1700: I – Patterns of Agricultural Production', *Agricultural History Review*, vol. 36 (1988), pp. 55–75, esp. graph on p. 60.
152. Ibid., pp. 60–2, esp. graphs on p. 61; these acreages are based on the cereal areas shown in summer probate inventories.
153. Ibid., pp. 62–3.
154. SAHAAS, *St Albans*, p. 146.
155. Ibid., pp. 145–7.
156. Quoted in ibid., pp. 153, 167. These two pages give different versions of this quote.

Notes to Chapter 6: Economy, society and government, 1700–1835

1. P. J. Corfield, *The Impact of English Towns 1700–1800* (Oxford: Oxford University Press, 1982), pp. 2, 7.
2. Ibid., pp. 21–2.
3. Ibid., p. 2.
4. Paul Slack, 'Great and Good Towns 1540–1700', in Clark, *Cambridge Urban History of Britain, Volume II*, pp. 352–3.
5. Herman Moll, *A New Description of England and Wales, with the Adjacent Islands* (London: H. Moll and Sons, 1724), p. 113. Perhaps not too much store should be set by Moll's opinion, as he described St Albans as being on the river Colne.
6. Alvey, 'Growth in the Population of St Albans', p. 155.
7. See above, p. 155.
8. Alvey, 'Growth in the Population of St Albans', pp. 152, 156; see SAHAAS, *St Albans*, p. 115, and above, p. 155; G. S. Minchin, 'Table of Population 1801–1901', *VCH Herts*, vol. 4, pp. 233–8.
9. Alvey, 'Growth in the Population of St Albans', p. 156.
10. Laszlo L. Grof, *Children of Straw: The Story of Straw Plait, a Vanished Craft and Industry* (Buckingham: Baron, 2002 [1st edn, 1988]), p. 13.
11. Nigel Goose, *Population, Economy and Society in Hertfordshire in 1851, Volume 2: St Albans and Its Region* (Hatfield: University of Hertfordshire Press, 2000), p. 33.
12. Thomas George Austin, *The Straw Plaitting* [sic], *Straw Hat and Bonnet Trade* (Luton: Patrick O'Doherty, 1871), p. 15.
13. N. E. Agar, *Hitchin's Straw Plait Industry* (Hitchin: Hitchin Historical Society and North Hertfordshire District Council Museums Service, 1998 [1st edn, 1978]), pp. 2–3.
14. Peter Clark, 'Small Towns 1700–1840', in Clark, *Cambridge Urban History of Britain, Volume II*, pp. 750–1.
15. Page *et al.*, 'City of St Alban', p. 482.

16. Gibbs, *Corporation Records*, p. 282.

17. Grof, *Children of Straw*, p. 14.

18. Ibid., p. 16.

19. Quoted in John G. Dony, *A History of the Straw Hat Industry* (Luton: Gibbs, Bamforth and Co., 1942), pp. 21–2.

20. Grof, *Children of Straw*, p. 19.

21. Ibid., p. 25.

22. Ibid., p. 26.

23. For a discussion of this, see Goose, *Population*, pp. 86–106.

24. S. G. Shaw, *History of Verulam and St Albans* (St Albans: S. G. Shaw, 1815), p. 162; quoted in Corbett, *History of St Albans*, p. 79.

25. Rose, *Historic Sandridge Revisited*, p. 38.

26. Pamela Sharpe, 'The Women's Harvest: Straw-Plaiting and the Representation of Labouring Women's Employment c.1793–1885', *Rural History*, vol. 5 (1994), pp. 134, 138–9.

27. Quoted in ibid., p. 136.

28. Ibid., p. 137.

29. Goose, *Population*, p. 71. See below, pp. 211–13.

30. Austin, *Straw Plaitting*, pp. 19–20.

31. Grof, *Children of Straw*, p. 13.

32. Austin, *Straw Plaitting*, p. 19.

33. Ibid., pp. 18–19. See Jennie Kitteringham, 'Country Work Girls in Nineteenth-Century England', in Raphael Samuel (ed.), *Village Life and Labour* (London: Routledge and Kegan Paul, 1975), p. 119.

34. Goose, *Population*, p. 73.

35. Michael Fookes, *Made in St Albans: Ten Town Trails Exploring St Albans' Industrial Past* (St Albans: Michael Fookes, 1997), pp. 15–16; see below, pp. 212, 226.

36. C. W. Chalklin, 'The South-East', in Clark, *Cambridge Urban History of Britain, Volume II*, p. 50.

37. *The Universal British Directory 1793–1798* (microfiche edition, Buntingford: Microfi Ltd, 1988), vol. 5, p. 179.

38. Ibid., pp. 180–1.

39. Fookes, *Made in St Albans*, p. 21; Chalklin, 'South-East', p. 62.

40. Shaw, *History of Verulam*, p. 159.

41. Goose, *Population*, p. 75.

42. See above, pp. 159, 162.

43. *Universal British Directory*, vol. 5, p. 180–1; Reynolds, *Short History of Bernard's Heath*, section 'The Bernard's Heath Brick Works'.

44. *Universal British Directory*, vol. 5, pp. 175, 179.

45. Ibid., p. 179.

46. H. C. F. Lansberry, 'Politics and Government in St Albans, 1685–1835', unpublished PhD thesis, University of London (1964), pp. 53–9.

47. *Universal British Directory*, vol. 5, p. 179.

48. Corfield, *Impact of English Towns*, p. 20.

49. Ibid., p. 21.

50. Chalklin, 'South-East', pp. 62–3.

51. Quoted in Corbett, *History of St Albans*, p. 79.

52. *Universal British Directory*, vol. 5, p. 175.

53. Corfield, *Impact of English Towns*, pp. 20–1.

54. Shaw, *History of Verulam*, p. 161.

55. Chalklin, 'South-East', p. 60; see Barker and Savage, *Economic History of Transport*, pp. 31–3.

56. Daniel Defoe, *A Tour Through the Whole Island of Great Britain* (Harmondsworth: Penguin, 1986 [1st edn, 1724–26]), p. 437.

57. Ibid., p. 340.

58. Corbett, *History of St Albans*, p. 73.

59. See p. 182.

60. *Universal British Directory*, vol. 5, p. 179.

61. Toms, *Story of St Albans*, pp. 125–6.

62. H. C. F. Lansberry, 'James McAdam and the St Albans Turnpike Trust', *Journal of Transport History*, vol. 7 (1965), p. 121.

63. Ibid.

64. Corbett, *History of St Albans*, p. 82.

65. Shaw, *History of Verulam*, pp. 160–1.

66. Lansberry, 'James McAdam', pp. 122–5; Toms, *Story of St Albans*, p. 126.

67. Toms, *Story of St Albans*, p. 126.

68. *Universal British Directory*, vol. 5, p. 179.

69. Lansberry, 'James McAdam', p. 121.

70. *Universal British Directory*, vol. 5, p. 178.

71. *The Journal of the Rev. John Wesley A. M.* (ed. Nehemiah Curnock, 7 vols, London: Culley, 1909–16), vol. 6, p. 380: Friday 6 December 1782.

72. Ibid., vol. 7, p. 123: Monday 31 November and Friday 4 December 1785.

73. Corbett, *History of St Albans*, pp. 72–3.

74. Ibid., pp. 77–8; Shaw, *History of Verulam*, p. 158.

75. Shaw, *History of Verulam*, pp. 158–9.

76. The Crown, the Goat, the Angel, the Blue Boar, the White Hart, the Peahen, the George, the Woolpack, the Fleur-de-Lys and the Chequers.

77. *Universal British Directory*, vol. 5, pp. 180–1.

78. Shaw, *History of Verulam*, appendix XIII.

79. Toms, *Story of St Albans*, p. 126.

80. Joanna Innes and Nicholas Rogers, 'Politics and Government 1700–1840', in Clark, *Cambridge Urban History of Britain, Volume II*, pp. 531–50.

81. Rosemary Sweet, *The English Town 1680–1840: Government, Society and Culture* (Harlow: Pearson Education Ltd, 1999), p. 41.

82. Lansberry, 'Politics and Government', p. 2

83. Ibid., pp. 22, 24–5.
84. Shaw, *History of Verulam*, pp. 166–7. For examples of Shaw's obsession, see uses of the word 'respectable' on pp. 155, 157, 161, 162.
85. Shaw, *History of Verulam*, appendix VI.
86. See above, pp. 139, 141.
87. Shaw, *History of Verulam*, p. 175.
88. Lansberry, 'Politics and Government', p. 26.
89. Ibid., p. 50. See above, p. 185.
90. Ibid., p. 49.
91. Toms, *Story of St Albans*, pp. 131–2.
92. Kilvington, *Short History of St Albans School*, pp. 28–31.
93. Lansberry, 'Politics and Government', pp. 67–72; for the sum after appeal see p. 72 n. 4.
94. H. C. F. Lansberry, 'A Whig Inheritance', *Bulletin of the Institute of Historical Research*, vol. 41 (1968), pp. 50–1.
95. Gibbs, *Corporation Records*, pp. 100–1; Toms, *Story of St Albans*, p. 45.
96. See above, p. 145.
97. Corbett, *History of St Albans*, pp. 68–9.
98. Sweet, *English Town*, p. 76.
99. Ibid., p. 78.
100. See p. 183.
101. Lansberry, 'Politics and Government', pp. 186–9.
102. Shaw, *History of Verulam*, pp. 159–60.
103. Lansberry, 'Politics and Government', pp. 186–8.
104. Shaw, *History of Verulam*, pp. 159–60.
105. 'Abstracts of Statements of Account of Boroughs in England and Wales from the 1st September 1842 to the 31st August 1843': Parliamentary Papers, 1844 (593) xlii, p. 3.
106. Lansberry, 'Politics and Government', p. 61.
107. Ibid., pp. 20–1.
108. Ibid., p. 21.
109. Corbett, *History of St Albans*, pp. 80–1.
110. See above, pp. 141, 145, 159.
111. Lansberry, 'Politics and Government', pp. 92–3.
112. Corfield, *Impact of English Towns*, pp. 87–8.
113. Ibid., p. 89.
114. Shaw, *History of Verulam*, p. 170.
115. Ibid., p. 172.
116. Innes and Rogers, 'Politics and Government 1700–1840', p. 567.
117. Quoted in Corbett, *History of St Albans*, p. 80.
118. Lansberry, 'Politics and Government', p. 3 (abstract).
119. See Bernard Harris, *The Origins of the British Welfare State: Social Welfare in England and Wales 1800–1945* (Basingstoke: Palgrave Macmillan, 2004), p. 44.
120. Innes and Rogers, 'Politics and Government 1700–1840', pp. 533–4, 548–9.
121. See above, pp. 151–3.
122. *An Account of Several Work-Houses for Employing and Maintaining the Poor; Setting forth the Rules by which they are Governed, Their Great Usefulness to the Publick, and in Particular to the Parishes where They Are Erected* (London: Jos. Downing, 1732 [1st edn, 1725]), pp. 111–12.
123. Ibid., pp. 113–14.
124. Ibid., p. 112.
125. Ibid., p. 119.
126. Corbett, *History of St Albans*, p. 85.
127. Rose, *Historic Sandridge Revisited*, pp. 51–3.
128. Ibid., p. 52.
129. Lansberry, 'Politics and Government', p. 81.
130. Rose, *Historic Sandridge Revisited*, p. 52.
131. Lansberry, 'Politics and Government', pp. 63–4.
132. Ibid., pp. 240–5.
133. On the establishment of parochial charities, see above, p. 154.
134. See above, p. 193.
135. Shaw, *History of Verulam*, pp. 206–8.
136. Lansberry, 'Whig Inheritance', p. 52.
137. Innes and Rogers, 'Politics and Government 1700–1840', p. 550.
138. Corbett, *History of St Albans*, pp. 71–2; Nathaniel Cotton MD, *Observations on a Particular Kind of Scarlet Fever that Lately Prevailed in and about St Alban's, in a Letter to Dr Mead* (London: R. Manby and H. S. Cox, 1749).
139. Corbett, *History of St Albans*, pp. 69–70.
140. Shaw, *History of Verulam*, pp. 202–3.
141. Ibid., p. 216.
142. Lansberry, 'Politics and Government', p. 94.
143. Ibid., pp. 131–9. On the turnpike trust, see above, pp. 186–9.
144. Ibid., pp. 139–46.
145. Ibid., conclusion.
146. Shaw, *History of Verulam*, p. 155.
147. Ibid., p. 157.
148. Ibid., pp. 156–7.
149. Quoted in Lansberry, 'Politics and Government', pp. 144–5.
150. Shaw, *History of Verulam*, p. 164.
151. Ibid., pp. 162–3.
152. Corbett, *History of St Albans*, pp. 85–7. See Part, 'Sport, Ancient and Modern'.
153. Shaw, *History of Verulam*, p. 61.

1. John Stevenson, 'Social Aspects of the Industrial Revolution', in Patrick K. O'Brien and Roland Quinault (eds), *The Industrial Revolution and British Society* (Cambridge: Cambridge University Press, 1993), p. 239.
2. Asa Briggs, 'The Victorian City', in Runcie, *Cathedral and City*, p. 105.
3. Ibid.
4. Ibid., pp. 105–6.
5. Corbett, *History of St Albans*, p. 104.
6. Goose, *Population*, p. 33.
7. Grof, *Children of Straw*, p. 29; Goose, *Population*, p. 71. See above, p. 179.
8. Grof, *Children of Straw*, p. 30.
9. Goose, *Population*, p. 41. See above, p. 180.
10. Ethel M. Hewitt, 'The Straw Plait, Hat and Bonnet Industry', *VCH Herts*, vol. 4, p. 254.
11. Goose, *Population*, pp. 34–8.
12. Ibid., p. 38.
13. Ibid., p. 39.
14. Ibid., pp. 39–42.
15. Ibid., pp. 90–1.
16. Quoted in Grof, *Children of Straw*, p. 29.
17. Quoted in Kitteringham, 'Country Work Girls', p. 126.
18. Nigel Goose, 'How Saucy Did It Make the Poor? The Straw Plait and Hat Trades, Illegitimate Fertility and the Family in Nineteenth-Century Hertfordshire', *History*, vol. 91 (2006), pp. 530–56.
19. Grof, *Children of Straw*, p. 28.
20. Ibid., p. 111.
21. Dave Thorburn, 'Gender, Work and Schooling in the Plaiting Villages', *Local Historian*, vol. 19/3 (1989), pp. 108–10.
22. Quoted in Kitteringham, 'Country Work Girls', p. 120.
23. John Burnett (ed.), *Useful Toil: Autobiographies of Working People from the 1820s to the 1920s* (London: Allen Lane, 1974), p. 70.
24. Grof, *Children of Straw*, p. 29; Goose, *Population*, p. 71.
25. Grof, *Children of Straw*, p. 103.
26. Stephen Royle, 'The Development of Small Towns in Britain', in Martin Daunton (ed.), *The Cambridge Urban History of Britain, Volume III: 1840–1950* (Cambridge: Cambridge University Press, 2000), p. 173.
27. Geoff Dunk, *Around St Albans with Geoff Dunk: Collected Articles on Local History First Published in the* Review (St Albans: SAHAAS, 1985), pp. 47–8.
28. *Census of England and Wales, 1871: Population Tables: Area, Houses and Inhabitants, Volume II: Registration or Union Counties* (London: HMSO, 1872, C.676-I), p. 123 n. j.
29. Vellacott, 'Industries: Introduction', p. 239.
30. Arthur Swinson, *Frederick Sander: The Orchid King: The Record of a Passion* (London: Hodder and Stoughton, 1970), pp. 24–5, 75–6.
31. Quoted in ibid., p. 75.
32. Ibid., p. 80.
33. Fookes, *Made in St Albans*, p. 52.
34. Swinson, *Frederick Sander*, p. 121.
35. Peter Fry, *Samuel Ryder: The Man Behind the Ryder Cup* (Weymouth: Wright Press, 2000), pp. 7, 11, 12–14.
36. Ibid., pp. 14–17.
37. Ibid., p. 1.
38. Fookes, *Made in St Albans*, p. 46; Plomer, 'Printing', pp. 263–4.
39. Plomer, 'Printing', p. 264.
40. Tony Billings, *Camp: A Local St Albans History* (St Albans: Tony Billings, 2002), p. 8.
41. Fookes, *Made in St Albans*, p. 65.
42. Ibid., p. 16.
43. Ibid., p. 53.
44. Toms, *Story of St Albans*, p. 170; Billings, *Camp*, p. 28.
45. Fookes, *Made in St Albans*, p. 63.
46. Ibid., pp. 9, 48. The remainder of this paragraph, except where other citations are given, is based on Fookes, *Made in St Albans*, pp. 17, 33, 40–1, 46–8, 51, 54, 64, 66, and Billings, *Camp*, pp. 26, 29, 38.
47. Tony Mercer, *Mercer Chronometers: History, Maintenance and Repair* (Ashbourne: Mayfield Books, 2003), pp. 15–16, 29, 38, 49.
48. Corbett, *History of St Albans*, p. 118.
49. Reynolds, *Short History of Bernard's Heath*, sections 'Early Brickmaking on Bernard's Heath' and 'The Bernard's Heath Brick Works'.
50. *Census of England and Wales, 1901: County of Hertford: Area, Houses and Population* (London: HMSO, 1903, Cd.1377; hereafter *Herts Census 1901*), p. 54.
51. Dunk, *Around St Albans*, pp. 47–8; Fookes, *Made in St Albans*, p. 12.
52. Fookes, *Made in St Albans*, pp. 55, 34.
53. Grof, *Children of Straw*, p. 52.
54. Fookes, *Made in St Albans*, pp. 15–16.
55. Billings, *Camp*, pp. 5, 12–14.
56. Corbett, *History of St Albans*, p. 104.
57. Rose, *Historic Sandridge Revisited*, pp. 139–40.

58. Mason, *Gibbs' Illustrated Handbook to St Albans, Containing a Sketch of Its History, and a Description of Its Abbey, Its Antiquities, and Other Objects of Interest* (St Albans: Gibbs and Bamforth, 1884), p. 43; also quoted in Corbett, *History of St Albans*, p. 104.

59. Billings, *Camp*, p. 38.

60. *Herts Census 1901*, p. 54.

61. Royle, 'Development of Small Towns', p. 153.

62. *Census of Great Britain, 1851: Population Tables II: Ages, Civil Condition, Occupations and Birthplaces of the People, Volume I* (London: HMSO, 1854, C.1691), p. 208; *Census of England and Wales, 1931: Occupation Tables* (London: HMSO, 1934), pp. 469–70.

63. Nigel E. Agar, *Behind the Plough: Agrarian Society in Nineteenth-Century Hertfordshire* (Hatfield: University of Hertfordshire Press, 2005), p. 148.

64. Ibid., p. 149.

65. Rose, *Historic Sandridge Revisited*, p. 42.

66. Hugh Aronson, *Our Village Homes: Present Conditions and Suggested Remedies* (London: Thomas Munby and Co., 1913), p. 131.

67. Agar, *Behind the Plough*, pp. 150–2.

68. Hertfordshire Federation of Women's Institutes, *The Hertfordshire Village Book* (Newbury: Countryside Books, 1986), pp. 149–50.

69. Rose, *Historic Sandridge Revisited*, pp. 43–5.

70. *Herts Census 1901*, p. 54.

71. Ibid., p. 54.

72. R. E. Pahl, *Urbs in Rure: The Metropolitan Fringe in Hertfordshire* (London: London School of Economics and Political Science, Geographical Papers, No. 2, 1965), p. 20.

73. Quoted in ibid., pp. 19–20.

74. Quoted in ibid., p. 20.

75. *Census of England and Wales, 1911: Area, Families or Separate Occupiers, and Population, Volume I: Administrative Areas* (London: HMSO, 1912, Cd.6258), p. p. 155.

76. Barry Doyle, 'The Changing Functions of Urban Government: Councillors, Officials and Pressure Groups', in Daunton, *Cambridge Urban History of Britain, Volume III*, p. 301.

77. Toms, *Story of St Albans*, pp. 151–3.

78. Doyle, 'Changing Functions', p. 295.

79. See above, p. 203.

80. The parishes of Abbey and St Peter's elected three guardians each; St Stephen's, St Michael's, Redbourn, Harpenden and Wheathampstead two each; and Sandridge one.

81. Goose, *Population*, pp. 580–5; *Herts Census 1901*, p. 29.

82. Dunk, *Around St Albans*, p. 46.

83. Corbett, *Secret City*, pp. 42–3.

84. Toms, *Story of St Albans*, p. 160.

85. Edward Moorhouse, 'Maple, Sir John Blundell, baronet (1845–1903)', rev. Wray Vamplew, *Oxford Dictionary of National Biography*.

86. *Herts Census 1901*, p. 29.

87. *Kelly's Directory of St Albans, Harpenden and Hatfield for 1913–1914*, p. 17: St Albans Central Library, Local Studies section.

88. Mason, *Gibbs' Illustrated Handbook*, p. 60.

89. *Herts Census 1901*, p. 29.

90. Toms, *Story of St Albans*, pp. 170–1; Dunk, *Around St Albans*, pp. 36–8.

91. Toms, *Story of St Albans*, pp. 180–1.

92. John G. E. Cox (ed.), *St Albans News of 1889* (St Albans: Eddington Press, 1989), pp. 13–16.

93. Kilvington, *Short History of St Albans School*, pp. 56, 62, 63. The word 'Grammar' was formally dropped from the name in 1930: see below, p. 270.

94. Ibid., p. 70.

95. Ibid., pp. 76–7.

96. Ibid., pp. 78–80.

97. Royle, 'Development of Small Towns', p. 175.

98. Toms, *Story of St Albans*, p. 144; *The Watford and St Albans Gas Company: Centenary, 1834–1934* (Watford: Watford and St Albans Gas Company, 1934), pp. 28–9: St Albans Central Library, LOC338.47.

99. P. J. Waller, *Town, City and Nation: England 1850–1914* (Oxford: Oxford University Press, 1983), pp. 301–2.

100. Fookes, *Made in St Albans*, pp. 36–7.

101. Quoted in Corbett, *History of St Albans*, p. 90.

102. Quoted in ibid., p. 89.

103. Dunk, *Around St Albans*, pp. 53–4; Briggs, 'Victorian City', p. 104; Corbett, *Secret City*, p. 62.

104. Dunk, *Around St Albans*, p. 33; Fookes, *Made in St Albans*, p. 24.

105. John Brodrick, 'A Man of Two Worlds: Frederick Kinneir Tarte 1858–1943', in Brian Moody (ed.), *A History in All Men's Lives: Essays on Events from 150 Years of the St Albans and Hertfordshire Architectural and Archaeological Society* (St Albans: SAHAAS, 1999), p. 25 n. 1.

106. See above, p. 226.

107. Quoted in Brodrick, 'Man of Two Worlds', pp. 19, 25 n. 2.

108. Letter from H. R. Wilton Hall, *Herts Advertiser*, 23 September 1905: quoted in Reynolds, *Short History of Bernard's Heath*, section 'Wiles and Lewis's Tallow Works'.

109. Toms, *Story of St Albans*, p. 183.

110. See Corbett, *Secret City*, chapter 9.

111. Brodrick, 'Man of Two Worlds', p. 25 n. 2.

112. Mason, *Gibbs' Illustrated Handbook*, p. 53.

113. Fookes, *Made in St Albans*, pp. 9–10.

114. Dunk, *Around St Albans*, p. 34.

115. Ibid., p. 34; Fookes, *Made in St Albans*, pp. 21, 25.

116. Toms, *Story of St Albans*, p. 162.

117. Ibid., p. 173; Toms gives the date as 1896.

118. Allen Eyles with Keith Skone, *Cinemas of Hertfordshire* (Hatfield: Hertfordshire Publications, 2002 [1st edn, 1985]), pp. ix, 91–4; Corbett, *History of St Albans*, p. 125.

119. Royle, 'Development of Small Towns', p. 174.

120. Richard H. Trainor, 'The Middle Class', in Daunton, *Cambridge Urban History of Britain, Volume III*, pp. 699–700.

121. Dunk, *Around St Albans*, pp. 53–4.

122. Ibid.

123. Corbett, *Secret City*, pp. 33–6.

124. Dunk, *Around St Albans*, p. 34; Brian Moody, *The Light of Other Days: A Short History of the St Albans and Hertfordshire Architectural and Archaeological Society 1845 to 1995* (St Albans: SAHAAS, 1995), p. 8.

125. Corbett, *History of St Albans*, p. 95.

126. Corbett, *Secret City*, pp. 30–1.

127. *Census of Great Britain, 1851: Religious Worship, England and Wales: Report and Tables* (London: HMSO, 1853, C.1690), p. 28. The figures include attendances at Sunday schools. Many people would have attended two or more services, and have been counted twice or more.

128. Toms, *Story of St Albans*, pp. 169–70; Corbett, *Secret City*, pp. 31–2. See above, p. 72.

129. Corbett, *Secret City*, chapter 5.

130. Dunk, *Around St Albans*, pp. 16–17.

131. Corbett, *History of St Albans*, pp. 75–6.

132. Dunk, *Around St Albans*, pp. 17–18; Fry, *Samuel Ryder*.

133. Corbett, *History of St Albans*, p. 107.

134. *Census of Great Britain, 1851: Education, England and Wales: Report and Tables* (London: HMSO, 1854, C.1692), p. 89.

135. The total of the figures for individual Sunday schools in St Albans given in Cox, *St Albans News of 1889*, p. 62. The figure for the Baptist Sunday school on Verulam Road was not known.

136. Fry, *Samuel Ryder*, p. 43; Dunk, *Around St Albans*, p. 34.

137. A. E. Gibbs, *The Corporation Records of St Albans* (St Albans: Gibbs and Bamforth, 1890), p. 295.

138. Toulmin's daughter published a volume of childhood reminiscences: Mary Carbery, *Happy World: The Story of a Victorian Childhood* (London: Longmans, Green and Co., 1941).

139. Cox, *St Albans News of 1889*, p. 23.

140. R. G. Simons, *Cricket in Hertfordshire* (Hertfordshire: Hertfordshire County Cricket Association, 1996), pp. 56–7.

141. Ibid., pp. 60–1.

142. Ibid., p. 62.

143. Briggs, 'Victorian City', p. 106.

144. Cox, *St Albans News of 1889*, p. 51.

145. Moody, *Light of Other Days*, p. 2.

146. Ibid., p. 7.

147. Waller, *Town, City and Nation*, p. 314.

148. Moody, *Light of Other Days*, pp. 8–9; Ashdown, *St Albans Historical and Picturesque*. Asa Briggs attributes the authorship of this history to Francis Kitton: Briggs, 'Victorian City', p. 114.

149. Charles H. Ashdown, *The St Albans Pageant, July 15th to July 20th 1907* (St Albans: Pageant House, 1907), preface.

150. Ibid.

151. Ibid., p. 49.

152. Paul Readman, 'The Place of the Past in English Culture, c.1890–1914', *Past and Present*, vol. 186 (2005), p. 172.

153. Ashdown, *St Albans Pageant*, p. 53.

154. Ibid., pp. 54–5.

155. Toms, *Story of St Albans*, pp. 179–80.

156. Corbett, *History of St Albans*, p. 125.

157. Readman, 'Place of the Past', pp. 154, 170, 174, 193, 197.

158. Ibid., p. 177.

159. Corbett, *History of St Albans*, pp. 122–4.

160. Quoted in ibid., p. 122.

161. Ibid.

162. Cox, *St Albans News of 1889*, p. 25.

163. Ibid., p. 27.

164. Charles H. Ashdown, *The City of St Alban [sic]: Its Abbey and Its Surroundings* (St Albans: Gibbs and Bamforth, 1907), p. 98.

165. Ibid., p. 144.

166. Ibid., pp. 144–7

167. Ibid., pp. 9–10.

168. See above, pp. 206–7.

1. John Stevenson, *British Society 1914–1945* (Harmondsworth: Penguin, 1984), p. 103.

2. Ibid., p. 113.

3. See above, p. 218.

4. Harris, *Origins of the British Welfare State*, p. 261 (sum of figures for 1930–39 in right-hand column of table).

5. Pahl, *Urbs in Rure*, p. 9.

6. Alice Goodman, *The Street Memorials of St Albans Abbey Parish* (St Albans: SAHAAS, 1987), pp. 4–5.

7. Ibid., p. 5

8. Mercer, *Mercer's Chronometers*, pp. 51ff.

9. Page, *Story of the English Towns*, pp. 107–8; Goodman, *Street Memorials*, p. 8.

10. *Annual report of the Medical Officer of Health of the St Albans Urban Sanitary Authority for the Year* (hereafter *MOH Report*) *1914*, p. 31. The MOH reports cited in this and the following chapter are in St Albans Central Library, LOC.362.109.

11. Page, *Story of the English Towns*, p. 108; also quoted in Corbett, *History of St Albans*, p. 128.

12. *MOH Report 1914*, p. 31.

13. Ibid., pp. 31–4; John G. E. Cox, *'Be Proud': Hertfordshire and the Great War: An Anthology* (St Albans: Eddington, 2002), pp. 8–9, 14–15.

14. *City of St Albans: Defence of the Realm (Consolidation) Regulations, 1914*: St Albans Central Library, LOC.942.585/STA.

15. Page, *Story of the English Towns*, pp. 108–9.

16. Cox, *Be Proud*, p. 220.

17. Goodman, *Street Memorials*, p. 10.

18. Page, *Story of the English Towns*, pp. 108–9; Toms, *Story of St Albans*, p. 182.

19. Goodman, *Street Memorials*, p. 15.

20. Cox, *Be Proud*, pp. 26, 31.

21. Goodman, *Street Memorials*, pp. 10–11.

22. Ibid., p. 20.

23. Cox, *Be Proud*, pp. 125–6, 183, 193–6, 198–201, 214, 219–22, 247–8 and passim.

24. The number of deaths was almost 19 per cent of the male population of the municipal borough aged 15–39 in 1911, but as the boundaries were extended in 1913, this is not a suitable figure. There was a significant excess of young females over young males in 1921. The sex ratio, and the overall population, was also affected by other demographic changes, including the extension of the borough boundaries (in 1911 the sex ratio was higher in the St Albans census registration district as a whole than in the borough), and by deaths from disease.

See *Census of England and Wales, 1911, Volume VII: Ages and Condition as to Marriage* (London: HMSO, 1913, Cd.6610), p. 63; *Census of England and Wales, 1911: County of Hertford* (London: HMSO, 1923), p. 30.

25. Goodman, *Street Memorials*. The memorials were on Albert Street, Bardwell Road, Fishpool Street, High Street, Holywell Hill, Lower Dagnall Street, Orchard Street, Pageant Road, Sopwell Lane and Verulam Road, and most remain in a good condition. They are thought to be 'unique survivals' as street memorials from the First World War.

26. *Kelly's Directory of St Albans, Harpenden, Hatfield and District* (hereafter *Kelly's*) *1922*, p. A39. The *Kelly's Directories* cited are in St Albans Central Library, shelfmark Y.234.52.

27. *MOH Report 1924*, p. 21.

28. Dony, *History of the Straw Hat Industry*, p. 181 n. 2.

29. Ibid., p. 176.

30. Fookes, *Made in St Albans*, pp. 12, 19.

31. Ibid., pp. 16–17, 19; *St Albans as a Visitor's Resort and Residential Town* (Cheltenham: E. J. Burrow and Co., 1923; hereafter *Official Guide 1923*), p. 52.

32. Dony, *History of the Straw Hat Industry*, p. 178.

33. Fookes, *Made in St Albans*, pp. 11, 39, 45–6.

34. *St Albans as a Visitor's Resort, Residential Town and Manufacturing Centre* (St Albans: St Albans Town Council [sic], 1919; hereafter *Official Guide 1919*), p. 9.

35. *St Albans: Official Guide* (1928; hereafter *Official Guide 1928*), p. 11: Beardsmore DA690. S13.032.1928.

36. Ibid., p. 50.

37. Ibid., p. 55.

38. Mercer, *Mercer Chronometers*, p. 52.

39. Fookes, *Made in St Albans*, p. 27.

40. See above, p. 225.

41. Fookes, *Made in St Albans*, p. 25.

42. Ibid., p. 64.

43. Ibid.

44. Ibid.

45. Ibid., p. 41.

46. Ibid., p. 28.

47. *Hatfield and Its People: The Story of a New Town, a Garden City, an Old Village, a Historic House, the Farms and the Countryside in a Hertfordshire Parish* (Hatfield: Workers' Educational Association, 1959–64), p. 1217. This source dates the establishment of de Havilland's to 1934, but Bailey, *Portrait of*

Hertfordshire, p. 120, gives the date as 1930.

48. Fookes, *Made in St Albans*, pp. 16–17.

49. Ibid., p. 55; Tom Doig, *St Albans: A History and Celebration of the City* (Salisbury: Frith Book Company, 2004), p. 96; Fry, *Samuel Ryder*, pp. 78–80.

50. Fry, *Samuel Ryder*, p. 139.

51. Fookes, *Made in St Albans*, p. 17.

52. See above, p. 226; *Official Guide 1923*, p. 54.

53. *Official Guide 1923*, p. 56; Fookes, *Made in St Albans*, p. 48.

54. *Official Guide 1923*, p. 54.

55. Fookes, *Made in St Albans*, p. 51.

56. Ibid., pp. 41, 54.

57. Ibid., pp. 36–7.

58. Mercer, *Mercer Chronometers*, pp. 57–72.

59. Toms, *Story of St Albans*, p. 184.

60. Corbett, *History of St Albans*, p. 132.

61. Stevenson, *British Society*, p. 273.

62. *MOH Report 1924*, p. 5; *MOH Report 1938*, p. 4.

63. *MOH Report 1924*, p. 5; *MOH Report 1938*, p. 4.

64. Harris, *Origins of the British Welfare State*, pp. 216–17, 242.

65. *MOH Report 1924*, pp. 13–16.

66. *MOH Report 1938*, pp. 11–13.

67. *Kelly's 1938*, p. A22.

68. *MOH Report 1924*, pp. 13–16; *MOH Report 1938*, pp. 13–14.

69. *Kelly's 1922*, p. A38.

70. *Kelly's 1938*, p. A22.

71. *MOH Report 1914*, pp. 30–1.

72. Harris, *Origins of the British Welfare State*, pp. 234–5.

73. *MOH report 1915*, p. 18.

74. *MOH report 1924*, p. 17.

75. *MOH report 1938*, p. 15.

76. Harris, *Origins of the British Welfare State*, p. 235.

77. *Watford and St Albans Gas Company*, pp. 28–9.

78. *Official Guide 1928*, p. 55.

79. I. C. R. Byatt, *The British Electrical Industry 1875–1914: The Economic Returns to a New Technology* (Oxford: Clarendon Press, 1979), pp. 21–3.

80. Fookes, *Made in St Albans*, pp. 64–5.

81. Rose, *Historic Sandridge Revisited*, p. 105.

82. Fookes, *Made in St Albans*, p. 40.

83. Billings, *Camp*, p. 26.

84. Toms, *Story of St Albans*, p. 180.

85. *Kelly's 1922*, p. A71.

86. See for example *Kelly's 1938*, p. A42.

87. *Official Guide 1928*, p. 53.

88. Billings, *Camp*, pp. 47ff.

89. Fookes, *Made in St Albans*, p. 33.

90. *Census of England and Wales, 1931: Occupation Tables*, p. 469.

91. Sue Bowden, 'The New Consumerism', in Paul Johnson (ed.), *Twentieth-Century Britain: Economic, Social and Cultural Change* (London: Longman, 1994), p. 246.

92. *MOH Report 1924*, p. 24.

93. Toms, *Story of St Albans*, p. 106; Doig, *St Albans*, p. 53.

94. *Official Guide 1928*, pp. 53, 59.

95. *Kelly's 1938*, p. 247.

96. Toms, *Story of St Albans*, p. 107.

97. *Census of England and Wales, 1931: Occupation Tables*, pp. 469–70. Not all those enumerated in St Albans will have worked in the city, but conversely, other employees may have commuted to St Albans from elsewhere. The inclusion of the rural district in the figures reduces the margin of error here; however, we do not know how many of these employees travelled to work in London or elsewhere.

98. *Official Guide 1919*, p. 26.

99. *Official Guide 1928*, p. 45.

100. Ibid., pp. 55–9.

101. See above, p. 244.

102. Eyles and Skone, *Cinemas of Hertfordshire*, pp. 91–6. The *St Albans Annual and Who's Who 1933* (St Albans: Sisley's Ltd, 1933), p. 7, claimed that the Capitol had 2,000 seats: St Albans Central Library LOC.942.585/STA.

103. See above, pp. 249–51.

104. *What to See in St Albans and Verulamium: Pictorial Guide to the Roman City, the Ancient Abbey and the Beauties of Mid-Herts* (revised edition, St Albans: Sisley's Ltd, 1932): St Albans Central Library, LOC942.585/STA.

105. *Official Guide 1919*, p. 20.

106. Moody, *Light of Other Days*, p. 13; Alan G. Crosby, 'Urban History in Lancashire and Cheshire', *Northern History*, vol. 42 (2005), p. 79.

107. See above, pp. 251–2.

108. R. L. P. Jowitt, *A Guide to St Albans and Verulamium* (London: Frederick Muller Ltd, 1935), p. 9.

109. Ibid., p. 105.

110. Ibid., p. 3.

111. See above, p. 251.

112. Fookes, *Made in St Albans*, p. 33.

113. Toms, *Story of St Albans*, p. 187.

114. Quoted in Corbett, *History of St Albans*, p. 133.

115. Jowitt, *Guide to St Albans*, p. 171.

116. *City of St Albans Year Book 1968–69*, pp. 62–3: Beardsmore DA.690.S13.Y4.

117. See chapter 1.

118. Sir Mortimer Wheeler and T. V. Wheeler,

Verulamium: A Belgic and Two Roman Cities (London: Society of Antiquaries, 1936), pp. iii–iv, 4.

119. Jane McIntosh, 'Wheeler, Sir (Robert Eric) Mortimer (1890–1976)', *Oxford Dictionary of National Biography*.

120. Moody, *Light of Other Days*, p. 13.

121. *St Albans Annual and Who's Who 1933*, advertisement on p. 35.

122. St Albans Museums, *Annual Review 2000–1*.

123. Toms, *Story of St Albans*, pp. 184–6.

124. Stephen G. Jones, *Workers at Play: A Social and Economic History of Leisure 1918–1939* (London: Routledge and Kegan Paul, 1986), pp. 87–100.

125. *City of St Albans Year Book 1968–69*, pp. 62–3. Toms, *Story of St Albans*, p. 186, and Corbett, *History of St Albans*, p. 133, both give the date as 1935.

126. Jones, *Workers at Play*, pp. 95–7.

127. *City of St Albans Year Book 1968–69*, pp. 62–3.

128. Harris, *Origins of the British Welfare State*, p. 243.

129. See above, p. 243.

130. Corbett, *History of St Albans*, pp. 129–30.

131. Ibid., p. 131; Toms, *Story of St Albans*, pp. 183–4.

132. *City of St Albans Year Book 1968–69*, p. 66. There were also 11 houses at Folly Mead, 36 on Shirley Road and 9 on Watling Way in Park Street. Corbett, *History of St Albans*, p. 139, gives the total figure as 646. The figure of 734 may refer to houses authorised before the war rather than those actually built.

133. Rose, *Historic Sandridge Revisited*, pp. 106, 141, each page giving different dates of construction.

134. Harris, *Origins of the British Welfare State*, pp. 254–9, 261. A little over 400,000 of the houses built by private enterprise had some state subsidy, mostly under the Housing Act (1923).

135. Pahl, *Urbs in Rure*, p. 22.

136. *MOH Report 1914*, p. 5; *MOH Report 1924*, p. 4; *MOH Report 1928*, p. 4; *MOH Report 1934*, p. 4.

137. Billings, *Camp*, pp. 44–5.

138. Ibid., pp. 15, 28, 38, 47.

139. Rose, *Historic Sandridge Revisited*, pp. 125–7, 139–44.

140. *Marshalswick: St Mary's Marshalswick Commemorative Brochure* (St Albans: St Mary's Marshalswick, 1993), p. 4: St Albans Central Library LOC.942.585; Rose, *Historic Sandridge Revisited*, p. 126.

141. *Official Guide 1928*, p. 11.

142. Ibid., p. 42; *Official Guide 1919*, p. 24 (quoted).

143. *MOH Report 1924*, p. 19.

144. Ibid., p. 25. The sanitary inspector's report, at pp. 29–30, gives different figures for the number of houses inspected.

145. *MOH Report 1938*, pp. 19–21.

146. *MOH Report 1924*, pp. 19–20; *MOH Report 1938*, pp. 16–17.

147. *St Albans Annual and Who's Who 1933*, pp. 15–16.

148. F. W. S. Craig, *British Parliamentary Election Results 1918–1949* (Glasgow: Political Reference Publications, 1969), p. 375.

149. *Kelly's 1938*, p. A36.

150. Clifford Crellin, *Where God Had a People: Quakers in St Albans over Three Hundred Years* (St Albans: Preparative Meeting of the Society of Friends, 1999), pp. 55–6, 59–60.

151. Ibid., pp. 63–4.

152. Elizabeth J, Gardner, *Marlborough Road 1898–1998* (St Albans: Marlborough Road Church Council, 1998), pp 39–46. St Albans Central Library, Local History, 287.142.

153. James Corbett, *Celebration: The Story of a Parish: SS Alban and Stephen 1840–1990* (St Albans: SS Alban and Stephen Church, 1990), pp. 31–2, 43.

154. F. A. J. Harding, *Three Hundred Years of Christian Witness in St Albans 1650–1950: The Independent Chapel (Congregational), Spicer Street* (St Albans: Gibbs and Bamforth, [1950]), pp. 8–9. The inside back cover of Harding's pamphlet has a list of the 87 members in 1950.

155. Derek Turner, *With Cheerful Zeal: A History of Dagnall Street Baptist Church, St Albans* (St Albans: Dagnall Street Baptist Church, 1999), pp. 104 (quoted), 110 (membership figures).

156. *Kelly's 1922*, pp. A67-A71.

157. The list was fuller than the list in *Kelly's 1938*, pp. A38-A42, which contained only 108 organisations: *St Albans Annual and Who's Who 1933*, pp. 52–65.

158. Ibid., p. 59; *Kelly's 1938*, p. A41.

159. *St Albans Annual and Who's Who 1933*, pp. 68–9.

160. Mark Freeman, *The Joseph Rowntree Charitable Trust: A Study in Quaker Philanthropy and Adult Education* (York: William Sessions, 2004), p. 154.

161. Anne Roach and Matthew Wheeler, *St Albans: The Home Front: Everyday Life in St Albans and District 1939–1945* (St Albans: St Albans Museums, 1995), p. 3.

162. Corbett, *History of St Albans*, p. 137; Toms, *Story of St Albans*, p. 187.

163. Roach and Wheeler, *St Albans*, p. 6.

164. Ibid., pp. 7, 15.

165. Ibid., p. 8; Toms, *Story of St Albans*, p. 187; Crellin, *Where God Had a People*, p. 63.

166. *Hatfield and Its People*, p. 1217.

167. Corbett, *History of St Albans*, p. 138; Roach and Wheeler, *St Albans*, p. 9; Crellin, *Where God Had a People*, p. 59; Kilvington, *Short History of St Albans School*, p. 102.

168. *MOH Report 1938*, p. 15; *MOH Report 1940*, p. 8, and p. 9 on the delay to house building and slum clearance.

169. Toms, *Story of St Albans*, p. 187.

170. Roach and Wheeler, *St Albans*, p. 9.

171. Crellin, *Where God Had a People*, pp. 60–3; Corbett, *Story of St Albans*, p. 136.

172. Roach and Wheeler, *St Albans*, p. 10.

173. Crellin, *Where God Had a People*, p. 63.

174. Roberts, *Hill of the Martyr*, p. 241.

175. Corbett, *History of St Albans*, p. 136; Roach and Wheeler, *St Albans*, pp. 26–8.

176. Mercer, *Mercer's Chronometers*, p. 76.

177. E. C. Pelham, *The Oaklands Story 1921–1971* (St Albans: Hertfordshire College of Agriculture and Horticulture', 1971), p. 109; Crellin, *Where God Had a People*, p. 59; Roach and Wheeler, *St Albans*, p. 29.

178. Roach and Wheeler, *St Albans*, pp. 9, 31.

Notes to Chapter 9: 'A terribly smug place': St Albans since 1945

1. *A Social and Economic Survey of St Albans City* (Association for Planning and Regional Reconstruction, 1946; hereafter *Social and Economic Survey*), pp. 16–17: St Albans Central Library, LOC.711.4.

2. Gordon E. Cherry, *Town Planning in Britain since 1900* (Oxford: Blackwell, 1996), p. 99 (p. 81 on the interwar development of the 'green belt').

3. 'St Albans in the Fifties', p. 4: supplement to *St Albans Observer*, 8 May 1996.

4. See Bob Mullen, *Stevenage Ltd: Aspects of the Planning and Politics of Stevenage New Town* (London: Routledge and Kegan Paul, 1980).

5. Bailey, *Portrait of Hertfordshire*, pp. 14, 49–50.

6. Christina Todd, 'The Mediation of Urban Change in a Historic Townscape: A Case Study of St Albans, Hertfordshire', unpublished BA (Hons) thesis, Bristol Polytechnic (1990; copy in St Albans Central Library, LOC.942.585/STA).

7. *Social and Economic Survey*, p. 17.

8. *St Albans: The Story of the City and Its People in the 1950s, Written by People of the City* (facsmile edition, St Albans: Paton Books, 1995; hereafter *Official Guide 1950*), pp. 32, 34.

9. *MOH report 1956*, p. 26.

10. This figure, and the figures given above, are all approximate, and taken from Fookes, *Made in St Albans*, pp. 16–17, 35, 41, 43, 51, 53–4, 64, 66.

11. Mercer, *Mercer Chronometers*, pp. 87–8.

12. *Census 1951, England and Wales: Occupation Tables* (London: HMSO, 1956), pp. 386–7. These figures refer to employment in occupation order XII: 'paper and printing'.

13. *Official Guide 1950*, p. 44.

14. *Social and Economic Survey*, p. 7.

15. Fookes, *Made in St Albans*, p. 35.

16. *Official Guide 1950*, pp. 34–44.

17. 'St Albans in the Fifties', p. 5.

18. *Official Guide 1950*, p. 44.

19. *MOH report 1956*, p. 26.

20. *Official Guide 1950*, p. 34.

21. *Social and Economic Survey*, pp. 6, 15–16.

22. Ibid., p. 6.

23. *Social and Economic Survey*, p. 6.

24. *Official Guide 1950*, p. 44.

25. *Census 1951: Occupation Tables*, pp. 386–7.

26. Richard Whitmore, *Hertfordshire: The Way We Were in the Forties, Fifties and Sixties* (Newbury: Countryside Books, 2002), p. 44.

27. *Social and Economic Survey*, p. xvi.

28. Cherry, *Town Planning*, p. 123.

29. Corbett, *Story of St Albans*, p. 141; *City of St Albans: Tenants' Handbook* (Gloucester: British Publishing Company Ltd, 1953–54), p. 9: Beardsmore PamBox DA690.S13.C51; 'St Albans in the Fifties', p. 15.

30. *City of St Albans Year Book 1968–69*, p. 66.

31. Ibid., p. 68; the number of households used as a basis for this calculation is the figure for 1971: *Census 1971, England and Wales, County Report: Hertfordshire, Part I* (London: HMSO), p. 3.

32. *City of St Albans: Tenants' Handbook*, pp. 11–13.

33. Ibid., p. 15: 'there are some tenants who take the view that even the limited regulations which are imposed are unnecessary and undemocratic'.

34. Rose, *Historic Sandridge Revisited*, p. 142.

35. *St Albans Rural District: The Official Guide* (Cheltenham: E. J. Burrow, 1964), p. 5.

36. *Marshalswick*, p. 14.

37. Rose, *Historic Sandridge Revisited*, pp. 127, 142.

38. Corbett, *History of St Albans*, p. 140.

39. 'St Albans in the Fifties', p. 5.

40. *St Albans Rural District: Official Guide*, p. 5.

41. 'St Albans in the Fifties', p. 14.

42. Toms, *Story of St Albans*, p. 187.

43. Brett, *St Albans*, p. 71.

44. *Marshalswick*, p. 20.

45. Ibid., p. 21.

46. Brett, *St Albans*, pp. 71–2.

47. Ibid., p. 73.

48. Ibid., pp. 72–3.

49. *St Albans and District Citizens' Guide 1991–92*, pp. 27–9: St Albans Central Library, LOC.942.585/STA.

50. Quited in Whitmore, *Hertfordshire*, p. 33.

51. Michael White and John Gribbin, *Stephen Hawking: A Life in Science* (London: Viking, 1992), pp. 8–10.

52. Kilvington, *Short History of St Albans School*, p. 112.

53. Ibid.; White and Gribbin, *Stephen Hawking*, p. 16.

54. Kilvington, *Short History of St Albans School*, p. 119. Pages 114–26 of this book were written by L. G. Walker.

55. *City and District of St Albans: Official Guide 1984* (hereafter *Official Guide 1984*), p. 34: St Albans Central Library, LOC.942.585/STA.

56. Kilvington, *Short History of St Albans School*, p. 115.

57. Quoted in Freeman, *Joseph Rowntree Charitable Trust*, p. 194.

58. Brett, *St Albans*, p. 74.

59. *Discover St Albans: A Historic Town Trail from 43 AD to 1997* (St Albans: St Albans Museums, 1997): copy in the author's possession.

60. Brett, *St Albans*, p. 75.

61. Ibid., pp. 74–6.

62. Ibid., p. 76.

63. *Social and Economic Survey*, p. xxiii.

64. Ibid., p. 119; see above, pp. 239, 240, 265.

65. *Official Guide 1950*, p. 10.

66. *MOH report 1956*, p. 11.

67. Corbett, *History of St Albans*, p. 141; 'St Albans in the Fifties', p. 13.

68. *MOH report 1956*, pp. 11–12.

69. Ibid., pp. 3–5; B. R. Mitchell, *British Historical Statistics* (Cambridge: Cambridge University Press, 1988), p. 59.

70. See *Kelly's 1956*, p. A15.

71. Brett, *St Albans*, pp. 88–9.

72. In ibid., pp. 92–3.

73. *City and District of St Albans: Official Guide 1976*, p. 15: St Albans Central Library, LOC.942.585/STA; *St Albans: What Your Council Is Doing 1975–76*, pp. 5, 5A, 8: St Albans Central Library, LOC.352.14

74. In Brett, *St Albans*, p. 93.

75. Ralph Glasser, *Town Hall: Local Government at Work in Britain Today* (London: Century Publishing, 1984), p. 22.

76. See below, pp. 323–4.

77. Glasser, *Town Hall*, p. 14.

78. *Review of Local Government, 1994: Hertfordshire*, section 7: St Albans Central Library, LOC.351.425.8. One seat was vacant.

79. *City of St Albans Year Book 1968–69*, p. 68; Brett, *St Albans*, p. 10.

80. Brett, *St Albans*, p. 67.

81. J. M. Richards, 'Gibberd, Sir Frederick Ernest (1908–1984)', *Oxford Dictionary of National Biography*.

82. Bailey, *Portrait of Hertfordshire*, p. 95.

83. *City of St Albans Year Book 1968–69*, p. 69.

84. Toms, *Story of St Albans*, p. 193.

85. Bailey, *Portrait of Hertfordshire*, p. 95.

86. *City of St Albans Year Book 1968–69*, pp. 62–4.

87. Toms, *Story of St Albans*, p. 174.

88. *City of St Albans Year Book 1968–69*, p. 64.

89. *City and District of St Albans: Leisure Handbook* [1978], p. 11: copy in the author's possession.

90. Ibid., p. 14.

91. Brett, *St Albans*, p. 63.

92. *St Albans Millenary Pageant 948–1948, Souvenir Programme, June 21st to June 26th 1948*, pp. 66–7: Beardsmore DA690.S13.M5.

93. *Social and Economic Survey*, p. xxii.

94. Ibid., p. 86.

95. *Official Guide 1950*, p. 47.

96. Ibid., pp. 45–50.

97. *City and District of St Albans: Leisure Handbook*, p. 25.

98. Moody, *Light of Other Days*, p. 14.

99. Ibid., pp. 15–16.

100. Corbett, *History of St Albans*, p. 145.

101. Toms, *Story of St Albans*, p. 191.

102. Ibid., pp. 145–6. Doig, *St Albans*, pp. 88–9, gives the date (wrongly) as 1972.

103. 'St Albans in the Fifties', pp. 23–4.

104. Quoted in White and Gribbin, *Stephen Hawking*, p. 7.

105. Corbett, *Celebration*, p. 69.

106. Ibid., p. 71.

107. Roberts, *Hill of the Martyr*, chapter 20.

108. Ibid., chapter 21.

109. Ibid., chapter 22.

110. *The Independent*, 2 July 2004, p. 16.

111. *Herts Advertiser (St Albans and Harpenden Edition)*, 3 August 2006, p. 1.

112. *Marshalswick*, foreword by Runcie, and passim.

113. Turner, *With Cheerful Zeal*, pp. 119–20, 125.

114. Gardner, *Marlborough Road*, pp. 56, 60, 74.

115. Corbett, *Celebration*, p. 59.

116. Crellin, *Where God Had a People*, pp. 67–71.

117. Ibid., pp. 71–2; Corbett, *Celebration*, p. 71; Rose, *Historic Sandridge Revisited*, pp. 128–31, 143–4.

118. These national figures are taken from Alec Cairncross, *The British Economy since 1945* (2nd edn, Oxford: Blackwell, 1995), pp. 231, 310–14. The table on pp. 312–13 gives an erroneous figure for service sector employment in 1964.

119. Quoted in 'St Albans in the Fifties', p. 20.

120. L. C. Hunter, G. L. Reid and D. Boddy, *Labour Problems of Technological Change* (London: Allen and Unwin, 1970), p. 43.

121. *1991 Census, County Report: Hertfordshire (Part 2)* (London: HMSO), p. 231. All occupation figures for 1991 are approximations, because only a 10 per cent sample was used in the calculations. Hertfordshire County Council, *Major Employers in Hertfordshire, Spring 1992*: St Albans Central library, LOC.338.702.542.58. For the 1951 figures, see above, p. 288.

122. Except where other sources are given, the account in this paragraph is based on Fookes, *Made in St Albans*, pp. 13, 16–17, 18, 19, 22, 27, 28, 35, 40–1, 42, 43, 51, 52, 64, 66.

123. Mercer, *Mercer Chronometers*, p. 92.

124. *St Albans Rural District: Official Guide* (Cheltenham: E. J. Burrow, 1969), p. 15:

125. *Official Guide 1984*, p. 49.

126. Glasser, *Town Hall*, p. 27.

127. Calculation based on *Census 1981, County Report: Hertfordshire, Part 2* (London: HMSO), p. 2.

128. For the British figure, see above, p. 312.

129. *Official Guide 1984*, p. 50

130. Ibid., pp. 50, 54–5.

131. Hertfordshire County Council, *Major Employers*.

132. Todd, 'Mediation of Urban Change', p. 39.

133. Ibid., p. 38.

134. Bailey, *Portrait of Hertfordshire*, p. 29.

135. *Official Guide 1984*, p. 50.

136. *1991 Census: Hertfordshire (Part 2)*, pp. 230–1, adding the figures for health professionals, health associate professionals and 'personal service occupations: health and related occupations'. See note 121 above for the reasons why 1991 figures are approximations only.

137. Ibid.; see note 121 on sampling.

138. *Official Guide 1984*, p. 39.

139. Hertfordshire County Council, *Major Employers*.

140. Todd, 'Mediation of Urban Change', pp. 46–7.

141. Glasser, *Town Hall*, p. 27.

142. *1991 Census: Hertfordshire (Part 2)*, pp. 230–1. See note 121 above on sampling.

143. Hertfordshire County Council, *Major Employers*.

144. *St Albans: The State of the Local Economy* (St Albans: City and District of St Albans, 2004), pp. 7–8.

145. Ibid., pp. 2, 5.

146. Ibid., pp. 2, 10.

147. *Stop Press* exhibition, St Albans Museum, 2006: 'Development and Change' panel. The figure of 20 per cent comes from Todd, 'Mediation of Urban Change', p. 36. According to the *Official Guide 1984*, p. 50, around 10 per cent of the working population of St Albans, some 3,000 people, worked in the capital, but this might have been an underestimate.

148. Todd, 'Mediation of Urban Change', p. 36.

149. Corbett, *History of St Albans*, pp. 149–50.

150. *St Albans: State of the Local Economy*, pp. 9–10.

151. Ibid., p. 2.

152. *Official Guide 1976*, p. 21.

153. Ibid., p. 17.

154. *Census 1981, County Report: Hertfordshire, Part 1* (London: HMSO), p. 80.

155. There were 'around 55,000' houses in the district: *St Albans City and District: Housing Strategy 2004–2007* (St Albans: City and District of St Albans, 2004), p. 5.

156. Ibid., p. 15.

157. At the latter date, there were 'around 55,000' housing units (see note 155 above); in 1981 (*Census 1981: Hertfordshire, Part 1*, p. 80), there were 42,927.

158. *Housing Strategy 2004–2007*, p. 5.

159. Rose, *Historic Sandridge Revisited*, pp. 128–31, 143–4. There was also a social development, by the Churches Housing Association, built in 1987: see above, p. 311.

160. Bailey, *Portrait of Hertfordshire*, p. 96.

161. *Housing Strategy 2004–2007*, p. 52. Calculated from the figures giving the total private-sector housing stock, and the numbers of terraced, semi-detached and detached homes.

162. Fookes, *Made in St Albans*, p. 33.

163. *St Albans: State of the Local Economy*, p. 4.

164. *Housing Strategy 2004–2007*, p. 25.

165. Ibid., p. 26.

166. Ibid., p. 25.

167. Ibid., p. 29.

168. Corbett, *History of St Albans*, pp. 138–9.

169. *Social and Economic Survey*, pp. xxiv–xxv.

170. Corbett, *History of St Albans*, p. 141.

171. Ibid., pp. 141–3.

172. Toms, *Story of St Albans*, p. 197.

173. Corbett, *History of St Albans*, pp. 144–5.

174. Ibid., p. 144.

175. 'St Albans in the Fifties', pp. 5–7.

176. Toms, *Story of St Albans*, pp. 192–3.

177. Bailey, *Portrait of Hertfordshire*, pp. 95–6.

178. Corbett, *History of St Albans*, pp. 149–50.

179. Todd, 'Mediation of Urban Change', pp. 41–2.

180. *Marshalswick*, pp. 16–17.

181. Todd, 'Mediation of Urban Change', p. 38.

182. Ibid., p. 46.

183. Ibid., pp. 40–1, 51–2.

184. Bailey, *Portrait of Hertfordshire*, pp. 96–7, partly quoted in Corbett, *History of St Albans*, p. 147.

185. Glasser, *Town Hall*, p. 19.

186. This paragraph is based on ibid., chapter 2, and Corbett, *History of St Albans*, p. 147.

187. Quoted in Glasser, *Town Hall*, p. 33.

188. *Herts Advertiser (St Albans and Harpenden Edition)*, 3 August 2006, p. 3.

189. Donald Pelletier (ed.), *St Albans Today: Personal Views* (St Albans: Mail Boxes Etc., 2004), passim.

190. Ibid., p. 24.

191. Ibid., p. 44.

192. Ibid., p. 2.

193. *The Idler Book of Crap Towns: The 50 Worst Places to Live in the UK* (London: Boxtree, 2003), p. 10.

194. Ibid.

195. *Herts Advertiser (St Albans and Harpenden Edition)*, 3 August 2006, p. 5; *St Albans and Harpenden Review*, 13 September 2006, p. 1.

196. *The Independent*, 2 July 2004, p. 16.

197. The Guardian, 25 September 2007, p. 6.

198. Glasser, *Town Hall*, p. 28.

Appendix:
Sources for tables and charts

Table 7.1: The population of St Albans, 1801–1911

Borough of St Albans. 1801-31: these refer to the 'ancient' borough and are derived from *Comparative Account of the Population of Great Britain in the Years 1801, 1811, 1821 and 1831...* (Sessional papers, 1831, vol. 8, no. 348), p. 115. 1841: *Abstract of the Answers and Returns Made Pursuant to Acts 3 and 4 Vic. c.99, and 4 Vic. c.7...: Enumeration Abstract MDCCCXLI, Part I: England and Wales and Islands in the British Seas* (London: HMSO, 1843), p. 122. This gives the population of the extended borough, giving the area as 320 acres; however, this was an error, as part of the parish of Tittenhanger was included in the borough at this date, which was not the case at previous censuses. The population of the part of Tittenhanger that was included in the borough was 723. Subtracting this from the population given would leave a population of 5,774 for the ancient borough. This report, p. 465, gives the population of the parliamentary borough of St Albans as 6,246. 1851: *Census of Great Britain, 1851: Population Tables, I: Numbers of the Inhabitants in the Years 1801, 1821, 1831, 1841 and 1851* (2 vols, London: HMSO, 1852), vol. 1, p. ccvi; and vol. 1, division 3 (South Midland Counties), p. 82. 1861 and 1871: *Census of England and Wales, 1871: Population Tables: Area, Houses and Inhabitants, Volume I: Counties* (London: HMSO, 1872, C.676), p. 145 (gives the area as 434 acres). 1881: *Census of England and Wales, 1881, Volume I: Area, Houses and Population: Couties* (London: HMSO, 1883, C.3562), p. 156 (p. 157 gives the area of the enlarged borough as 997 acres). 1891: *Census of England and Wales, 1891: Preliminary Report and Tables of the Population and Houses in England and Wales* (London: HMSO, 1891, C.6422), p. 142. 1901 and 1911: *Census of England and Wales, 1911: Area, Families or Separate Occupiers, and Population, Volume I: Administrative Areas* (London: HMSO, 1912, Cd.6258), p. 155.

Census registration district. 1801-51: *Census of Great Britain, 1851: Population Tables, I: Numbers of the Inhabitants in the Years 1801, 1821, 1831, 1841 and 1851* (2 vols, London: HMSO, 1852), vol. 1, division 3 (South Midland Counties), pp. 4-5. 1861 and 1871: *Census of England and Wales, 1871: Population Tables: Area, Houses and Inhabitants, Volume II: Registration or Union Counties* (London: HMSO, 1872, C.676-I), p. 113. 1881 and 1891: *Census of England and Wales, 1891: Area, Houses and Population, Volume II: Registration Areas and Sanitary Districts* (London: HMSO, 1893, C.6948-I), p. 189. 1901: *Census of England and Wales, 1901: County of Hertford: Area, Houses and Population* (London: HMSO, 1903, Cd.1377), p. 19. 1911: *Census of England and Wales, 1911: Area, Families or Separate Occupiers, and Population, Volume II: Registration Areas* (London: HMSO, 1912, Cd.6258), p. 62.

The population data given by Asa Briggs in 'The Victorian City', in Robert Runcie (ed.), *Cathedral and City: St Albans Ancient and Modern* (London: Martyn Associates, 1977), p. 104, are taken directly from G. S. Minchin, 'Table of Population 1801-1901', *VCH Herts*, vol. 4, pp. 233–8. Although Minchin's data is labelled 'St Albans Borough', it actually comprises the population of St Albans or Abbey parish, St Peter's parish and 'part of' St Michael's parish. From 1881, *none* of St Michael's parish is included in these figures, which partly accounts for the very low rate of growth shown for the period 1871-81. In fact, during this period the population of *St Peter's* parish grew from 5,261 to 6,562 (24.7%), although the growth of the population of the Abbey parish itself was minimal. The expansion of St Peter's, and hence of St Albans as a whole, is masked by the removal of St Michael's. The full data given by Minchin and Briggs are as follows:

	Population	Growth (%)
(%)		
1801	3,872	
1811	4,362	12.7
1821	5,733	31.4
1831	6,582	14.8
1841	7,745	17.7
1851	8,208	6.0
1861	9,090	10.7
1871	10,421	14.6
1881	10,659	2.3
1891	12,478	17.1
1901	16,181	29.7

Table 7.2: Sex ratios in St Albans (males per 100 females)

The sources for the borough of St Albans and the census registration district are as given for table 7.1 above, except for the sex ratios for the borough of St Albans in the period 1801–41. These are not available for the 'ancient' borough. The sex ratios given for these dates relate to an area almost exactly co-extensive with the post-1835 municipal borough, as given in *Census of Great Britain, 1851: Population Tables, I: Numbers of the Inhabitants in the Years 1801, 1821, 1831, 1841 and 1851* (2 vols, London: HMSO, 1852), vol. 1, division 3, pp. 18–19.

The UK sex ratios are calculated from B. R. Mitchell, *British Historical Statistics* (Cambridge: Cambridge University Press, 1988), p. 9.

Table 8.1: Population of St Albans, 1901–1971

The source of the data for 1901 and 1911 is as given for table 7.1 above (p. 157 for the rural district). For 1921 and 1931, the figures are from *Census of England and Wales, 1931: County of Hertford (Part I)* (London: HMSO, 1932), pp. 3–5. The estimates for 1939 and 1945 are from *A Social and Economic Survey of St Albans City* (Association for Planning and Regional Reconstruction, 1946), p. 23: St Albans Central Library, LOC.711.4. For 1951–71, the figures are from Office of Population Censuses and

Surveys, *Census 1971, England and Wales, County Report: Hertfordshire, Part I* (London: HMSO), p. 1.

Table 9.1: Population of the City and District of St Albans, 1961–2001

The figures for 1961 and 1971 are for the area covered by the district, which was created in 1974, at those two earlier censuses. They, and the figure for 1981, are for the population present on census night (not the usually resident population), and are taken from Office of Population Censuses and Surveys, *Census 1981, County Report: Hertfordshire, Part I* (London: HMSO), p. xvi. The population for 1991 is from *1991 Census, County Report: Hertfordshire (Part 2)* (London: HMSO), p. 29. For 2001, the figure is from *St Albans City and District: Housing Strategy 2004–2007* (St Albans: City and District of St Albans, 2004), p. 24.

Charts 9.1 (a)–(c)

Calculations based on *Census 1951, England and Wales: Occupation Tables* (London: HMSO, 1956), pp. 386-7. This table divides occupied workers into 27 categories or 'occupation orders', and these have been aggregated into the nine categories used in the table: Fishing, agriculture, mining (I, II and III); manufacturing (IV–XIII); construction/painting and decorating (XIV and XV); transport (XVII); commerce and finance (XVIII); professional and technical (XVI and XIX); personal service (XXII); clerks, typists, etc. (XXIII); and other (XX, XXI and XXIV–XXVII). Some of those in the 'professional and technical' and 'clerks, typists, etc.' were probably also working at these occupations in the manufacturing, construction and transport sectors.

Chart 9.2

Calculations based on *1991 Census, County Report: Hertfordshire (Part 2)* (London: HMSO). Note that these figures are based on a 10 per cent sample. The categories are those given in the report.

Bibliographical note

The full references to sources used in this book are given in the 'Notes and references' section. This bibliographical note is intended to give an overview of just the principal sources for further reading.

There have been surprisingly few histories of St Albans in the past century. There is a very full account in William Page (ed.), *The Victoria History of the County of Hertford* (4 vols, London: Constable, 1902–14); and William Page, *The Story of the English Towns: St Albans* (London: Society for Promoting Christian Knowledge, 1920) is very difficult to find. I consulted it in the Beardsmore local history collection in the Hudson Memorial Library. More recent accounts are Elsie Toms, *The Story of St Albans* (St Albans: Abbey Mill Press, 1962), a useful but very anecdotal book, and James Corbett, *A History of St Albans* (Chichester: Phillimore & Co., 1997), which has recently been republished in a new, but not updated, edition. The same author's *Secret City: Hidden History of St Albans* (St Albans: McDermott Marketing, 1993), has some interesting short studies of particular episodes in the history of St Albans. Eileen Roberts, *The Hill of the Martyr: An Architectural History of St Albans Abbey* (Dunstable: The Book Castle, 1993), is also useful and covers a very long period.

There is a larger and more recent literature covering specific periods of the history of the city. Of particular note for the earliest periods are Rosalind Niblett, *Verulamium: The Roman City of St Albans* (Stroud: Tempus Publishing, 2001), and Rosalind Niblett and Isobel Thompson, *Alban's Buried Towns: An Assessment of St Albans Archaeology up to AD 1600* (Oxford: Oxbow Books, 2005). The latter is a mine of very detailed, and very specialised, information, whereas the former is more accessible to the general reader. Two collections of essays covering longer periods should also be mentioned: Robert Runcie (ed.), *Cathedral and City: St Albans Ancient and Modern* (London: Martyn Associates, 1977), and Martin Henig and Phillip Lindley (eds), *Alban and St Albans: Roman and Medieval Architecture, Art and Archaeology* (Leeds: British Archaeological Association and Maney

Publishing, 2001). A useful account of one period in the history of the medieval abbey of St Albans can be found in Michelle Still, *The Abbot and the Rule: Religious Life at St Alban's 1290-1349* (Aldershot: Ashgate, 2002).

Although this book is primarily based on secondary sources, for chapter 4, the recent edition of Walsingham's chronicle – John Taylor, Wendy R. Childs and Leslie Watkiss (eds), *The St Albans Chronicle: The* Chronica Maiora *of Thomas Walsingham, I: 1376-1394* (Oxford: Clarendon Press, 2003) – proved invaluable.

For the early modern period, two sources, separated by almost forty years, are particularly useful. The first is H.C.F. Lansberry, 'Politics and Government in St Albans, 1685–1835', unpublished Ph.D. thesis, University of London (1964), which gives a wealth of detail about the government of the town. Lansberry also wrote two short articles on more specific features of the period: 'James McAdam and the St Albans Turnpike Trust', *Journal of Transport History*, vol. 7 (1965), pp. 120–7; and 'A Whig Inheritance', *Bulletin of the Institute of Historical Research*, vol. 41 (1968), pp. 47–57. The second useful source is St Albans and Hertfordshire Architectural and Archaeological Society (SAHAAS), *St Albans 1650-1700: A Thoroughfare Town and Its People* (ed. J.T. Smith and M.A. North, Hertford: Hertfordshire Publications, 2003). Moving into the nineteenth century, a key primary source for the 1810s is S.G. Shaw, *History of Verulam and St Albans* (St Albans: S.G. Shaw, 1815). Nigel Goose, *Population, Economy and Society in Hertfordshire in 1851, Volume 2: St Albans and Its Region* (Hatfield: University of Hertfordshire Press, 2000) contains a complete transcript of the census enumerators' books for the area, and a long analysis of the findings of a detailed examination of them. On the straw plaiting and straw hat industry, Laszlo L. Grof, *Children of Straw: The Story of Straw Plait, a Vanished Craft and Industry* (Buckingham: Baron, 2002 [1st edn, 1988]), deals mostly with Buckinghamshire, but has some useful general information. I would also like to single out Michael Fookes, *Made in St Albans: Ten Town Trails Exploring St Albans' Industrial Past* (St

Albans: Michael Fookes, 1997), a meticulously researched description of the modern industrial history of the city.

Primary source material has been used more intensively in the later chapters of the book. Some local and national newspapers have been used, as have the published reports of the decennial census of population. Full sources for the figures used are given in the endnotes, and the sources for the tables and charts are in the appendix. Reports of the medical officers of health for St Albans, local government publications, guide books, souvenir programmes for the city pageants, trade directories and other sources can be found in St Albans Central Library and in the Beardsmore collection. Census reports are published by HMSO. I have also used some sources in my own possession, which may not be easily obtainable elsewhere; where this has been the case, the fact has been reported in the endnotes.

Many local historians have produced interesting histories of their neighbourhoods, villages, churches and organisations, and these have proved especially useful in the research for this book. Among the plethora of publications – many of which I have probably overlooked completely – I would like to point especially to Janet R. Rose (ed.), *Historic Sandridge Revisited* (Sandridge: St Leonard's Publishing, 1999), an updated version of an older history of Sandridge written by Edward Giles and Richard W. Thrale. Others that deserve particular mention include Alice Goodman, *The Street Memorials of St Albans Abbey Parish* (St Albans: SAHAAS, 1987); Tony Billings, *Camp: A Local St Albans History* (St Albans: Tony Billings, 2002); James Corbett, *Celebration: The Story of a Parish: SS Alban and Stephen 1840–1990* (St Albans: SS Alban and Stephen Church, 1990); Derek Turner, *With Cheerful Zeal: A History of Dagnall Street Baptist Church, St Albans* (St Albans: Dagnall Street Baptist Church, 1999); and F.I. Kilvington, *A Short History of St Albans School* (no publisher given, 1986 [1st edn, 1970]). I must also mention two unpublished thesis, which I consulted in St Albans Central Library: Susan Flood, 'Wealth and Piety in St Albans in the Late Fifteenth and Early Sixteenth Centuries', unpublished M.St. thesis, University of Cambridge (1997; shelfmark LOC.942.585.05); and Christina Todd, 'The Mediation of Urban Change in a Historic Townscape: A Case Study of St Albans, Hertfordshire', unpublished BA (Hons) thesis, Bristol Polytechnic (1990; shelfmark LOC.942.585/STA).

Acknowledgements

Many have assisted with the writing of this book. In particular, I am grateful to colleagues, past and present, in the Department of Economic and Social History at the University of Glasgow, who have provided encouragement and comradeship over many years. These thanks are also extended to Robin Pearson and James Taylor, with whom I have worked since 2003, and to all at Carnegie Publishing, especially Alistair Hodge, Anna Goddard and Judith Franks. Carnegie's local history editor, Dr Alan Crosby, read the first draft of the manuscript, and provided many very useful suggestions for alteration and improvement; I am grateful to him, and to Stephen Marritt, who also read sections of the manuscript. Tamsin Beal also read most of the chapters in draft form, and suggested several improvements. In addition, Louise Wannell provided invaluable assistance by obtaining census data for St Albans. Naturally, I remain responsible for any omissions, and for any errors of fact or interpretation in the book.

For assistance with obtaining illustrations, and for permissions to reproduce them, I am grateful to St Albans Central Library, St Albans Museums, Hertfordshire Archives and Local Studies, St Albans Cathedral (who also kindly allowed Alistair to take photographs inside the cathedral), the British Library, the National Library of Scotland, the National Archives, the National Portrait Gallery, Glasgow University Library, the Board of Trustees of Trinity College Dublin, the Science and Society Picture Library, Jonathan Webb at www.webbaviation.co.uk, Tony and Christine Baxter, Gavin Deas, Francesca Hammond, Marianne Blaauboer and James Taylor. For their encouragement throughout the writing of the book, I thank Lucy and Dave Brennan and Christine Cheepen; and, for their company on many enjoyable occasions in St Albans and elsewhere, Giles Cooke, Jacob Sharpe, Emily Mackley and Tamsin and David Gammie. I would also like to thank my mother and father, Catherine and Alec Freeman, who have lent me a number of useful books and pamphlets about St Albans, helped with obtaining illustrations, and been constant and unfailing sources of support.

Mark Freeman, October 2008

Index

Index entries in *italic* type refer to information given within the illustration captions